D1346691

THE ARGYLL BOOK

Books Edited/Written by Donald Omand

The Caithness Book	Inverness	1972
The Moray Book	Edinburgh	1976
Red Deer Management	Edinburgh	1981
The Sutherland Book	Golspie	1982
The Ross & Cromarty Book	Golspie	1984
A Kaitness Kist (with J. P. Campbell)	Thurso	1984
The Grampian Book	Golspie	1987
The New Caithness Book	Wick	1989
A Northern Outlook:		
100 Essays on Northern Scotland	Wick	1991
Caithness Crack	Wick	1991
Caithness: Lore and Legend	Wick	1995
The Borders Book	Edinburgh	1995
The Perthshire Book	Edinburgh	1995
Caithness: Historic Tales	Wick	2001
The Fife Book	Edinburgh	2001
The Orkney Book	Edinburgh	2003

Monograph
The Caithness Flagstone Industry
(with J. D. Porter)   University of Aberdeen   1981

THE ARGYLL BOOK

edited by
Donald Omand

BIRLINN

First published in 2004 by
Birlinn Limited
West Newington House
10 Newington Road
Edinburgh
EH9 1QS

www.birlinn.co.uk

This edition published in 2006

Copyright © The Editor and Contributors severally 2004

All rights reserved. No part of this publication may be reproduced,
stored, or transmitted in any form, or by any means, electronic,
mechanical or photocopying, without the express
written permission of the publisher.

ISBN10: 1 84158 480 0
ISBN13: 978 1 84158 480 5

British Library Cataloguing-in-Publication Data
A catalogue record is available from the British Library

Designed and typeset by Carnegie Publishing Ltd, Lancaster
Printed and bound by MPG Books Limited, Bodmin

Contents

List of Plates, Figures and Maps

Plates

Figures

Maps

Conversion: Metric/Non-metric

1 metre = 3.28 feet   1 foot = 0.30 metres

1 kilometre = 0.62 miles   1 mile = 1.61 kilmetres

1 hectare = 2.47 acres   1 acre = 0.40 hectares

Preface

THIS BOOK, lively and scholarly at the same time, comes at the right moment to support a popular movement which seeks, in a variety of ways, to restore Argyll's damaged sense of identity.

To understand Argyll, which means to understand the way in which its people have considered it throughout most of its human past, a number of epithets have to be dispelled. These epithets are misleading, originally imported descriptions of Argyll which became current only in the last few centuries.

'Argyll is remote.' Remote from where? Glasgow is a hundred miles away from Lochgilphead, the main administrative centre and the site of the Council. Campbeltown is a hundred miles further on. Arinagour in Coll is accessible only by ship. The pass over Rest And Be Thankful, leading down to Loch Fyne and the strange micro-climate of Mid-Argyll, is sometimes snowed up or blocked by landslides. These are distances which matter now, when Argyll is an ill-integrated part of centralised Scotland within a centralised United Kingdom. But for most of time, they were of no consequence. Very few people – cattle drovers, marching soldiers, a few pedlars – used the tracks going east into the barren mountain spine which walled off Argyll from the rest of Scotland. The distances which did matter were almost all concerned with sea travel off the west coast: the passage down the Sound of Jura to Ireland; the Sound of Mull leading out towards the ocean and the islands; and the Firth of Lorne, through which boats sailed on a rising tide up past Lismore to the foot of the Great Glen.

'Argyll is marginal, peripheral, disadvantaged.' Today, many inhabitants have come to think of their land in those terms. But the whole cultural and historical nature of Argyll has been its identity as a centre, not a periphery. For thousands of years, Argyll was an integral part of a wide, Gaelic-speaking world which stretched from Kerry to the Hebrides and was interconnected by seaways. In the earliest times, Mesolithic settlers found their way to the western coasts, with their rich supplies of fish and molluscs in shallow seas and rivers. While upland and central Scotland were inhospitable, life was relatively easy along the shores and the low, forested hills which ran down to them. When agriculture began, it was simple to cultivate the light soils of the *machair* soils and the glacial terraces left at the heads of the sea-lochs by the last Ice Age. This choice of the western coasts as sites for human settlement carried on into the Bronze Age, with its warmer and drier climate. It explains the extraordinary concentration of ritual monuments in seaward Argyll – evidence, perhaps, of large and secure social units able to mobilise and feed the labour forces required to build the sacred places, the cairns and the circles or files of standing stones such as those in Kilmartin Glen.

This centrality of Argyll carries on into the period beginning in about 1000 BC and continuing for almost two millennia, a period misleadingly partitioned between The Iron Age and early mediaeval times. The climate grew wetter and colder, and there is some evidence that society disintegrated into smaller, mutually hostile units. Stone fortlets studded the landscape, and new ritual practices led to the abandonment of the great monuments. The tale of how 'the Scots' migrated from northern Ireland to Argyll and founded the Dalriada kingdom seems to suggest a colonial enterprise, casting Argyll as marginal territory. But the archaeologist Ewan Campbell is one of those who now question this version. For him, the evidence suggests that Argyll had always been a part of a greater cultural sphere uniting it with Ireland and the Hebrides, and that the arrival of 'the sons of Erc' from what is now County Antrim in the sixth century AD was no mass migration but – if it happened at all – the exchange of one small governing elite for another.

This Gaelic–Atlantic world survived for many centuries. Argyll's connections were primarily with Ireland, although excavations at Dunadd have shown that Argyll Dalriada was on early medieval trade routes whose ships brought high-quality goods from Merovingian France and possibly from the eastern Mediterranean. Far from being 'peripheral', Argyll was a source of cultural and political influence. From Iona, Columban Christianity sent its missionaries and, probably, its material culture in the form of illuminated manuscripts across northern Britain. In the course of the ninth century, Dalriadic princes moved eastwards to establish hegemony over the Pictish kingdoms, to lay the foundations of the 'Alba' which was to become Scotland and, for a time, to spread Gaelic speech and place-names over much of central and eastern Scotland.

Weakened by Norse raids and conquests, Argyll now indeed became 'peripheral' to the medieval Kingdom of the Scots. But the ancient Irish–Gaelic connection fitfully survived, flowering once more in the Lordship of the Isles, based on Islay. It was not until the Reformation and the destruction of Gaelic Ulster in the sixteenth and seventeenth centuries that the Irish link was finally severed. From then on, Argyll was gradually assimilated into the general concept of 'the Highlands'. The collapse of the clan system, the introduction of modern commercial farming and the Clearances drove Argyll's dazzling Gaelic culture – the myth-cycles, proverbs and songs revealed, for instance, in J. F. Campbell's *Popular Tales* – into almost terminal decline. Today, the very factors which gave Argyll its continuity and strength – its enormous coastline, its reliance on sea communication – are seen as its weaknesses in an age which enforces urban standards of convenience and economic 'sustainability'.

But there are signs of hope and revival, some of them based on history. A reconstruction of Argyll identity is taking place, including a new exploration of links with Ireland in culture and sport. There is a new interest in the Gaelic language. In this revival, *The Argyll Book*, with its powerful and unsentimental recovery of the past brilliance of this beautiful land, will make a major contribution.

Neal Ascherson
September 2004

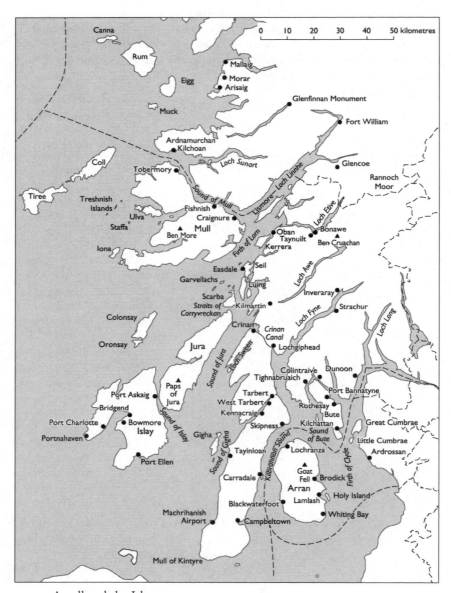

MAP I Argyll and the Isles

CHAPTER ONE

Geology and Landscape

Introduction

The Argyll and Bute district of Scotland contains a remarkable wealth of rock types, landscapes and scenery. Ancient crystalline rocks in Coll, Tiree and Iona are amongst the oldest in Europe, together with similar rocks in the Outer Hebrides and in north-west Sutherland. Much of the rest of the district, including the islands of Colonsay, Islay, Jura and Bute, consists of the folded slates and other rocks belonging to the great Caledonian mountain chain that stretches from the west of Ireland through Argyll and north-eastwards into the Grampian Mountains, then towards Shetland and western Norway. Three of Scotland's most important faults – the Great Glen Fault, the Moine Thrust and the Highland Boundary Fault – cut across Argyll (Map 2). The youngest rocks of all are found in Mull – these are the volcanic lavas around Tobermory and the Ardmeanach peninsula, and the central volcano of Ben More. Argyll's landscape and scenery were shaped by the moving glaciers of the last great Ice Age, which was responsible for gouging out the floors of the deep narrow sea lochs and fiords, and for smoothing the mountain tops. Altogether, Argyll has seen nearly 3,000 million years of history, and for its size shows perhaps the greatest diversity of any of Scotland's regions. This chapter outlines that history, and gives an account of the riches that lie beneath the soil. Table 1 provides a summary of the geological development of Argyll and the Isles.

Geology of Argyll in outline

Most of Argyll lies within the Caledonian belt, the remnants of a great chain of former mountains, now greatly reduced, which crosses Scotland from Ireland in a south-west to north-east direction (Map 3). Within this belt, the rocks are folded sediments and lavas that once formed on an ancient sea floor. Heat and pressure associated with earth movements around 400 to 500 Ma (million years ago) were responsible for converting these sediments – mud, sand, silt and limestone – into metamorphic slates and schists during intense compression and shortening of the Earth's crust.

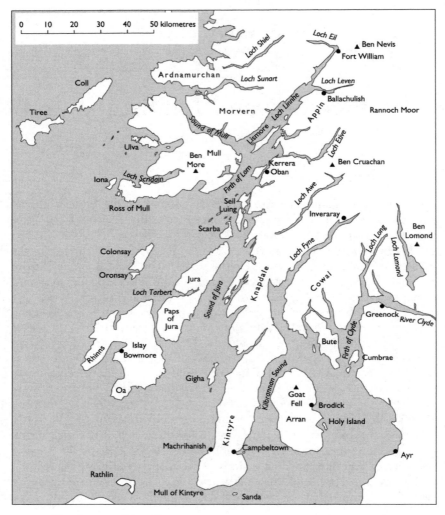

MAP 2 Sketch map of Argyll

Rocks of the ancient basement

The metamorphic rocks belonging to the Dalradian were forced into place against much older rocks, which formed the so-called basement to the Caledonian mountain belt (Map 4). Iona, Coll and Tiree are part of this ancient block of crust and the rocks are intensely folded and highly metamorphosed gneisses, similar to those in the Outer Hebrides and belonging to the 2,000 to 3,000-million-year-old Lewisian Gneiss complex, named after the isle of Lewis. The Lewisian Gneiss underwent a long and complex history of folding and high temperature metamorphism deep within

TABLE I   Geological timetable for Argyll

Geological Period	Age, millions of years	Main rock types and geological events
Quaternary	1–2	Glacial erosion and deposition
Tertiary	2–65	Extensive erosion and formation of river system; eruption of lavas, intrusion of dyke swarms and central volcanic complexes
Cretaceous	65–144	Chalk and sandstone, Mull & Lochaline
Jurassic	144–213	Shallow marine sediments, Mull
Triassic	213–250	Pebble beds, Mull
Permian	250–286	(desert sandstones on Arran)
Carboniferous	286–360	Coals and lavas, Machrihanish and Bute
Devonian	360–408	Old Red Sandstone sediments, Kerrera, Oban, south Kintyre, Lorne Plateau lavas; granite intrusions
Silurian	408–438	Highland Border Complex, Loch Lomond, Cowal & Bute; closure of Iapetus Ocean, folding, faulting, uplift, formation of Caledonian mountain belt, Highland Boundary Fault, Great Glen Fault
Ordovician	438–505	Highland Border Complex, Loch Lomond & Bute (Loch Fad Conglomerate & Innellan group)
Cambrian	505–590	Top of Dalradian may be Cambrian in age
Dalradian	590–800	Slate, grit, quartzite, greenstone (lava), limestone
Colonsay Group	>600?	Mud rocks on Colonsay & Islay; rocks on E. Iona may be of this age; could be equivalent to Dalradian
Moinian	800–1,200	Quartzite & schist (Mull)
Torridonian	800–1,200	(Northwest Sutherland; previously thought to be same as Colonsay, Islay and Iona sediments)
Rhinns Complex	1,800	Gneiss (Rhinns of Islay)
Lewisian	1,750–3,300	Gneiss, marble, ironstone on Iona
Age of the Earth	4,560	

the Earth's crust, and probably formed part of a continent that also included large areas of North America, Greenland and Scandinavia. The Scottish part of this supercontinent (sometimes referred to as Laurentia) became detached during the opening of the present North Atlantic Ocean and is now separated from the Scandinavian part by the Caledonian fold belt. Typically, the gneisses are coarse-grained, banded or striped rocks,

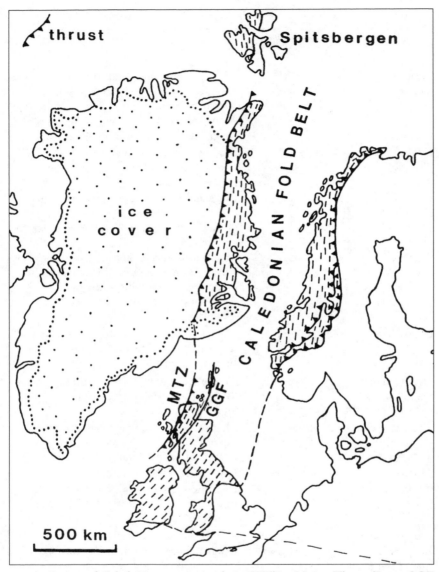

MAP 3 Extent of Caledonian mountain chain (MTZ – Moine Thrust Zone, GGF – Great Glen Fault)

pink, white and cream with quartz, white mica (muscovite) and feldspar, interbanded with darker layers, usually rich in dark green or black hornblende and black mica (biotite). They are invariably folded and often contain lenses, sheets, patches and dykes of granite and pegmatite. In addition to the gneisses, there are also rocks that were once sediments (probably shale, mudstone, sandstone, limestone and ironstone) which have

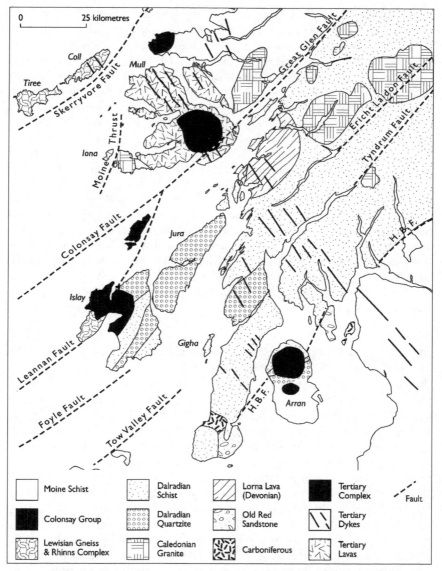

MAP 4 Outline geological map of Argyll (H.B.F – Highland Boundary Fault)

been transformed into schist, quartzite and marble under extremely high pressures and temperatures. Particular examples are the famous green marbles of Iona and Tiree and the ironstone of Iona, which is found adjacent to the marble in the same quarry.

Other parts of this ancient basement are also found in the islands, particularly in Islay and Colonsay (at Balnahard Bay), where the rocks are referred to as the Rhinns Complex after the Rhinns of Islay. Here we find intensely deformed igneous rocks, once molten granites and gabbros, that were added to the crust around 1,800 Ma. Folding and metamorphism of these rocks took place at the same time as the Lewisian rocks found around Loch Laxford in Sutherland. Previously, these rocks had been thought to belong to the Lewisian Gneiss Complex, but they are now known to be quite different and may in fact be present in a large area beneath western Scotland and northwest Ireland. A tiny outcrop is found on the island of Inishtrahull off the Donegal coast.

On Colonsay, the Rhinns of Islay and on the east coast of Iona there is a 5,000-metre-thick sequence of very dark brown to black slaty mud rocks, over 600 million years old, i.e. younger than the Rhinns Complex, and known as the Colonsay Group. The junction with the underlying basement is partly sheared and partly contains a conglomerate with pebbles of Rhinns gneisses. The rocks on Iona cannot definitely be correlated with the Colonsay Group, but are possibly equivalent; a conglomerate at the base has pebbles of Lewisian Gneiss. Previously these rocks were shown on maps as belonging to the Torridonian Sandstone of north-west Scotland, but they are now regarded as being quite distinct, and may belong to a separate crustal block.

Moine Schists

Metamorphosed Moine rocks cover most of northern Scotland east of the Moine Thrust Zone and north of the Great Glen Fault. They occur as three groups or divisions – Morar, Glenfinnan and Loch Eil – in a series of Caledonian thrust sheets, rather like a pack of cards that was pushed westwards during mountain-building around 400 Ma. Most of the rocks belonging to the Moine Supergroup are thick units of grey and white striped quartzites (originally sandstones) and quartz-mica schists (originally muddy sands), representing shallow-water marine sediments. Sedimentary structures such as ripple marks and cross bedding (formed by currents in shallow water) are frequently preserved. They are completely unfossiliferous, and the banding is often intensely folded. As a result of folding, stretching and faulting, it is very difficult to give an overall thickness for the Moine sequence of rocks, but it may have been around 5 to 10 km thick. Moine rocks occur in the Ross of Mull at Ardalanish, within the Morar and Glenfinnan Groups. Metamorphic ages of 1,050 million years have been obtained, and it is possible that the Moine rocks were laid down some 1,200 to 1,300 million years ago, after the last metamorphic event in the Lewisian Complex (which was 1,750 million years ago in the Hebrides), then metamorphosed at 1,050 million years ago.

Dalradian Schists

In contrast to the somewhat monotonous grey Moine rocks, the Dalradian represents a highly varied sequence of metamorphosed late Precambrian

(600–750 million-year-old) rocks, with a total thickness of 25 km. Rock types in the four groups – Grampian (oldest, found on Islay), Appin, Argyll and Southern Highland (youngest) – include quartzite, schist, limestone and marble, slate, phyllite, grit and conglomerate, volcanic rocks, including pillow lavas, and glacial tillite (boulder beds). Together they form a Supergroup that extends from Shetland in the north-east through the Grampian Highlands to Argyllshire in the south-west, then on to Ireland, occupying a total area of some 48,000 km². Dalradian rocks crop out between the Great Glen Fault and the Highland Boundary Fault (see Map 3), and are nowhere in contact with the Moine schists. They range in age from around 750 Ma to 600 Ma, with the Tayvallich Volcanics (596 million years old) near the top of the Southern Highland Group (Table 2) possibly representing the first rifting and opening of the ancient Iapetus Ocean, a precursor of the modern Atlantic. Most of Argyll is occupied by the Dalradian, where the best and most complete sections are found, and from where the names of the rock units are derived (based on place names). In the Scottish Highlands, the Dalradian strata generally become younger towards the south-east, with the youngest rocks at or near the Highland Border, so that the Kintyre peninsula, Cowal and northern Bute are made of Southern Highland Group rocks, while Knapdale is mostly in the Argyll Group. Extensive research has been done on the geology of the Dalradian, and the names in Table 2 reflect the subdivisions made possible by detailed work across the Highlands. The Dalradian schists are everywhere folded and metamorphosed. In general terms the northern part of the outcrop in Argyll belongs to the Cowal Flat Belt, while to the south along the Highland Boundary Fault the rocks are in the Highland Border Steep Belt, with some of them actually turned right over, where they have been pulled into a vertical position by movements on the fault.

The Dalradian rocks formed as mud, sand, silt, shale and limestone in an ancient ocean. This ocean closed 500 million years ago when a northern continent collided with a southern continent, and the sediments were squeezed, folded and heated in the building of the Caledonian Mountains, converting the muddy shales into the phyllites and schists of today. Generally speaking, the lowest grades of metamorphism (mainly lowest temperatures, also in part low pressure) are found in the south, around the Highland Boundary Fault, where slate and phyllite (papery, contorted, shiny greenish rocks) occur. Farther north, the grade increases and the rocks are mostly quartz-mica schist, often with the dark red metamorphic mineral, garnet. Other rock types besides schist are present. The island of Lismore, for example, is made of Dalradian limestone, and gives fertile soils, hence its name – Lios Mór in Gaelic, 'the big garden'. Gigha consists mostly of greenstones (chlorite schist and amphibolite), which are metamorphosed lavas and igneous sills or sheets. One unit in the Dalradian that forms a notable landmark from many viewpoints on the west is the Jura Quartzite, a very white metamorphosed shallow-water sandstone

TABLE 2 Subdivisions of the Dalradian Supergroup in Argyll

Group	Subgroup	Beds and rock types
Southern Highland		Aberfoyle Slate; Dunoon Phyllite
		Ben Ledi Grit; Beinn Bheula Schist
		Green Beds (metamorphosed volcanic rocks)
		Glen Sluan Schist
		Tayvallich Volcanics (595 million years old)
Argyll	Tayvallich	Loch Tay Limestone
		Tayvallich Slate & Limestone
		Kilchrenan Conglomerate
	Crinan	Ben Lui Schist
		Crinan Grit
	Easdale	Shira Limestone
		Ardrishaig Phyllite (= Craignish Phyllite) &
		Ben Lawers Schist
		Scarba Conglomerate
		Ben Eagach Schist & Easdale Slate
		Carn Mairg Quartzite
	Islay	Killiecrankie Schist
		Schiehallion & Islay (= Jura) Quartzites
		Port Askaig Tillite & Schiehallion Boulder
		Bed (glacial sediments, 650 million years old)
Appin	Blair Atholl	Islay Limestone
		Mullach Dubh Phyllite
		Lismore Limestone
		Cuil Bay Slate
	Ballachulish	Appin Quartzite
		Appin Limestone
		Ballachulish Slate
		Ballachulish Limestone
	Lochaber	Leven Schist
		Binnein Quartzite
Grampian	Glen Spean	Eilde Flags; Bowmore Psammite (Islay)
	Corrieyairack	
	Glenshirra	

that is much tougher than the surrounding schists on east Jura and so stands out in the landscape.

Dalradian rocks appear to have been deposited in a sedimentary basin, which evolved as the Earth's crust thinned and stretched in relation to the break-up of a great supercontinent. As thinning progressed, the basin sank and initially shallow-water sediments (sands and limestones) gave way to deep-water muds. By the time of the formation of the Southern Highland Group around 600 million years ago, the ancient continent had completely ruptured and volcanic rocks were erupted on the floor of the newly-formed Iapetus Ocean.

Two highly distinctive and extremely important horizons are present in the Dalradian of Argyll – a boulder bed at the base of the Argyll Group (Port Askaig Tillite and Schiehallion Boulder Bed, 650 million years old) representing the deposits of an ice sheet or swarm of icebergs, grounded on the floor of a shallow sea; and a volcanic horizon at the base of the Southern Highland Group (the Tayvallich Lavas, 595 million years old), representing pillow lavas erupted onto the floor of the Iapetus Ocean at a mid-ocean ridge.

The Argyll Group in the Dalradian is important in economic terms, since the rocks host a number of mineral deposits – ores of copper, nickel, lead, silver, barium, zinc, iron, molybdenum and gold. Many of these metals occur as sulphides in individual rock units, and they are usually referred to as 'stratabound deposits', the formation of which may have been related to the activity of hot metal-rich brines bubbling onto an ocean floor during sediment deposition. Some of the deposits may have been later remobilized along fault lines to become the source of metals in vein deposits.

The Caledonian mountain-building episode

Northern and western Scotland can be viewed as a geological jigsaw puzzle, with the various pieces locked together around 400 Ma, in the final stages of the Caledonian orogeny or mountain building episode. Briefly, the events that took place 410–405 Ma were the intrusion of granite bodies, including the Cairngorm massif, Ben Cruachan and the Ross of Mull granite, into the folded metamorphic rocks of the Highlands. Separate crustal fragments containing Moine, Dalradian and Highland Border Complex rocks were then slid into place along the Great Glen Fault and Highland Boundary Fault, and the entire mass was transported north-westwards over the Moine Thrust onto the Lewisian and Torridonian basement or foreland. Collision between the two great supercontinents of Laurentia (Scotland, Scandinavia, Greenland) and Avalonia (England and western Europe) some 478 million years ago marked the final closure of the Iapetus Ocean, which had up until then separated Scotland from England. The latest event in the mountain building episode was the formation of major faults, including the Great Glen Fault, the Highland Boundary Fault and the Moine Thrust.

Highland Border Complex

Sporadically along the Highland Boundary Fault are narrow fault-bounded lens-shaped outcrops of weakly metamorphosed Cambrian to late Ordovician sediments – limestone, black shale, sandstone, conglomerate and chert or jasper, with igneous serpentinite, volcanic tuff (fine ash) and pillow lavas in places, such as at Stonehaven, Balmaha and Bute in the Highland

Boundary Fault zone. This tectonically disrupted rock sequence is unique and is difficult to correlate with other units in the Caledonian belt. The lower part of the Highland Border Complex may represent a fragment of an ocean floor, which was thrust as a slice onto Dalradian rocks. Later the entire complex was slid along the Highland Boundary Fault by a series of sideways-moving faults. In Argyll these rocks are seen at Rosneath, Innellan (Bullrock Greywacke and Innellan Group) as well as in Bute at Loch Fad (the Loch Fad Conglomerate and serpentinite), which lies along the line of the Highland Boundary Fault.

The Highland Boundary Fault

The Highland Boundary Fault can be traced from Stonehaven to Conic Hill (by Balmaha on the east side of Loch Lomond) then through the islands on Loch Lomond to Helensburgh, Kilcreggan, Innellan, Bute and Arran. It represents a major crack in the Earth's crust and is the northern margin of the Midland Valley of Scotland, which dropped down to the south. Major movements on the fault took place around 375 million years ago and resulted in the Highlands being pushed up 2,500 to 3,000 metres to the north-west, relative to the younger sediments in the Midland Valley lying to the south-east. To the south and east against the fault are the very coarse rocks (boulder conglomerates) of the Old Red Sandstone, sediments deposited in desert conditions during the Devonian period, 410 to 390 million years ago. There is a marked change in scenery across the fault, from Highland schist and granite with rugged landscapes, to the younger sedimentary rocks with much smoother, rounded and low-lying features.

The Moine Thrust Zone

Moine schists are in contact with rocks of the basement along an important fault-line known as the Moine Thrust Zone, which marks the western edge of the Caledonian mountain chain. The thrust is located along the bedding planes of the Durness Limestone, which acted as a kind of lubricating plane to facilitate movement around 400 million years ago. The line of the thrust runs from Loch Eriboll in north Sutherland through Assynt, the Sleat peninsula on Skye, then down to the Sound of Iona. Westward thrusting was the last great event in the mountain building episode and resulted in great piles of overfolded rocks being pushed up like a pack of cards. Altogether there are four major thrusts, from base to top (and oldest to youngest) the Sole Thrust, Ben More Thrust, Loch Glencoul Thrust and Moine Thrust. Each thrust may have had 10 to 20 km westward movement on it, and a total displacement of around 80 km may not be an unreasonable estimate. The line of the Moine Thrust lies along the Sound of Iona, juxtaposing Moine rocks on the Ross of Mull against the Lewisian Gneiss and Iona Group rocks of the foreland or basement. The trace of the Moine Thrust was later masked or obscured by the intrusion of the Ross of Mull granite at 414 Ma, an event which also caused heating and hardening of the Iona Group sediments. The line of the thrust continues to the south-west beyond Iona and the Ross of Mull, but its actual location becomes speculative.

The Great Glen Fault

Loch Linnhe, between Kentallen and Port Appin, follows the line of the Great Glen Fault and is the only sea loch within the Great Glen; it runs between Lismore and the mainland of Morvern. Moving ice was responsible for gouging out the loch floor. Bands of quartzite, schist and limestone run north-east to south-west, parallel to the loch shore, and in places these Daldradian rocks are intruded by igneous bodies, for example at Kentallen. On the north-west side of Loch Linnhe is the Strontian granite, 435 million years old. This was previously thought to have once been connected to the Foyers granite lying 80 km to the north-east on the opposite side of the Great Glen Fault, but this comparison is no longer valid, since the two granites are actually quite different in composition. The Great Glen Fault is referred to as a tear fault, i.e. with a vertical fault plane; movement of the northwest side was sideways to the southwest. The fault continues into Mull, around Loch Don and Loch Spelve, and can be traced to the south-west as the Dubh Artach Fault and the Colonsay Fault. The main fault has a curved trend between Duart Bay, Loch Don, Loch Spelve and Loch Buie due to the intrusion of the Ben More central complex on Mull during the Tertiary volcanic episode, around 55 million years ago.

Devonian and Old Red Sandstone

Following the formation of the Caledonian mountains, the chain was rapidly worn down by erosion in desert conditions. Huge amounts of coarse sediment were removed from the treeless landscape into the Midland Valley by intermittent, fast-flowing rivers and flash floods. In early Devonian times there was a period of explosive volcanic activity. Around Oban are the Lorne lavas, andesite and basalt erupted 420 million years ago. These lavas form the Lorne plateau and cover an area of 300 km² and are up to 800 metres thick. They form step-like terraces in the landscape. Similar rocks are found just to the north, at Glencoe and Ben Nevis. Lower Old Red Sandstone deposits and volcanic agglomerate are found in southern Kintyre. In Bute, the Upper Old Red Sandstone is coarse conglomerate and red sandstone, laid down by a series of braided rivers which brought material from the mountains to the north-west.

Carboniferous

As Scotland drifted northwards from desert latitudes some 30° south of the equator to nearer equatorial regions, the climate and geography changed in the Carboniferous period (360 to 286 Ma) to densely-forested tropical swamps, river deltas and coastal lagoons that were frequently flooded by the sea, producing marine limestone bands. In the early part of the

Carboniferous there was extensive eruption of basaltic lavas around the Clyde area, including Bute and Kintyre. Also present are numerous volcanic vents, sills and dykes, especially in southern Bute. The weathering of the lava flows has produced the characteristic stepped topography. Many of the lavas show columnar jointing, as at Dunagoil on Bute, which formed as the lavas cooled rapidly at the Earth's surface. Sedimentary rocks are best represented in Kintyre, around Machrihanish, where the four-metre-thick coal seam was worked for centuries. The coal represents the compacted remains of ancient vegetation – huge fern-like trees and giant club mosses that grew in profusion in coastal swamps. Late Carboniferous to early Permian igneous activity is marked by the intrusion of a number of east-west dykes, including those near Rothesay on Bute.

Permian to Cretaceous

Following the deposition of the Carboniferous rocks, there was a return to desert conditions during the Permian and early Triassic, when the New Red Sandstone formed, present in Ayrshire and Arran but missing from Argyll. Offshore, in the Inner Hebrides Basin, there are thick Permian–Triassic sediments against the Camasunary Fault, east of Coll and Tiree, and north-east of Colonsay. Triassic, Jurassic and some Cretaceous sedimentary rocks are found extensively in the Inner Hebrides, Ardnamurchan and Morvern (at Lochaline), preserved under the protective cover of the Tertiary lavas. Triassic conglomerates and sandstones are found in south-east Mull, around Loch Spelve. Jurassic marine sediments – limestone, sandstone and shale – are found in Mull around the Loch Don area. These rocks are richly fossiliferous, with brachiopods, bivalves, corals, ammonites and belemnites, indicating clear, warm, shallow sub-tropical seas. Sandstones represent river delta-deposits that built out into the shelf sea. Estuaries and lagoons became established also, in the Middle Jurassic. It is worth pointing out that these rocks are much more abundant and thick in the North Sea and Moray Firth, where they form the source rocks and reservoir rocks for our oil and gas deposits.

Compared with the Jurassic, younger Cretaceous and Tertiary sediments are much thinner and sparser onshore. Cretaceous rocks are found at Carsaig and Loch Don in Mull, and on the north side of the Sound of Mull at Lochaline is found the well-known pure white sandstone that is still mined for glass manufacture. During the Cretaceous, the famous white chalk cliffs of Dover were formed, and it is probable that these rocks extended right around the Inner Hebrides, but erosion has now removed almost all of them. After the Cretaceous sediments were deposited, the land was uplifted and eroded, prior to the formation of some Tertiary sediments and the eruption of the great thickness of Tertiary basalt lavas. On Mull there are a few local patches of Tertiary conglomerate, sandstone, shale and lignite (poor-quality coal). The most famous of these are the Ardtun Leaf Beds of western Mull. Here, fossil leaves are exquisitely preserved in intricate detail on the surfaces of paper-thin shales, indicating a warm humid climate and dense vegetation on a land surface. Equally famous is MacCulloch's tree near Burg on the Ardmeanach peninsula of western Mull. This fossil tree, now sadly removed by collectors, was engulfed in its growing position by a sudden outpouring of lava and petrified instantly, some 55 million years ago.

Tertiary volcanic activity

After the deposition of the chalk and other Cretaceous sediments, the land surface was elevated and eroded. Then quite suddenly in the early Tertiary Period (63 to 52 Ma) the whole of the Inner Hebrides region, from St Kilda to Ailsa Craig and Antrim in Northern Ireland, was overwhelmed with volcanic activity. In contrast, the North Sea area and south-east England continued to experience marine and deltaic sedimentation. Vast outpourings of basaltic lava flows covered the land surface; in Mull the total thickness of these flows is around 1,800 metres. Skye, Rum, Eigg, Ardnamurchan and Arran were volcanically active areas. Vents were located where the present-day central complexes are located, e.g. Ben More in the case of Mull. These central intrusions are closely associated with areas where thinned crust intersects major fault lines – the Great Glen Fault in the case of the Mull volcano, and the Highland Boundary Fault in the case of Arran. Generally, the central intrusions consist of gabbro and basalt, although Goat Fell in Arran is made of granite (as are the Red Hills in Skye). As well as lava, the volcanic regions also contain layers of ash and bombs. Sometimes the tops of lava flows were weathered red in the tropical climate of the Tertiary period, to form fossil soils that were preserved when the next flow was erupted. Some of these red horizons contain fossil leaves, indicating a relatively long, quiet period between eruptions. The great piles of lava flows have given northern and western Mull and Ulva a highly characteristic stepped landscape – partly a reflection of the weathering out of these rather weaker red horizons (see Plate 1).

Arguably the most famous geological locality in the world is Fingal's Cave on Staffa, which demonstrates to spectacular effect the columnar cooling joints so typical of basalt lava. These are nearly perfectly hexagonal, and formed when the lava cooled rapidly and evenly from top to bottom after being erupted onto the land surface (see Plate 2). Many of the flat skerries and islets off western Mull are also fragments of lava flows, such as the Dutchman's Cap and the other Treshnish Isles. The Giant's Causeway not far to the south on the Antrim coast is identical in age and formation to Fingal's Cave.

During this volcanic episode, the Earth's crust was considerably distorted and weakened. As a result, circular and radial cracks opened up and allowed lava to penetrate to the surface, possibly to feed lava flows; dipping sheets and horizontal sills are also abundant. Today, all around the Mull volcano we see parallel sets of ring dykes and cone sheets, as well as an impressive and far-reaching swarm of radial dykes, rather like the spokes of a wheel. These north-west to south-east trending dykes cross much of Argyll, and those originating in Mull can be found all the way from the Outer Hebrides to north-east England. Mull can be said to have the most complex geology in the entire Tertiary volcanic province, particularly since the volcanic activity shifted from centre to centre over a period of around three million years – the Glen More centre, the Ben Chaisgidle centre and finally the Loch Bà centre, also know as the Late Caldera. The volcanism ceased as abruptly as it began 52 Ma. Intrusion of the Mull central complex caused radial folding of the Triassic and Jurassic sediments around the volcanic centre. This is especially evident around Loch Don and Loch Spelve, and in fact the semi-circular shape of eastern Mull is a result of this folding.

One consequence of this activity, particularly the intrusion of the central complexes, was to force up the Earth's crust in western Scotland. Torrential rain and profoundly deep sub-tropical weathering removed vast quantities of rocks and caused the land surface to tilt to the east. At this period, the main river pattern of Scotland was established, with all our major rivers flowing to the east, carrying sediment to be deposited into the Moray Firth and North Sea.

Landscape development

By two million years ago, Scotland had reached its present position, i.e. close to the North Pole. Climate change led to the rapid onset of cold conditions in the northern latitudes and widespread sheets of ice became established on the continental landmasses, giving rise to the great Ice Age, which lasted until around 10,000 years ago. During that period, four successive cold and warm events affected Scotland. Ice cover was at its maximum 18,000 years ago and Scotland was buried under a sheet possibly 2,000 metres thick. The main centre of the thickest ice was the Rannoch Moor–Loch Lomond area. Certainly all of Argyll would have been submerged beneath this ice sheet. Glacial erosion was to a large extent controlled by the underlying geology, which as we have seen is predominantly Caledonian in origin, i.e. the main strike of the rocks is north-east to south-west, the same as the main folds and faults. So, deep erosion of different hardnesses of rocks has created the highly-indented coastline, with many north-east to south-west sea lochs and long narrow peninsulas and islands. The Paps of Jura provide a stunning example of differential erosion – the tough quartzite is much more resistant than the mica schists to the east, and glaciation had the effect of rounding the peaks (see Plate 3). They may look conical, but they were never volcanoes.

Whilst the ice was moving, loose boulders and rocks were picked up and transported at the base of the ice sheet, causing scouring and scratching of the bare rock surface, rather like sandpaper on a large scale. When the ice melted, these blocks were deposited over the ground, together with finer clay and sand particles. Some of the transported boulders are huge, e.g. the 'Jim Crow' rock at Hunter's Quay, which was dropped at the base of such an ice sheet or glacier. The sediment is referred to as till and the obliterating cover is known as drift. Many parts of western Argyll, especially the islands, have very little drift, and the bare rocky knolls of basement rock are exposed as a flat, low-lying plateau.

The enormous weight of the 2,000-metre-thick ice sheet caused the Earth's crust to be depressed for almost two million years, but melting occurred relatively rapidly and the sudden outpouring of melt water caused a rise in sea level at first, leading to extensive flooding of coastal areas. Once the ice had completely melted, the land surface began a slow process of recovery or rebound, and this gradual rise is still continuing today, more particularly in Scandinavia, but also in parts of Scotland. Uplift took place in a series of pulses over the last 8,000 years as the land regained its previous level and the sea again retreated. This has given rise to a series of raised beaches around the coast, which are particularly well seen in Jura, Islay and Colonsay (see Plate 3). One of the best stretches in the Cowal Peninsula is between Innellan and Toward, while other raised beaches occur at the head of many of the sea lochs – e.g. Holy Loch and Loch Riddon.

Post-glacial changes

Soon after the main melting of the great ice sheets 13,000 years ago, lowland Scotland was clear of glaciers, although ice remained in the west and in the Highlands for several more thousand years. The bare landscape was rapidly colonised by trees, shrubs, mosses, lichens and grasses. Conditions initially would have been similar to the Arctic and sub-Arctic tundra found in northern Canada and Scandinavia. Dwarf willow, birch and juniper were the first trees to invade. Around 11,000 to 10,000 years ago, there was another sudden deterioration in the climate and in the Highlands ice reappeared in the valleys. This period has been called the Loch Lomond Readvance. Trees were killed off and the arctic tundra landscape was reestablished for another thousand years. Thereafter, the climate improved and average temperatures rose steadily, resulting in the reappearance of birch and hazel. The climate around 7,500 to 5,000 years ago provided optimum conditions for tree growth throughout Europe. Conifers were the first migrants to arrive, followed by broad-leaved woodlands with birch and hazel, eventually giving way to oak and elm, and areas of coniferous forest. Most of the lower ground then would have been tree-covered. From about 5,000 years ago, the decline of elm and the rapid spread of blanket peat, heath and grassland over previously forested areas can be connected with a climatic deterioration to cooler, wetter conditions, and the effects of humans, who started to clear the native forests. Peat is common in Argyll, especially on the acid rocks (gneisses) of the islands in the west, although Tiree is not well endowed with this resource, and islanders in the past crossed to Coll to gather their peat.

No visitor to Argyll and the islands can fail to notice the spectacular white sandy beaches around the west coast especially in Colonsay and Tiree, and the machair lands that fringe the coastal bays and inlets (see Plate 4). This sand has been derived from the skeletons of minute marine planktonic animals that were abundant in the waters prior to being killed off by the sudden drop in temperature brought on by the start of the Ice Age. Thick banks of shell debris piled up in the Minches and the material is now being carried onshore by currents, then sorted and moved by the wind. Being of carbonate, the soils that form in the machair lands by the mixing of the shells with organic matter and quartz sand are usually quite fertile and where not grazed are host to an amazing range of plants. Many of the post-glacial dunes have now been stabilized and have stopped moving across the land.

The most recent landscape effects have been created by human cultivation and building. Here too the local geology has been of great benefit – in particular the Dalradian limestones have made for fertile soils, as at Kilmartin, and the slates from Easdale have been put to good use throughout the region. Another Dalradian rock of great significance is the greenstone used in the carving of the Kildalton Cross on Islay, an exquisite piece of work which is slowly being weathered – the rain and wind affect the minerals differently, so that the white or creamy feldspar are standing proud and the green chlorite and hornblende are weathering back and obscuring the carvings (see Plate 5). Dalradian hornblende schist in the Kilmartin glen area is tougher than the limestone, and upstanding knolls have been important landmarks, e.g. the famous fortress of Dunadd between Lochgilphead and Kilmartin. Clearly, geology has played an extremely important part in the shaping of Argyll and the islands.

CHAPTER TWO

The Early Peoples

Introduction

Some 20,000 years ago Scotland was completely covered by deep ice and there was virtually no plant or animal life. Climatic conditions gradually changed, the ice cover melted, and around 15,000 years ago plants and animals recolonized, only to be largely extinguished once again during the tundra conditions of a 'mini-Ice Age' between 13,000 and 11,500 years ago. Thereafter warmer conditions rapidly set in.

As far as is currently known there was no human presence in Scotland before the extreme glacial conditions of the last Ice Age (Saville 1997), nor during the relatively short episode of warmer climate 15,000 to 13,000 years ago. It was only after the onset, from about 11,500 years ago, of climatic conditions similar to those of the present day that people arrived, following in the wake of recolonizing plants and animals.

Environmental change during the following millennia was marked. The melting of huge amounts of ice returned large volumes of water to seas and lochs, with consequent submerging of land. On the other hand, the removal of the great weight of ice led to some uplift of the land mass. As a result of these two factors, sea levels generally rose in the period from 11,500 to 8,000 years ago until a maximum high shore-line was reached. Since around 6000 BC there has been a general fall in sea level.

Change in the natural vegetation is best documented in terms of the dominant tree and shrub species through time. The initial spread of juniper, birch and hazel woodland gave way to elm, oak and alder on the mainland by around 7000 BC, though this happened rather later and more patchily on the islands. Maximum forest cover was attained by around 5000 to 4000 BC, after which there was a marked decline in elm, probably as a result of disease, and a gradual reduction in forest density. This was partly as a result of a long period of generally wetter and stormier conditions and the expansion of blanket bog, but also of the increasing effect of human influence on the landscape.

The early peoples of Argyll shared the land with various large animals, such as the wolf, red deer, brown bear, wild boar, beaver, elk, bison, and lynx. Apart from the red deer, these are all now extinct and, while some survived into historic times, others, such as the elk, were probably quite rapidly hunted out of existence by the early peoples.

Radiocarbon dating is the technique on which archaeologists rely for understanding the sequence of events in prehistory. The earliest radiocarbon dates for human presence in Scotland – at about 8500 BC – are from burnt hazelnut shells found with flaked stone tools at Cramond, on the outskirts of Edinburgh (Denison 2001). On this evidence it is probable that settlement throughout the central belt of Scotland had occurred by this time. Radiocarbon dates from elsewhere in the country make it likely that the spread of people across most of the mainland and the islands (the chief exceptions being Shetland, the Western Isles and St Kilda) happened relatively rapidly, almost certainly by 7500 BC.

So sketchy is our knowledge of this early period, however, that we cannot yet say whether people are likely to have arrived in Argyll earlier or later than in the central belt. The radiocarbon dates currently available from Argyll are quite late, but the probability is that people were there as early, if not earlier, perhaps by shortly after 10,000 BC. The most likely route of the peoples who first colonized Argyll is that they arrived from the south along the coast, making most of their progress north by boat through inshore waters.

The first peoples

The earliest peoples in Argyll were nomadic hunter-fisher-gatherers, living entirely off the natural resources of the sea, rivers, lochs and land. The people of this period, which is conventionally termed the Mesolithic (or Middle Stone Age), were skilled seafarers, and all the main islands, from Islay to Mull, reveal traces of their presence (see Finlayson 1998 and Wickham-Jones 1994 for general introductions to the Mesolithic period in Scotland). These traces are predominantly in the form of characteristic flint and stone implements, which have the benefits for the archaeologist of being both virtually indestructible and readily recognizable. The forms of these implements are fairly standardized, and the great majority of Mesolithic artefacts found throughout Argyll probably date to what appears to have been the main period of hunter-fisher-gatherer activity between 7500 and 5000 BC. Only one collection of artefacts, from a now-destroyed cave at Kilmelfort, near Oban, has been identified as possibly dating to a very early phase, perhaps before 9500 BC, on the basis of some unusual flint tools, but there is no direct dating evidence (Coles 1983).

Also on purely typological grounds, from an assessment of some of the flint implements known as microliths found on Jura (Plate 6), it is possible that an Early Mesolithic phase – later than the objects from Kilmelfort but before 8500 BC – is represented at Glenbatrick and Lussa Bay (Mithen ed. 2000). Otherwise, most of the Mesolithic artefacts found throughout the region belong to the so-called Later Mesolithic, from 8500/8000 BC

onwards. Microliths, the most diagnostic type of Mesolithic flint implement, were mainly used as the tips and barbs for wooden arrowshafts.

Argyll's earliest well-dated settlement site is at Staosnaig on Colonsay,
where recent excavations have revealed the extensive remains of a
Mesolithic encampment from around 6500 BC (Mithen 2000). The infill of
one large circular pit at Staosnaig was found by the excavators to contain
over 49,000 flint artefacts. Although the vast bulk of these comprised the
waste chippings from tool manufacture, they did include nearly 200
microliths and other tools. As is common on archaeological sites throughout Scotland, the acidic nature of the soil at this location has prevented the
survival of any organic remains other than those burnt or charred at the
time, as was the case with thousands of hazelnut shells. This means it is
not possible to say much about the economy of these early settlers, though
it can be assumed they were hunting and fishing and exploiting other plant
foods besides hazelnuts, nutritious though these may be.

At this site, as at all other Mesolithic encampments throughout the
region, people erected temporary shelters, established hearths, prepared
and cooked their food, and made tools and other equipment and clothing
as required, before moving on to establish another camp in order to exploit
a fresh suite of resources. Many camps were returned to, perhaps as part
of an annual territorial cycle, over periods which may in some cases be
reckoned in centuries.

Most of these Mesolithic sites were open-air, but on occasion caves and
rock-shelters were utilised, as for example was a small cave on the island
of Ulva, off the west coast of Mull (Bonsall et al. 1994). The importance
of this type of site is often exaggerated in the archaeological record simply
because caves can provide good conditions for the preservation of archaeological remains. Such was the case at two of the most famous Mesolithic
sites in Argyll, MacArthur Cave and Druimvargie Rockshelter in Oban,
which produced rare examples of barbed points made of red deer antler,
which were used as the tips of harpoons (Anderson 1895 and 1898)
(Plate 7). The earliest well-dated artefact from Argyll so far, a small bone
tool from around 7400 BC, was found at Druimvargie Rockshelter.

Another site which has produced some important bone and antler artefacts, as well as flint tools, is on the small island of Risga in Loch Sunart
(Pollard et al. 1996). Further south in Argyll, the islands of Islay and Jura
have proved to be particularly rich in hunter-fisher-gatherer sites, which
have yielded many hundreds of thousands of flint artefacts (Searight 1984
and Mithen 2000). It is not entirely clear why some of the islands have such
prolific traces of settlement during this period when the mainland does not.
In the case of Islay, however, part of the explanation may be that on its
western coast the beaches were rich in flint pebbles, which provided an
obvious attraction for Mesolithic people looking for raw material for
implements (Marshall in Mithen 2000).

Evidence for the final stages of the Mesolithic in Scotland is scanty, though Argyll has produced most of what is available. In particular, sites on the small island of Oronsay and in the vicinity of Oban have yielded important information. On Oronsay, no fewer than five shell-middens (Figure 1) dating to the later part of the Mesolithic period, around 5500 to 4000 BC, indicate the extensive exploitation of limpets, probably as bait used in fishing for saithe (Mellars 1987). The thousands of discarded limpet shells in these middens have created an environment suitable for the preservation of organic remains, and the very frequent bones of saithe (or coalfish) suggest that catching these fish was the main focus of activity. The presence of fragments of the antlers and bones of red deer has sparked much debate as to their source, since neither Oronsay nor the adjacent island of Colonsay are thought likely to have had deer populations at this time. This being the case, it is odd that no sites of this same phase have been found on the nearby islands of Islay and Jura, nor on the neighbour-ing mainland. Only to the north, around Oban, have sites such as the rockshelter at Carding Mill Bay (Connock et al. 1992) also produced com-parably late or even later remains. Both Carding Mill Bay and some of the Oronsay middens have produced small perforated cowrie-shell beads, the only evidence that survives for personal ornament at this period.

Another fascinating aspect of the shell-middens on Oronsay is that archaeologists have found some human bones and teeth scattered within them (Richards & Sheridan 2000). A possible explanation is that these bones, dated to around 4000 BC, come from formal burials in cemeteries, which have then been disturbed by continuing re-use of the same location for the activities which created the shell-middens. Cemeteries of this kind dating to the late Mesolithic have been found associated with Mesolithic coastal settlements elsewhere in Europe, especially in Scandinavia (Larsson 1989). If this were the case on Oronsay, it would indicate the beginnings of a concern for the disposal of the dead which becomes a significant fac-tor in the life of subsequent communities in Argyll.

Early farmers

Given the paucity of late Mesolithic remains in Argyll, it is very uncertain whether there were pre-existing populations at around 4000 BC capable of adopting new technologies, or whether the succeeding Neolithic (New Stone Age) period represents the influx of new settlers. Whatever the case, after about 4000 BC we see the presence in Argyll of people with a new way of life, involving for the first time agriculture (domesticated cattle and sheep and cultivated cereals), the construction of ceremonial and funerary monuments, and a new technology which embraced the manufacture of pottery vessels and polished stone axeheads (see Ashmore 1996 and Barclay 1998 for general introductions to the Neolithic period in Scotland).

Inevitably, it is the monuments — principally the chambered tombs —

FIGURE 1 Nineteenth-century engraving from a photograph, showing a large Mesolithic shell-midden on Oronsay. Reproduced from S. Grieve, *The Great Auk, or Garefowl: its History, Archaeology, and Remains* (1885, London, Thomas C. Jack).

which loom largest in any consideration of this period in Argyll. As we have seen, apart from the few scraps of human bones found in the Oronsay shell-middens, there is no evidence for individuals or of burial practices during the Mesolithic period.

The earlier part of the Neolithic period, however, is marked by a rite of collective burial, which required the construction of elaborate stone tombs, many of which still survive in Argyll. One of the best-known is the cairn of Nether Largie South (Plate 8) in the Kilmartin Valley (RCAHMS 1998, 48–51), with its impressive rectangular burial chamber constructed, in characteristic fashion, of large upright stones. Lintel slabs, which can in some tombs be very large, and dry-stone walling complete the chamber, which is then encased in a large cairn of boulders. Nether Largie South, like many other chambered cairns, was entered and disturbed long before detailed archaeological records could be made, and it is now difficult to tell exactly how the chamber related to the cairn.

However, by piecing together information gained from other tombs in and around the region, such as Blasthill and Gort na h'Ulaidhe in Kintyre (RCAHMS 1971, 33 & 35) and Glenvoidean on Bute (Marshall & Taylor 1977), we can see that, fundamentally, this type of monument comprised a long cairn with a chambered area opening onto a forecourt at one end of the cairn. The burial chamber may be a simple rectangular stone 'box', or be elaborated by subdivision into segments. Numerous individuals were buried in the chambers, as inhumations much more often than as cremations, sometimes accompanied by pottery bowls and flint implements. Such monuments are known as Clyde cairns and are common throughout much of south-west Scotland (Henshall 1972 and Scott 1969a).

In addition to the Clyde cairns there are a few examples of another tomb type in the far north of the region, for example at Achnacree just north of Oban (RCAHMS 1975, 37–8). These are so-called Hebridean tombs, which have a chambered area at or near the centre of a round cairn, with access provided by a long, narrow, low passageway connecting the chamber and the outside of the cairn. In addition to these two main types there are numerous examples of vaguely categorized 'long cairns', which exhibit no clear structural features but which are presumed to be tombs of Neolithic date.

Apart from the tombs, the other major category of surviving monuments in Argyll consists of the stone circles, other standing stones and alignments, and decorated rocks. These types of site are difficult to date, and in many cases they probably straddle the Neolithic and succeeding Bronze Age periods.

At Temple Wood, very close to the tomb already mentioned at Kilmartin, two stone circles have been extensively excavated (Scott 1989). They demonstrate a complex history of construction, both starting as timber circles which were replaced in stone (Plate 9). Close by is the enigmatic setting of standing stones at Nether Largie, some of which are decorated with cup-marks or cup-and-ring marks. Two of the stones from the south-west circle at Temple Wood are also decorated, one with concentric circles, the other with a double spiral.

Also close by are the standing stones at Ballymeanoch, which again have cup- and cup-and-ring marks (RCAHMS 1988, 127–9). These sites lie within a relatively small area around Kilmartin, which has a remarkable concentration of some of the most impressive cup-a nd-ring decorated rock surfaces in Scotland, for example at Achnabreck, Cairnbaan, and Kilmichael Glassary (Butter 1999 and Stevenson in Ritchie 1997) (see Plate 10). What these decorated rock surfaces actually mean will never be known, but their very mystery helps evoke the strangeness of the prehistoric past.

Elsewhere in Argyll there are other stone circles, for example at Cultoon, Islay; Hough, Tiree; Lochbuie, Mull; and Strontoiller, Lorne (Burl 2000). These, together with all the other standing stones and stone settings, some of which, such as Kintraw, Mid-Argyll (RCAHMS 1988, 64–7), are associated with burial cairns, attest the importance of the ritual aspect of life for societies in the latter part of the Neolithic period (see Plate 11). There is a strong probability that rituals were linked to significant celestial phenomena occurring during the year, the observation and recording of which conditioned the siting of some stone settings. It is also likely that many similar settings existed entirely in timber, as at Temple Wood, but very few of these survive in any fashion, apart from those identifiable from distinctive cropmarks visible in aerial photographs, as with a timber circle and avenue recently excavated at Upper Largie, Kilmartin.

A final type of Neolithic ritual site, known as a henge monument, is represented by only one known example in Argyll, again at Ballymeanoch, near Kilmartin. Ballymeanoch henge consists of two crescentic banks with matching internal ditches, demarcating a circular central area with entrances to the north and south (RCAHMS 1988, 52). Excavations in the nineteenth century recovered evidence of burials within this monument, but these relate to subsequent usage in the Early Bronze Age and the function of the original monument is not established.

The presence of Neolithic peoples is also evident from chance finds throughout the region of polished stone axeheads and leaf-shaped flint arrowheads (Scott 1969b). Stone axeheads fall into two categories: those which were functional, providing the blades used in a variety of wood-working tasks, in particular, we presume, house- and boat-building; and those which were prestige or ceremonial items. Functional axeheads, often found discarded in fragments after having broken during use, are in the majority. But an outstanding prestige example is the axehead found at Appin, north of Oban, made of jadeite, which must have originated far away in southern Europe (Clarke 1968). Axeheads are usually made from stone, which is sometimes of a locally available type; other axeheads may have been imported from well-known Neolithic quarry locations in the Lake District and Northern Ireland, where the stone was of superior quality (Bradley and Edmonds 1993). Flint, not a common resource within the region except as small pebbles, was only occasionally used for axeheads in Argyll, though one spectacular find of a cache of imported Irish artefacts at Auchenhoan, near Campbeltown, included five examples (Plate 12), together with over a hundred flint flakes (Saville 1999).

Leaf-shaped arrowheads, normally made of flint, attest the importance of the bow and arrow at this period. There is little evidence to suggest, however, that hunting, as opposed to animal husbandry, was of any significance during the Neolithic, and it is likely that the main use of the bow and arrow was in warfare, which, albeit at a low level, seems to have been endemic to society at the time.

This would fit with a picture of scattered, relatively self-contained communities (of perhaps a few hundred people each), which needed to interact with neighbouring groups for sexual partners and other social and economic purposes, but between and among which violence could often occur. The actual settlement sites of these people are extremely difficult to discover, but at least three have been located by chance during the excavation of more recent structures. Two of these locations in Cowal, at Ardnadam near Dunoon (Rennie 1984) and Auchategan in Glendaruel (Marshall 1978), produced traces of timber houses with associated spreads of flint and stone artefacts and fragments of pottery vessels. A third site, at Balloch

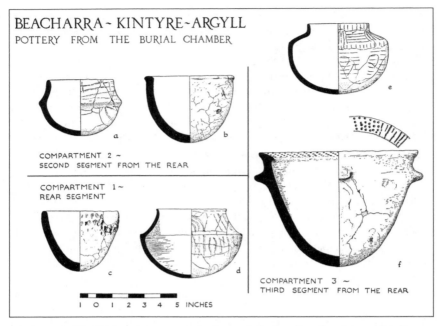

BEACHARRA ~ KINTYRE ~ ARGYLL
POTTERY FROM THE BURIAL CHAMBER

COMPARTMENT 2 ~
SECOND SEGMENT FROM THE REAR

COMPARTMENT 1 ~
REAR SEGMENT

COMPARTMENT 3 ~
THIRD SEGMENT FROM THE REAR

1 O 1 2 3 4 5 INCHES

FIGURE 2 Neolithic pottery vessels from the chambered cairn at Beacharra, Kintyre. Scale in inches. Reproduced from Scott (1964, fig. 8), by permission of The Prehistoric Society.

Hill, Kintyre (Peltenburg 1982), had a hilltop setting and may well have been a defended settlement. In addition to the normal inventory of finds of flint, stone and pottery, the Neolithic people at Balloch Hill made use of a number of artefacts of pitchstone, a volcanic raw material with similar properties to flint, which must have been imported from the island of Arran.

The pottery used by Neolithic people is best known from finds made during the excavation of some chambered tombs. Various names have been given to types of Neolithic pottery in the region, such as Beacharra ware, called after the tomb at Beacharra in Kintyre where six vessels were found in 1892 (Scott 1964 and Scott 1969a). These Neolithic pots are mostly simple round-based bowls and cups, sometimes completely plain and hemispherical, sometimes with an angular profile or an elaborate rim, and sometimes decorated with limited patterns made by incision or impression (Figure 2).

Few other elements of everyday tools and equipment survive from the Neolithic period, chiefly because these artefacts were made of organic materials such as bone, antler, skin, wood, twine, straw, reed, and so on – materials which decay rapidly in Scotland's acid soils without special conditions for preservation such as we have found in the Mesolithic middens of the west coast. Nevertheless, it is important when visiting the remaining Neolithic stone monuments, or looking at the flint and stone implements of the period in museum displays, to remember that a rich variety of buildings and monuments in timber, and of artefacts in organic raw materials of all kinds, once existed but have not survived.

It is difficult to pinpoint specific changes in material culture, economy or ritual through the Neolithic period in Argyll. In general terms the chambered tombs appear relatively early, whereas the henge monument, stone circles, and rock art are probably later, perhaps all after 3000 BC. One of the few types of artefact which does seem specific to the later Neolithic is the enigmatic carved stone ball (Marshall 1977). These balls are most often found in north-east Scotland, but there are Argyll examples from Dunaverty, Kintyre; Castle Sween and Dunadd, Mid-Argyll; and Glen Massan, Cowal. Care must be taken over the interpretation of their presence, however, since the examples from both Castle Sween and Dunadd could have been brought to the region in early historic times rather than in the Neolithic.

The end of the Neolithic period, at around 2500 BC, is signalled in the archaeological record by the first appearance of the new technology of metalworking, in the form of copper and bronze axeheads and daggers. The latter are often found as grave-goods, associated with burials which are also accompanied by a distinctive new type of pottery vessel known as a Beaker. Argyll seems to have been at the forefront of the adoption of this pottery in Scotland, since a particularly early example was found in a grave at Sorisdale on Coll (Ritchie and Crawford 1978).

During the Neolithic the countryside underwent distinct changes. Before this period there was no major human interference with the landscape — there were for example no fields or other major clearings and there had been no need for substantial trackways. Such changes may not have been marked throughout the whole of Argyll during the Neolithic: some areas, such as the islands of Jura, Mull and Tiree, or Morvern on the mainland, have produced little evidence from this period. In general, however, it was during the Neolithic that the impact of farming and a more settled way of life began the process of transforming the rural landscape into the Argyll countryside we know today.

CHAPTER THREE

The Bronze Age: from Sacred Landscapes to Warrior Society

Introduction

This chapter surveys aspects of the archaeology of Argyll from approximately the mid-third millennium BC to the 7th century BC. The start of this period is marked by the introduction of the earliest metalwork, in the form of copper artefacts, followed relatively soon by the development of full bronze metallurgy, and it closes with the adoption of iron as the principal raw material for edged weapons and tools. Conventionally, this span of time encompasses the 'Bronze Age', but, as has long been recognised, the 'Three Age' system must now be seen as convenient shorthand. By and large, the technological changes which the terms Stone, Bronze and Iron Age reflect did not neatly coincide with major changes in settlement and economy, or archaeologically detectable social and political upheavals. The first artefacts of copper probably circulated among the late Neolithic communities in Scotland prior to the formal introduction of metallurgy itself, while the transition to widespread use of iron may also have been a gradual one.

For much of the period under review, the legacy of some two centuries of discovery, survey and excavation still consists principally of artefacts and data relating to ceremonial and funerary practices. However, during the later part of the Bronze Age the balance shifts in favour of evidence relating to settlement and economy. Even then the picture is far from even, for there are marked variations in the quality of the evidence across Argyll as a whole; in part, this is a reflection of the fact that Argyll is an amalgam of sub-regions of differing character rather than a single geographical entity.

Making an appearance: Beaker users and the earliest metalwork

The middle of the third millennium BC saw the appearance in Britain of the so-called 'Beaker phenomenon', characterised by the presence in individual graves of a new and distinctive highly-decorated style of fine quality pottery, along with related artefacts. These types are found widely over western and central Europe and have their origins there. Rather than marking a wholesale folk movement, as once thought, it is now considered that the appearance of Beaker pottery and associated artefacts may have been associated with the spread of a new ideology or new beliefs. The Beaker user went to the grave accompanied by symbols of personal status – the pot itself and, in richer graves, a range of prestige artefacts manufactured by skilled craftsmen or made from exotic materials. Archery equipment is a recurrent feature of the richer male graves: a notable find from Argyll is the fine ceremonial stone wristguard or archer's bracer from Callachally on Mull (see Map 5 for location of sites mentioned in the text).

Although some metal objects, particularly copper axes, may have been in circulation prior to the formal introduction of metallurgical skills, it is among such Beaker graves that we find the first dateable evidence of metalwork in Scotland, in the form of small copper knives and gold ornaments. In due course, continuing contact with the continent led to the introduction of full bronze technology, involving the alloying of copper and tin, an innovation that can be dated to around 2100 BC.

Whatever the precise nature of the phenomenon, the west of Scotland soon appears to have felt the wind of the social changes associated with the spread of the Beaker 'package' of artefacts. A sample of human bone from a skeleton found with a cord-decorated Beaker at Sorisdale on Coll was submitted for radiocarbon dating; falling within the range 2468–2197 in calibrated years BC, the result is among the earliest for any Beaker burial in Scotland (owing to the statistical nature of the method, the date is expressed in terms of a span within which there is a 95 percent chance that the true date lies).

Finds of the distinctive Beaker vessels are known from across Argyll. Fragments have been found eroding from old soil horizons in a number of coastal sandhills in Ardnamurchan and Coll; these probably reflect fugitive traces of occupation on light sandy soils. However, Early Bronze Age settlement sites are very rare and, in most cases, Beakers have been found associated with burials. Discoveries of Beaker pottery in a number of chambered cairns suggest the continuing use and veneration of these, by then ancient, monuments, in some cases involving re-use of the chamber, in others the insertion of slab-built cist graves into the body of the cairn or the extension of the cairn to incorporate burials on its periphery.

The Earlier Bronze Age: a landscape of the dead

Apart from a few sites which have survived in coastal locations, settlement evidence is largely lacking for the earlier part of the Bronze Age. In the absence of domestic sites, an indication of the consolidation and expansion

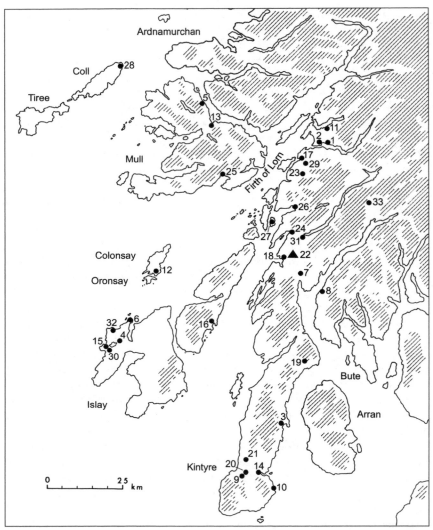

MAP 5 Location of sites and finds mentioned in Chapter 3. 1. Achnaba; 2. Achnacree;
3. Achnasavil; 4. An Sithean, Islay; 5. Ardnacross, Mull; 6. Ardnave & Kilellan, Islay;
7. Badden; 8. Ballimore; 9. Balloch Hill; 10. Balnabraid; 11. Barcaldine; 12. Beinn
Arnicil, Colonsay; 13. Callachally, Mull; 14. Campbeltown; 15. Coul, Islay; 16. Cul
a'Bhaile, Jura; 17. Dalrigh; 18. Duntroon; 19. Glenreasdell; 20. Killeonan;
21. Kilmaho; 22. Kilmartin Valley; 23. Kilmore; 24. Kintraw; 25. Lochbuie,
Mull; 26. Melfort; 27. Shuna, Nether Lorne; 28. Sorisdale, Coll; 29. Strontoiller;
30. Sunderland, Islay; 31. Torran; 32. Traigh Bhan, Islay; 33. Tullich, Glen Aray.
(Map drawn by Marion O'Neil)

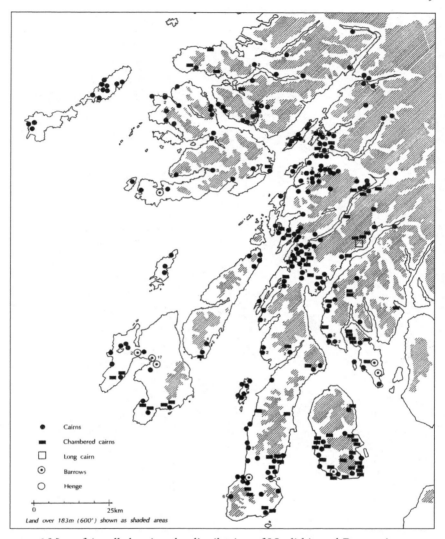

Cairns

Chambered cairns

Long cairn

Barrows

Henge

0   25km

Land over 183m (600') shown as shaded areas

MAP 6 Map of Argyll showing the distribution of Neolithic and Bronze Age monuments, including chambered cairns, long cairns, barrows, henges and round cairns. Reproduced by courtesy of Dr Graham Ritchie.

of settlement is provided by funerary monuments such as cairns and cists. Maps in the volumes of the Argyll *Inventory* convey the distribution of sites area by area and they combine to indicate that, by the mid-second millennium, settlement by small farming communities probably extended to all parts of the region – including remote mainland glens such as Glen Creran and Glen Etive and all of the major Inner Hebridean islands. The

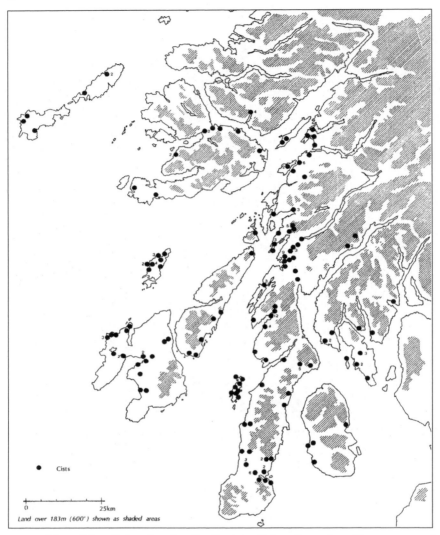

Cists

0   25km
Land over 183m (600') shown as shaded areas

MAP 7 Map of Argyll showing the distribution of cists. Reproduced by courtesy of
Dr Graham Ritchie

best-known concentration of sites occurs in the Lochgilphead/Kilmartin
area, but there are also notable groups of monuments in Benderloch and
Lorne, as well as smaller clusters on several of the islands (Maps 6 and 7).

By the middle of the third millennium BC, chambered cairns had long
since ceased to be built, although they continued to be venerated. At the
risk of over-simplification, the communal burial rite of the Neolithic was
replaced by interment in individual graves, most commonly consisting of

small slab-built cists, usually only large enough to accommodate a single flexed or crouched inhumation. In practice, there is a great deal of variety in the treatment of the dead. In some cases, the graves were covered by round cairns of stone or earthen barrows but in others they were left unmarked; some burials occur singly, while others are grouped into small cemeteries, as at Poltalloch, where at least two separate groups of cists lie on the gravel terraces on the west side of the Kilmartin valley. Modern systematic excavation has often revealed that cists were reopened for the insertion of later burials: for example, a cist excavated at Traigh Bhan on Islay had been used on two occasions, the skeletal remains of the earlier interment being carefully moved to one end so as to accommodate the second burial, which was accompanied by a pottery vessel.

Round cairns and barrows are not exclusive to the Bronze Age but the majority are assumed to belong to this period. In Argyll as a whole, over 350 cairns have been recorded. They range in size from diminutive kerb cairns, only a few metres in diameter, to the remains of massive monuments over forty metres across. The majority of the larger monuments have suffered damage from stone-robbers or treasure-seekers in the past, but some of the best preserved examples still stand to a height of two metres or more. The important group of monuments at Kintraw, on a terrace at the head of Loch Craignish, comprises a large cairn, a smaller kerb cairn and an impressive standing stone, easily visible from the main Oban-Lochgilphead road as it rises towards the Bealach Mór.

Only a few earthen barrows have been recorded – but, in view of their vulnerability to destruction, these may be the unrepresentative rump of a class of monument that was once more numerous. They are a useful reminder that what survives from the prehistoric past has always to be viewed against the background of succeeding landscape changes – a pattern of destruction that accelerated in pace with the onset of agricultural improvements during the eighteenth and nineteenth centuries. Even allowing for fallible memories, one account of the Kilmartin valley soon after the turn of the nineteenth century hints at just what has been lost:

> The valley is studded with cairns, megaliths, inscribed stones, forts and other monuments of antiquity. The number of these is but a tithe of what existed two centuries ago: old men alive at the beginning of the last century spoke of more than a score of cairns and many standing stones being removed to make room for the plough or to build dikes and farm steadings. (P. H. Gillies, *Nether Lorn and its Neighbourhood*, 1909, pp. 147–8)

Modern excavations have shown that the superficially simple surface appearance of cairns and barrows can mask complex sequences of use and re-use. Sometimes the cairn represents a final stage, amounting to closure of a monument that may have been used as centre for ceremonial and burial activity for centuries. Unfortunately, relatively few of Argyll's major cairns have been investigated and, of those, only a small proportion has been excavated systematically.

The cairn at Balnabraid in Kintyre is one of the few funerary monuments in Argyll to have been excavated completely, although the early twentieth-century excavations were inadequate by more modern standards. Nevertheless, the results provide an impression of burial practices and artefacts from the later third to the mid-second millennium BC. The monument appears to have been in use as a burial place over a period of several centuries. At least eleven burial cists were discovered beneath the cairn material or just outside the stone kerb defining its perimeter. Grave goods accompanying the burials included one beaker, three food vessels and two cinerary urns, exemplifying the main ceramic traditions that were current in the region at various times between c. 2500 and 1400 BC, together with objects of flint, bone, bronze and jet.

The location of the dead within the landscape was a complex matter, frequently involving re-use of earlier monuments to create areas of sacred space. This is seen most strikingly in the Kilmartin valley (Map 8), where the Neolithic chambered cairn at Nether Largie South forms the origin for an impressive linear arrangement of cairns. To the NNE are the large cairns of Nether Largie Mid and North with the Kilmartin Glebe Cairn beyond. To the SSW lie the cairn known as Ri Cruin and possibly the remains of a further two severely robbed sites, represented by the remains of cists at Rowanfield and Crinan Moss. The most complex of these monuments appears to have been the Glebe Cairn, excavated by the well-known antiquary Canon Greenwell in 1864. Two concentric circles of stones were found beneath the cairn, and it has been suggested that it might have incorporated an earlier monument, perhaps comparable with Temple Wood. Two cists were found: one of them contained a splendidly decorated bowl (Figure 3) and a jet necklace, which no longer survives.

In a number of cases, the construction of the burial cists in the Kilmartin group of monuments not only reflects the abilities of their builders in the handling and working of stone, but also hints at otherwise invisible carpentry skills. At Nether Largie Mid and Ri Cruin, for example, the side-slabs of the burial cists have carefully pecked-out grooves, designed to allow the end-slabs to slot neatly into position – long recognised as a translation of a wood-working technique into stone. The most remarkable example of a cist slab treated in this manner is that from Badden, which is decorated with double and triple lozenges – the grooves being added after the original designs had been cut (Figure 4). In some cases, the edges of slabs have been rebated or chamfered to make a more precise joint.

Cist graves with these features have a very restricted distribution in Britain: a dozen examples of such 'grooved and rebated cists' are known from the Kilmartin area alone, while single examples are known from Kintyre and Bute. At the site at Glenreasdell Mains in Kintyre, one of a group of five cists had its single surviving end-slab grooved at either end to

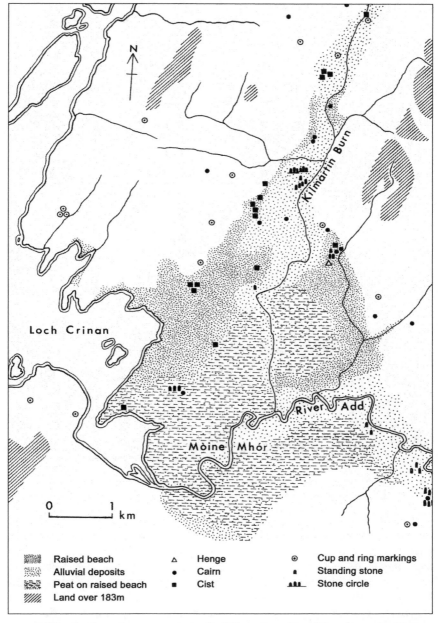

Loch Crinan

Kilmartin Burn

River Add

Mòine Mhór

0   1
└─────────┘ km

	Raised beach	△	Henge	⊙	Cup and ring markings
	Alluvial deposits	●	Cairn	▪	Standing stone
	Peat on raised beach	■	Cist	⚏	Stone circle
	Land over 183m				

MAP 8 Distribution of monuments in the Kilmartin valley. (Map drawn by Marion O'Niel after RCAHMS 1988)

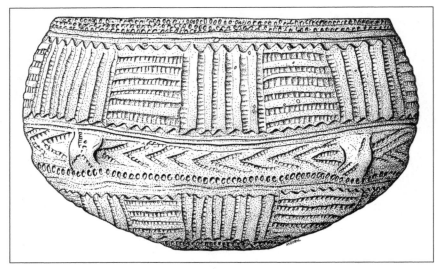

FIGURE 3 Pottery bowl from the Glebe Cairn, Kilmartin. Drawing by Marion O'Neil.

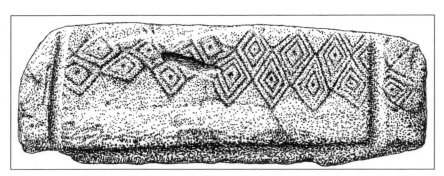

FIGURE 4 Decorated cist slab, Badden Farm, Kilmichael Glassary. Reproduced by courtesy of Dr Graham Richie.

receive the side slabs. Cists showing similar construction techniques have been noted in the Scilly Isles and in Brittany. Connections with SW England may well have developed once the adoption of full bronze metallurgy had created a demand for tin; as noted above, this technological change can be dated to the closing centuries of the third millennium BC.

Ironically, we know relatively little about the construction, use and landscape setting of the Kilmartin cairns, which have come to epitomise the richness of the Bronze Age archaeology of Argyll. The nineteenth- and early twentieth-century investigators of the cairns probably only discovered the most easily recognised features such as burial cists and stone kerbs; given the quality of the excavations, dug graves or cists set in deeper pits could have been overlooked by earlier excavators. Given the presence of grooved and rebated cists, there is a very real possibility that systematic excavation might reveal traces of dug graves containing traces of log or plank-built coffins. A remarkable log coffin was discovered in 1878 during peat cutting at Dalrigh, near Oban. It had been hollowed out of a trunk of oak and its ends were composed of pieces of wood inserted into prepared grooves at either side; the coffin, therefore, plausibly represents a timber prototype for the grooved cists described above. A surviving fragment of what may have been the birch bark cover has been radiocarbon dated to the first quarter of the second millennium BC.

A sacred valley?

The large numbers of cairns, standing stones and rock art sites in the Kilmartin area indicate intense activity in the third and second millennia BC. The combination of ceremonial and funerary monuments on the one hand and the apparent absence of domestic settlements on the other has led to suggestions that the valley was a ceremonial centre or sacred area. In the light of excavations at Temple Wood and the recently-discovered ceremonial complex on the gravel terrace at Upper Largie, it is clear that the ritual and funerary landscape of the valley developed over a very long period of time.

While the idea of a sacred valley is a seductive one, the apparent absence of settlement sites may simply reflect biases in the evidence. Early Bronze Age domestic sites may have lacked the permanence of the funerary monuments and are almost universally rare. Clearance activity presumably lies behind the acquisition of stones for the construction of the cairns and raises the possibility that the monuments lay near or within an agricultural landscape. Pollen analysis can provide a proxy indication of the extent and nature of human impact on the environment, but a detailed picture of what might be termed the Bronze Age 'cultural landscape' is as yet unavailable for the Kilmartin Valley.

However, these gaps in our knowledge scarcely detract from the impact that the monuments make on the visitor today. In Rachel Butter's evocative words, the Kilmartin valley and its monuments represent 'the remnants of a landscape which once bristled with power and meaning.' Formal burial is likely to have been restricted to those entitled to such treatment by their status. Through their links with the dead and their association with sacred sites, the living would doubtless have reinforced their right to status, land and territories.

The number of round cairns and cist burials on the gravel terraces are testimony to the relative importance of Kilmartin; the density of the sites and the quantity and quality of the artefacts found in them suggest a concentration of wealth unmatched elsewhere in Argyll. However, other

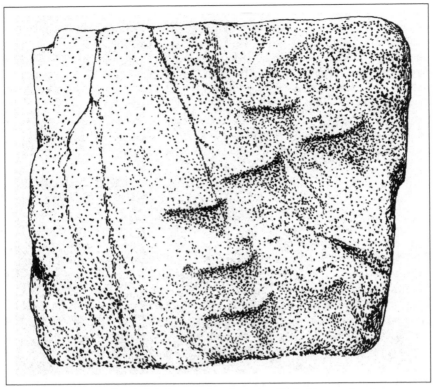

FIGURE 5 Decorated end-slab from a cist, depicting Early Bronze Age bronze axe-heads. Ri Cruin cairn, Kilmartin. Reproduced by courtesy of Dr Graham Ritchie.

striking groups of monuments are known. At Kilmore in Lorne, for example, an alignment of cairns forms a linear cemetery comparable to that at Kilmartin. Four round cairns extend NNW-SSE over 1.8 km in an almost straight line, an alignment that also takes in what may be assumed to be the 'ancestral' Neolithic chambered cairn at Dalineun. In Benderloch, too, there is a further alignment, composed of a string of large cairns at Balure, Achnamoine and at Barcaldine. Clusters of cairns are also known, for example, at Achnaba and on and around the Moss of Achnacree.

Powerful possessions: pots, bronze and jet

In the past, it has been suggested that local copper sources – particularly around Loch Fyne – may have lain behind the apparent wealth of the early Bronze Age in Argyll; but, as yet, there is no firm evidence that those resources were worked in prehistory. Metal almost certainly did play a part,

FIGURE 6 Bronze armlet from Melfort, Lorne, after *Proceedings of the Society of Antiquaries of Scotland.*

but on available evidence it was the control and transmission of Irish copper to other parts of northern Britain that is likely to have led to the enrichment of the region. In particular, the Kilmartin/Lochgilphead area may have benefited from control of the important porterage from Loch Fyne to Loch Crinan.

Paradoxically, relatively little Early Bronze Age metalwork has been discovered in the heart of mid Argyll – the most significant artefact being a halberd from the Poltalloch area. However, the fundamental importance of metalwork, probably both symbolically and economically, is reinforced by the well-known carvings of axeheads found on capstones and cist slabs at the Nether Largie North, Mid and Ri Cruin cairns. The association of actual axes with burials is extremely rare in Britain – making the presence of naturalistic carvings at these sites unusually potent symbols of the status of the individuals buried in these graves. Additionally, at Ri Cruin, an enigmatic carving has been interpreted as an oared boat or as a halberd bedecked with pennants. In the context, either explanation lends weight to the suggestion that the community or communities who buried their dead in the valley were keyed in to a network of contacts that extended across the North Channel and into Ireland. The highly ornamented pots, known as Irish Bowls, found in a number of the cists are closely comparable with examples found in Northern Ireland, where the style appears to have emerged in the centuries around 2000 BC.

Although not on the scale of the Kilmartin area, occasional rich graves suggest that control of resources, trade and exchange may have led to the aggrandisement of favourably placed communities elsewhere. In Lorne, for example, a group of three cists was discovered in 1878 at Melfort House, near the head of Loch Melfort. One was exceptionally large and contained a extended inhumation accompanied by a pair of bronze armlets, of which only one now survives (Figure 6), as well as parts of four or five necklaces made of jet (or related materials). Further north at the head of Loch Feochan, at Kilmore, a fine bronze dagger was recovered from a cist when one of a series of round cairns was opened by antiquarians in the nineteenth century. Modern systematic re-excavation revealed that the original excavators had missed an earlier burial accompanied by flint flakes! In Kintyre, a significant number of Early Bronze Age burials have been discovered in and around Campbeltown. In a small cemetery of three cists discovered at Kilmaho, for example, one inhumation was accompanied by an unusually rich assemblage of grave goods, comprising a food vessel, a riveted bronze knife, a bronze awl and two flint knives. Around Campbeltown itself, several burials have produced fine examples of elaborate jet necklaces.

The striking crescentic necklaces composed of beads and intricately-made spacer-plates of jet (or related substances such as cannel coal or lignite) have long been recognised as among the most technically accomplished prestige items of the Early Bronze Age in Britain and Ireland (see Plate 13). Argyll and the Firth of Clyde represent one of the areas of Britain with a significant concentration of finds of necklaces made from jet and they provide some of the most telling evidence of the involvement of the region in long-distance networks of trade and exchange. Such ornaments were destined for wear by the local members of what Dr Alison Sheridan of the National Museums of Scotland has wittily described as the Bronze Age 'jet set': they reflect a concern with personal finery, bodily adornment and the use of visible markers of status. Analysis has shown that the finest necklaces are made of jet from Whitby and that they were almost certainly manufactured in east Yorkshire. A number of necklaces show evidence of replacement of beads and plates with inferior raw material and workmanship, suggesting local repairs.

It is thus the grave goods deposited with the dead that provide us with some of the most telling and remarkable insights into the lives and wider connections of the Bronze Age communities of the region. The range of artefacts found in graves combine to demonstrate that communities in the west of Scotland around four thousand years ago were fully in touch with other regions of Britain and Ireland, and add weight to the suggestion that trade and exchange may be the key to the wealth implied by the density and sophistication of the monuments and associated artefacts.

In parts of Argyll, the later second millennium saw the construction and use of a distinctive class of small cairns known as kerb-cairns, characterised by the strikingly large size of the ring of stones forming the perimeter in proportion to the relatively small diameter of the cairn. A key site is

FIGURE 7 The impressive standing stone, known as Clach Diarmid, and the kerb-cairn at Strontoiller, Lorne. According to tradition, they mark the burial place of the Irish hero Diarmid. Reproduced from R. Angus Smith, *Loch Etive and the Sons of Uisnach* (1885, London & Paisley).

Strontoiller in Lorne, where this class was first recognised by the RCAHMS. On Mull, kerb-cairns form components of small, but locally significant, groups of monuments at Ardnacross and Lochbuie. By about 1400 BC, many of the traditions of the Earlier Bronze Age had come to an end. The pattern of treatment of the dead changed: cremation burials, deposited without grave goods, increasingly became the norm.

Survival and loss: Bronze Age houses and settlements

During the earlier Bronze Age, settlement evidence is at a premium over most of Argyll and, as noted above, it is necessary to look to the distribution of funerary and ritual monuments to gauge the extent and density of settlement across the region as whole. The processes of formation of coastal machair deposits and sandhills have favoured the preservation of occupation sites; however, the processes of erosion which have promoted discoveries have also sown the seeds of their destruction. Eroded scatters of pottery and flint in the sand-hills of Coll, Tiree and Islay and along the coastline of Ardnumurchan hint at occupation, but for the most part the location of actual settlement sites has proved elusive.

Rare examples of early Bronze Age domestic sites include Sorisdale on Coll, where an arc of stones and an area of floor deposit represented all that survived of a small house otherwise severely truncated by erosion. At Kilellan and Ardnave on Islay, excavations revealed more substantial structures and rich midden deposits dating from the earlier second millennium.

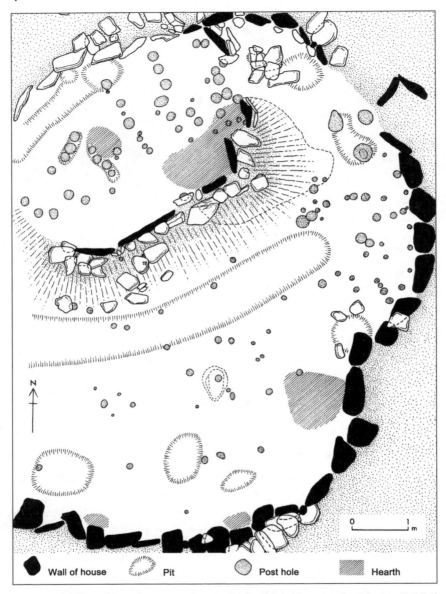

Wall of house   Pit   Post hole   Hearth

FIGURE 8 Plan of house excavated at Ardnave, Islay. Drawing by Marion O'Neil after Ritchie amd Welfare, 1983.

At Ardnave, in particular, excavations revealed the remains of a house built within a hollow in the sand and faced with dry stone walling (Figure 8). Some time after 2000 BC, part of the interior had been reused to form a smaller house measuring about 3.3 m by 4.5 m internally, with stone walls outlining the interior and distinct settings of post-holes, which indicate several periods of rebuilding. The house may eventually have been deliberately sealed with midden deposits prior to abandonment.

Over much of Argyll, the evidence of settlement has doubtless been effaced by centuries of subsequent agricultural activity. Elsewhere in Scotland, aerial survey has transformed our knowledge of past settlement-patterns; in Argyll, where arable agriculture is more restricted, the pattern of land-use mostly precludes the widespread formation of cropmarks and resists detection of ploughed-out sites from the air. However, chance can occasionally play a part in site location, as at Achnasavil in Kintyre, where a vigilant local amateur archaeologist happened to observe pits and other features in gravel terraces that were being eroded by a stream. Subsequent field survey and excavation revealed traces of occupation dating to between 1000 and 500 BC; the very diffuse nature of the site emphasises the problems of site detection in areas of agricultural improvement.

However, on the islands of Islay, Jura and Colonsay the picture changes markedly. When these areas came to be surveyed by the RCAHMS, much fuller traces of the prehistoric settlement pattern were discovered, ranging from hut-circles and enclosures to the remains of field systems. At Beinn Arnicil on Colonsay, for example, the remains of a complex cellular house were discovered, associated with low stone walls which formed a series of terraces on the flanks of the hill. At Cul a'Bhaile on Jura, a well-preserved hut-circle was located; it was set within an enclosure, now largely covered by the blanket peat that has formed over the site. As is the case with cairns, excavation reveals that hut-circles are almost invariably more complex than surface appearances would suggest. At Cul a'Bhaile, excavation revealed that the house had undergone major reconstruction at least twice during a lengthy occupation from the late second to the early first milllennium BC. Such sites owe their survival to their marginal situation on tracts of rough grazing or moorland, a reflection of the extent to which later land use determines survival or destruction.

Until the first millennium BC, the overall picture is of small, undefended settlements; it is only towards the end of the Bronze Age that fortified settlements make an appearance. In Argyll, the date of the earliest hillforts and duns is still largely unknown. One of the few hillforts to have been investigated is Balloch Hill in Kintyre, where the earliest known defences were constructed around the mid-first millennium BC. The fort at Duntroon overlooking Loch Crinan is a strong candidate for being a major late prehistoric territorial centre in mid Argyll – perhaps until it was supplanted by Dunadd in the mid-first millennium AD.

The farming landscape

During the period under review, evidence for the subsistence economy ranges from surviving examples of field systems and enclosures to actual traces of cultivation, and from plant and animal remains to cultivation implements.

Patterns of farming doubtless varied, but the evidence is too partial to permit any distinctions to be drawn. Traces of prehistoric field systems were found during the survey of Islay, Colonsay and Oronsay. In particular, excavations at An Sithean on Islay pointed to relatively sophisticated organisation and management of the farming landscape. Just as surface remains of houses or hut circles can mask complex patterns of re-use and remodelling, so the evidence of field systems may be much more complicated than surface indications suggest. Field-walls found emerging from the peat moss at Achnacree in Lorne appear to form part of an extensive land enclosure system, dating to the later second millennium BC and possibly associated with the control of stock.

At Ardnave on Islay, the sandy soil conditions favoured the preservation of animal remains, throwing light on the economic basis of the community that lived there. In addition to the bones of cattle and sheep, red deer bones indicated some use of wild resources, while the remains of shell-fish and crabs pointed to exploitation of the local shores. Evidence of cereal cultivation at Ardnave included barley and emmer wheat, although by the second millennium the latter would have been at the limits of its environmental range.

The principal cultivating implements appear to have been simple wooden ploughs of the type known as ards. Actual traces of cultivation have been recovered at a number of sites: during the excavation at Cul a'Bhaile on Jura, for example, traces of ard marks were found below the wall of the house, showing that the area had been under the plough prior to the construction of the building. A wooden ox yoke found late last century in a bog at Loch Nell has recently been radiocarbon dated to between 2000 and 1500 BC, making this one of the earliest pieces of direct evidence found in Britain for animal traction – as well as demonstrating vividly how peat deposits can preserve artefacts made from organic materials, which normally do not survive.

By the first half of the first millennium BC, the enclosure system at Achnacree was becoming blanketed with peat – a reminder of the problems associated with the over-exploitation of poor soils. Where agriculture was no longer tenable on the more marginal land, farms and fields would have been abandoned. Soil degradation due to over-use, combined with climatic deterioration, may have reduced the availability of agricultural land in many areas by the first millennium BC – and this may well have been a factor in creating stresses in society, as communities competed for diminishing resources.

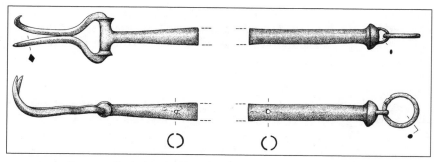

FIGURE 9 Bronze flesh hook; the wooden central portion has not survived.
Drawing by Marion O'Neil.

Later Bronze Age metalwork: offerings to the gods?

Tools and weaponry figure prominently among the finds of artefacts that
form one of the main sources of evidence for the later Bronze Age in the
region, around 1000–800 BC. Examples include a large hoard discovered
when an ornamental pond was being excavated at Ballimore House in
Cowal: its contents included eight axeheads, seven spearheads, two swords
and a cast tube of unknown function. In another instance, bronzes were
found on two separate occasions under a rocky scarp at Torran, near the
south end of Loch Awe. The original find consisted of two spearheads and
a gouge, found in 1885 in the course of 'digging out a ferret'. Serendipity
very often plays a role in archaeological discovery. Equally remarkably,
axeheads, rings and a knife were found when the site was visited in 1962
during a systematic archaeological field survey! The little woodworking
gouge from Torran provides a hint of the increasing evidence for craft
specialisation that emerges around this time.

While their discovery has usually been due to chance, many such finds
of metalwork appear to have been committed to the ground as deliberate
offerings or sacrifices. Casual loss can hardly explain the discovery of three
Late Bronze Age swords found on the small island of Shuna in the Firth
of Lorne, close together and sticking vertically in peat with their points
downward. It is tempting to wonder if this remarkable group might
represent the ritual demarcation of some political boundary of the time.

Two groups of bronze objects found on separate occasions during
drainage work on the farm of Killeonan in Kintyre may originally have
belonged to a single sizeable hoard. The earlier find was made around 1884
and comprised five swords, a chape (the tip of a sword scabbard), a spear-
head and eleven flint flakes, while the later discovery in 1908 consisted of
a fragmentary sword and the metal fittings of a bronze flesh hook – the
only Scottish example of a type of artefact associated with feasting equipment (Figure 9). With a leap of the imagination, it is possible to visualise

the hook in use, with the host perhaps picking out some choice piece of meat from a great sheet bronze cauldron for a particularly favoured guest – perhaps a visitor from across the Irish Sea or even further afield? During the later Bronze Age, the west of Scotland was once again a nodal point within networks of trade and exchange stretching from Ireland to Scandinavia.

Gold ornaments provide some of the most telling evidence of contact with Ireland at this time, as well as clues to the fashions and markers of status of contemporary 'high society'. Among the rare surviving finds are examples of bracelets and cup-ended ornaments, Irish in form and probably also manufacture, from Sunderland on Islay and Tullich in Glen Aray. Sadly, many of the gold finds from the region are now lost – melted down or dispersed at the time of discovery – and are known only through tantalisingly incomplete records made at the time. They include the largest gold hoard known from Scotland, found on the farm of Coul on Islay in 1780, and comprising thirty-six gold bracelets said to have been looped together to form a bunch. What appears to have been the sole surviving ornament from this hoard was sold to a jeweller in Edinburgh, from whom it was acquired by the National Museum in 1883.

The significant numbers of weaponry deposits dating to the early centuries of the first millennium BC carry with them connotations of prowess in combat, raiding, and warfare. In turn, they hint at a more warlike society and an increasing emphasis on the control of resources and ownership of areas of land – aspects of social organisation that eventually take on a more tangible form with the development of hillforts and duns. Together with the image of boozy feasts conjured up by the Killeonan flesh hook – occasions doubtless accompanied by storytelling, music, song and laughter – the evidence combines to suggest the gradual emergence of the type of warrior society celebrated in much later Celtic tales.

Sources of information

The Bronze Age archaeology of Argyll is exceptionally rich and, in the space available, it has not been possible to do more than highlight some of its main aspects and to note some of the main sites and finds. Fortunately, there is a wealth of readily accessible information about the archaeology of the region.

Building on the immediate foundations laid by Marion Campbell and Mary Sandeman's field-survey of mid Argyll, the work of the Royal Commission on the Ancient and Historical Monuments of Scotland (RCAHMS) from the 1960s onwards was to make Argyll one of the most intensively surveyed regions of Scotland. The stately volumes of the Argyll Inventory incorporate the results of some three decades of detailed fieldwork and research, presented area by area. One drawback of the inventory series was the absence of an overview of the county, but this deficiency was subsequently admirably addressed with the publication of *The Archaeology of Argyll*, edited by Dr Graham Ritchie. This provided an opportunity to consider various aspects of the prehistoric and Early Historic archaeology of the county as a whole and to make the results of the survey of Argyll accessible to a wider public. Over the lifetime of the survey programme, archaeology had seen many changes and Ritchie's book also offered a chance to view the region in the light of developments in chronology and new approaches to the interpretation of the evidence (for example, rock art) – new approaches frequently made possible by the quality of the data gathered and presented by the Commission. The monuments of Colonsay and Oronsay, and more recently, the Kilmartin area have also been published separately as more affordable booklets. These meet the needs of the local community and visitors by combining extracts from the relevant inventory with specially-written introductions to the archaeology.

In the archaeological heart of the county, the creation of the Kilmartin House Museum has provided an excellent interpretive centre and museum, where visitors are introduced to one of the richest prehistoric landscapes in Britain, and can readily explore the monuments with the aid of Rachel Butter's lively guidebook. Finally, thanks to the stunning changes in technology that have taken place over the last decade, much information about individual sites and monuments is now also available on the web, particularly in the form of CANMORE, the online database of the National Monuments Record of Scotland.

CHAPTER FOUR

The Iron Age

Introduction

In common with much of Scotland, the Iron Age of Argyll is dominated by its settlement record. While we can identify the remains of many hundreds, if not thousands of settlements that were apparently occupied between around 700 BC and AD 500, it is exceptionally difficult to elaborate the picture with evidence for other aspects of human activity (RCAHMS 1971, 1975, 1980, 1984, 1988). Thus we have few, if any, overtly religious monuments which can be dated to the Iron Age and remarkably little evidence for the disposal of the dead. While we can point to the remains of enclosures and fields in close proximity to Iron Age settlements (Nieke 1990, 139), we are far from being able to claim these as unambiguous evidence of Iron Age farming landscapes. The persistent re-use of derelict stone buildings in areas such as Argyll, where the same favoured pockets of land remained the most attractive settlement locations century after century, has meant that many Iron Age houses were re-inhabited sporadically into recent centuries.

This problem of continual re-use and re-modelling of settlements is common to the whole of Atlantic Scotland; the western and northern seaboard from Argyll through the Western Isles to Caithness, Orkney and Shetland. What creates particular difficulties in Argyll, however, is the absence of modern excavation on any significant scale. This leads to serious problems of interpretation, regarding even some of the most basic questions concerning the chronology of the various building forms. Time and again we are forced to address such questions through analogy with better understood areas such as Orkney, Shetland or the Western Isles, despite some significant differences in the character of the Argyll material. Indeed in a recent review of the British Iron Age, Argyll was identified as one of several 'black holes' where 'archaeological understanding of the Iron Age has barely begun,' and where even the most basic chronological frameworks remain to be established (Haselgrove *et al.* 2001, 24–5).

Settlement and subsistence

The Iron Age settlement record for Argyll is dominated by drystone, thick-walled structures often built in prominent locations such as on rock outcrops or low hills. They tend to be solid and imposing and were clearly intended to dominate the tracts of land in which they were located and to provide clear statements of authority over land and resources. As such they seem to represent the habitations of land-holding groups. Indeed the concern to establish and give physical expression to control of land seems to be a unifying characteristic of the Iron Age settlement record in Argyll, setting it apart from earlier periods, when settlements were considerably less conspicuous in the landscape.

The specific nature and organisation of land-holding no doubt varied between different parts of Argyll, and between different periods within the Iron Age. At a very basic level the occurrence of relatively large forts in the Early Iron Age (EIA, 700–200 BC) might suggest land-holding either by a sizeable corporate group, or by an elite presiding over such a group, while the dominance of Atlantic roundhouses in the Middle Iron Age (MIA, 200 BC-AD 200) might suggest the holding of land at a more devolved level, perhaps equating to an individual household (as has been argued for the MIA in parts of the Western Isles, Armit 1997).

The sheer numbers of Iron Age settlements in Argyll suggest that they were by no means exclusively elite dwellings. Even allowing for the fact that they were clearly not all contemporaneous, the minimum figure of around 500 forts, enclosures and Atlantic roundhouses greatly exceeds the likely number of elite households that could ever have been supported in the area (figures from Nieke 1990, table 8.1). In no case is it possible to demonstrate any form of settlement hierarchy, e.g. a fort or broch tower at the centre of a scatter of lesser, satellite settlements. Indeed, more modest settlement forms of any kind are remarkably scarce in Argyll. Excavated hut circles, such as Cul a' Bhaile in Jura (Stevenson 1984) and An Sithean, Islay (Barber and Brown 1984) have produced dates in the second millennium BC and there is little positive evidence that this tradition continued into the EIA on the west coast as it did further north in Caithness and Sutherland. A sand-hill site at Balevullin, Tiree, was clearly occupied during the EIA (MacKie 1963) but few such sites have been systematically explored.

Our understanding of the economic basis of Iron Age society remains extremely limited. From the many finds of querns for grinding grain at a wide range of sites, and from the presence of cereal grains in the MIA levels at Dunadd (Lane and Campbell 2000), we can assume that cereal cultivation was practised. Its importance relative to pastoralism, however, is difficult to gauge, as is the potential role of wild resources. A range of innovations was adopted during the Iron Age in Atlantic Scotland and there is no reason to think that the inhabitants of Argyll were any less receptive than their neighbours. The adoption of iron, for example, ultimately made available a range of more efficient tools, although there is little positive evidence for its early use in Argyll itself (the one exception being an early form of socketed axe from the Atlantic roundhouse of Rahoy, see below). Later, around 200 BC, the rotary quern displaced the traditional saddle quern, greatly improving the efficiency of grain processing.

Although local environmental conditions would always have limited the economic possibilities open to Iron Age communities, exploitation of available resources did not always follow the most obvious pattern. The high proportion of deer remains from Dun Mor Vaul on Tiree (MacKie 1974), an island most unlikely to have been able to sustain deer herds of any size, suggests significant deviation from expected subsistence strategies. Interestingly, deer are the only animals depicted on Hebridean decorated pottery, as at Dun Borbaidh on the neighbouring island of Coll (Lethbridge 1952, 189), and this suggests the animal may have had some special significance. Coll and Tiree are, however, the only parts of Argyll in which decorated pottery is commonly found. Indeed, from a ceramic point of view they belong firmly within the cultural milieu of the Western Isles (Lane 1990, figure 7.7), while the rest of Argyll was apparently aceramic throughout the Iron Age, the only notable exception being a small decorated pottery assemblage from the enclosure of Dun Cul Bhuirg in Iona (Ritchie and Lane 1980).

Forts and enclosures

Although substantial hilltop enclosures are generally rare in Atlantic Scotland, they are found in some numbers in Argyll (Map 9 and Figure 10). The hillforts of Argyll are, however, a thoroughly mixed bag in terms of their size, layout, topographic location and modes of construction. Most are located reasonably close to pockets of relatively favourable land, and few are wholly removed, either by distance or altitude, from the day-to-day farming landscape.

It is only the relative lack of evidence which allows us to treat these sites as a group, and it seems highly probable that they occupy a wide chronological and functional range, albeit of broadly later-prehistoric character. For example, in Kintyre alone the 2.5 ha triple-ramparted enclosure of Cnoc Araich (RCAHMS 1971, no. 161) is some twenty times larger in enclosed area than the second-phase fort on Bealloch Hill (*ibid.*, no. 158, see Fig. 10). The smaller forts, however, are much more common, with the average internal area being as small as 0.15 ha for Kintyre (*ibid.*, 16). The use of the term 'fort' for these sites is rather problematic, as there is no clear distinction between the smaller forts and the larger examples of the class recorded by the RCAHMS as 'duns'. The RCAHMS justified the distinction on the grounds that the forts were large enough to have 'served

MAP 9 Distribution of forts in Argyll (based on the definition used by the RCAHMS).

the needs of small communities', while the duns were essentially fitted for the requirements of a 'single family group' (*ibid.*), although it was quickly recognised that this rather arbitrary division has little meaning in terms of our interpretations of these monuments (e.g. RCAHMS 1975, 16).

It makes more sense to distinguish the few large forts such as Cnoc Araich, and perhaps the multivallate ones such as Ranachan Hill (RCAHMS 1971 no. 173), from the smaller, univallate examples. Indeed the latter may more usefully be considered alongside the monuments defined by Harding (1984) as 'dun enclosures'. Harding's division usefully distinguishes these irregular, and clearly never-roofed structures from those more regular circular or oval 'duns' that do appear to have been roofed structures (i.e. Atlantic roundhouses; see below). The dun enclosures themselves are far from being a homogenous group and are poorly dated, but on balance probably have their origins in the EIA.

Of the larger forts, Cnoc Araich (Figure 10) has been tentatively identified as a 'minor oppidum' (Feachem 1966, 82), implying its use as a tribal centre in the last few centuries BC. In the absence of excavation, however, there is nothing beyond its size to justify this claim: there is, for example, no surface evidence for the former presence of internal buildings. Indeed, evidence from other forts in the area suggests that their *floruit* may have been many centuries earlier. Occupation on the site of the vitrified fort at Dunagoil on Bute, for example, seems to have begun in the Later Bronze Age, judging from the nature of the metal-working debris found in the early excavations (Mann 1915 and 1925; Marshall, 1915). Other objects, however, including a La Tène 1C brooch, attest activity in the EIA, which is perhaps the most likely date for the construction of the timber-laced ramparts.

The plan of Dunagoil shares its characteristic elongated form with the timber-laced forts of eastern Scotland and clearly forms part of that wider tradition (Ralston 1979 467). Unfortunately the nature of the early twentieth-century excavations was such that virtually nothing can be said regarding the character of the activity on the site. More recent excavations of the fort on Balloch Hill revealed that it too was built in the EIA, but continued in occupation until the end of the first millennium BC (Peltenburg 1982). Similarly, the preponderance of saddle querns from Duntroon, mid-Argyll (RCAHMS 1988, no. 257), might suggest that it was built and occupied before the local introduction of the rotary quern, around 200 BC. Two radiocarbon dates from a small timber-laced island enclosure, Eilean an Duin, may suggest construction during the EIA or MIA, but there are too many uncertainties both in the archaeological context and the nature of the samples to give much confidence in their reliability (Nieke and Boyd 1987).

It seems improbable that the forts of Argyll all served the same function. Although excavations at Balloch Hill revealed the remains of numerous circular house foundations inside the ramparts (Peltenburg 1982), not all of Argyll's hillforts are likely to have been settlements. Recent excavations at the Brown Caterthun, in Angus, have suggested that even some of the most visually impressive hillforts of eastern Scotland, which must have consumed huge resources of time and effort to construct, were devoid of human occupation during the pre-Roman Iron Age (Dunwell and Strachan 1995 and forthcoming), and the same may be true even of supposed 'oppida' like Traprain Law in East Lothian (Armit *et al*, forthcoming). Thus the lack of evidence for internal structures within the majority of Argyll forts may reflect a genuine absence of occupation on these sites.

Some of the larger forts on the west coast seem to have been replaced

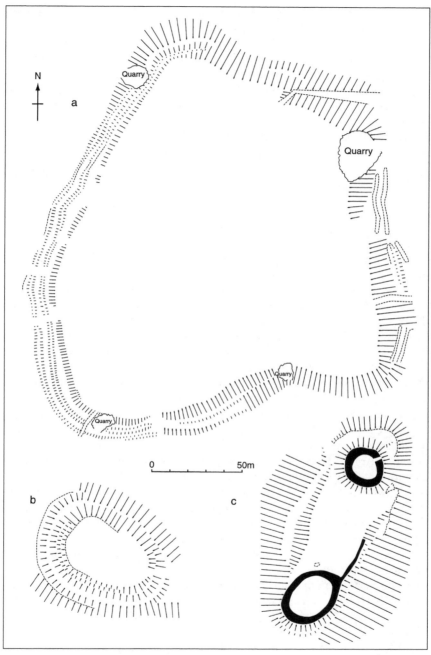

FIGURE 10 Forts and enclosures: a. Cnoc Araich, Kintyre. (RCAHMS 1971, no. 161), b. Kildalloig, Kintyre (RCAHMS 1971, no. 166), c. Dun Skeig, Kintyre (RCAHMS 1971, no. 165).

by smaller enclosures or by Atlantic roundhouses (Nieke 1984). Although
unexcavated, Dun Skeig in Kintyre (RCAHMS 1971, 18 and no. 165) displays a clear sequence of this type (Figure 10). Here a fairly large,
stone-walled fort has been replaced by a much smaller, timber-laced (and
vitrified) enclosure, and finally by an Atlantic roundhouse. This site may
well represent a more general development of settlement, from fort to
timber-laced enclosure to Atlantic roundhouse, but much fieldwork
remains to be done to test this hypothesis. Activity on at least some of
Argyll's hillforts continued during the MIA and LIA, as indicated by some
of the objects recovered from Dunagoil, including fragments of Roman
Iron Age glass bangle (Stevenson 1966, 21), and metal-working debris of
the mid-first millennium AD.

Atlantic roundhouses

Atlantic roundhouses comprise a range of massive-walled drystone roundhouses in Atlantic Scotland often referred to as brochs, duns, galleried
duns, island duns, semi-brochs, etc (Armit 1991 and forthcoming). They
are found throughout the north and west of Scotland, although the most
distinctive and elaborate forms, the broch towers, appear to be most common in the north mainland and Northern Isles. Seen from a wider
perspective, Atlantic roundhouses form a distinctive regional manifestation
of the wider tradition of substantial roundhouse building in Britain during
the last two millennia BC. Like the large timber roundhouses of southern
and eastern Scotland, they were essentially roofed domestic buildings: in
other words strongly built farmhouses.

Aside from the obvious, well-preserved examples, which survive to several storeys in height (e.g. Dun Carloway in Lewis, Mousa in Shetland or,
closer to Argyll, Dun Troddan and Dun Telve in Glenelg) it can be difficult to establish whether any given structure was originally a multi-storey
broch tower or a complex Atlantic roundhouse of more modest proportions. Later modification and systematic stone-robbing will have removed
the vital evidence in an unknowable number of cases. Identification of
a broch tower would most commonly be indicated archaeologically by
the survival of a first-floor gallery, or by voids above the entrance lintel
indicative of a massive superstructure (e.g. Loch na Beirgh in Lewis,
Harding and Gilmour, 2000). In Argyll, broch towers can only be identified with reasonable certainty at a handful of locations, the clearest case
being the site of Tirefour Castle, Lismore (RCAHMS 1975, no. 147, see
Map 10, Figure 11 and Plate 14). More typical are the complex roundhouses, such as Dun Rostan (RCAHMS 1988, no. 315), overlooking Loch
Sween, which incorporate features such as intra-mural galleries and a well-
built entrance with door rebates and bar-holes, but which was probably
never of tower-like proportions (Figure 11).

MAP 10 Distribution of Atlantic roundhouses in Argyll, excluding Arran and Bute (definite examples of complex roundhouses marked as encircled dots, others as solid dots; data adapted from Gilmour 1994).

On the basis of evidence drawn mainly from Orkney and the Western Isles, it has been suggested that Atlantic roundhouses may emerge around 700 BC, with the complex roundhouses developing by around 400 BC (e.g. Armit 1990). Although there is little independent dating evidence from Argyll, a much-disputed series of radiocarbon dates suggests that the complex roundhouse of Dun Mor Vaul on Tiree was first occupied in the EIA, probably in the fourth or fifth century BC, with occupation continuing to the end of the MIA (Armit 1991, 210; MacKie 1974 and 1997). Rare

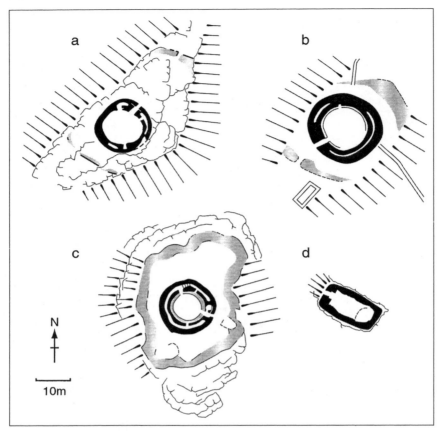

FIGURE II Atlantic roundhouses and rectilinear stack 'duns': a. Dun Rostan, mid Argyll (RCAHMS 1988, no. 315), b. Tirefour Castle, Lismore (RCAHMS 1975, no.147), c. Dun Mor Vaul, Tiree (RCAHMS 1980, no.167), d. Dun Fhinn, Kintyre (RCAHMAS 1971, no. 203).

artefactual evidence for an EIA date for an Atlantic roundhouse (in this case probably third century BC) comes from a La Tène IC brooch found at Rahoy, in Morvern, while a socketed iron axe from the same site suggests even earlier occupation, around the period of the LBA/EIA transition (Childe and Thorneycroft 1938; Stevenson 1966, 20). There is some evidence, then, that a complex roundhouse tradition was present in Argyll in the EIA, broadly contemporary with similar structures elsewhere in Atlantic Scotland.

Taken as a group, however, Atlantic roundhouses in Argyll are somewhat different in character from those in other parts of Atlantic Scotland. Generally the Argyll examples display a rather lower incidence of complex architectural traits than their counterparts to the north and west (Nieke 1990) and seem to include a correspondingly greater number of apparently solid-walled structures. Given the possibility that there was a general trend towards greater complexity in these structures over time, this may suggest that Argyll contains a greater proportion of EIA roundhouses than other parts of Atlantic Scotland. Another peculiarity is the occasional use of timber-lacing in the walls, as is the case for many of the hillforts and enclosures of the region. It seems likely that this represents the retention of a local building preference, perhaps reflecting a readier availability of timber in Argyll than was the case further north.

The isolation and generally small scale of Atlantic roundhouses suggests that overt social differentiation was limited in Iron Age Argyll, although the occasional broch towers may reflect the social aspirations of wealthier members of society. Argyll lacks any evidence for the growth of nucleated broch villages, like those at Gurness and Midhowe in Orkney, where the broch tower is the focus of a densely clustered group of much smaller houses. Indeed it appears that the increasing social stratification that these highly formalised settlements represent may not have occurred to any significant extent in Argyll.

Crannogs

Another settlement form that may have its origins in the EIA is the crannog. Significant numbers of these artificial islets have been identified in Argyll, their numbers increasing wherever targeted underwater survey is applied (Holley 2000). Since the majority of available radiocarbon dates for Scottish crannogs lie broadly within the Iron Age (Barber and Crone 1993) it is probable that many of the Argyll crannogs were constructed during this period. Evidence from Argyll itself is, however, extremely limited (Holley and Ralston 1995; Holley 2000) and the study of crannogs in this region remains in its infancy.

Contacts with the Roman world

The social, military and political upheavals associated with the Roman incursions into Scotland in the first to third centuries AD have left little obvious mark on the archaeological record of Argyll, and there is nothing to suggest direct military incursions into the area. Culturally, if not geographically, Argyll lay wholly north of the various Roman frontier systems, though the Antonine Wall was sufficiently near to suggest that there must have been at least some direct contact with the Roman army. The gazetteer compiled by the Greek geographer Ptolemy in the second century AD listed a few place-names and tribal names of relevance to Argyll, the most notable of the latter being the *Epidii*. This name, roughly trans-latable as 'horse people', seems to apply to the occupants of Kintyre and adjacent areas.

In archaeological terms it appears that settlement patterns in Argyll continued much as they had before. The use of Atlantic roundhouses extended well into the first millennium AD, though often with structural modifications. Gilmour (2000 160–1) has identified MIA remodelling within existing complex roundhouses such as Druim an Duin (RCAHMS 1988, no. 293); this seems generally to have been intended to create smaller, less monumental secondary roundhouses with smaller internal diameters. This might be a response to problems in the timber supply, since smaller diameters can be spanned by shorter rafters. The same suggestion has been made in the Western Isles where Atlantic roundhouses with sub-stantial internal diameters were replaced by wheelhouses which could be roofed using only shorter timbers such as might be available as driftwood.

New architectural forms, however, were also beginning to appear. Sherds of Roman Samian Ware recovered from rectilinear, coastal stack 'duns', such as Dun an Fheurain, Lorne (Ritchie 1971; RCAHMS 1975, no. 164), and Dun Fhinn (RCAHMS 1971, no. 203) suggest that these may have been a distinctive architectural development of the period (Figure 11), although none has yet been excavated. It is not entirely clear how the occasional objects of Roman manufacture found at sites like these came to be in the possession of the inhabitants of Argyll. They may have been obtained, for example, by raiding within the Romanised areas to the south, through service in the Roman army, or through trade with the Roman garrisons in central and south-west Scotland.

In this context it is worth mentioning the alternative view that this Roman material may not reflect any genuine contact with the Roman world at all. Leslie Alcock has argued that the consistent occurrence of Early Historic material from many of the sites discussed should be taken to indicate actual construction in the Early Historic period (Alcock 1987). In his view the occasional finds of Roman material could have been intro-duced long after the Roman period (although the precise mechanisms for this are unclear). The balance of evidence suggests, however, that the great majority of these structures were in fact constructed during the Iron Age with some being re-used as elite residences in the Early Historic period. The Iron Age pedigree of the Atlantic roundhouses at least is demonstrated by their clear architectural parallels with Iron Age buildings in other parts of Atlantic Scotland, as well as the few available radiocarbon dates. Indeed, the recently-published radiocarbon dates from the summit enclosure at Dunadd show that even this archetype of Early Historic fortifications in Argyll was founded on a pre-existing Iron Age settlement (Lane and Campbell 2000). Nonetheless, Alcock's views remind us of the problems and ambiguities in dating many of the poorly-understood enclosures and small forts of the region.

External links: Ireland and beyond in the Later Iron Age

Given the current controversies surrounding the Irish pedigree of the Scottic kingdom of Dalriada, the question of Iron Age links between Argyll and Ireland is clearly of some interest. Ewan Campbell has recently cast doubt on the conventional view that the Dalriadic presence was established by invasion from north-east Ireland, traditionally led by Fergus Mor around AD 500 (Campbell 2001). Rather than resulting from a single dynastic conquest or folk migration, Campbell sees the perceived 'Irishness' of Early Historic Argyll as representing much deeper-rooted cultural links across the North Channel. In his view, the Goidelic or 'Irish' branch of the Celtic language evolved in a zone which encompassed both Ireland and Argyll, rather than being exported from one to the other.

Travel back and forth across the modest body of water which separates Argyll from Antrim would probably have been much more convenient than the tortuous land journeys required to access the central Scottish lowlands. Certainly, the inhabitants of Argyll appear to have been insulated from the social and political processes which led to the formation of the nascent Pictish kingdom from around the third century AD on the other side of Druim Alban. It may even have been the threat posed to the autonomous communities of Argyll by the gradual emergence of a Pictish state that helped create a separate Dalriadic identity which deliberately turned its face across the water to Ireland.

As yet there is no very clear archaeological evidence for a 'special relationship' between Iron Age Argyll and Ireland, although there are signs of at least periodic contact. Of some relevance here are the fragments of moulds used to make distinctive knobbed spearbutts which have been identified among the metal-working debris from the hillfort of Dunagoil and the complex Atlantic roundhouse of Dun Mor Vaul (MacKie 1974, 152–5). The artefact type produced in these moulds is found widely in Ireland, and other moulds have been found in a number of locations in Atlantic Scotland. Andrew Heald has recently re-dated these artefacts to the fourth to fifth centuries AD (Heald 2001), which might, at first glance, suggest cultural links between Ireland and Atlantic Scotland in the generations leading up to the 'historical' migration. The wide distribution of these objects, however, which extends as far as southern England, makes it unwise to use them as evidence of close connections across the North Channel. Other rare examples of Irish links in the material culture of Iron Age Argyll include cast ring-headed pins from Coll and Sassaig (Warner 1983, 166).

The occurrence in Ireland of a series of largely undated stone ring-forts or cashels, with intra-mural features reminiscent of broch architecture (Warner 1983, 178–81), provides a further tantalising link between the two areas, although the limited chronological evidence on both sides of the north channel limits any serious discussion. A few Irish cashels, such as Altagore, Co. Antrim (Warner 1983, 178), incorporate elements of architectural complexity, such as intra-mural galleries, and could easily be 'lost' in the pages of the RCAHMS Inventories of Argyll. The chronology of Irish cashels is, however, even less well-established than that of Iron Age Argyll, so it is not yet possible to do much more than highlight these occasional parallels.

Death and religion

Beyond the settlement landscape a scatter of evidence exists for Iron Age ritual activity in Argyll. A series of simple inhumation burials from MacArthur Cave have been dated to the EIA, and a similar date for burials in other nearby caves seems quite likely (Saville and Hallen 1994). It is not clear, however, how far these burials might illuminate wider patterns of disposal of the dead, since the caves themselves may have had a specific religious significance that dictated an unusual form of burial. Keil Cave, a large natural cave at the southern end of the Mull of Kintyre, has produced evidence for activity during the LIA (and possibly slightly earlier) including Roman pottery sherds, a Roman toilet implement and various bone combs (Ritchie 1967). The quality of the items recovered from the 1930s excavations suggests that this cave may best be interpreted as a votive site used over an extended period, although at other times it may have been used for industrial practices such as iron-smithing. Roman pottery has also been found at St Columba's Cave, Ellary in Mid-Argyll (Tolan-Smith 2001, 46–7).

Perhaps the most striking of all the Iron Age objects from Argyll is an almost life-sized female oak figure, radiocarbon dated to around 700–500 BC, which was found below more than 3 m of peat at Ballachulish in 1880 (Coles 1990). The figure was apparently found underneath a collapsed wicker structure, and its fresh condition at the time of its discovery suggests that it had been deliberately submerged rather than being allowed to rot on the surface. This seems to suggest the decommissioning of some form of shrine or cult site, but in isolation it is difficult to know how far this might be representative of Iron Age religious practice in the region. Similarly enigmatic is a carved stone head which was found in a vegetable garden in Port Appin in the early 1980s (Cowie 1986). This crudely-carved object was found with no obvious archaeological context but does seem to belong to a wider tradition of Iron Age 'Celtic' heads found widely across Britain, Ireland and parts of mainland Europe (Ross 1967). Similarly, a bronze armlet of a type well known in north-east Scotland was recently discovered in spoil from a building site at Newfield, Lismore (NMS 1995 66). Like the Ballachulish figure, these stray and unpredictable finds may denote the former presence of Iron Age sanctuaries, shrines or simply places imbued with religious or supernatural power.

Conclusion

Despite the extraordinary density of Iron Age settlement within Argyll and the exceptional preservation of many of the sites, the area remains woefully neglected by archaeologists. In part this may be due to the sheer amount of effort and resources which will be required to address some very basic questions of site characterisation and chronology. Nonetheless, the quantity of archaeological survival, at the level of landscapes as well as individual sites, suggests that a well-focused and systematic programme of research could transform this area from an Iron Age 'black hole' to one of the key areas for understanding the social and economic dynamics of Iron Age society.

CHAPTER FIVE

Secular Society
from the Iron Age to Dál Riata
and the Kingdom of the Scots*

RECORDED HISTORY begins in Argyll around 500 AD when, if we believe the sources, the Irish leader Fergus Mór and his sons migrated here from northern Ireland. Between the years 500 and 800 Argyll became the cradle of the future kingdom of Scotland. During this period we find the first written sources, the first kings, and the beginnings of state formation, along with tax collection and the creation of military forces. Christianity also establishes itself as the main religious force within the area. Overall, we see the transition from the earlier local, tribal societies which had inhabited the area for millennia, to a brave new heroic era. This provided the firm foundation from which the great medieval kingdom of Scotland was to spring.

Scholars have debated interpretation of the initial Irish colonisation of western Scotland (Bannerman 1974; Nieke and Duncan 1988; Campbell 1999, 2001). Given the close proximity of Argyll and northern Ireland, and the known expertise of early sea-farers, it seems most probable that there was extensive contact and movement between the two areas from earliest times. What the sources seem to record around 500 is the transfer of a family of Irish aristocrats who were, for some reason, motivated to move and establish themselves as the dynastic rulers of the new Scottish kingdom of Dál Riata. Interestingly, the very name of the kingdom hints at an earlier Irish presence. It translates as the 'portion of Riata' rather than the 'portion of Fergus Mór', as might be expected. Bede's *History of the English Church*, written in the early eighth century, attributes the founding of the kingdom to 'Riata'. Irish sources suggest that one Cairpre Riata, whom we assume was the same person, was a pseudo-historical figure who lived some ten generations before Fergus Mór (Bannerman 1974).

The territorial extent of this kingdom equated roughly with historic

---

* This chapter uses Old Irish accented name forms, e.g. Dál Riata for Dalriada.

Argyll and early genealogies tell us that the area was divided into three, each sub-division being held by a separate lineage or *Cenél*. We need to understand that the early people of Dál Riata saw, and recorded themselves, as belonging to large extended family groupings, all of whom traced their origins back to one important male ancestor. The three main *Cenéla* were the *Cenél nGabráin*, the *Cenél Loairn* and the *Cenél nOengusa*, and each traced its origin back to Fergus Mór or one of his brothers. We also know roughly the area that each group occupied. Around 700 a new group, the *Cenél Comgaill*, who occupied the Cowal peninsula, split away from the *Cenél nGabráin*. Throughout the history of Dál Riata a single king, drawn from one of these groups, ruled over the whole kingdom. A word of caution is useful here: in modern sources the Dál Riata are often referred to as Scots. This is a translation of *Scoti* or *Scotti*, names first used in Classical sources for one of the groups involved in assaults on Roman Britain. In fact, the Classical authors used this term to denote Gaelic speakers in Britain and Ireland. It is only after about 900 that events and circumstances allow us to use the term 'Scots' in its modern sense.

Our understanding of Scottish Dál Riata can be pieced together from fragmentary documentary sources and evidence from archaeological discoveries across the area. Both need to be interpreted in the light of wider changes taking place in post-Roman Britain, a period which saw a variety of diverse and new peoples and cultures all competing for land, resources and power. The years 500 to 800 were vibrant and distinctive, marked by ethnic, linguistic, political and religious conflict and change. Leaders, whether of church or state, were portrayed as heroic warriors, whose activities inspired poetic record. Craftsmanship flourished in a wide variety of media and works of international note were created. As we will see, Dál Riata was firmly enmeshed in this network of energy and change.

The authors and patrons of some of our early documentary sources were obsessed with genealogy and fully exploited the new powers the written record gave them to set their version of ancestry in stone (Nieke 1988). Happily for us, this has resulted in reasonably detailed king-lists for substantial periods. Contemporary annals – records of significant events compiled year by year, probably in the monastery of Iona – provide further insight into the activities of the kings and other members of the aristocracy. A particular theme of these records is warfare: battles; sieges; the taking of hostages, plunder and prisoners; the wasting of hostile land – all the stuff of the heroic warrior king (Alcock 2003). There is much debate about the origin and composition of military forces at this time, but for Dál Riata, very unusually, we have a survey of the civil, military and naval strength of the kingdom. Contained in the *Senchus Fer nAlban* or 'History of the Men of Scotland' and originally compiled in the seventh century, this is the earliest known census in Britain (Bannerman 1974; see also Sharpe 2000 for discussion of a slightly later date). It was probably written down to record and justify what was considered due to the king in military

MAP 11 The approximate areas inhabited by the *cenéla* of Dál Riata.

support from his kingdom in time of trouble. From this, we know that for every twenty houses the *cenéla* were expected to provide a crew for two 'seven-bench' ships for a sea-expedition. It is assumed that these oared ships had a crew of fourteen rowers and a steersman, and that these men would fight on land as well as sea. Other calculations in the document suggest an overall armed force of some two thousand (Alcock 2003).

This was surely a realistic assessment of military strength; otherwise, there would have been little point in compiling the survey. Apart from anything else, the survey confirms that the king's rights to military service extended across Dál Riata and that there was an established administration which could calculate and record the king's due force. It also suggests that mechanisms to raise and manage the force existed.

The existence of some form of literate governmental bureaucracy is also indicated by the civil survey which is also contained within the *Senchus Fer nAlban*. This details the number of 'houses' belonging to the *Cenéla* and their various branches. The house was not only the unit that underpinned the system of military service in the kingdom; it was also the unit on which a king could expect to raise rent or tribute. Essentially, it was the taxation unit across the land.

None of this should surprise us. Contemporary sources, in particular those from the Irish homelands of the Dál Riata, provide us with a picture of a developed secular society, in which kings ruled supreme and were supported by extensive and traditionally-defined laws and rights. Throughout, the support of the kindred group, the equivalent of the *Cenéla*, was fundamental. Whilst the king might expect a range of support from his people, he was also under obligation to protect them, to judge disputes and to provide largesse through assemblies, feasting and gift-giving. Sadly, our written sources, which were compiled for specific, often political, purposes, do not colour in the full detail of the day-to-day activities of the kings and their people. Here, however, we can turn to the evidence of archaeology to augment our understanding and, most importantly, to provide new insights into the nature of this early kingdom.

A key starting point is provided by the evidence for settlement in Dál Riata. We know that a variety of enclosed or otherwise 'secure' structures were occupied across the area. These include at least some of the stone-built forts and duns which are so characteristic of the area and also the crannog sites built in many lochs. The origins of this enclosed and protected settlement tradition are still debated. Whilst they may stretch back into pre-history, it is also clear, as we shall see, that major building projects were being undertaken in Dál Riata. It is worth noting that this pattern of small enclosed settlements is also characteristic of the Irish homelands of Fergus Mór, although the wider distribution of such sites in Scotland makes it clear that they were not a specifically Irish introduction.

Some two hundred duns have been recorded across Argyll (RCHMS 1971–1992) usually located on knobbly, craggy hilltops. A variety of constructional form and detail is evident and it is clear that all of these sites required a considerable labour force to construct. A significant group (perhaps two thirds) of these duns exhibit a regularity of shape and constructional details (including intra-mural cells) which strongly suggest they were totally roofed homesteads (Harding 1984; Alcock 2003; Nieke 1984, 1990). These would have been substantial and impressive buildings, not

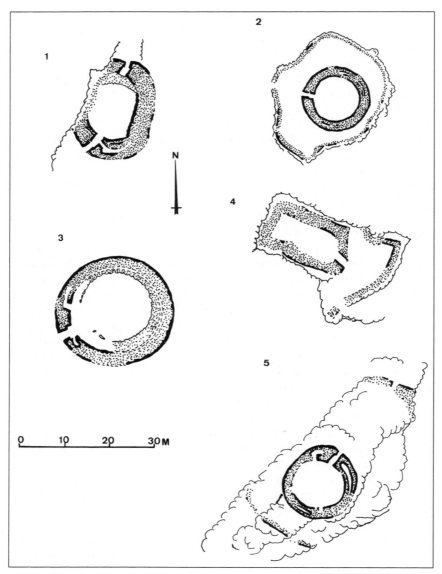

FIGURE 12 Representative Argyll duns: 1. Druim an Dùin; 2. Dùn Aisgain; 3: Ardi-fuir 1; 4. Dùn Mucaig; 5. Dùn Rostan. All these examples may have been totally roofed. After RCAHMS, copyright © Margaret R. Nieke.

least because of their careful placing in prominent positions in the land-scape. The external enclosures and terraces seen at many sites would have provided additional space for activities which could not be conducted in the domestic interior. The handful of sites which have been investigated have yielded pottery, glass and metalwork from the sixth to eighth centuries. As we will see, this material is distinctive in being associated with high status and wide-ranging contacts. The inhabitants of these duns clearly had access to the labour required to build their homes and to fine goods to use within them. Crannogs, of which around a hundred are known, can be seen in the same light as duns. Again, few have been excavated, with the notable exception of Loch Glashan, where, alongside comparable high-status items, a wide range of leather and wooden items have been preserved in the water-logged conditions (Scott 1960, 1961; Nieke 1984; Campbell 1999). Forth-coming publication of the Loch Glashan excavations and recent analysis of the finds promise a major new insight into this site (Crone and Campbell, forthcoming). Both crannogs and duns usually lie in close proximity to areas, albeit sometimes only pocket-sized, of cultivable land; we also know that cattle, pigs, sheep and goats were kept, and this suggests that the settlement network was supported by a mixed agricultural economy. Wild resources, not least those harvested from the sea, must also have been important.

Whilst duns and crannogs formed a major part of the settlement patch-work of Dál Riata, it seems obvious that this was only one element of a more complex network. As we noted, the *Senchus Fer nAlban* contained a survey based on the number of 'houses' in the kingdom. It is unclear exactly what type of 'house' was being referred to, but we can be sure that the duns and crannogs made up only a small proportion of the hundreds of 'houses' noted in the document. It seems, therefore, that the settle-ments of the vast majority of the population have yet to be identified. We can envisage that the majority of these were lesser settlements, linked by bonds of clientage and obligation to the dun- and crannog-living aristoc-racies. Tantalising glimpses of what appear to be open (unenclosed) settlements of the period have been noted (RCAHMS 1980, 1984, 1988), but proper analysis of this evidence poses one of the major challenges for future fieldworkers in the area.

We must now turn to consider those forts known to have been occupied by the higher level of the settlement hierarchy within the kingdom. We have noted the emphasis on military activity in the historical sources. The annals are especially interesting in recording sieges and other happenings at named sites. Careful detective work (Alcock 1981) has identified several of these sites as forts of some type. Thus we hear of the siege, in 712, of *Aberte*, identified as the coastal fort of Dunaverty at the southern end of Kintyre. In 712 and again in 731 we hear of the burning of *Tairpert Boittir*, identified as Tarbert, Loch Fyne. The exact location of the fort here is not certain, but the obvious site appears to be the rocky knoll occu-pied by the later royal castle. *Dun Ollaigh*, identified as Dunollie just north of Oban, is referred to several times and was clearly an important site. It was burned in 698 and then in 701 destroyed by Selbach. The same Selbach, who was ruler of the *Cenél Loairn* if not of the whole of Dál Riata, rebuilt the site in 714. Subsequently, we learn that, in the conflict with the neighbouring Picts in the 730s, Talorcan, son of the Pictish King Drustan, 'was taken and bound near Dunollie' in 743. *Dun Att*, Dunadd in mid Argyll, is recorded to have been besieged in 683, while in 736 a Pict, Oengus son of Fergus, captured the site.

Of these sites, Dunollie and Dunadd have both been archaeologically investigated and have provided important insights into royal power and authority in Dál Riata. At Dunollie, limited excavations confirmed that there was activity in the seventh and eighth centuries within the small headland fort now occupied by the ruins of the later fifteenth-century Dunollie Castle (Alcock and Alcock 1987). Bone combs and pins, and imported French pottery and glass were found, along with evidence of bronze-working: crucibles for melting the metal and moulds for casting pins, rings and other small objects. The finds from Dunollie suggest that it was a royal centre of activity, whose inhabitants had access to cattle, sheep, goats and pigs for the table and to high-status craft products.

From Dunadd we have our most extensive and important evidence, as a result of which the site is the best-known early historic fortification in Scotland. The fort site is on a distinctive craggy hill rising up from the Mòine Mhór, the Moss of Crinan, and has a clearly visible series of stone defences (see Plate 15). On the highest point of the hill is an enclosed 'citadel', from which ramparts extend to enclose a series of lower pendant enclosures – a plan which has been classified as 'nuclear' (Stevenson 1949). Excavations in 1904, 1929 and, most recently, 1980–1 (Christison 1905; Craw 1930; Lane and Campbell 2000) have provided a wealth of material and other evidence for activity there. Of these, the recent excavations have provided our most detailed insight, in particular, clarification of the sequence of defences on the site. It now appears that the site began in the fifth century as a small dun, probably fully roofed, on the summit. Over the next couple of centuries, the site was gradually enlarged as the range of activities taking place there increased.

A range of evidence indicates that Dunadd was one of the royal forts of Dál Riata, and possibly the main one. It seems unlikely that the site was permanently occupied by the royal household, despite the presence of the house-dun on the summit. Evidence from comparable contemporary king-doms suggests that making royal progresses around their lands was an all important way for the kings to maintain links with their people. Such royal tours provided opportunities for the king to be seen presiding over judicial cases, distributing largesse – often, it seems, through lavish feastings – and, most importantly, collecting tribute and local taxes. Whilst perhaps not a permanent residence, Dunadd was certainly a major ceremonial site, at which kings were inaugurated into office. The evidence for this is provided primarily by a footprint carved into the living rock on a terrace near the summit of the site. Other associated carvings include a boar, a rock-cut basin and an inscription in ogham – a form of writing invented in Ireland. Various accounts of medieval Irish and Scottish inauguration rituals

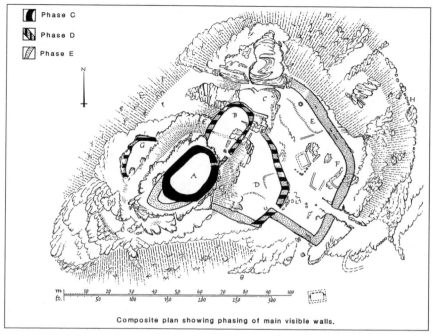

Phase C
Phase D
Phase E

Composite plan showing phasing of main visible walls.

FIGURE 13 The sequences of defences at Dunadd, showing how a dun grew into a large, multiple-enclosure fort. Copyright © Howard Mason.

survive; these typically involve the placing of the royal foot in a carved depression, thereby bonding him firmly to his land. The choice of Dunadd for such rituals is especially interesting given its close proximity to Kilmartin Glen. That this area was seen as very special from earliest times is strongly suggested by the cluster, one of the densest in Britain, of prehistoric burial and ceremonial monuments there. The kings' use of ancient pagan traditions and centres of power to justify their own status and position comes as no great surprise; it was commonplace in contemporary Ireland. In Scottish Dál Riata it may have had the additional benefit of firmly linking the Irish 'newcomers' with the ancient traditions of their new kingdom. The significance of the inauguration rituals is also demonstrated by the appropriation of the ceremony by the early church. We know that St Columba, the driving force behind the establishment of Christianity in Dál Riata, ordained King Áedán as king around 574 (Anderson and Anderson 1961). This is an instance of the early church taking over established rituals and practices to further establish its own position and to forge crucial links with the royal household.

Evidence from the excavations reveals that Dunadd was a hive of activity. Other contacts with the early church and early literacy are indicated by the distinctive cross-marking on a corn-grinding quern, suggesting that it was an ecclesiastical gift and had been blessed (Campbell 1987), and by a small pebble inscribed 'Inomine' – the opening words of a blessing (see Plate 16). A fragment of Mediterranean orpiment, a pigment used to produce vibrant yellow colours in manuscript illustration, is also tantalising; it is normally assumed that manuscript production was confined to monasteries. Was this piece lost from a consignment destined for Iona or is it a hint that illuminated texts were compiled at Dunadd itself?

Agricultural activities are indicated by the fifty-four rotary querns found in early excavations. These would have been used to grind the barley and oats which charred grains indicate were brought to the site. Bones from butchered animals indicate meat consumption, mainly of cattle but also of sheep and pigs. It is tempting to link both the meat and cereals with the food due in tribute to the king. The pottery vessels recovered included a range of drinking beakers and jugs. None of this pottery was produced locally, possibly because wood, leather and other materials were readily available and preferred. The pottery was imported from France, probably as containers. One vessel is known to have contained the dyestuff, madder. At other sites, imported seeds of coriander and dill have been found associated with such pottery. Interestingly, this collection of French pottery, of a type known to archaeologists as E-ware, is the largest collection known from any British site. Other imported goods are likely to have included French wines, nuts and dates. We have written evidence of Gaulish traders visiting the region: Adomnán's seventh-century *Life of Saint Columba* mentions Gaulish merchants coming to the 'chief place of the region' – quite possibly Dunadd itself (Anderson and Anderson 1961). Glass vessels, probably also imported from France, were an appropriate accompaniment to the fine wines. It is worth reflecting here on the implications of these imported goods. All were quality items affordable only by the highest members of society. The vision we have is of the kings dressed in exotically coloured cloth and entertaining their nobles with spiced Mediterranean foods and fine wine served in expensive glasses. What is noteworthy is the early date (late sixth and seventh centuries) at which this was happening – a good century before we know of comparable imports reaching the English kings (Campbell 1999). Quite how this trade network developed is still debated, but it seems likely that its origins lie with the developing Christian church. Wine was used in early services and comparable imported goods are also known from early monastic sites. We also know that many early ecclesiastics were well travelled and had well-established contacts with France, Italy and beyond. In making contacts with the secular rulers of Dál Riata, Gaulish merchants were probably seeking to acquire high-quality northern goods to trade. We have no direct evidence for these, but gold, copper, silver, freshwater pearls, furs, leather and woollen goods have all been proposed as likely commodities, as have human cargoes of slaves (Alcock 2003).

The weaponry found at the site is an exceptional discovery. Fragments include a sword, spearheads, arrowheads and crossbow bolts. Such weapons would not have been casually lost and the size of this collection is paralleled only at Lagore in Ireland, a roughly contemporary royal site. Whilst the weapons may have been brought to Dunadd for recycling, it is tempting to link them with the defensive nature of the site and the military action we know took place there.

Other evidence from Dunadd also indicates wide-spread contacts, numerous craft workshops and high-status products. Iron-working produced a wide range of tools and other items; polished stones suggest leather-working; it is also likely that objects were fashioned from wood, bone, jet and stone. But it is the fine metalworking which is the most important. Copper, silver and gold working is indicated by the hundreds of crucible and mould fragments found (see Plate 17). Tin was imported from Cornwall; other metals were recycled from earlier pieces, some of which also appear to have been imported from England and beyond. The broken mould fragments indicate that a wide range of small decorative pieces of very fine quality were being produced. Hooped brooches of a type known as penannular were a main product. Cast in metal, these brooches and other items could then be further embellished with gold filigree, enamel work and insets of glass or semi-precious stones. The range of techniques in use was impressive and it is clear that all the processes from initial design to final ornamentation of pieces were carried out at Dunadd. In addition to this fine metalworking, some very high-quality beads were produced by a glass-working process which utilised recycled glass. The great flowering of activity in metal-working was in the seventh century; the quality and sophistication of craftsmanship cannot be overstated. Contemporary ideas, and indeed metalwork, were imported to the site from Ireland, Anglo-Saxon England and beyond, and were used to help develop a distinctive Dunadd style; examples of this include the bird-headed brooches, which drew on Anglo-Saxon designs adapted to an Irish/Celtic style (see Plate 18).

The presence of highly skilled craftsmen adds to our understanding of the importance of Dunadd. It is assumed that they were working under royal patronage and that this gave the kings some control over their products. We know that fine brooches were prized possessions, often given as kingly gifts and worn as symbols of status (Nieke 1993). The ability of the kings to control this whole process of craft production and gift-giving may well have provided crucial support for their position both within Dál Riata and beyond.

Whilst we know that Dunadd was a thriving place in the seventh century, it is not so clear what happened later. We know of some major rebuilding and further extension of the site in the eighth and ninth centuries and there are suggestions that the site continued in use until at least the tenth century, but the scale of this later activity is not fully understood. Sadly, the lack of archaeological evidence for these later years is compounded by a dearth of documentary sources. In the years up to the mid-ninth century we know that the kings were able to establish and maintain an extensive kingdom. These years were not without incident: the lineages controlling the kingdom changed, and conflict is recorded within and without the territory. In the early eighth century, as we have seen, the neighbouring Picts were able to invade the kingdom, ravaging it as they went and capturing Dunadd itself. Some argue that this was followed by a period of Pictish overlordship of Dál Riata. Whatever happened, the kings clearly enjoyed a later resurgence of power, which culminated in 843 when Cináed mac Alpín (also known as Kenneth mac Alpín) was able somehow to effect the union of Dál Riata with Pictland, thereby creating the large territorial unit which evolved into the medieval kingdom of Scotland. Quite how this unification occurred is poorly documented, not least because the Iona annals end around 740, possibly as a result of disturbance by viking raiders. It used to be thought that Cináed took control in Pictland through military conquest. However, careful consideration of the limited documentary sources now suggests that links with the east were already well established and that during the early ninth century several kings of Dál Riata had already also been kings of Pictland (Broun 1994, 1998). This in turn suggests that there may have been early dynastic marriages between east and west – no great surprise, given what we know of links between other kingdoms of the period – and perhaps also that there was a history of Dalriadic settlement in Pictland. It appears, then, that Cináed was able to seize control in Pictland with the support of an extended network of kin and clients. A major impetus for the move may have been provided by the Norse presence on the west coast of Scotland; a couple of decades of Norse incursion and settlement may have left Dál Riata ravaged and reduced. If so, the lure of new lands and opportunities may have seemed all the more tempting. Whatever the details, Cináed rapidly established himself as a permanent presence in the east; documentary sources tell us that he 'led the Scots from Argyll into the land of the Picts'. Interestingly, Cináed chose to develop a new royal centre and inauguration site at Scone. In doing so, he took over an established Pictish centre which itself had prehistoric origins, thus perpetuating the tradition of deliberately adopting pre-existent power centres. All of this had a major impact on the rich tapestry of Scottish history; but that is another story.

CHAPTER SIX

The Early Christian Period

Dalriada

The period between the sixth and the ninth centuries saw the establishment in Dalriada of a monarchy, a language and a religious tradition which were to make major contributions to the future kingdom of Scotland. The church in these first centuries of Christianity played a mission role which went far beyond racial and linguistic boundaries. The work of the monastic founders, Columba and Moluag, and of their successors at Iona and Lismore, is commemorated by dedications throughout the Pictish areas of northern and eastern Scotland. Historical records of Lismore are scanty but its founder was a kinsman of St Comgall of Bangor, the east Ulster monastery from which the great missionary Columbanus travelled to the continent in the decade of Moluag's death (*c.* 592). Colum Cille or Columba (521–97) was of royal birth in west Ulster, but his own monastic foundations and his recorded connections with other saints covered all the provinces of Ireland, and his *paruchia* or federation of monasteries in Ireland and Scotland remained important for centuries. For three decades from about 635 the conversion of the Angles of Northumbria was led by Aidan and other monks from Iona based at Lindisfarne. In the ensuing century there was a lively interchange of intellectual and artistic ideas between the peoples of north Britain and Ireland, which on Iona was to produce such masterpieces as the high crosses and the Book of Kells. At a more local level, the sites chosen by monastic founders or itinerant priests in this early epoch were to shape religious organisation into the medieval and post-Reformation periods. The medieval cathedral of Argyll on Lismore – now the parish church – and the restored Benedictine abbey of Iona stand at the hearts of ancient monastic enclosures (RCAHMS 1975, 156–63, no. 267; 1982, 31–152, nos 3–4) (Plate 19; Figure 14).

The Early Church

The early church in Argyll has exceptionally rich documentation for a period in which, throughout Britain, historical sources are rare and often obscure. The English historian Bede (d. 735) recorded Columba's arrival on Iona, his travels among the Picts, and even the Irish form of his name, 'Columcelli' (*Colum Cille*, 'Colum of the church'). Most of the other sources originated on Iona itself, including a series of annals recorded during the seventh and eighth centuries and incorporated in later Irish collections. These laconic entries record the deaths of abbots and kings, as well as the battles and sieges of Dalriada and its Pictish, British and Anglian neighbours. The miracles of Columba were chronicled by Abbot Cumméné (d. 669), but only a few sentences survive, quoted in the *Life of Columba* by Abbot Adomnán (d. 704), himself a great ecclesiastical statesman and legislator. This work, presented as a collection of miracles and visions, is full of valuable details on religious and everyday life (Anderson 1961; Sharpe 1995). It concludes with the famous chapters in which the saint bids farewell to his island home in the weeks before his death. Earlier tributes to Columba in Irish verse survive from soon after his death, while an alphabetic Latin poem attributed to the saint himself recounts biblical history from Creation to the Last Judgement (Clancy and Markus 1995, 195–207). Adomnán's less-known work, *On the Holy Places*, based on the narrative of a Gaulish pilgrim, gives a detailed account of the holy places of Palestine and the eastern Mediterranean including Jerusalem and Constantinople. This interest in the homeland of Christianity among monks who were often belittled for living on its remote western fringe is matched by artistic features in the Book of Kells and some of the sculpture of Argyll. The record of sea-faring in these sources, with constant journeying between Scotland and Ireland, is complemented by the arrangements for naval service in the *Seanchas Fir n'Albainn*, and the coastal or insular distribution of many ecclesiastical sites.

Ecclesiastical place-names supplement the historical sources and give a more detailed impression of the wide distribution of early ecclesiastical activity. Many sites have names in 'Kil-' (Gaelic *Cill*, 'church', or 'burial-ground'), often compounded with a personal name (Watson 1926). Dedications to Columba of Iona, Moluag of Lismore, and Maelrubha of Applecross are widespread, but the most numerous dedications, usually anglicised as 'Kilbride', are to the Irish female saint *Bríd* or Brigid. A more obscure saint from her native province of Leinster was Abbán moccu Corbmaic, commemorated at 'Kilvickocharmick' or Keills in Knapdale and the nearby Eilean Mór in the 'MacCormac Isles' at the mouth of Loch Sween (Maclean 1983). Several examples are preserved of the name *Annat*, 'an old church', and there is continuing debate as to whether this name indicates high status, as in Ireland, or refers to abandonment, perhaps during the period of Norse activity (Macdonald 1973; Clancy 1995). Other less common elements include *disirt*, 'hermitage'; *cladh* and *reilig*, 'burial place', and *teampull*, 'church'. Two of these names are combined on Iona in Cladh an Dísirt, a secluded chapel-site near the shore (RCAHMS 1982, 242–3, no. 7). Clachan Dysart, the older name of Dalmally (Lorne), commemorated the hermitage of St Conan, whose well is preserved nearby (RCAHMS

1975, 124, no. 242). *Annat, disirt* and *reilig,* from Latin *antiquitas, desertum* and *reliquiae* (relics), testify to the Mediterranean contacts of the church in Ireland and Argyll.

Later tradition held that burial-grounds such as Reilig Odhrain on Iona were sanctified with soil brought from Rome (RCAHMS 1982, 250), and a fragment of porphyry found at Kilberry was probably a memento from one of the churches of the imperial city. The Irish church also created its own relics; these brought faithful worshippers and pilgrims into direct contact with their saintly patrons, and the churches that possessed them enjoyed high prestige. They were considered to bring healing and protection, and could be used to enforce the church's moral and social teaching. At the highest level, the relics of Columba and Adomnan were taken on circuit through Ireland, and no doubt also Dalriada, to renew their 'laws' when fines were levied and tribute received. Columba's crozier, the *Cathbuidhe* ('battle-victory'), was one of the relics taken to Dunkeld in the ninth century; it was carried in a victory over the Danes, in the same way as were the Monymusk Reliquary and the arm of St Fillan at Bannockburn. At a more mundane level, the keeper of St Fillan's crozier was authorised to carry it throughout Scotland in the search for stolen cattle.

Lismore preserves a precious relic of its founder: his *bachuil mór* or staff. This curved length of yew, with nails which formerly secured a metal casing or shrine, is displayed in Bachuil House, the home of its hereditary keeper, the 'Baron of Bachuil', along with a charter of 1544 by which the Earl of Argyll confirmed this office to an earlier member of the Livingstone family. At the same period, a bell of St Moluag was kept at a crannog a few miles east of Oban, and two early iron bells were encased in later shrines, now in the Museum of Scotland. The one found in 1814 at Kilmichael Glassary near Dunadd has a fine bronze casing in twelfth-century Romanesque style (Glenn 2003, no. H2, 100–4). The Guthrie bell-shrine, probably originally from Iona, has bronze figures of the same period re-used with silver plates which bear the name of John son of Alexander, perhaps the John MacDonald who was Lord of the Isles from 1449 to 1493 (Glenn 2003, no. H1, 94–9). Later traditions recorded a crozier of St Munn kept near Kilmun (Cowal), and bells at Keil, Lochaline (Morvern) and at Kilberry (Knapdale). Other saints' relics on the borders of Argyll include the bronze bell on Eilean Fhianain in Loch Sheil and the magnificent bell and crozier of St Fillan, which were retained by hereditary keepers in Strathfillan and Glen Dochart (Glenn 2003, nos. H5–6, 106–15). The third of the classic Irish trinity of monastic relics was the book; the Book of Kells, 'the great gospel-book of Columcille', was probably created on Iona in honour of the saint in the second half of the eighth century. Adomnán related that readings from books written by Columba's own hand helped to end a drought eighty years after his death, when his white garment, also preserved as a relic, was carried as a processional banner. We may imagine that a fine copy of the *Life of Columba* was preserved beside the ornate metalwork shrine in which his remains were placed in the eighth century, and which was the target of a murderous Norse attack in 825.

The archaeology of the early church in Argyll (Fisher 1997), and throughout the Irish culture-area, is marked by the widespread use of timber, with the consequent lack of surface-remains. Bede recorded that the church on Lindisfarne was enlarged about 651 'in the Irish manner, not of stone but of sawn timber and thatched with reeds', and Adomnán describes the collection of boatloads of wattles in Columba's time. A century later, large timbers for building and boat-building were rafted to Iona from mainland Argyll by a fleet of wooden and skin-covered boats. However, in treeless areas of Atlantic Ireland and Scotland drystone masonry was used, and stone cells survive on the small island of Eileach an Naoimh (Figure 15). In some cases stone or earthwork enclosures are preserved, but carved stones offer the most widespread evidence for Christian activity. These range from simple crosses incised on pillars, slabs or natural rock-surfaces, to great free-standing crosses. In sculpture, as in the other monastic arts, there was a vast development in technique and ambition between the age of the monastic founders and the artistic 'Golden Age' of the eighth century. Simplicity, however, is no certain indicator of age, for crosses had many functions and most were carved by amateurs. Even on Iona, many of the surviving carvings reflect the ascetic tradition of Columba rather than the capabilities of a great literary and artistic centre (Fisher 1997; Fisher 2001).

Iona

The island of Iona is situated on the major sea-route west of Mull and, although the summit of Dun I is only 100 m high, it provides a panorama extending from Islay to Skye, east to the Argyll mainland and north-west to Coll and Tiree. Barely 5.5 km by 2.5 km, Iona comprises a wide variety of terrain: uplands of barren gneiss intersected by valleys of green pasture; fertile sandy machair soils to west and north; more solid glacial soil on the eastern plain, the main settlement-area both in Columba's time and at present; and sea-cliffs or rocky shores interrupted by sandy bays. Adomnán gives a detailed and credible picture of interlocking sacred and domestic activity within this landscape. Communal worship, solitary meditation and pilgrimage alternate with pastoral and arable farming, seal-hunting and the collection of building materials. Columba regularly came to meditate on the natural mound at Sithean, the 'little hill of the angels', which was the target of the procession intended to end the spring drought in Adomnán's time. It overlooks the Machair or *Campulus Occidentalis* ('little western plain'), where the monks had their arable fields and from which they carried home the heavy sacks of grain. The celebrated incident of the white horse, which carried vessels of milk from the pasture and came to bid farewell to the dying Columba, occurred after the saint had inspected the grain stored in a barn near the monastery. The spot was later marked by a cross set in a millstone or quernstone, and the tradition of using these as cross-bases continued at Iona into the late middle ages.

The topography of the monastic area, centred on the later Benedictine abbey, is partially known from field remains, aerial and geophysical survey, and excavation. These again give a picture consistent with Adomnán's account, which describes numerous features within the *vallum* or rampart that formed the spiritual boundary of the monastery: a church large enough to house the community at the time of the founder's death; a *platea* or open space, perhaps corresponding to the existing area where the high crosses stand in front of the medieval church; a monastic cemetery which was probably separate from the present Reilig Odhrain; large communal buildings and small living and writing cells, all of timber; craft workshops and peripheral agricultural structures. Internal divisions of the *vallum* enclosure may represent its growth along with the size and wealth of the community, but also the separation of these various functions. The rampart and outer ditch visible west and north-west of the abbey belonged to a roughly rectangular enclosure, which measured at its greatest extent at least 8 hectares and was bounded on the east by rough ground above the shore (Plate 19; Figure 14). Excavation north of Reilig Odhrain in 1979 revealed a massive ditch and an entrance-causeway whose alignment was preserved by a medieval paved road. The ditch was beginning to fill with peat in the decades after Columba's death in 597, and pollen and plant-remains preserve a detailed record of the local environment (Barber 1981). A nearby circular or round-ended structure built with large post-holes was re-used and repaired over a long period, extending into the eighth century (Figure 14). Excavation in the 1950s found remains of a rectangular timber building south of the rocky mound of Torr an Aba, and there were traces of a circular structure on the summit of the hillock itself. Rubbish dumped in the excavated ditch from nearby workshops included building timbers and other worked wood, fragments of about thirty alder-wood bowls turned on pole-lathes of traditional type, and leather objects including a purse and many shoes. Excavated craft-material includes crucibles for making glass or enamel and clay moulds for large glass studs decorated with an interlaced motif found in the Book of Kells.

It is likely that the early churches lay under the medieval one, but a tiny oratory comparable in plan with the earliest Irish stone churches survives in rebuilt form as 'St Columba's Shrine' a few metres to the west. This chapel, which stands close to St John's Cross, was pointed out in seventeenth-century tradition as 'St Columbus's Tomb', and may indeed mark the spot where his stone pillow was set 'as a memorial beside his grave'. In the eighth century the saint's remains were transferred to an elaborate

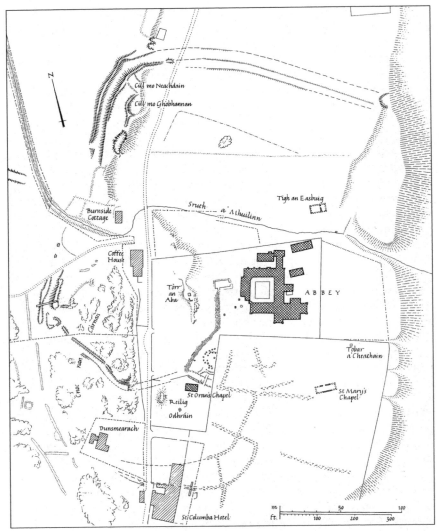

FIGURE 14 Iona Abbey. The early Christian monastic vallum survives to the
north of the abbey. The medieval paved road is the stippled band to the north of
St Oran's and the circular post structure is to the north-east of the chapel.
(RCAHMS)

metalwork shrine, which was to be the target of a Viking raid in 825, when
the monk Blathmac was martyred for refusing to reveal its hiding-place.

Smaller Monasteries

Historical sources indicate a wide hierarchy of smaller monasteries in Dalriada, some of them independent and others linked to the major foundations of Iona, Lismore and, beyond the boundaries of present-day Argyll, Kingarth (Bute) and Applecross (Wester Ross). Lismore's enclosure, as preserved in eighteenth-century estate maps and present-day field boundaries, was an oval about 2 ha in extent, compared with the monastic area of at least 8 ha on Iona. A large but fragmentary cross-slab, perhaps of the ninth century and only recently identified, is the only monumental sculpture from the site.

The fertile island of Tiree (*Ethica Terra*) had other monasteries beside the Columban daughter-house at *Campus Lunge* (?Soroby), and medieval traditions recorded attempted settlements there, even before the foundation of Iona, by the celebrated Irish saints Brendan and Comgall. The small enclosed site at St Patrick's Temple, Kenvara, between the shore and an inland cliff in the most remote and rugged part of the island, preserves a turf-and-stone wall and hut platforms. The ruined chapel is of medieval date, but three simple cross-marked stones of early type remain at the site. It is possible that this site was occupied by a small group of hermits from one of the larger houses or from Iona itself, which is visible to the south. This pattern would match Adomnan's account of the island monastery of Hinba, an unidentified daughter-house of Iona which had its own 'place of the anchorites' at Muirbolc Mar. On Iona itself, a 'head of the hermitage' is named in 1164, and the chapel at Cladh an Dísirt has been mentioned above.

The most extensive remains of a small monastic site are on the rocky and treeless island of Eilach an Naoimh in the Garvellach group (RCAHMS 1984, 170–82, no. 354) (Figure 15). A series of cross-walls span the gully that rises from the boat-landing to the oval inner enclosure with its rebuilt chapel. Early cross-marked stones stand in a nearby burial-ground and in a small circular enclosure known as 'Eithne's Grave' which overlooks the site. The central area has been robbed to build post-medieval agricultural structures, but among the rocks near the shore there stands a double cell. In its corbelled 'beehive' technique and its figure-of-eight plan it closely resembles examples at monastic sites in Co. Kerry, some of which have a similar arrangement of terraces rising to an inner enclosure. Most of the identifiable sites of this period, however, are circular or oval enclosures within thick drystone or stone-and-turf walls, such as that at the head of a beach on Nave Island, off the Ardnave peninsula of Islay (RCAHMS 1984, 225–8, no. 383). The most elaborate example lies north of Argyll, at Sgor nam Bàn-naomha on Canna (RCAHMS 1999), but that at Cladh a' Bhearnaig at the north end of Kerrera has an internal dividing-wall like that found at several Irish sites (RCAHMS 1975, 119–20, no. 232). Situated opposite the Cenel Loairn fortress of Dunollie, and identified on an

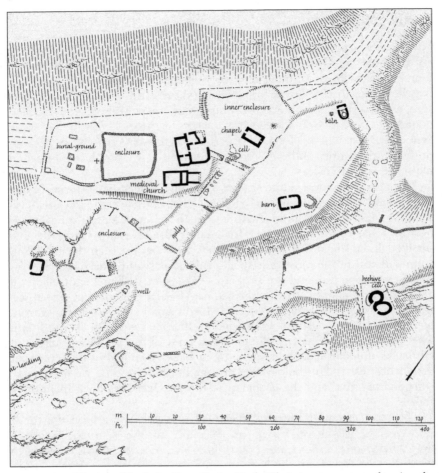

FIGURE 15 Eilach an Naoimh, Garvellachs. Early Christian monastery showing the location of the beehive cell. (RCAHMS)

eighteenth-century map as 'Clyvernock, an old monastery', the dedication may be to St Ernan or 'Marnock'. However, the remarkable collection of nearly thirty early carved stones at Cladh a' Bhile near Ellary in Knapdale occupies an irregular enclosure of uncertain origin.

Caves

A particular feature of Argyll is the number of caves with early graffito crosses on their walls, which may result from early occupation by hermits and later pilgrim cults in their honour. The largest numbers of carvings, which continue into the post-medieval period, are found in two caves in the Ross of Mull, at Carsaig and Scoor (RCAHMS 1980, 159, no. 318; 166–7, no. 326). Smaller groups are found in the caves associated with Saints Columba and Ciaran, in Knapdale and Kintyre, while the marigold and Chi-rho carvings in a cramped and almost entirely dark cave on Eilean Mor afford a vivid insight into the ascetic devotion of the early hermits (RCAHMS 1992, 66–74, no. 33). Similar crosses are found in caves in other parts of Scotland but are rare elsewhere; hermits from this area may have inaugurated the tradition of artificial caves and graffito crosses in southern Iceland, whose chronology is the subject of current research.

Sculpture

The sign of the cross was in everyday use in Columba's monastery for blessing practical objects (Sharpe 1995, 166–7, 177–8), and an interesting application of this is a cross-marked quernstone from Dunadd (RCAHMS 1992, 526). It was also in universal use for sanctifying places of worship and burial, and on individual grave-markers. Almost all of the three hundred pre-Romanesque carved stones from Argyll listed in a recent survey (Fisher 2001) bear incised or relief crosses, and many are of cruciform shape. Moreover, these forms are often combined, or a simple type repeated, as on many of the stones at Cladh a' Bhile, Ellary (RCAHMS 1992, 53–61, no. 20). This site has a fine pillar with a six-petalled 'marigold' pattern, also found elsewhere in southern Argyll and the Clyde islands and perhaps derived from Gaul (Plate 20; Figure 16).

The collection of over one hundred carved stones on Iona (RCAHMS 1982, 179–219, no. 6 (1–108)) contains examples of most of the types found in the area, ranging from small grave-markers with the simplest of incised crosses to some of the largest of Irish high crosses. Dating of simple crosses, here and elsewhere, is notoriously difficult, but many are probably of seventh- and eighth-century date (Figure 17a). Many of the simple stones resemble those found at small monastic sites, hermitages and burial-grounds, but there are also a number of large recumbent graveslabs, mostly bearing ringed crosses, of a type that rarely occurs elsewhere in the West Highlands. Seven of these bear simple Irish inscriptions and a wedge-shaped gravemarker is incribed in Latin LAPIS ECHODI ('the stone of Echoid') (Plate 21). However, the small number of inscriptions and their amateur character suggest that personal commemoration was a low priority in eighth-century Iona, in contrast to the splendour of the high crosses erected to the glory of God.

Adomnán mentions three crosses on Iona during or soon after Columba's lifetime, one of them standing in a millstone and presumably of timber. The earliest of the high crosses, St Oran's and St John's (Figure 17b), show this ancestry in the carpentry joints used to link massive

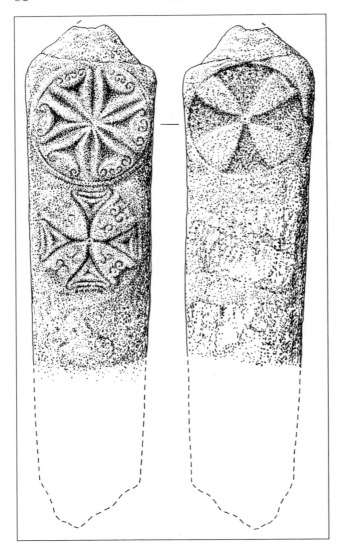

FIGURE 16
Cladh a'Bhile,
Ellary: 'marigold'
cross. (scale 1:15)
(RCAHMS)

slabs of stone imported from Mull and Knapdale. Both were originally ringless, but the 'ring of glory' to which so much symbolism has been attached was probably introduced in St John's Cross during repairs after an early fall. These crosses, with St Martin's on Iona (Plate 22) and the closely related Kildalton Cross on Islay (Figure 18), share elaborate spiral and geometrical patterns, and most bear figure-scenes. These include instances of divine salvation such as Abraham sacrificing Isaac and Daniel in the lions' den (also seen on the Keills Cross in Knapdale). Repeated images of the Virgin and Child and the elaborate spirals and

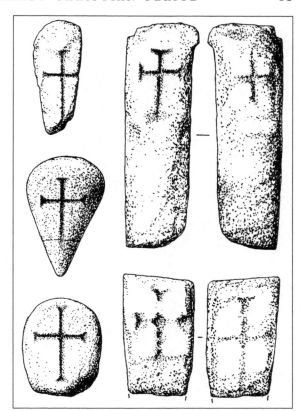

FIGURE 17a
Iona: a selection of
linear incised crosses.
(scale 1:15) (RCAMHS)

'snake-and-boss' ornament which are unifying features of the group link the crosses with the Book of Kells, the richest of Irish manuscripts. This was probably being decorated on Iona in the second half of the eighth century at the same time as St John's Cross, one of the tallest of all Irish crosses and the widest in span. Both were probably created in honour of St Columba and may reflect the ornament of the metalwork shrine to which the saint's remains were transferred at that period. This enhancement of Iona's status as a centre of pilgrimage (Fisher 1994) is attested particularly by the retirement to Iona in the late eighth century of two Irish kings, from Ulster and Connaught.

Laity

The religious provision made for the laity is much more obscure than the activities of the monastic world. For the Columban period one can extrapolate from Adomnán and from Bede's account of the enthusiastic

FIGURE 17b
Iona: St John's Cross.

evangelising of Irish missionaries in Northumbria to build a picture of itinerant monks, but no archaeological picture emerges. The most prominent
lay group in Adomnán are those penitents who spent years under strict
monastic discipline, in some cases, no doubt, in the small eremitic sites
which have been described above. The sculpture of the area shows little
evidence of the aristocratic patronage that is so obvious on the Pictish
cross-slabs, with their constant depictions of riders and hunting scenes.
The Kilnave Cross on Islay, however, stands close to an area of early settlement, and may mark a centre of lay worship, perhaps served from the
enclosed site on Nave Island.

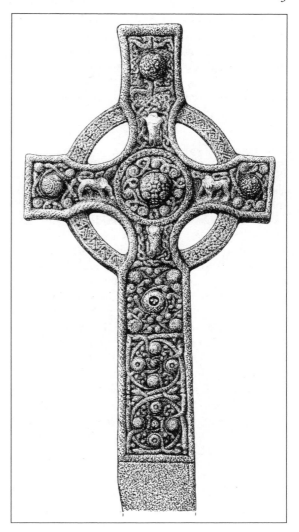

FIGURE 18
Kildalton Cross, Islay.

Many of the medieval churches and chapels throughout the area occupy ancient sites, usually with 'Cill-'prefixed names, but it is not known whether they originated as monasteries or as secular burial-grounds. Early drystone or clay-mortared rural chapels in very small burial-grounds are particularly common on Islay (RCAHMS 1984, fig. 26; 1992, fig. 6), but most are likely to belong to the Christian Norse period, from the tenth century onwards, rather than to the Columban one. A small chapel identified below St Ronan's Church, Iona (O'Sullivan 1994) and that at St Ninian's Point, Bute (Aitken 1955) overlay Christian burials, but neither produced evidence for close dating, nor for timber predecessors.

Adomnán offers some glimpses of popular religion, of the type common among Celtic peoples, and the Reformation has not entirely eliminated such traces, including the veneration paid to holy wells. In some cases these are associated with carved stones, notably at Kilmory Oib, Mid Argyll (RCAHMS 1992, 172–3, no. 78). The evidence for pilgrimage to places on Iona and to certain caves has been mentioned.

Vikings and After

Norse raids on Iona in 795 and 802, and particularly that of 806 when sixty-eight members of the community were killed, led to the establishment of Kells (Co. Meath) as a more secure centre for the Columban family of monasteries. When raiders again attacked Iona in 825, there was no resident abbot and it was a senior monk, Blathmac, who was martyred for refusing to say where Columba's shrine had been hidden. Relics of the saint were transferred to Kells and to Dunkeld (Perthshire) during the ninth century, and Iona retained only a local importance. However, it came to attract the devotion of the converted Scandinavian settlers of the Hebrides, and once again an Irish king from Dublin, this time of Norse descent, came 'in penitence and pilgrimage' in 980. This period of Norse Christianity is represented by cross-shafts at Iona and Doid Mhairi (Islay), and by an Iona graveslab bearing an interlaced cross and a runic inscription naming Olvir and his sons Kali and Fugl. This period may have seen the origins of many of the small rural chapels described above. When Somerled, 'king' of Argyll, tried to reform the monastery of Iona in 1164, it retained several of the officials of a typical Celtic community, and they continued to maintain the Columban tradition until the arrival of the Benedictines about 1200.

CHAPTER SEVEN

The Medieval Church in Argyll

T HE START of the Middle Ages in Argyll can be defined by changes in
the Church. From the eleventh century, reforms in the Latin Church
spread through Europe, triggering a surge in the founding of new monastic orders. The influx of the reformed Latin Church did not take place
effortlessly in Argyll. This was an area where the 'Irish' Church held great
sway; St Columba's Iona was its spiritual heart. It is therefore not surprising that when the Benedictine abbey was founded in the heart of the old
monastery on Iona in 1203, it elicited a strong reaction. 'The clergy of Ireland ... came together and destroyed the monastery according to the law
of the Church' (Marsden 2001, 124). This destruction of the new Latin
monastery by figures from the old 'Irish' Church is the most remarkable
manifestation of a struggle which characterises the start of the Middle Ages
in Argyll.

The Church reforms brought about by St Margaret and her sons, David
I in particular, are well recorded. Through the eleventh and twelfth centuries these Canmore kings founded monasteries for orders originating on
mainland Europe. This encouragement of these cosmopolitan orders was
not only pious but wise, since they had a civilising and centralising influence on the areas in which they were established. The patronage of
monastic orders was paralleled by the formation of dioceses and parishes
along continental lines. The dioceses in Scotland appear to have been
based on the great earldoms, and it is likely that the parishes followed similar secular subdivisions. As in the system of feudalism which David and his
brothers were also encouraging, every member of the new ecclesiastical
structure was aware of his role in a hierarchy which acted through chains
of delegation and duty, passing protection and patronage down the chain
and services and goods up.

David I enabled this reformed structure to be adequately funded by the
institution of the system of teinds. This allocated to each parish church one
tenth of the parish's production in order to support the parson, pay for the
upkeep of the church and manse (which was meant to be of a sufficient
standard of comfort to offer hospitality to the bishop) and fund the care
of the poor and sick of the parish. The parson was also expected to pay
episcopal dues out of these revenues.

A variation on this system – vicarage – quickly arose and was canonised by the Fourth Lateran Council in 1215. Under the vicarage system institutions such as monasteries could acquire the parsonage of a parish and the teind income which went with it. The holder of the parsonage would then provide the parish with a vicar, who received a small portion of the teind or a small stipend.

On the western seaboard, these reforms penetrated slowly, if at all. Until 1266 the Hebrides were still subject to the superiority of Norway rather than Scotland; this had been reaffirmed in 1098 by the campaign of Magnus Barelegs. While mainland Argyll was part of the diocese of Dunkeld until towards the end of the twelfth century, culturally it had more in common with the Hebrides than with central and eastern Scotland. The western seaboard can be understood as being distinct from the rest of Scotland at this stage. It was not so much a far-flung fringe of Canmore Scotland as a major element in a cultural grouping of territories around the Irish Sea, which also included Galloway, the Isle of Man and Ireland. Norse influence in the area was still strong; Man and the Isles were still Norwegian territories, albeit with a local ruler, the King of Man.

From 1156, Argyll and the Isles began to have a greater coherence under Somerled, *rí Innse Gall* (King of the Isles), and his descendants, known as the MacSorleys. Somerled has been portrayed as a conservative potentate on the Celtic fringe, resisting the influence and the reforms of the Scottish kings. He did, though, seek reforms of his own choosing. In 1164, the year of his death, he unsuccessfully invited Flaithbertach Ó Brolchán, the abbot of Derry, to become abbot of Iona. Building on the extensive reforms of St Malachy across Ireland, Abbot Flaithbertach had successfully reinvigorated the monastery at Derry and re-established the coherence of the *familia* of Columban establishments. These reforms rejuvenated an indigenous, Columban Church, rather than bringing in continental orders. It seems that Somerled, in inviting Abbot Flaithbertach to become abbot of Iona, was encouraging reforms which arose from local, rather than continental, models.

Somerled may have been unsuccessful in his patronage of the Church but changes were also being carried forward by others. In a charter of 1134, Olaf, King of Man, Somerled's father-in-law, re-established the existing diocese of Sodor and the Isles, granting the right to elect the bishop of Sodor to the Cistercian monks of Furness in Cumbria. His motive for re-establishing a diocese which coincided with his territories appears to have been political: he expressed concern about 'strangers' and 'mercenaries' (McDonald 1997, 208). Like the Scottish kings, Olaf seems to have been making use of the organisation of the Church to reinforce his secular power.

Man and the Isles became subject to the suzerainty of Scotland in 1266, but the loss of Man to England in 1333 split the diocese between England and Scotland, dividing the Hebrides from the cathedral at Peel, on Man. The Great Schism in 1387 cemented this division by producing two lines of bishops, one on Man and the other in the Isles. This seems to have been the final act in a division which had had a long history. A group of the canons of Snizort and clergy on Skye elected a bishop and sought his confirmation in 1331. This may have been a reflection of an older tradition; a bishop of Skye was recorded in the eleventh century. Snizort emerged as the cathedral church of the Isles in the fourteenth century. Enough survives on the site to make it clear that, while the buildings were more complex than most church sites in the area, the cathedral of Snizort was, in comparison with most cathedrals, a very modest affair. In 1433 Bishop Angus de Insulis sought to move the cathedral from Snizort to 'some honest place', and tried to establish a proper cathedral chapter. This attempt was not successful and was followed by a petition in 1498 to make Iona Abbey the cathedral of the Isles. This was not successful either but the following year the bishop of the Isles was granted the abbey *in commendam* and from that point on the abbey church may have functioned as a *de facto* cathedral.

About 1189 the diocese of Argyll was formed out of the western territories of the diocese of Dunkeld. Its formation was prompted by a petition to the pope by Bishop John, the Scot, of Dunkeld, on the basis that the western half of his diocese was difficult to administer because of the inhabitants being Gaelic speakers. The real impetus is more likely to have been the influence of the sons of Somerled, Ranald and Dugald. Like Olaf, they may have seen the creation of a diocese of Argyll, under their patronage, as a tool in their increased control of their mainland territories.

Patronage of the see seems to have rested mostly with Dugald MacSorley and his descendants, in whose territory lay the cathedral on Lismore. It has been suggested that this patronage may have lain behind the long and frequent vacancies of the see in its first sixty years, the revenues of the bishopric being siphoned off by Dugald and his descendants. Alexander II's invasion of 1249 seems to have been prompted not just by Ewen MacDougall's assumption of the title King of the Isles, but also by a concern regarding Argyll's repeated episcopal vacancy. In the same year, papal approval was given for the cathedral of Argyll to be moved to a site on the mainland, to be chosen by the bishops of Glasgow and Dunkeld. The crown was to pay part of the costs, and the king, shortly before his death on Kerrera, gave the church of Kilbride in Glen Feochan to the bishop of Argyll, presumably to act as the new mainland cathedral. In the event, the cathedral stayed at Lismore and was rebuilt in the early fourteenth century.

The rebuilding of Lismore may have been related to reform within the diocese. While members of a cathedral chapter first appear on record in the second quarter of the thirteenth century, as late as 1357 Bishop Martin stated that the chapter did not have a seal because the bishop is elected by the entire clergy. This probably refers back to the practice of bishops being elected by the 'clergy of the city and the diocese', in other words the deans and the parish priests. However, it is about this time that the parochial clergy seem to have been deprived of their electoral rights, and that a properly instituted chapter starts to appear.

The establishment of parishes in Argyll is remarkably poorly recorded, but it is safe to assume that it took place as part of the diocesan reforms of the late twelfth century. Before the twelfth century, the organisation of the Church does not appear to have been so clearly pyramidal. The distinction between monastic establishments and the secular clergy was less marked, with groups of clergy based at major centres carrying out pastoral duties over a large area. Clearly, most communities would have a place of worship and burial, but they were served from a central minster. Minsters in Argyll and the Hebrides have not been easy to identify although Snizort and Iona have been suggested.

The identification of minsters has been made difficult by the lack of archival evidence and the widespread practice, not unique to the west coast, of using existing sites for the new parochial churches. This is indicated by a variety of evidence: the high proportion of parish churches with 'Kil-' prefixed place names, indicating sites venerated from the sixth to tenth centuries; the frequency of dedications to saints from the 'Irish' Church, such as St Columba, St Brendan or St Bride; and the existence of features attributed to Early Christian sites, such as holy wells and sub-circular burial enclosures.

That parishes were established in the late twelfth century is borne out by the archaeological evidence of the parish churches of Argyll. However, in looking at the origins of the buildings identified as being parish churches, a note of caution must be struck. The twelfth century sees the widespread introduction of lime mortars in building work. This transformed both secular and ecclesiastical architecture, enabling stone structures to be both more elaborate and more durable than their predecessors, which were made of timber or unmortared stone. Therefore some caution must be taken in assuming that when the earliest parts of a church date to the twelfth century, this is because the parish was created then. That said, patterns do emerge across Argyll which permit generalisations to be made. For example, several of the Medieval parish churches of Kintyre contain twelfth-century elements, while such features can be ascribed to only one church in Lorne – Kilchattan. This difference is clearly not due to a variation in technical possibilities, and can be seen as a mark of the spread of ecclesiastical reorganisation. Kintyre, controlled by Somerled's son Ranald MacSorley and closer to the heavily feudalised lands of the Stewarts, appears to have established parishes before such a change is seen further into the MacSorley heartlands controlled by Dugald.

In the diocese of Sodor, lying within the province of Trondheim in Norway, a pattern reminiscent of Norwegian models has been traced. In this system, the administrative unit was not the parish but the 'priest's district' (*prestegjeld*). This could include up to four principal churches in a grouping which could vary with time. Such groupings have been identified for Rothesay and Kingarth on Bute, Kilmory and Kilbride on Arran, and pairings of Kilnaughton, Kildalton and Kilarrow, Kilmany on Islay. Mull was divided into three districts of three churches each (Inch Kenneth, Kilfinichen and Kilvikeon; Pennygown, Killean and Laggan; Kilninian, Kilcolmkill and Ulva) while Tiree and Coll formed a single district. It is not clear how long such a pattern of organisation lasted. While the ceding of the Isles to Scotland in 1266 clearly resulted in a dramatic decline in Norwegian influence, the diocese of Sodor remained subject to Trondheim until 1472, when the province of St Andrews was created.

As with parishes and dioceses, the foundation of monasteries in Argyll and the Isles in medieval times never quite fulfilled the potential of the continental models. While they were the most impressive churches in Argyll, the tally of five monastic houses (only one of which was of any size) in an area the extent of Argyll and the Isles is remarkably low. There are a variety of reasons for this, of which a lower concentration of population is only one. Monasteries do not generate spontaneously. They require the will and generosity of a patron to give them a site and sufficient endowments, normally in the form of land, to establish a house; no patron, no monastery.

As with the creation of the diocese of Argyll and the formation of parishes, the influx of the reformed continental orders was the work of the MacSorleys, in particular Ranald. Saddell Abbey in Kintyre, a daughter house of the Cistercian abbey of Mellifont in County Louth, appears to have been the first foothold of the reformed continental orders in Somerled's territories. However, the date of its foundation is not clear: some time in the latter half of the twelfth century and possibly as early as 1160. Ranald is recorded as the founder of Saddell, and the abbey lies within the territories he inherited in 1164, after Somerled's death at Renfrew. Of Somerled's three heirs, Ranald appears to have become the most dominant. His patronage of Saddell was not an isolated example of his interest in the Church. It was probably under Ranald that St Oran's Chapel on Iona was built as a mausoleum for Somerled and the MacSorleys. Iona, though, was not within Ranald's territories, forming part of the inheritance of Dugald which included Lorn, Benderloch, Lismore, Mull, Coll and Tiree. Dugald was no stranger to ecclesiastical patronage himself, making donations at St Cuthbert's shrine at Durham on 23 August 1175, and it must be supposed that he was involved in any establishments on Iona, at least tacitly.

Ranald is also reputed to have been the patron of the Benedictine monastery and the Augustinian nunnery on Iona, the former being the cause of so much consternation in the 'Irish' Church. According to the *Annals of Ulster* the monastery was founded in 1203, with the nunnery probably being founded about the same time, with Bethag, Ranald's sister, as its first prioress. In 1231 Ranald's nephew, Duncan MacDougall, founded Ardchattan Priory on Loch Etive for the Valliscaulians. In their treatment of the see of Argyll at this time the MacDougalls had shown themselves to be not the greatest supporters of the Church and it has been suggested that this was a political move to placate Alexander II.

Oronsay Priory, an Augustinian house, was founded by John, first Lord of the Isles, at some point between 1325 and 1353. It may therefore be the last monastic house, other than those for the mendicant orders, to be founded in Scotland. By the end of the thirteenth century enthusiasm for founding religious houses had waned among patrons across Scotland. The new mendicant orders (primarily the Franciscans, Dominicans and Carmelites) did found later houses in Scotland, but their preference for towns meant that their interest in Argyll was slight. During the fifteenth century the collegiate church became a popular alternative to monasteries as a form of ecclesiastical patronage, partly because of disillusionment with the state of the monastic orders, and partly because they were less expensive to endow.

Argyll received only one collegiate church, that at Kilmun. In 1442 the parish church was re-established as a collegiate church by Sir Duncan Campbell of Lochawe, and served as the family mausoleum until the end of the nineteenth century. The rise of the Campbells has often been attributed to their adept straddling of two worlds; the western seaboard and lowland Scotland. It comes as little surprise, therefore, that Argyll's only collegiate church, a type of establishment popular further east, should be a Campbell foundation, nor that the effigies of its founder and his wife should be carved by sculptors from outside Argyll, rather than by one of the renowned schools of carving in Argyll.

As elsewhere in Scotland, parishes were appropriated by a variety of institutions; they supplemented the income of monasteries, they funded the prebendaries of cathedral chapters and they helped supplement the funds of bishops themselves. The dioceses of the Isles and Argyll were notoriously poor, and special provision was given to the bishops of the Isles to receive one quarter of the teinds in each parish in their diocese. In 1203, the bishops of Argyll received a similar privilege, receiving one third of the teinds of each parish. However, of the fifty or so parish churches in the diocese of the Isles, eight were entirely appropriated by the bishop, thirteen were held by Iona Abbey, two by Iona Nunnery and two by Oronsay Priory. Establishments outside the diocese also held parsonages; on Bute, the teinds of Kingarth formed part of the prebend of the chancellor of the Chapel Royal, Stirling, while Rothesay was appropriated by the collegiate church of Restalrig near Edinburgh. Generally, those parishes which were remote from ecclesiastical institutions elsewhere in Scotland fared better because of the difficulty in staking and enforcing claims of appropriation at a distance.

The picture is similar in the diocese of Argyll, where, by the time of the Reformation, the bishop and the collegiate church of Kilmun each held six churches, Ardchattan Priory held five, Paisley Abbey four, Iona Abbey three, Inchaffray Abbey two, and Kilwinning Abbey and Fail Priory one each. Saddell appears to have appropriated three churches, that of Kilchattan on Gigha, Kilkivan and Inchmarnock. However Inchmarnock lost its parochial status, and when, in 1507, Saddell was granted to the bishop of Argyll *in commendam* in 1507, Kilchattan, being in a different diocese, became independent.

The system of appropriation required that vicars should be appointed to carry out the pastoral work of the parish. In the case of the Abbey of Iona and Ardchattan Priory, which both lay within parishes appropriated by them, they simply provided one of their number to carry out the duties of the vicar. In other cases adjoining parishes had to share a vicar which was particularly difficult given the large size of parishes in Argyll and the Isles. Vicarages were not much sought after, and the standard of the parochial priests was notoriously poor. In 1466 it was necessary to request that vicars should not be appointed in Argyll unless they could at least speak Gaelic, the language of their parishioners.

The monasteries survived on the revenues of their estates and appropriated parishes. In the case of Saddell, its endowments proved to be insufficient, and by 1507 it was said that the monastery had ceased to function, and that its revenues amounted to only £9 sterling. The Abbey of Iona, though, could count on the income from a steady stream of pilgrims. St Columba was a popular saint throughout Scotland and, although there were major shrines at both Dunkeld Cathedral and Inchcolm Abbey, Iona could rely on a significant number of visitors. The abbey church, with an undercroft beneath the high altar which communicated directly with the north and south choir aisles, was designed to allow the smooth flow of pilgrims. In 1428 the Pope granted an indulgence of three years' remission of purgatory for pilgrims to Iona. Such a move was intended to help fund the repair and rebuilding of the church, by making Iona a more popular destination for pilgrims.

While Iona was the most important pilgrimage site in the west, there were other local places of pilgrimage. Two of the most remarkable are on Eileach an Naoimh in the Garvellachs, south of Mull, and Eilean Mór in the MacCormac Isles, at the mouth of Loch Sween. Both of these sites probably started as early Christian retreats. Eileach an Naoimh seems to have been associated with St Brendan, and its popularity in the Middle Ages, demonstrated by the construction of a mortar-built church, may derive from the popularity of the tenth-century *Brendan's Voyage*, which tells of how the saint found a beautiful land of promise in the Atlantic.

Ecclesiastic life on Eilean Mór appears to have started as a hermitage for the Leinster saint, Abbán moccu Corbmaic, to whom the neighbouring church at Keills on the mainland is also dedicated. Like Eileach an Naoimh, Eilean Mór also has a medieval church, probably dating from the thirteenth century, adjacent to an ornate tenth-century cross. The site was patronised by John, Lord of the Isles, who created the vaulted chancel in the small chapel. His daughter-in-law, Mariota of Ross, erected a fine disc-headed cross (now in the Museum of Scotland) on the highest point of the island.

It is not surprising that the Lords of the Isles, the most powerful figures in Argyll, were patrons of the Church. Conscious of the role of Iona as the burial place of kings, and of their renowned ancestor Somerled, the Mac-Donald lords appear to have used St Oran's chapel as their mausoleum. Donald, Lord of the Isles, gave the abbey lands on Mull and Islay, as well as providing a new silver and gold casket for the relic of St Columba's arm. Donald had also provided the Church with a bishop of the Isles, his son Angus. However, one family had a greater impact on Iona than the Mac-Donald lords. The MacKinnon family probably provided many of the abbots of Iona, and developed a proprietorial attitude to the abbey. In 1426 Abbot Dominic complained of his MacKinnon predecessors that 'certain noble abbots ... kept noble women as concubines, had offspring by them and dowered them with the goods of the said monastery' (Steer and Bannerman 1977, 101). Donald, Lord of the Isles, threatened to remove from Iona the relics of his ancestors and the gifts Iona had received in the past, in protest at the entry of a monk called Finguine MacKinnon into the abbey. This Finguine was the grandson of Abbot Finguine, 'the Green Abbot', who was described as a 'subtle and wicked councillor'. It was under this abbot's tenure that Iona reached its lowest ebb with the buildings falling into almost complete disrepair as the abbot sequestered up to £400 silver merks of the abbey's wealth.

While the corruption of the MacKinnons was remarkable, they were by no means unique in having a tight hold on a monastic house. The MacLeans provided many of the abbesses of the nunnery on Iona. Ard-chattan presents an even more extreme example of this, with the family of MacDougall of Dunollie retaining the right to nominate the prior and, apparently, always choosing one of their own kinsmen. In 1506 the prior of Beauly Priory was commissioned to carry out a visitation on Ardchat-tan. As a result of this visitation Eogan MacDougall, prior of Ardchattan, was deposed. Later in the century, there were several local MacDougalls who referred to themselves as Mac a' Phrior, or 'son of the prior', thereby suggesting a reason for the deposition of Prior Eogan. It has been suggested that such concubinage in the Argyll Church was a legacy of the 'Irish' Church, where views on celibacy were not so strict. However, given the lack of evidence for the survival of other elements of the 'Irish' Church in Scotland, this must be questioned. The distance of the monastic houses of Argyll from their mother houses made them far more susceptible to the influence of local families and the relaxation of centrally enforced rules of conduct.

The history of the Church in Argyll is clearly one of comparative dis-organisation and poverty. However, the condition of institutions such as the dioceses should not be confused with the experience of those who attended the churches and chapels of Argyll and the Isles. While the vicars in each parish were, in general, a fairly mediocre lot, respect for the Church appears to have been largely undiminished. The castles of Skipness and Dunstaffnage both had fine chapels situated well beyond their defensive circuit, safe in the knowledge of the taboos which surrounded those who molested churches. When Allan MacRuari of Clanranald attacked both Iona and Eilean Finan at the turn of the sixteenth century, he was described as a 'demon of the gael', 'fierce ravager of church and cross, the bald head, heavy, worthless boar', and a 'worthless, cruel son of Ruari' (MacDonald 1997, 28–9).

Given the size of most parishes, it can be assumed that most worship took place in the chapels or holy places local to each settlement. These holy places could range from holy wells, such as that in the township of Kilmory Oib in Knapdale, to fine chapels such as that at Kilmory Knap further south. In the latter case, not only did the community support a building as fine as their parochial church at Keills, but they left a great legacy of memorials. These memorials are examples of the West Highland schools of carving, whose work is found in cemeteries and churches throughout the western seaboard. At Kilmory the collection contains only one figure in military dress and, judging by the tools shown on several of the slabs, indicates that Kilmory Knap was a trading centre specialising in finished cloth (see Plate 27). The people of Kilmory were merchants rather than aristocrats, but the church was still the centre of their community and the recipient of their most lasting legacy.

The Age of Sea-Kings: 900–1300

CURIOUSLY, in Scotland, the second half of the 'Dark Ages' are even darker than the first and this contrast is nowhere more obvious than in Argyll. Lit up by the writings of Adomnán of Iona and the annalists of that monastery who succeeded him, Argyll between the mid-sixth and the mid-ninth century is one of the best documented parts of Britain. After the relics of Columba left Iona in 849, however, the region is plunged into obscurity for three hundred years, only gradually emerging from the gloom in the time of Somerled, his sons and grandsons.

The Coming of the Vikings

A clue to the fate of the region in the mid-ninth century is to be found in the Frankish chronicle compiled at this time by Prudentius, Bishop of Troyes, and known today as the *Annals of St-Bertin*. Prudentius wrote, under the year 847, 'the Northmen also got control of the islands all around Ireland and stayed there without encountering any resistance from anyone.' This account almost certainly refers to the southern Hebrides, the island portion of Dál Riata, which from now on formed a base for viking attacks on Ireland and northern Britain. That the islands of Dál Riata suffered a more traumatic fate that the mainland portions is indicated by the preservation of the names of two of the four leading kindreds of the kingdom – Cenél Comgaill and Cenél Loairn in the districts of Cowal and Lorne – while the names of the remaining kindreds – Cenel nGabráin (based in Kintyre and Arran) and Cenél nOengusa (based on Islay) – have disappeared without trace. It may well be that the accounts written in Iceland in the twelfth and thirteenth centuries that record Scandinavian ancestors of the Icelanders, such as Olaf the White and his son Thorstein the Red, ruling 'half of Scotland' refer to a partitioning of Dál Riata. Such a sharing of a kingdom between incoming vikings and native dynasties also occurred in several parts of England, Mercia, in the Midlands, was split with the old rulers keeping the west and the vikings the east; in Northumbria the vikings got the southern half of the kingdom and there is some evidence for a north/south division in East Anglia and perhaps an east/west division in Wessex. Such a division of Dál Riata may well provide an explanation for the Gaelic terms Innse Gall and Airer Gaedel, 'Islands of the Foreigners' and 'Coastline of the Gael'. The latter term was anglicised as Argyll.

The long-term effect of the loss of the islands to a viking dynasty was to reduce the contact between Gaelic Scotland and Ireland. Indeed the *Annals of Ulster* record under the year 871 that there was a 'storming of Dunseverick, which had never been done before: the foreigners [i.e. vikings] were at it and the Cenél nEogain.' Dunseverick was the chief fortress of Dál Riata in Ireland and Cenél nEogain were the leading dynasty in the north of Ireland. It seems likely that by 900 Cowal and Lorne had passed into the protection of the kings of the Picts, who were themselves the descendants of the Dál Riata dynast Cinaed mac Ailpín.

If something like a formal division of Dál Riata between Norse kings and natives did occur on the pattern better recorded for parts of England then it probably contributed to the continuity of language and culture that seems to distinguish the southern Hebrides, Kintyre and Arran from the northern Hebrides, the Northern Isles and Caithness. North of Ardna-murchan the place-name evidence seems to suggest total replacement by Norse of the local languages (presumably Pictish but perhaps Gaelic in some districts), while in the southern Hebrides Gaelic survived with only a handful of Norse place-names taking root. The one exception to this general rule is in the western portion of Islay, which may have formed the political centre of the Norse realm. It seems likely that on the whole the vikings took over the tributary structures of the Dál Riata and attempted to stress continuity in governance. Their main desire at this stage was for a secure base from which they could raid the more prosperous lands to the south and east.

The Uí Ímair *imperium*

From the late ninth century to the twelfth almost no events can be securely located within Argyll. By the middle of the tenth century the islands seem to have fallen within the *imperium* of the dynasty claiming descent from Ímar (known to the Icelanders as Ivarr the Boneless) who had died in 873 as 'King of all the Norsemen in Britain and Ireland'. Ímar was probably a Dane and possibly originated from the Danish colony on the island of Walcheren in the mouth of the Scheldt (the English sources refer to his kinsmen as 'Scaldingi' and the Scheldt as 'Scald'). By the 930s and '40s, however, all the leaders of the vikings in the Irish Sea region and Argyll had not only been born in Britain and Ireland but were probably the sons of men who had been born here. Many, perhaps most, would have had native mothers and grandmothers. The descendants of Ímar ruled the whole of this region, including Dublin and the other 'Scandinavian' *long-phuirt* ('ship-ports') of Ireland, together with the Isle of Man and the coastal littoral of northwest England and southwest Scotland. They were also able sporadically to control the greater part of Northumbria until the final West Saxon conquest of York in 953 or 954.

This said, however, it would be a mistake to imagine the Uí Ímair *imperium* as a unitary empire. Strong kings like Olaf Guthfrithsson (d. 941) and his cousin Olaf Cuarán (d. 981) could bring all the territories together under their rule, but often the different portions of this far-flung sea-kingdom were ruled by a 'brood' of cousinly princes who squabbled amongst themselves for the over-kingship – a situation perhaps not so dissimilar from that prevalent among the Gaels of Ireland and Dál Riata in an earlier age. The natural tendency to fission was partly the result of the flexible arrangements for royal succession that Scandinavian and Gaelic culture shared in this period, as well as the simple geographical dispersal of the territories, but an increasingly important factor was that, although the royal family and the leading chieftains beneath them were all, in the male line, of Scandinavian origin, they were in fact the product of a variety of fusion cultures that were growing up from the different mixes of Scandinavian, Anglian, Gaelic, British and Pictish in each province. Of late scholars have coined the terms 'Anglo-Danish' and 'Hiberno-Norse' to cover two of these fusion cultures but another term, genuinely found in medieval documents, is worth reviving and certainly applies to some of the peoples of our area: *Gallgaedel*.

The Origins of the Gallgaedel

The term *Gallgaedel*, literally 'foreign Gael', first appears in a couple of entries in the Irish chronicles relating to the 850s when this group are said to be allied to the Irish high king Maelsechnaill mac Maile Ruanaid. In the second of these entries the leader of the Gallgaedel is named as Caittil the White and he has been identified by modern historians as the Icelandic ancestor figure Ketill Flatnose. In the Icelandic tradition Ketill is said to have been a war-chief from Romsdal in the Norwegian Westland and to have made himself ruler over a portion of the Hebrides. In any case these annals do not explain the term Gallgaedel, although a much later eleventh-century literary account of the same events says that the Gallgaedel were 'Gaels fostered by Norsemen'. Modern historians have tended to describe these Gallgaedel as people of 'mixed race', although some have been sceptical about the likelihood of having an army of such people available in the mid-ninth century, i.e. so close to the earliest likely dates for Norse settlement (and thus intermarriage) in these islands. More probably the term refers to Gaelic natives of a kingdom ruled by a Scandinavian dynasty, some of whom may have been of mixed descent. Unfortunately these two ninth-century references are all we have to go on for nearly two centuries. When, however, the term re-emerges in the eleventh and twelfth centuries it is clear that the Irish writers imagine it to cover the inhabitants of Kintyre, Arran and Bute as well as some of the other islands and, by then, also Ayrshire. In fact this word is the Gaelic term that lies behind the modern English 'Galloway' although the modern usage of this name, confined to the Stewartry of Kirkcudbright and Wigtonshire, is misleading. It is quite likely that both these counties were late in coming under the control of the Gallgaedel and it is the use of the title 'Lord of Galloway' by the rulers of this rump territory that has led to the modern usage.

It seems most likely that the term Gallgaedel emerged as a way of designating 'Norse Dál Riata' and that even when this *regnum* was absorbed into the Uí Ímair *imperium* it maintained, and perhaps continued to develop, its own cultural identity in which language, and apparently religion, drew upon the Dál Riatan heritage while the male-oriented aristocratic culture had its roots in Viking-Age Scandinavia.

Dál Riata and the Kingdom of the Picts

What was happening on the mainland territories of Cowal and Lorne whilst the Gallgaedel were developing their distinct social and political identity in the later ninth and early tenth centuries? The truth is that we have little clear idea. Either gradually, or as the result of a specific political action, these territories seem to have become incorporated into the large kingdom to the east which in the ninth century was known as Pictavia but which had, by the early tenth, become known in Gaelic as *Alba* and in English as *Scottland*. The fate of Argyll is intimately bound up with the fate of the Picts in this period but that subject goes far beyond the scope of the present volume. While Cinaed mac Ailpín, who was king of the Picts from *c.* 843 to his death in 858, was almost certainly of Dál Riatan origin the popular idea that he conquered or destroyed the Picts is not easy to verify from the early sources. Contemporaries saw him as king of the Picts, not of Dál Riata, and the kingdom continued to be self-consciously Pictish until the time of Cinaed's grandson Causantín mac Aeda (*c.* 900–943), when the terms Alba and its Latin equivalent Albania (whence 'Albany') appear in the sources. At some point there was clearly a major influx of Gaelic speakers into Pictland and a conquest or something very like a conquest took place, but whether we should see this as happening in Cinaed's time or in that of his grandsons is unclear. The fate of Dál Riata in this period is very obscure, although it clearly makes a great difference to our reading of events to know whether the 'conquest of the Picts', if such it was, was a pre-Viking-settlement victory by a resurgent Dál Riata, or an act of desperation by fleeing refugees.

One event that may possibly be relevant here is noted in the text variously known as *The Chronicle of the Kings of Alba* or *The Older Scottish Chronicle*. This text is preserved only in the fourteenth-century 'Poppleton

Manuscript' but appears to be a genuine late ninth and early tenth-century chronicle from Scotland, modified somewhat in both the late tenth and the late twelfth centuries. It comprises one or two sentences on each king, noting how long he reigned, where and how he died and occasionally one or two other details. The account of the reign of Cinaed's brother Domnall (858–862) reads: 'In his time the laws and rights of the kingdom [of Aed mac Echdach] were made by the Gaels and their king at Forteviot.' Most recent historians have presumed that 'their king' refers to Domnall mac Ailpín but it seems an odd way to refer to him when the sentence starts by a direct reference to him: 'in his time'. A more likely explanation is that the king referred to as the 'king of the Gaels' is the ruler of a rump Dál Riata, presumably Cowal and Lorne, who is submitting to, or entering into a treaty with, the king of the Picts, Domnall, whose royal centre was at Forteviot. The Aed mac Echdach referred to may have been the king of that name who ruled Dál Riata before his death in 778, or another of the same name, otherwise unattested, who was in fact the king of the Gaels referred to in the passage. Unfortunately this kind of source material is extremely difficult to interpret.

One other set of evidence may hint at some aspect of the relationship between Dál Riata and Pictavia in this period. It was noted above that Kintyre and the islands do not preserve the names of the dominant *cenéla*, or kindreds, who ruled them, Cenél nGabráin and Cenél nOengusa. The names of these two kindreds may be preserved in the east of the country, however, in the provinces of Angus (Forfarshire) and Gowrie (north-east Perthshire). If this is more than simple coincidence, it probably relates to this period, but what might it tell us? At first sight it might reinforce the refugee hypothesis. The island *cenéla* had fled east whilst those on the mainland, Comgaill and Loairn, remained where they were. There is, however, some evidence to suggest that some sort of eastern movement was also made by some members of these mainland *cenéla*. Irish texts of the eleventh and twelfth century refer to the area around Culross and Strathearn as being in *Comgaillaib* and the rulers of Moray in the eleventh century claimed descent from the Cenél Loairn. Dunblane, the eventual seat of the bishops of Strathearn, appears to commemorate Blaan, whose original cult site was Kingarth on Bute, in Cenél Comgaill territory. Rosemarkie on the Moray Firth claimed in the later middle ages to have the body of Saint Moluag who died on the island of Lismore in the territory of the Cenél Loairn. This fragmentary evidence hints that much of Pictavia may have been divided up amongst the *cethri prímchenéla Dál Riatai*, the 'four chief-kindreds of Dál Riata'. The evidence of the transfer of saints' relics as part of this process inclines one to think that this links in again with the events of the 840s, when not only does Prudentius of Troyes tell us that the Vikings took control of the islands but the *Chronicle of the Kings of Alba* claims that Cinaed mac Ailpín moved the relics of Colum Cille to Dunkeld. The fact that the provincial names of only two of the *cenéla* were taken up in the east may simply reflect the fact that after Viking annexation of the islands these two names were redundant in the west and available for recycling.

The Gallgaedel in the Late Viking Age

It was noted in passing above that by the twelfth century the Gallgaedel also occupied Ayrshire. This was certainly the result of a conquest of that region from Argyll but at what point this took place is unclear. Indeed it is not even clear from whom they conquered this territory. At the beginning of the Viking Age most of Ayrshire may well have been part of the kingdom of Northumbria but it is possible that it formed one of the Northumbrian provinces taken into the lordship of the kings of Strathclyde in the late ninth or early tenth century when they spread out from their Clydesdale homeland and extended their rule as far south as the Carlisle and Penrith. Be that as it may, by the end of the eleventh century Gaelic language and saints' cults associated with Argyll had been introduced into the area.

From the late tenth century we can tentatively associate some 'Viking' rulers with this area. From the 970s two brothers, Maccus and Gofraid mac Arallt (possibly brothers of the Yric Haraldsson who had been expelled from York in 953 or '54), seem to have used the region as a base for attacks on the Irish Sea zone, rivalling the hegemony of Olaf Cuarán and later his sons. Olaf seems to have asserted himself in the region at the end of his reign, however, for in his last great battle at Tara, in 980, he was aided by Conmael mac Gilla Airi, 'tributary king of the Gall', whose name suggests that he was probably Gallgaedel. After his defeat at that battle, Olaf retired to Iona, which he may have refounded. Maccus seems to have been little more than an annoyance to Olaf and the neighbouring kingdoms but after Olaf's retirement, while his sons fought amongst each other for dominance, Gofraid asserted himself more forcefully. He was eventually killed 'in Dál Riata' (an extremely late use of this name, and usually taken to mean the Irish portion of the old kingdom) in 989, when the Irish obituaries give him the title *Rí Innsi Gall*, 'King of the Hebrides', probably the earliest surviving contemporary use of the term. His son Ragnall, of whom nothing else is known, was also accorded this title at his death in 1005.

The next king of whom we have any record who may ruled in these region is Echmarcach mac Ragnaill but his kinship and thus location is far from clear. He first appears sometime between 1027 and 1031 (probably in the latter year) when, along with Mael Coluim mac Cinaeda, king of Alba, and Macbethad, king of Moray, he met with Cnut the Great when this powerful king of Denmark and England took submission from the rulers of Scotland. His parentage is unclear. It is tempting to see him as a son of Ragnall mac Gofraid, and thus an Argyllsman, but there are reasons for doubting that parentage. Firstly Echmarcach appears as a king from at least 1031 until his death, on pilgrimage in Rome, in 1064, but 1034 sees the death of Suibne mac Cinaeda, king of the Gallgaedel. Secondly he appears to be far more successful than his putative Innse Gall kinsman, playing a dominant role in the Uí Ímair *imperium* for most of his reign, ruling Dublin and Man for significant periods. This makes it more likely that he is the son of Ragnall mac Ímair, a grandson of Olaf Cuarán. He certainly ruled 'the Rhinns' a territory roughly equivalent to Wigtonshire, but further north we cannot say.

Suibne mac Cinaeda (d. 1034) is the first person to be given the title *rí Gallgaedel*, 'king of the Gallgaedel', in our sources, and is the first person since the collapse of Dál Riata whom we can be fairly certain ruled in our area. It is an interesting coincidence that he bears the same patronymic as the King of Alba who died in the same year, Máel Coluim mac Cinaeda (1005–1034). This has led some to suppose that Mael Coluim conquered Argyll and put a brother on the throne. The rather odd and frustrating pseudo-prophetic poem about the kings of Ireland and Scotland known as the *Prophecy of Berchan* describes Mael Coluim, amongst other things, as 'Voyager of Islay', which might back up this hypothesis. Such a hypothesis might also restore Echmarcach's chances of being the son of Ragnall mac Gofraid, if we imagine that he was king of Innse Gall in 1031 and expelled from there by Mael Coluim between then and 1034. Against this argument is the name Suibne, which is otherwise unattested in the Scottish royal house, but this is not an insuperable obstacle to the identification. The truth is that we know so little about this region in this time period that any number of interpretations of our fragmentary evidence is possible.

What we can say, on the evidence of renewed ecclesiastical sculpture turning up across Argyll and Bute, is that by the mid-eleventh century organised Christianity has definitely been re-established in the region.

Gofraid Crobán and Magnus Barelegs

One of Echmarcach mac Ragnaill's rivals for the kingship of the Uí Ímair was a man named Ímar mac Arallt (Ivarr Haraldsson). Ímar ruled parts of the territory for brief periods in the mid-eleventh century before dying in 1054. His brother (or just possibly son) Gofraid, however, was to have a more interesting career. He first appears as one of the participants in the ill-fated attempt by the king of Norway, Harald Sigurðsson, to conquer England in 1066. Fleeing from the battlefield of Stamford Bridge he came to the Isle of Man and was given refuge by his cousin Gofraid mac Sitriuc. After King Gofraid's death in 1070 his son Fingal proved less popular. First he faced an invasion from Munster, in Ireland, in favour of his cousin Sitric mac Amlaíb and then in 1079 Gofraid mac Arallt led three attempts to conquer the Isle of Man and eventually succeeded. This Gofraid, known as Gofraid Crobán ('white-claw') or Gofraid Méránach ('of the finger'), succeeded in re-uniting the Uí Ímair *imperium*, even holding Dublin for a while. He died of the plague on Islay in 1095. On his death the kingdom was riven once more by internecine strife and his enduring legacy was not reunification but the elimination of rivals. From now on all serious contenders for the kingship of the Isles (as we can probably begin to call the kingdom now) would be his descendants.

A combination of Gofraid Crobán's reputation and the chaos which followed his death probably combined to encourage direct intervention in the region by the Norwegian king Magnus Barelegs. Popular history often presents the Norwegian claims to sovereignty over the Western Isles as a relic of the Viking Age but this expedition in 1098 probably marks the beginning of such a relationship. Norway itself had barely existed before Harald Sigurðarson's reign (1044–66) and although his son Magnus had appeared in the Irish Sea in 1058 this had been in connection with ambitions relating to England rather than through any hegemonic claims to the Western Isles. The younger Magnus' expedition of 1098 genuinely seems to have been aimed at asserting authority in the region. His activities included the expulsion of the Normans from Anglesey, where a uterine kinsman of the Uí Ímair, Gruffydd fab Kynan was struggling to maintain a toehold. On his way back north, the sagas tell us, Magnus met with the Scots king, somewhere between Man and Kintyre, and here, famously, they agreed to divide the west coast, the Scots getting the mainland and Magnus the islands and Kintyre. This account, though entrenched in the popular psyche, is deeply suspect. The kings' sagas were written at precisely the time in the early thirteenth century when Scoto-Norwegian tensions over the Hebrides were at their height. Suspiciously, the Scots king is named as Malcolm, when in fact Edgar ruled at this time (1098–1107); the southwest, where the meeting was said to have taken place, was not under his rule but was dominated, probably, by his brother Alexander. If any meeting of this sort took place it may perhaps have concerned a division of over-lordship of the Gallgaedel territory, the 'Scots' (Edgar or Alexander?) being recognised as overlords of the lands on the eastern shore of the outer Clyde, and Magnus as 'King of the Isles' being recognised as ruler of the islands and the western shore of the firth.

Attempts by Muirchertach king of Munster to interfere in the kingdom of the Isles led to Magnus' return in 1102. The two sides reached an agreement and Magnus set off back north the following summer but was killed in a skirmish whilst raiding Ulster for provisions. No Norwegian king was to return to the west for a century and a half. Once more the kingdom of the Isles collapsed into chaos for a decade.

Somerled

In the course of the twelfth century the darkness that envelops Argyll gradually recedes. The earliest reference to Argyll in Scottish administrative documents comes from a charter recording grants by David I (1124–53) to Holyrood Abbey issued at some point between 1141 and 1147. Amongst other grants, mostly in Lothian, David gave the canons of Holyrood the right to half the *teind* (tithe) of his *cáin* (tribute) from Kintyre and Argyll. The distinction between the two districts probably indicates that the term Argyll was confined to Cowal, Lorne and 'mid-Argyll' and that Kintyre was still thought of as some kind of island. This charter is the earliest allusion to royal control of this area. Interestingly a slightly later charter in favour of Dunfermline Abbey, dating from between 1150 and 1152, grants away the other half of the *teind* of the king's *cáin* from Kintyre and Argyll, 'in whatever year I should receive it'. This *caveat* would seem to suggest that at the time of issue these territories had slipped from effective royal control. Exploring what may have happened brings us to the most famous Argyllsman of all: Somhairle mac Gillebrigte.

Somerled's origins and early career are now obscure but it is unlikely that he came from lowly stock. At the beginning of his reign David I was challenged for the succession by one Mael Coluim, the illegitimate son of his brother and predecessor Alexander I. After considerable military action, which included bringing in help from England, Mael Coluim was eventually captured in 1134 and imprisoned in Roxburgh Castle for the rest of his days. The sequel to these events occurred on David's death, in 1153, when Mael Coluim's sons led an invasion of the kingdom aided by their uncle, Somerled. The most likely explanation of the relationship between Somerled and the sons of Mael Coluim is that they were his sister's sons, although one cannot exclude the outside possibility that Somerled and Mael Coluim were uterine brothers. Assuming, as most scholars have done, that Mael Coluim married Somerled's sister this must have taken place before his incarceration in 1134. This does not mean, of course, that Somerled himself was already a ruler of distinction by this date but it does suggest that his family was of considerable standing if a potential king of Scots was to marry into it. Unfortunately, although we know that Somerled's father was called Gillebrigte we know little else about him. The stories told in the seventeenth century linking him to Morvern are almost certainly late fabrications and Somerled's own base and that of his son Ragnall seems to have been Kintyre. Almost certainly he sprang from amongst the leading families of the Gallgaedel and it was in this general region that Mael Coluim and his sons seem to have gained their support. The English forces which came to David's aid in the war against Mael Coluim gathered a fleet at Carlisle; Mael Coluim's son Domnall was captured at Whithorn in 1156 and Somerled himself was killed at Inchinnan near Renfrew in 1164. In 1160 David's grandson Mael Coluim IV led an invasion of

Galloway that unseated Fergus, self-styled 'king of Galloway', and this may have been linked to these troubles.

It is extremely tempting to link Somerled in some way to Fergus, who first appears witnessing royal charters issued in favour of Glasgow at Glasgow and Cadzow in or around 1136. It is possible that these grants, which include rights to the kings *cáin* in Carrick, Kyle, Cunningham (all in Ayrshire) and Strathgryfe (the bulk of Renfrewshire), represent a part of the division of the spoils of the war which resulted in the capture of Mael Coluim. As well as heralding the appearance of Fergus, who seems to have held Carrick, these charters also mark the first appearance of Walter fitzAlan, who was to hold Strathgryfe as part of his honour of Renfrew. It may well be that before this time these lands had been part of a unified kingdom of Gallgaedel, albeit one tributary to the king of Alba.

Fergus of Galloway's parentage is unrecorded but his oldest son was called Gilbert, almost certainly representing Gaelic Gillebrigte, the same name as that borne by Somerled's father and oldest son. It is extremely tempting to see Fergus and Somerled as brothers or cousins, the former profiting from David's vengeance on the supporters of his nephew Mael Coluim. It seems unlikely that Somerled himself was the leader of the opposing faction but he may well have been marginalized if his father, perhaps, was ousted from the rulership of the Gallgaedel by David and his Anglo-Norman friends, and indeed if Ayrshire and Kintyre, and presumably the islands of the Clyde, came into direct Scottish lordship at this time.

Somerled's marriage connections were not restricted to the Scottish royal house. At some point prior to 1153 he had married the daughter of Olaf king of the Isles. The youngest son of Gofraid Crobán, Olaf had restored order to the kingdom of the Isles after his succession in 1113/14. Like David of Scotland he seems to have been a protégé of Henry I of England and began to introduce reformed monasticism and other Anglo-Norman innovations into his kingdom. According to later clan histories Somerled was rewarded with the king's daughters for the military assistance he gave Olaf in his campaign to conquer the northern Hebrides. While there is no contemporary account of these campaigns circumstantial evidence does suggest that the outer Isles at least may have come under the control of the kings of the Isles in this period, having previously fallen within the orbit of the earls of Orkney. It is possible that Somerled was an exile from the Gallgaedel territories living at Olaf's court in the early part of his career.

The evidence of David's charters suggests that he had lost control of mainland Argyll at some point in the period between 1141 and 1152. It is quite likely that this loss of territory marks the beginning of Somerled's rise to power, and that it was one of the results of the strange rebellion of Wimund bishop of the Isles. Wimund was a Sauvignac monk from Furness abbey who had been appointed bishop of the Isles by King Olaf at some point in or just after 1134. In about 1148 he seems to have led an armed invasion of Scotland, claiming that he was being deprived of his inheritance as the son of the earl of Moray, presumably King David's nephew William fitzDuncan, who seems to have died about this time. The war is said to have cost David heavily and he eventually granted Wimund the lands in Furness and Lancaster that he had taken from King Stephen in the English civil war (Wimund may perhaps have also gained William fitzDuncan's estates in west Cumberland). Although Wimund's triumph was short-lived, and the men of Furness captured and mutilated him, it may well be that Somerled had taken advantage of the situation to begin the restoration of his own family's fortunes.

On David's death, in 1153, Somerled led an invasion of Scotland in support of Malcolm, the Prisoner of Roxburgh. Despite the capture of Malcom's son Domnall in 1156 the war seems to have continued until 1159, when it appears Somerled made peace with King Mael Coluim. Mael Coluim, who had ceded his sovereignty in Cumberland to Henry II, possibly because this area was extremely exposed to Somerled's aggression, may have been eager to make peace with Somerled and to recognise his holdings in Argyll in return for a promise to drop support for the Prisoner of Roxburgh. In the event Mael Coluim's expedition to Toulouse in support of Henry in 1160 encouraged the rebels to re-open hostilities and on his return from France Mael Coluim was forced by his earls to subdue Galloway and force Fergus into retirement at Holyrood. The pacification of Argyll seems to have been beyond the reach of the Scottish crown at this stage.

Meanwhile Somerled was fighting a war on a second front. King Olaf had been assassinated in the same year as David had died and had, after the usual succession crisis, been succeeded by his son Gofraid. This new king, however, proved unpopular. Towards the end of 1155 a nobleman of the Isles, Thorfinn mac Ottir, came to Somerled and asked if one of Olaf's grandsons could be presented as a rival king to Gofraid. Somerled agreed and gave over one of his sons – Dubgall according to the *Manx Chronicle*, but perhaps actually Ragnall. Thorfinn took the boy around the different islands and had him acclaimed king by each local assembly in turn. Gofraid got wind of this and began to raise a fleet. Somerled brought his own fleet to meet Gofraid's and an inconclusive naval battle occurred on Twelfth Night 1156. Following the battle the two rulers seem to have called a truce but, two years later, in 1158, Somerled brought a fleet to Man and drove Gofraid out of the kingdom altogether, sending him into exile in Norway. From now until his death in 1164 Somerled ruled the whole of the kingdom of the Isles together with the lordship he had created on mainland Argyll and he may have exerted considerable influence in Galloway, theoretically divided between Fergus' sons at this point.

In 1164 Somerled raised a fleet from across his kingdom and from Dublin and invaded the kingdom of the Scots, landing near Inchinnan on the Clyde. Despite the great size of his force he was slain in the first encounter by a lucky spear, cast by one of a small defending force made up of the bishop of Glasgow's followers and perhaps the forces of Walter fitzAlan, the Stewart. Somerled's now leaderless fleet seems to have given up the fight and fled. What the motives of the 1164 invasion were is unclear. It may have been yet another attempt to promote the claims of the Prisoner of Roxburgh, or to 'liberate' greater Galloway, but it has also been suggested that the Stewarts had already begun to threaten Somerled's interests in Argyll.

The Sons of Somerled

Although the *Manx Chronicle* claims that it was Somerled's son Dubgall who was chosen by the Islesmen for their king there is no evidence that he ever acted in this role. He appears once, together with his own sons, in the company of Scottish nobles who had accompanied William the Lion to York in 1175 but that record does not accord him any title. Instead all the evidence suggests that after Somerled's death Dubgall's brother Ragnall took over the headship of the kindred. Perhaps some palace revolution had occurred, but it is just as likely that Dubgall's claim was being made retrospectively at the time the chronicle was composed in the late thirteenth century when his descendants, the MacDougalls, were definitely in the ascendant.

Ragnall faced renewed conflict with Gofraid son of Olaf, who had returned from exile in Norway on Somerled's death. Gofraid got control of Man and some of the other islands, probably the outer Isles and Skye, but the two continued to struggle until Gofraid's death in 1187. Both men used the style *Rex Insularum* but Ragnall seems to have been based in Kintyre. He was a great patron of the Church. Charters recording his donations were preserved at Paisley Abbey and at some point he founded the Cistercian house of Saddel on the east side of Kintyre. Saddel's mother house was not one of the other Scottish Cistercian houses, or even Rushen or Furness, two houses closely linked to the kingdom of the Isles, but Mellifont in Co. Louth in Ireland. This house had been founded by Donnchad Ua Cerbaill, King of Airgialla, in 1142, and the monastic connection may reflect some tie between these two men. By the end of the middle ages the descendants of Somerled were claiming that Somerled's father had spent years of exile amongst the Airgialla and, since Donnchad (d. 1168) and his son Murchad (d. 1189) were the only rulers of this land-locked kingdom whose territories ever stretched as far as the sea, they were most likely his hosts. Later traditions suggest that Ragnall eventually went on crusade but there is no evidence for this. It seems likely that he fell from power following his defeat in battle by his brother Aongus in 1192. Aongus himself was killed by Ragnall's sons in 1210 and little is known of his period as leader of his kindred.

Ecclesiastical Changes

Somerled seems to have conceived of a plan to return the leadership of
the Columban familia to Iona. In Ireland the comarbship of Colum
Cille had, by the twelfth century, passed from the abbot of Kells in the
Midlands to that of Derry in the northwest. In 1164, the *Annals of Ulster*
tell us, Augustín the *sagart mór* ('arch-priest') of Iona together with Dub-
side the *fer leiginn* ('teacher of students'), the hermit Mac Gilladuib and
the head of the Céli Dé, Mac Forcellaig, on the advice of Somerled
went to Derry to offer the abbacy of Iona to Flaithbertach Ua Brolcain
bishop and abbot of Derry. The annals tell us that Flaithbertach was prevented from accepting the offer by the archbishop of Armagh and by
Muirchertach MacLochlainn, the most powerful king in the north of
Ireland. This episode, which might have met with more success had
Somerled not been slain in the same year, informs us that Iona was once
again (or still?) a significant church with pastoral responsibilities, a regular
monastic community and a school. A strange sequel to these events
occurred in 1204 when, the same chronicle tells us, Cellach, the abbot of
Iona, 'built a monastery, in the centre of the enclosure of Iona, without
any right, in dishonour of the Community of Iona, so that he wrecked the
place greatly.' One can only imagine that what is meant is that Cellach had
a modern cloister constructed for his monks to live in whereas the tradition may have been that only churches stood within the enclosure and
domestic buildings lay outwith the *vallum*. In any event Florentius bishop
of Tyrone and Mael Isu bishop of Tirconnaill, together with the abbots of
Armagh and Derry, led a great expedition of the clergy of the north of Ireland to Iona where they destroyed Cellach's monastery. Amalgaid abbot of
Derry then took the abbacy of Iona 'with the consent of the Gall and the
Gael'.

The other great ecclesiastical event of this era was the creation of the
see of Argyll. Following the death of Bishop Cristin of the Isles (who may
have been the same person as Bishop Christian of Galloway who died in
1186) both Ragnall son of Somerled and his Manx rival seem to have
attempted to appoint successors. Thus Harald became bishop in the lands
of the sons of Somerled and a Manxman, Michael, in the other parts of the
kingdom. Eventually the two dioceses regularised their boundaries and
seats, Argyll being confined mainly to the mainland of Scotland with its
cathedral on Lismore, and the Isles taking the islands with its seat on Peel
Island, Isle of Man. Some of Argyll's territory was made up of land taken
from the Scottish kingdom by Somerled and detached from the see of
Dunkeld, and, perhaps, Dunblane.

Ragnall Son of Ruaídrí and the Rise of the MacDougalls

From about 1210 until some point towards the middle of the thirteenth century the most significant figure in Argyll was Ragnall, son of Somerled's son Ruaídrí. Ruaídrí seems to have enjoyed good relations with Alan of Galloway, who held the office of Constable of Scotland, and at some point he appears to have patched up the feud with his Manx cousin Ragnall mac Gofraid, marrying his daughters to this king and to his brother Olaf the Black. The extended civil war in the kingdom of the Isles that had raged since the death of Somerled had been to the advantage of the king of Scots but this new rapprochement seems to have worried Alexander II. In 1221 and 1222 he led expeditions into Argyll which resulted in the creation of a lordship in Lorne for Donnchad (Duncan) son of Dubgall son of Somerled. Ruaídrí may also have been expelled from Kintyre at this time. Olaf repudiated Ruaídrí's daughter and, marrying instead Christina of Ross, threw his lot in with the King of Scots. Civil war returned to the kingdom of the Isles, this time with Olaf and Donnchad acting as agents of the Scottish interest and Ragnall and Ruaídrí for the independence party.

Following Ragnall's murder in 1229 those in the Isles who feared Scottish intervention took the dangerous step of appealing to King Hákon of Norway. Although it was over a century since a Norwegian king had shown any serious interest in the west of Scotland the long civil wars that had riven Norway were now over and the kingdom was experiencing expansion in various directions. In spring 1230 a small Norwegian fleet was sent west. After inconclusive fighting and negotiations with Donnchad mac Dubgaill off Islay the fleet rounded Kintyre and attacked Stewart-held Bute. Here the Norwegian commander Uspak was slain and the fleet took refuge on Man; the following spring it sailed home, ravaging Kintyre on the way. In many ways this Norwegian expedition was counter-productive. Intervention by a significant foreign power awakened in Alexander the realisation that instability on his western frontier was indeed a potential threat to the kingdom in a way that it had not been since the days of Somerled. It also demonstrated to Donnchad of Argyll that his interests lay in loyalty to the crown.

It is through Donnchad and his MacDougall descendants that Argyll began to become part of Scotland once again. The MacDougalls were consistently loyal to the crown and were only to fall from grace in the fourteenth century because they remained loyal in their allegiance to King John in the face of Robert Bruce's usurpation. Their principal castle was Dunstaffnage and they founded the Valliscaulian priory of Ardchattan close by. The proximity of both these sites to the episcopal centre on Lismore emphasises that this region was becoming regarded as the geographical core of the lordship of Argyll. Until this time 'Argyll' had been a loose term for the whole west coast from Dumbarton to Cape Wrath, but the use of the style *de Ergadia*, 'of Argyll', by the MacDougalls, presumably reflecting their ambitions, gradually led to the term being confined to Lorne and its environs. 'Northern Argyll' was, in any case, gradually falling into the hands of the earls of Ross at this period. In some sense it is in this era that the history of Argyll really begins. The distribution of power in the islands at this period is very unclear and it seems likely that local communities kowtowed to whichever claimant to overlordship turned up with a fleet, and at other times measured their loyalty according to the situational factors on any given day.

Norwegian Interventions

Donnchad mac Dubgaill lived into ripe old age, at least until 1244 when he last appears on record. In 1247 a descendant of Somerled, described as 'king of the Isles' by the Irish chronicles, was slain fighting against the English in Ireland. The identity of this man is uncertain but since Donnchad was too old to go on active service (we first hear of him as early as 1175!) it was probably Ruaídrí, whose recent activities had been obscure. The following year Donnchad's son Eogán (Ewen) sailed to Norway to state his claim to be the dead man's successor. His bid was successful and on his return to Scotland he controlled not only his inherited Scottish lordship of Lorne or 'Argyll' but also the southern Hebrides. Despite Eogán's protestations that holding the islands from Hákon and the mainland from the king of Scots did not create a conflict of interests, Alexander II saw things differently. In 1249 the king led his army to Oban and crossed to Kerrera in preparation for an expedition against Eogán. God, however, sided with Eogán and Alexander died suddenly and the army returned to the East. Eogán, however, remained in exile in the Isles and Norway until 1255 when he made peace with the new king Alexander III. In the following year we hear for the first time of his kinsman Aongus mac Domnaill, as lord of Islay.

The conflict with Norway came to a head in 1263. The previous year William Earl of Ross had invaded Skye, part of the northern Hebridean kingdom of Dubgall mac Ruaídrí. Hákon led his fleet into the Firth of Lorne and then to Gigha, off Kintyre. Eogán mac Dubgaill attempted to mediate but was arrested by the Norwegians and his kinsman Aongus of Islay was intimidated into joining them. The outcome of the expedition is well known. Bad weather beset the fleet when it entered the outer Clyde and the massacre by local levies of a small portion of the fleet who were driven ashore at Largs during the storm badly affected Norwegian morale. The king may already have fallen sick at this stage for the fleet turned back for Orkney, where he died. Norwegian lack of nerve and bad luck undoubtedly saved Scotland from an extremely serious threat. Three years later, however, the new Norwegian king, Magnus, surrendered all claims over the Isles to the Scots in return for a cash payment; this agreement is recorded in a document known as the Treaty of Perth.

Although the position of Dubgall MacRuaídrí (d. 1268) and his heirs, who ruled the Outer Isles and the mainland between Ardnamurchan and Skye, is unclear, and into the fourteenth century Scottish sources are very coy about giving the MacRuaídrí rulers titles, Eogán, Aongus and the other rulers of the Hebrides became Scottish lords and ceased to use royal titles. Man was annexed by a royal expedition led by Eogán, amongst others, in 1269.

Eogán had been succeeded by his son Alexander by 1275. Alexander was fully integrated into the Scottish nobility. In 1293 King John created two sheriffdoms in the modern area of Argyll: one, called Lorne, to be held by Alexander and extending from Ardnamurchan to Knapdale; the other, called Kintyre, including both Kintyre and Bute was held by the Steward, who also dominated Cowal. Thus the scene was set in Argyll, now fully part of the Scottish kingdom, for the wars of Bruce and Balliol.

CHAPTER NINE

Rural Settlement:
an Archaeological Viewpoint

A MAJOR ECONOMIC AND SOCIAL UNIT in the rural landscape of Scotland in the later- and post-medieval period was the joint-tenancy farm township also referred to as the town, 'fermtoun' or farm. It survived in the Highlands and Islands well into the nineteenth century and, in a few cases, into the twentieth. In the past few decades the application of archaeological techniques in the investigation of these sites has added a great deal to our knowledge of a level of rural society which was never prominent in the historical record (Fairhurst 1960, 1967). In particular, the Royal Commission on the Ancient and Historical Monuments of Scotland (RCAHMS) has now given us a corpus for future archaeological research with their inventories supplying plans and details of the better preserved townships and settlement clusters, starting with the Kintyre Inventory in 1971, and now completed for the whole of Argyllshire with the publication of the Mid Argyll & Cowal (Medieval and Later Monuments) Inventory in 1992.

The township consisted of the arable and grazing lands used by the tenants below or inside the head dyke. Within this area the settlement form was usually one or more clusters (sometimes referred to as 'clachans') of buildings and enclosures, whose main function was to shelter the tenants, subtenants, crofters or cotters with their animals and farming tools. In a study of settlement evolution in south-west Argyll between 1841 and 1961, Robertson (1967, 51) states:

> The most frequent settlement form in 1841 was the clachan, a group varying in size from 3 to 18 families. Almost 300 of these clusters, many of which were probably swollen group (multiple-tenancy) farms, can be distinguished. Some were purely agricultural in structure, housing tenants, cottars, farm servants and labourers, but many included craftsmen, in particular shoemakers, masons, weavers, tailors, joiners and carpenters.

A more remote or detached part of this set-up was the shieling or grazing-ground and the remains of the associated transitory shelters or bothies, which were usually located well above or outside the head dyke that separated the rough grazing from the better land within.

For the archaeologist, the best surviving elements of these units are the ruins of the buildings of the settlement clusters on the townships. As might be expected, the remains of these settlements in Argyll vary in form and state of preservation. The later sites might be roofless but with upstanding walls, whereas the older remains might consist of a couple of courses of dry-stone walling or turf- or peat-covered outlines only. Some will show an amorphous scatter of buildings, others will be more regular in layout. Without doubt many sites remain to be discovered and recorded.

The shape and architecture of the buildings on the farm townships of Argyll depended on a number of factors. Function was a major control in the appearance of these structures: dwellings, byres, barns, sheds for farming tools, corn-drying kilns or barns with a kiln built into one end, mill buildings. In some deserted and ruined townships it is still possible to deduce the functions of some of the individual remains from the surviving shapes.

Climate also had an effect on the construction and orientation of some buildings – the thick-walled, wind-resistant 'black house' of the Hebrides is a good example of adaptation to a difficult environment. Many buildings were positioned with the long side away from the prevailing winds, although barns were often placed side-on so that the wind would blow through opposing doorways to winnow the grain. The selection of a dry point in a wet or marshy area would also have been an important consideration; the remains of many settlements now appear to be located in wet areas, but this is probably due to deterioration of the natural drainage of the site since abandonment. The county of Argyll has a wide range of landscapes – mountain and coastal, peninsular and insular. It might be expected that settlement forms would be to some extent adapted to this variety of locations. An example of two different forms of township buildings on neighbouring islands can be seen in the remains on the islands of Coll and Tiree. On Tiree the main dwelling structure was the Hebridean black house, with its double walls and specialised 'streamlined' hipped roof, which did not overhang the wall head; on the neighbouring island of Coll the single-walled dwelling with overhanging roof is the norm. There is little doubt that environmental factors were important here – the flat, exposed landscape of Tiree as opposed to the hilly, more sheltered conditions on Coll. But we must always be careful with single causes and assumptions as to the control of physical geography over settlement forms or economy. Even in extreme circumstances, choice, tradition, economic and social controls, or the decisions of landowners can still be important, and it has been suggested that the differences between the two islands might have more to do with Tiree having had an absentee landlord from the seventeenth century onwards, while Coll was managed by resident lairds who were introducing changes in dwellings and field layout (Boyd 1978).

The availability and quality of building materials will also determine form and size. Timber was always a scarce commodity in the Highlands and we read in the post-medieval Baron Court books of quarrels in some regions between landlord and tenants over the 'taking away' of structural timbers and doors upon the removal of the tenant to a new location. In the dry-stone dwellings and outhouses of the tenant-farmers the important wooden elements were the cruck-couples rising from floor-level or higher to support roofs which could not rest directly on the unmortared walls. Turf was, as noted below, used extensively for roofing, but in some areas it was also used in the walls:

> Formerly sod huts were the common habitations of the tenantry of the Central Highlands, and they are still in use in the more northern districts. Those huts were built of sods or thick turf, taken from the pasture lands, and having remained a few years in the capacity of walls, were pulled down and spread over the arable field as manure; another square of rock being laid bare, and another set of sods piled up for the same purpose. (Marshall 1794)

There are also references to buildings with walls made of alternate layers of turf and dry stone (e.g. Fenton 1968), or with walls with two or three courses of dry-stone walling as a foundation with the upper part entirely of turf. An eighteenth-century writer, referring to houses in northern Argyllshire and southern Inverness-shire, stated:

> The houses in which they live they call basket-houses. The method of building them is this, they first make out both length and breadth of the house, then drive stakes of wood at nine inches or a foot distance from each other, leaving four or five feet of them above the ground, then wattle them up with heath and small branches of wood upon the outside of which they pin on very thin turf, much in the same manner that slates are laid. Alongst the top of these stakes runs a beam which supports the couples and what they call cabers (thin rafters or scantlings stretching from wall-head to ridge-pole), and this either covered with turf, heath or straw. (Robertson 1788)

The are other references to 'basket-walled' houses or to the use of what would appear to have been wattle and daub structures, but none of this survives on the ground and there are few traces even in the evidence from archaeological excavation, a rare example being the turf house excavated at McEwen's Castle, Kilfinnan in 1968 by Dorothy Marshall (Marshall 1983).

Attempts have been made to classify or regionalise types of house-form in the Highlands, most notably the study by Sinclair (1953) which listed three types: the 'Hebridean' type, the 'Skye' type and the 'Dalriadic' type. This classification now seems rather rigid and limited, as more fieldwork has shown that the geographical distribution of these types is not restricted to the areas stated and that the triple classification covers a much wider range of shapes and materials as well as building techniques (Walker 1989).

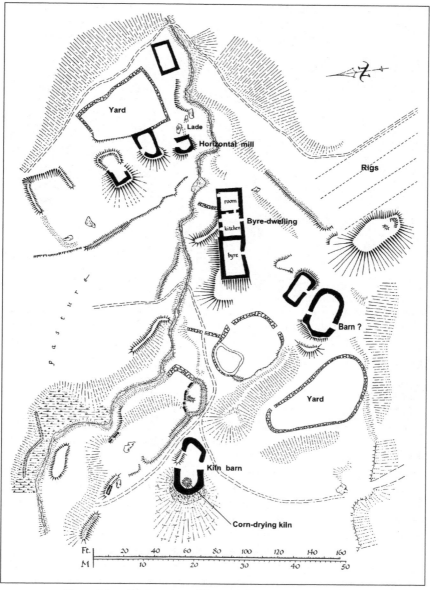

FIGURE 19 Township of Balmavicar, Kintyre. (Crown copyright: RCAHMS)

A good example of a deserted settlement group is the township of Balmavicar (Figure 19), just north of the Mull of Kintyre, the name recorded by Timothy Pont between 1583 and 1596 and shown in Blaeu's Atlas in 1654 as 'Balmackvicar'. It is not a large cluster, but it contains a

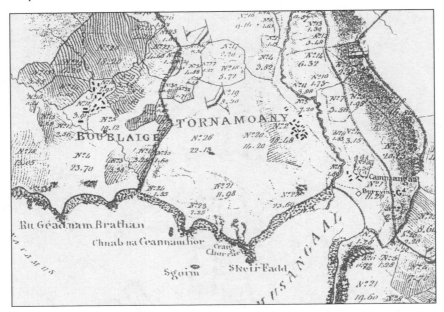

FIGURE 20 William Bald's plan of the townships of Bourblaige, Tornamoany and Camusangaal, in Ardnamurchan, 1806–07. (National Archives of Scotland, RHP 72)

variety of structures not always found on the same site. Traces of the lade bringing water from the nearby burn to power the small horizontal mill (RCAHMS 1971, fig. 183) have survived, as have remains of a kiln barn with its interior corn-drying kiln. This structure has opposed openings in the side walls, between which the grain would have been winnowed in the through-draught. Another building appears also to have opposing door-ways, and this too may have been a barn.

Early estate plans are of great assistance in the field identification of set-tlement clusters. Bourblaige on the south coast of Ardnamurchan, was surveyed by William Bald in 1806–07 and his plan (Figure 20) shows dif-ferent areas of arable and grazing with their acreages (Storrie 1961). The buildings are represented by seventeen black rectangles. The latest surviv-ing remains of the buildings on the farm (Figure 21) belong to the period between 1806 and about 1829, after which Bourblaige was joined with the neighbouring townships of Tornamoany (Ordnance Survey: *Torr na Mòine*) and Mingary to form one large grazing farm held by a single tenant (Scot-tish Record Office AF 49/3). There may be more than one explanation for the fact that there are only seventeen buildings shown on Bald's plan but over thirty on the modern plan. The scatter of rectangles may simply have been a way of indicating where the settlement was located, without giving accurate numbers; the surveyor may have ignored the various outbuildings

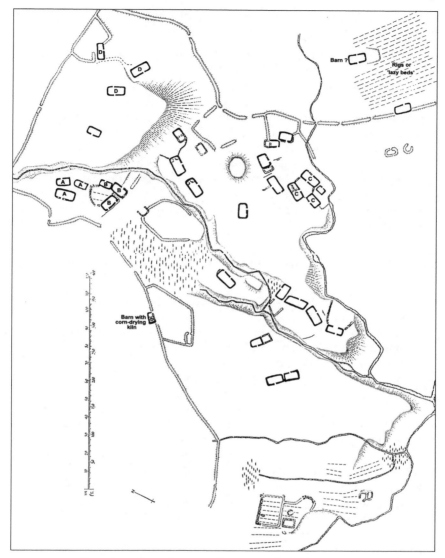

FIGURE 21 Remains of settlement cluster on Bourblaige township. (Crown copyright: RCAHMS)

and shown only dwellings; some of the structures on the modern plan may have been already ruined or abandoned in 1806 and therefore not recorded by the surveyor. Buildings appear to have been grouped into threes (perhaps dwelling + barn + byre or shed), shown by AAA, BBB, CCC, DDD in Figure 21, but this pattern is not continuous over the whole settlement and may have been altered by later 'infilling' of individual structures such as crofters' or cotters' dwellings, before the site was abandoned. The houses on the estate were described in the 1807 valuation:

> Many of the Farm Houses on the Estate are very poor and mean, and almost the whole of those occupied by the small Tenants and Crofters are miserable Huts ... it would certainly be pleasant to the Proprietor and to Travellers to see the people better lodged, especially at a place where there is a Prospect of People being wanted for many Ages on account of the Mines and Fisheries ... It would be worth while to take the Crofters ground as their present Houses fall down (which will be the case at no very distant period with many of them) to remove to the Road-side and build them with stone and lime. The Landlord, in this case, should find the lime at his own expense, and if, by any compromise betwixt him and the Tenant the Houses could be slated, so much the better.

That conditions were still unchanged well into the nineteenth century in some areas of Argyll can be seen in the comment of another observer in 1813:

> ... the lower, which are the more numerous class of tenants, are still very poorly lodged. Their houses are generally low, narrow, dark, damp and cold. The walls are built sometimes with dry stones, and sometimes with clay or mud for mortar; couples are set about six feet asunder; ribs are laid on these couples (The couples consist sometimes of one piece, with a natural bend, sometimes of two pieces fixed together at the eaves. The feet are built up in walls, which is apt to shake them. If the walls were of stone and lime, the couple soles might as well rest on the top of them, over a flag, like those of slate and tile roofs. This mode, which is less troublesome and expensive, has been lately followed in several instances in Kintyre); poles or brushwood across these ribs; divot, or thin turf, covers these poles; and then the whole is covered with a coat of thatch. The thatch, which commonly consists of straw, sprots, or rushes, is laid on loosely, and fastened by ropes of the same materials, or of heath; except in Kintyre, where the straw is fastened by driving the one end into the roof with a thatcher's tool, as in the low country. A few roofs are covered with ferns, and fewer still with heather. (Smith 1813)

Occasionally the sites of the settlement clusters seem to be badly chosen – in damp surroundings, exposed to the elements or in cramped circumstances. But this may not have been due to bad choice on the part of the tenants; there were often constraints on where the settlement could be located, avoiding the better land required for arable or dictated by the instructions of the landowner. The inhabitants would perhaps have chosen better sites if that had been possible; many are located in what we still regard as sheltered or picturesque landscapes.

Traces of the old fields and their plough rigs are still visible in some areas, but they are a more fragile element of the former cultural landscape, best observed in aerial photographs or when the sun is low. A good example of this can be seen on the Bourblaige site (Figure 21). In the 1807 valuation of the estate, under 'land classification' are listed 'arable' and 'spade arable'. The remains of this 'spade arable' can still be traced on the ground as a series of ridges much narrower than would be produced by ploughing and these spade-dug 'lazy beds', to use an overworked misnomer, still show more prominent edges than the nearby eroded plough rigs. That this method of working the land was regarded as unsuitable, because of the associated removal of turf, can be seen from this comment in the Riddell estate valuation in the 'Articles of Lease as to the Management of Arable Land': 'No land on the Stock Farms ought to be allowed to be cultivated by the Spade, except where it joins closely that which may be cultivated by the Plough ...' The drastic effect on the land of removing turf in large quantities, spoiling the surface and losing much of the soil through erosion, is also reflected in the further comment: 'Casting muck Fail [i.e. turf] ought to be forbid, and it would be of consequence to the Estate to encourage the Tenants and Crofters to cover or thatch their Houses with Braichens or Ferns, Slates or Tiles in place of doing it with Straw, thatch and Divots.'

A township neighbouring Bourblaige in Ardnamurchan is Camusingall or Camusangaal (Ordnance Survey: *Camas nan Geall*) (Figure 20). The buildings were situated not far from the shore of the bay. The remains of a Neolithic chambered cairn lie beside the traces of the settlement cluster. The surviving cairn structure is very shallow and limited in extent, and it was undoubtedly used over centuries as a quarry for stone for buildings and enclosure dykes. About 500 m along the coast from the settlement are the ruins of a fort or dun. Some settlement sites were obviously favourable enough to be valued as 'higher status' locations by some surveyors, and here at Camusangaal, in the 1806–07 survey of the Riddell estate, the assessor noted: 'The low Lands of Camusingal will make a beautiful Situation for a Villa and Hunting Seat, but too confined for a Place.' Some better house may have existed here, perhaps in the tree-lined enclosure adjoining the ruined buildings. Immediately to the south of the former settlement cluster is a graveyard, shown as a rectangle on Bald's plan. The words 'Burrying Gd.' are printed beside it, but it is unclear whether this refers to the Camusangaal graveyard or something on the neighbouring farm of Ardslignish. Within the graveyard are two headstones of the first half of the eighteenth century, but just outside is a standing stone, of possible prehistoric origin, with cross carvings on its western, seaward-facing side (Figure 22a). The archaeological and historical evidence thus shows that this particular location has been used at various times over the last five thousand years for burial and ritual, agriculture and settlement. It would be interesting indeed if we could discover what the last few generations of

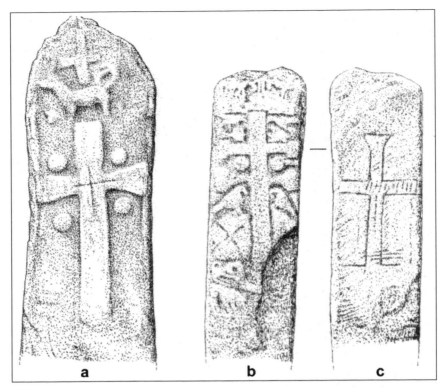

FIGURE 22 Standing stones with carvings from settlement sites: a. Camusangaal, Ardnamurchan; b. & c. the two sides of the stone from Kilmory Oib, Mid Argyll. (Crown copyright: RCAHMS)

inhabitants of the area thought of these traces of earlier activities so close to their dwellings!

One of the best preserved examples of the farm-township settlement is that at Auchindrain, about 8 km south of Inveraray; it is an interesting and useful source of information for the history of rural settlement in Argyll. The maximum population here was reached in the mid-nineteenth century, but the site continued to function well into the twentieth century, the last occupant leaving in 1963. The site is now preserved as the Museum of Farming Life (Figure 23). The buildings here follow the axis of the Eas a' Chorabha burn, mostly on its northern side, and there is a strong suggestion from the existing remains that, as at the Bourblaige site, the structures at one time may have been distributed in a dwelling + barn + enclosure or yard grouping. Having a long history of occupation, the settlement and its structures would have experienced many changes in shape and function. Some of the buildings still have, from a time when the walls would have been built of dry-stone, the lower members of cruck couples embedded in the former cruck-slots in the now-cemented walls, but sawn off at wall-head height. Another building has a surviving, cruck-supported, thatched roof covered by a more recent roof of corrugated iron. Photographs of Auchindrain from the late nineteenth century show some corrugated iron roofs, so this building technique is as much a part of the township's history and structural evolution as the earlier cruck couples.

Excavations in Auchindrain at the gable-end of a building that had latterly served as the township's 'bull's house' yielded evidence of a corn-drying kiln running under the existing building, suggesting that at some time in its history there may have been a kiln-barn on the site (Morrison 1984). A good example of a free-standing corn-drying kiln was excavated on the neighbouring township of Brenchoillie in 1981–82 (Grant et al. 1983). Another indication that these Auchindrain township buildings underwent various changes throughout the history of the settlement is that at least one structure (marked 'enclosure' on Figure 23) which had probably been a small dwelling was later used as an enclosure or yard. In his letters to London from the Highlands in the first half of the eighteenth century, Edward Burt noted:

> One thing I observed of almost all the Towns I saw at a Distance, which was, that they seemed to be very large, and made a handsome Appearance; but when I passed through them, there appeared a Meanness which discovered the Condition of the Inhabitants; and all the Out-Skirts, which served to increase the Extent of them at a Distance, were nothing but the Ruins of little Houses, and those in pretty great numbers. Of this I asked the Reason, and was told, That when one of those Houses was grown old and decayed, they often did not repair it, but, taking out the Timber, they let the Walls stand as a fit Enclosure for a Cale-Yard, i. e a little Garden for Coleworts, and they built anew on another spot. (Burt 1754, Letter II, 32–33)

The settlement cluster of Kilmory Oib is situated on the western shore of Loch Coill á Bharra in Mid-Argyll. It consists of the ruins of about eight dry-stone buildings, some still standing to wall-head height, some more ruinous, all completely unroofed. This settlement was occupied into the nineteenth century, but was shown as unroofed on the first OS 1:10,560 maps. The most interesting and important feature of the group, near its southern end, is a natural spring, which has been converted into a well with a stone-lined basin. Just behind this basin is a standing stone with incised designs on both faces. One side has a cross in false relief and the other an incised cross (Figure 22 a and b). The carvings have been tentatively dated to the eighth or ninth century but perhaps, as at Camusangaal, human use of the stone itself might be older, this area of Argyll having many examples of prehistoric standing stones. The Kilmory Oib cross stone may not be in its original position. Many carved stones in Mid-Argyll have

FIGURE 23 The northern area of Auchindrain farming township. (Crown copyright: RCAHMS)

undoubtedly been removed from their original locations, for example some of the Poltalloch collection of stones in Kilmartin Church and churchyard. In some regions the carved stones will have been removed from ruined sites, perhaps even burial grounds in the vicinity. Outside our region, on the island of Hirta, St Kilda, a cross-inscribed stone frames part of the window opening in the end house (No. 16) of The Street, built in 1860–61. The stone probably came from the old burying ground, just north of The Street. Another such stone on Hirta is in use as a roofing-slab in a cleit behind The Street, again in the vicinity of the island's main burying ground (Harman 1977).

Many of the ruins in the Argyll landscape represent the end product of the intermittent use of the same locations over a long period of time, through more than one style of building and using different materials.

There is no doubt that buildings of perishable materials and even early dry-stone structures must have frequently fallen into disrepair. In some areas the sites were abandoned and rebuilding took place at other locations with fresh materials; in others the very building stones may also have been removed to the new site, leaving nothing behind. Re-allocation of house stances could also mean re-shaping of settlement clusters.

Travellers' accounts, landscape drawings, estate papers and ministers writing in the Old Statistical Account about the earlier eighteenth century offer useful information about the nature of some structures. These descriptions of settlements may not be completely reliable, especially where the word 'primitive' is used to cover an ignorance of local environmental, economic and social conditions, but they do indicate a general recognition of the impermanent nature of many buildings. Outsiders might also have described structures that were necessarily temporary, such as the bothies used for summer transhumance on the shieling grounds, assuming them to be permanent houses.

An interesting example of such misinterpretation is Thomas Pennant's description of the 'Sheelins in Jura': '. . . a grotesque group; some were oblong, many conic, and so low that entrance is forbidden, without creeping through the little opening, which has no other door than a faggot of birch twigs, placed there occasionally: they are constructed of branches, covered with sods' (Pennant 1790). This is a reasonably accurate description of the types of bothy remains found on shieling grounds and recorded by field survey or archaeological excavation. But the illustration of the 'Sheelins' (Figure 24) shows large, very high wigwam-like or beehive structures out of all proportion to known sites and with no 'creeping' necessary to gain entrance. Pennant's tour of Scotland in 1772 was illustrated by Moses Griffiths, who drew some of the sites and landscapes visited. Although he may have recorded many sites accurately, it is also possible that he did not see all of the landscapes himself, and some might have been described to him. There is also a possibility that changes were made to the original drawings at the time of etching, in an attempt to make the scenes more 'realistic'.

Changes in the agricultural economy and abandonment in many areas meant that the township settlement form was disappearing rapidly in the later nineteenth century. In summing up her study of settlement change in south-west Argyll, Robertson (1967, 43) notes: 'By 1891 most clachans had been replaced by individual farms or had been abandoned. A few had become hamlets acquiring a church, school or hotel and enjoying a brief intermission until they also became out of phase with changing social and economic conditions.'

It is interesting to note how many of these deserted settlement sites have remains of much earlier human presence close by. The carved cross-stones at Kilmory Oib and Camusangaal have been mentioned. Camusangaal also has a Neolithic chambered cairn, and other sites have traces of hut circles,

FIGURE 24 Illustration of outsize shieling bothies on Jura, from Pennant's *A Tour in Scotland and Voyage to the Hebrides* (1772)

souterrains, duns, brochs and other prehistoric structures in the vicinity. There is also documentary evidence for the existence of some of the settlement place-names in medieval times, but there are few remains which can be ascribed with certainty to the period before the eighteenth century. The remains visible now are perhaps only a last instalment in stone of a much longer history of occupation and, while in some regions and at some periods the houses and other buildings may have been constructed of impermanent materials, there is good reason to believe that the existence of the settlements themselves was not temporary, although unbroken occupancy would be difficult to prove.

There are settlement sites whose names occurred in medieval documents, of which no material traces have yet been found. But more intensive archaeological field survey and excavation techniques, particularly in those areas that have traces of very early and much later periods of settlement in close proximity, may well in many instances lead to the unravelling of a much longer history of occupation of the surrounding landscape.

CHAPTER TEN

The Lordship of the Isles: 1336–1545

IN MOST WAYS, the year 1336 was unremarkable in the history of Argyll and the Isles. While much of Scotland was convulsed with civil war between supporters of David Bruce and Edward Balliol, and ravaged by the armies of Edward III of England, the Gaelic West escaped the worst of the conflict. The significant event of 1336 was not a battle or the death of a ruler, but the first recorded use of the title *dominus Insularum* – Lord of the Isles – by John of Islay, head of the MacDonald kin.[1] It was a bold claim, a statement more of ambition than of reality, adopted without reference to either of the individuals who claimed to be king of Scots and his overlord. But John turned ambition into reality and founded a line of lords who ruled the Isles and dominated the Highlands for over 150 years until their ruin at the hands of James IV. Even then, the *idea* of a Gaelic lordship in the West remained a potent symbol in the crown's struggle for authority in the Isles, feeding a conflict that festered into the seventeenth century.

Of the kindreds descended from Somhairle mac Gillebrigte (Somerled), the mid-twelfth-century ruler of Argyll and the southern Hebrides, the MacDonalds had been the least successful in comparison to their Mac-Dougall and MacRuaridh relatives. By the end of the thirteenth century, all three families had been absorbed into the Scottish polity and were active participants in the progressive hybridisation of Scottish culture and society that was the hallmark of that time. Integration into the Scottish political and social elite, however, did not promote stability within their territories, for the effective reach of royal government failed to break into the Isles, where the crown lacked any landed resource upon which to build a power base. Instead, the most powerful of the kindreds, the Mac-Dougalls, could capitalise on their links with the heads of Scotland's governing elite to entrench and extend their authority at the expense of their relatives. Conflict with the MacDougalls, therefore, ensured the Mac-Donalds' alignment with Robert Bruce after his coup in 1306, for their more powerful kinsmen were members of the Balliol-Comyn party. Under Angus Óg, the MacDonalds were key players in the campaigns that led to the destruction of the power of the MacDougalls of Lorne and, while Bruce was careful to keep strongholds such as Dunstaffnage in royal hands, his allies were established as the new power in the West. From Robert, Angus Óg received charters of the lands of Ardnamurchan, formerly Mac-Dougall property, and of Lochaber, Duror and Glencoe, the first a possession of the Comyns.[2] The Hebridean poor relations had become a major power on the mainland, but one whose status was founded on royal patronage.

John, 1st Lord of the Isles, 1336–86

Angus Óg's loyalty to Robert I did not bind his son to the Bruces. In the shifting politics of the 1330s, John displayed the mix of pragmatism and opportunism that became the hallmark of his career and the foundation upon which he built his lordship. Like many Scottish magnates, John hedged his bets by negotiating with both Bruce and Balliol parties in the civil conflict of the 1330s. In 1336, Edward Balliol appeared to win the contest for MacDonald support with the confirmation of John's original possessions, and the grant of Kintyre, Knapdale, Gigha, Colonsay, Mull, Skye, Lewis, Morvern, and the wardship of Lochaber, lands mostly held by David II's supporters.[3] In return, John promised Balliol aid against his ene-mies and acknowledged the overlordship of Edward III of England.[4] Despite this, John played no active part in the war.

The collapse of Balliol's position in Scotland and Edward III's diversion to war in France rendered the 1336 agreement redundant; by 1343, John had made his peace with David II and received confirmation of his posses-sions.[5] Greater things followed. In early October 1346, John's brother-in-law, Ranald MacRuaridh, was murdered.[6] John's wife, Amie MacRuaridh, was Ranald's sole heir, which brought the lordship of Gar-moran, a sprawling domain that stretched from Knoidart and Glenelg on the mainland to the Uists, into MacDonald hands. The Lordship of the Isles now extended on the mainland from Morvern to Loch Hourn and encompassed all of the Hebrides except Skye.

With David II a prisoner in England from 1346 to 1357, John was free to capitalise on the weakening of royal government in the Highlands. He aligned himself with David's nephew and heir, Robert the Steward, and the two men began to carve up the earldom of Moray, which stretched from the Moray Firth to Lochaber. To strengthen the bond between them, in 1350 John divorced Amie – although he retained control of her inheritance – and married the Steward's eldest daughter, Margaret.[7] It was a political union and one over which Robert called the shots: for, although John had children by Amie, their sons were passed over in the succession to the Lordship in favour of the children of this new marriage, who now carried royal blood in their veins. Although excluded from the main succession, Amie's sons were not slighted, eventually succeeding to their mother's lands to form a MacDonald cadet branch, the Clanranald MacDonalds.[8]

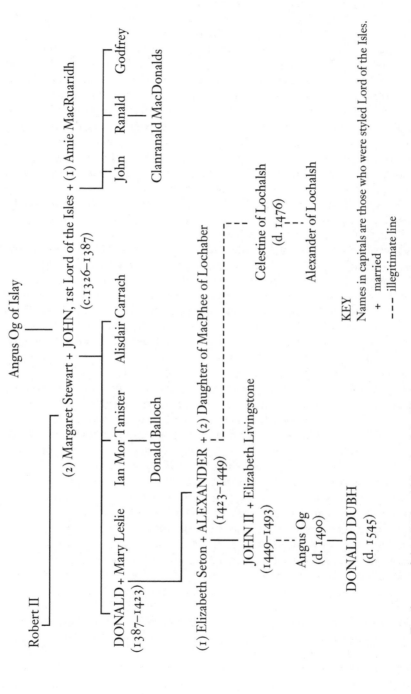

FIGURE 25 Family tree of the Macdonald Lords of the Isles.

With the Stewart marriage came Knapdale and Kintyre, which Robert perhaps gave as Margaret's dowry. John had now reassembled most of the
maritime empire once ruled by Somhairle.

For John, the Stewart connection meant greater influence. Robert had
been expanding his power in the Highlands since the 1330s, and his ties
with the MacDonalds and Rosses worried David II. The king's concerns
were sharpened by knowledge of John's dealings with Balliol and the English, and his refusal to attend parliament or implement royal plans for a valuation of his lands, from which his 'contributions' towards the king's
ransom could be calculated.[9] When David took personal control of the
earldom of Moray in 1367–8, he adopted a forceful policy towards this
intransigence:[10] in 1369, David brought an army to Inverness and secured
John's submission.[11] Just over a year later, however, David was dead and
John's father-in-law had succeeded to the throne as Robert II. Immediately,
the threat of an extension of royal administration into the Isles disappeared
and John looked forward to the benefits of his kinship with the new king.

Robert II, with his strong ties to the Gaelic West and his understanding
of and sympathy for Gaelic culture and society, faced a dilemma. While his
background and personal experience put him at ease with that culture and
society, he had succeeded to the throne of a kingdom whose centres of
political power and economic wealth were bedded firmly in regions where
a different tradition had become established. By the later fourteenth
century, the cleavage of the kingdom into two distinct cultural and linguistic zones was an evident reality, with the balance of influence tilted firmly
in favour of the anglicised and anglophone lowlands. Consequently, the
crown was increasingly dependent on the political support of the nobility
and burgesses of this dominant tradition – men who displayed a deepening
distrust and contempt for what they regarded as an alien and inferior culture. While maintaining and, wherever possible, strengthening his bonds
with the Gaelic north and west, Robert was obliged to recognise and
accommodate the views of his Lowland lords. As a consequence, Stewart
support added little to John's position in the Isles.

The growing chasm between Highland and Lowland cultures in the
later fourteenth and fifteenth centuries has tended to be presented as a
cause rather than a symptom of the development of the Lordship of the
Isles. To some historians, the Lordship became the political expression of
Gaelic culture, a response to the marginalising of the remaining regions of
the kingdom that were predominantly Gaelic. Certainly, it formed the
chief cultural focus of the Scottish Gàidhealtachd; the Lords of the Isles
were patrons of Gaelic musicians, poets and sculptors. Indeed, it is in that
role that the MacDonalds were cast by their McMhuirich *seannachies* in the
eulogies to them composed throughout the Lordship era, and beyond. Yet,
on a political level, what the careers of John and his descendants confirmed
was the greater integration of both their Lordship and the wider Gaelic
cultural zone into the kingdom of Scotland. Although operating within a

Gaelic milieu, the MacDonalds, in their actions and social behaviour, were little different from the wider Scottish nobility within which they were operating. What set them apart was the extent of their territories and their seeming ability to keep royal authority at arm's length. Furthermore, their geographical location, and the blurring of political boundaries where the Irish and Scottish Gàidhealtachd merged, has enabled them to be portrayed as peripheral to the kingdom and operating outwith its political sphere. In many ways, however, their position was paralleled by that other great regional magnate family, the Black Douglases, whose authority developed in a zone from which royal power had likewise retreated during the Wars of Independence, and who had assumed many of the roles within that region formerly exercised by the crown. Like the MacDonalds, they occupied a frontier position where the spheres of Scottish and English authority blurred into each other. They too dominated the social and cultural life of their domain, as patrons of the Church, of the arts, and as the apex of a spreading social pyramid.

As with the Douglases, MacDonald power within their vast domain rested on two pillars: lordship and patronage. Throughout most of his territories, John exercised superior lordship over vassal lords, clan chieftains in their own right. The emergent clans of this period were new phenomena, militarised kindreds whose reserves of professional mailed warriors gave their captains great power and influence. These were *ceatharn*, infamous in later tradition as 'Highland caterans', standing forces maintained by the imposition of heavy demands for quarter and maintenance on the tenants of their master's lordship. While utilising junior branches of his family to consolidate MacDonald influence throughout his domain, John drew many of these militarised kindreds into his service. Principal amongst them were the Macleans, who acquired former MacDougall lands in Mull, centred on Duart Castle, and the Mackintoshes, who received Glenloy and Locharkaig.[12] But John's patronage embraced more than secular lordship, and control over the Hebridean Church constituted a major prop to his power.

By 1350, John was patron of all the religious communities within the Lordship. This gave him great influence throughout the diocese of the Isles for, although the seat of the bishopric itself – based at Snizort in Skye since the loss of Man to the English in 1333 – lay outwith his power, his grip on Iona, the oldest, wealthiest and most influential of the monasteries, gave him a symbol of greater potency. Robert I had sought to use the bishop of the Isles as a royal agent and counterbalance to MacDonald influence, appointing his chancellor, Abbot Bernard of Arbroath, to the see in 1328, a policy continued on Bernard's death in 1331 with another Lowlander, Thomas, installed, and again in 1349 with William Russell.[13] But Iona provided the Isles with a spiritual focus that no 'foreign' bishop could challenge.

The MacDonalds' relationship with Iona was ancient, dating from

Somhairle's rise in the 1150s. Somhairle had aimed to use his control of Iona to underpin his authority in his Hebridean kingdom; his descendant John sought to do the same. Throughout the fourteenth century, the abbey was controlled, with MacDonald approval, by the MacKinnons, who ran it more as a secular lordship than a religious community. Ambition to expand this power perhaps prompted Abbot Finguine MacKinnon to conspire after John's death in 1386 to overthrow the new lord, Donald, and replace him with his younger brother, John Mór. Although the rebellion failed and Donald curbed Finguine's power, the abbey remained under MacKinnon domination to the end of the fifteenth century.[14]

John was no mere cynical manipulator of the Church. He was deeply pious, and conservative in the expression of his beliefs. At a time when monastic foundations had virtually ceased to be a feature of religious patronage, John established a community of Augustinian canons on Oronsay some time before 1358.[15] The priory buildings record the continued support of John's descendants for the canons and offer insight on the resources available to John to fund such a venture. The inroads made into the family's wealth, however, probably ensured that it was the last example of such patronage in the Isles.

The accession of Robert II in 1371 opened a new episode in the development of the Lordship. By that date, John was already elderly and preoccupied with the settlement of the succession and arrangements for the future of his brood of sons. First, he established the legality of his control of the MacRuaridh lands, which Robert now confirmed by charter.[16] His right to Garmoran secure, he granted it to Ranald, his eldest surviving son by Amie MacRuaridh, presumably as compensation for Ranald's exclusion from headship of the family.[17] This was followed in 1376 by a series of crown charters that settled Colonsay, lands in Kintyre and Knapdale, and Lochaber on John and Margaret Stewart jointly, and confirmed their future descent to their sons only.[18] By this date, it is clear that John had designated their eldest son, Donald, as heir to the lordship. Around this time, eastern Lochaber was settled on their youngest son, Alexander, whose descendants were the Keppoch MacDonalds.[19]

It is possible that by 1376 Donald was already *de facto* Lord during his father's lifetime. Certainly, no charters of John exist from after that date and there were no further royal acts in his favour. However, he lived for a further decade, dying *c.* 1386 at Ardtornish Castle in Morvern, and receiving burial at Iona.[20] John's death marked the closing of an era of unparalleled growth and is itself symbolic of both the continuity and change that characterised his career. Burial at Iona re-affirmed MacDonald ties with the spiritual focus of Gaeldom and his family's continuing role as protectors of the community there, while his death at Ardtornish underscored the dramatic expansion of MacDonald power out of their ancestral heartland in Islay.

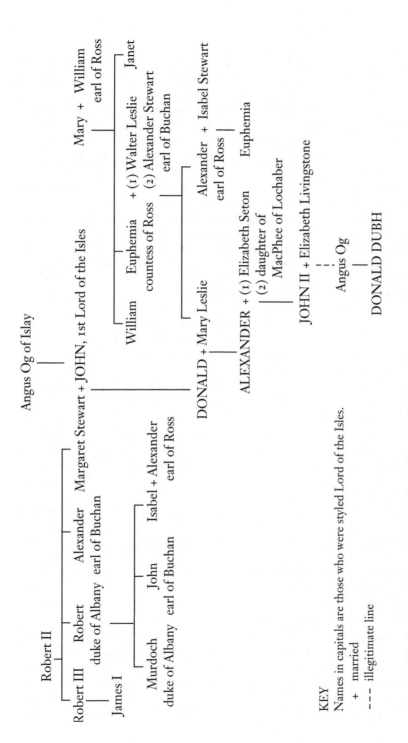

FIGURE 26 Family Connections of the Macdonald Lords of the Isles

Donald c. 1386 to c. 1423

It is easy to overstate the distinctiveness of the Lordship of the Isles as it emerged in the course of the fourteenth century within the wider Scottish polity and to misrepresent the significance or implications of its strongly Gaelic character. While John was actively 'state-building', the fact that he sought confirmation of his rights to his acquisitions from a superior authority – whether the Scottish or English crown is irrelevant – emphasises that he was content to operate within the established political hierarchy of northern Britain. Even during the episodes of English domination of Scotland that coincided with the collapse of the Bruce regime, while John attempted to capitalise on his position as a warlord of the first degree, he was also seeking to regulate his position within what he saw as the widening sphere of the English monarchy. He was not creating a 'state within a state', nor was he attempting to establish an independent domain: that is a fiction in the minds of modern historians. Indeed, throughout his career, John pursued a course that stressed his integration into Scottish political society rather than any diminution of that relationship. If anything, his links with the Stewarts accelerated that trend and set a pattern that was to be followed closely by his successor, Donald.

John's settlement of portions of his lordship on his sons produced tensions within the family that exploded into conflict on his death. While the lion's share and the title went to Donald, his eldest surviving half-brother, Ranald, had received Garmoran, from which the Uists were detached for Ranald's younger brother, Godfrey.[21] Donald's youngest brother, Alexander, had likewise been established in eastern Lochaber. John Mór, Donald's younger brother, however, although recognised as his *tanaiste*, or heir, received only a portion of the Kintyre estates and land centred on Dunyvaig in Islay.[22] Resentment at this unequal arrangement made John Mór a focus for malcontents within the Lordship and fuelled rebellion against Donald in 1387. This had repercussions beyond the Isles, for in 1389 their uncle, John, earl of Carrick, presented a complaint in parliament which spoke of the wrongs committed against his sister, Margaret, by her own sons and their adherents.[23] The rebellion dragged on into the early 1390s but collapsed when John Mór and his Maclean allies submitted to Donald. Expelled from the Lordship, by early 1395 the erstwhile rebel was in Ireland, where he entered the service of Richard II of England. He eventually found a bride there in the heiress to the Bisset lands and established a MacDonald lordship in Antrim.[24]

The end of John Mór's rebellion coincided with a revival of MacDonald expansion on the mainland. While Donald was clearly proud of his royal descent, and was permitted to incorporate the royal tressure into his coat of arms, there is little overt sign of co-operation between him and his Stewart uncles. Indeed, Donald's territorial ambitions clashed with those of his uncles, John, earl of Carrick, Robert, earl of Fife, but especially Alexander, earl of Buchan, whose control of Badenoch, Urquhart, Skye and Ross curbed further expansion. From 1389, however, Buchan was under sustained attack by Fife, and their MacDonald nephews capitalised on the decline in Buchan's power. There are indications that Fife drew his nephews into his designs, but it proved a dangerous liaison in the long run.[25]

The decline of Buchan's position was underscored in September 1394 when Donald's youngest brother, Alexander of Lochaber, entered a seven-year indenture with the earl of Moray for the protection of the earl's lands and those of the church of Moray, a service previously offered by Buchan. As part-payment for his protection, Alexander gained Bona at the northern end of Loch Ness, originally granted to Buchan in 1386.[26] MacDonald power stood on the threshold of the Moray lowlands. Soon after 1395, Urquhart, another of Buchan's former properties, fell into MacDonald hands and, to secure control over this strategic fortress, a cadet of the Macleans of Duart was established there. Further blows to Buchan's power fell in Skye and Wester Ross, but there the Macleods repulsed Godfrey MacDonald.[27]

Thus far the MacDonalds had been useful allies in Fife's schemes, but by 1398 their interests had diverged and collision was inevitable as complaints to the king about the depredations of their caterans mounted. In the summer of 1398, Fife, newly created duke of Albany, and his nephew, David, duke of Rothesay, campaigned in the Highlands and Islands to check expanding MacDonald power, but met with little success. Although Donald came to terms, his relationship with his Stewart kin never recovered and in the early 1400s he was again at loggerheads with Albany.

The cause of the conflict was the earldom of Ross and lordship of Skye. In 1402, Alexander Leslie, earl of Ross, Albany's son-in-law, had died, leaving as his only direct heir a young daughter, Euphemia. Albany took control of his granddaughter and her inheritance, and by 1405 had secured possession of Dingwall and the sub-Highland portions of the earldom. Donald, as husband of Euphemia's aunt, Mary Leslie, had his own interest in the Ross succession and feared that Robert would simply absorb it into the growing landed holding of the Albany Stewarts. Soon after 1402 he began to press his wife's claim to the earldom and before 1411 had seized the political centre of Ross, Dingwall Castle.[28] It was against this background that in August 1407 Donald sent emissaries to meet with the captive James I in London, this being followed in 1408 by a mission from Henry IV of England to negotiate an alliance with Donald and his kinsmen.[29] MacDonald was clearly looking for any allies he could in the growing crisis over Ross. The conflict reached a climax in 1411 when he marched east to challenge the power of the current royal strongman in the north, his cousin, Alexander Stewart, earl of Mar. At Harlaw, near Inverurie in Aberdeenshire, the armies fought to a stalemate, and, while the heavier casualties were inflicted on Mar's men, Donald fell back into Ross.[30]

Withdrawal was a fatal mistake, for Albany seized the initiative. By autumn 1411, Albany had driven Donald from Ross and retaken Dingwall, and in 1412 a series of campaigns in the West forced Donald to submit. In June 1415, Albany's victory seemed complete when Euphemia resigned her earldom and entered a nunnery for, while Donald was provoked into fresh warfare and proclaimed himself lord of the earldom of Ross, he could not prevent his uncle from granting Ross to his own son, John Stewart, earl of Buchan.

It is difficult to reconcile the efforts made by Donald to achieve recognition of his rights to a Scottish earldom with traditional depictions of the Lords of the Isles as Gaelic separatists. There can be no clearer demonstration of his personal perception of his place in the political geography of Scotland. To represent his ambitions with regard to Ross as being motivated by greed – Ross was the greatest territorial earldom in Scotland – is extremely simplistic and fails to recognise the powerful symbolism which still attached to the title of earl at this date. Earls still stood at the head of the social and political hierarchy of the kingdom and, as a consequence, exercised immense influence at both regional and national levels. Donald's pursuit of the title should be viewed in the context of the Stewart family's progressive accumulation of earldoms through the fourteenth and early fifteenth centuries, which provided the foundation upon which their domination of the kingdom was founded. For Donald, an earldom would not only have given him the status befitting a grandson of Robert II and provided a proper reflection of his power, it would have staked him a place at the top table of government.

Donald's aspirations in Ross were part of a general shift in the centre of gravity within the Lordship that had begun under his father. While Islay, or rather the MacDonald stronghold at Finlaggan, remained the chief place of the Lordship, where the lords were inaugurated through the fifteenth century and where their advisory council – the Council of the Isles – met in a purpose-built chamber on the Eilean na Comhairle, Donald and his descendents showed a marked preference for residences acquired during the lifetime of John. Aros and Ardtornish castles, which faced each other across the Sound of Mull, lay on the axis around which the Hebridean lordship pivoted, and also offered easy access via Loch Linnhe into Lochaber and the Great Glen. Here was the new political heart of the Lordship, a role reflected in the fact that of the eight charters of Donald that survive, four were issued at Ardtornish and one at Aros, while none were produced at Finlaggan.[31] Nevertheless, it appears to have been in the cradle of MacDonald power on Islay that Donald died in about 1423.

Alexander c. 1423–1449

The rivalry of the MacDonalds with the Albany Stewarts over Ross continued beyond the death of Duke Robert in 1420 and ensured that the new lord, Alexander, was a willing ally of James I in his destruction of the Albany kin. In May 1425, Alexander attended the Stirling parliament that sealed the fate of Robert's son, Duke Murdac – testimony to his closeness to the king. This, however, did not last and by 1426 there was a widening breach between them, fuelled by Alexander's involvement in various feuds and private wars in the north-west Highlands, and by his uncle John Mór's harbouring of Albany's rebellious son, James the Fat. Ross, again, proved the flash point. Alexander clearly controlled much of the earldom by this date. Skye, certainly, was within his orbit, for in 1426 MacDonald influence secured the election of Angus, Alexander's bastard half-brother, as bishop of the Isles by the chapter based at Snizort.[32] His election underscored how reduced royal power had become in the region, for his predecessors since the 1320s had generally been Lowlanders, installed as royal agents to counterbalance MacDonald power. By early 1428, Alexander had assumed the style 'lord of the earldom of Ross', a highly provocative move given that the king had held the earldom since the death of John Stewart in 1424. James arranged a meeting with Alexander and his mother at Inverness in August 1428 and, in a breath-taking breach of faith, arrested them and fifty leading men of the Highlands and Islands, including John Mór MacDonald. It was a stunning coup and James was convinced of victory, but it was soon clear that he had merely caught a tiger by the tail.[33]

James attempted to by-pass Alexander and subvert John Mór, who was again *tanaiste* to the Lordship, but John's death at the hands of the king's agent in the negotiations shattered the illusory peace.[34] Alexander, at liberty before the end of 1428, joined forces with John Mór's son, Donald Balloch, and with Alasdair Carrach of Lochaber, and in 1429 launched a series of attacks around the fringes of MacDonald power. In spring 1429, Alexander burned Inverness. In June, however, a royal army, aided by the defection of clans Cameron and Mackintosh, defeated Alexander's army in Lochaber and forced him into a humiliating submission.[35] Although the king held the MacDonald lord prisoner and was able to curb the power of Bishop Angus by removing Iona from his control, their kinsmen and most of their Hebridean vassals refused to come to terms. One striking success for the king was the separation of Lachlan Maclean of Duart from his family's long-standing loyalty to the MacDonalds. Sometime around 1430, Lachlan married Mar's daughter, and was associated closely with his new father-in-law in the campaigns in the west and north. Despite this body-blow so close to the heart of MacDonald power, for two years Donald Balloch and Alasdair Carrach harried the king's men and in summer 1431 inflicted a stinging defeat on Mar at Inverlochy in Lochaber.[36] The king faced a hard choice: raise funds to continue the war or come to terms with Alexander MacDonald. Although parliament grudgingly granted him a tax to finance a campaign, on 22 October 1431 James abandoned his aggressive stance towards the Lord of the Isles and staged a public reconciliation of king and subject.

Alexander returned to his Lordship a more cautious man. Although events showed that he harboured grudges against those of his vassals who had deserted him – the Macleans of Duart, Camerons and Mackintoshes – James obliged him to accept them back into his peace.[37] The door, too, had been closed on Ross, which James entrusted to the administration of Alexander's rival for power in the Highlands, Mar. Mar's death in 1435 transformed that situation, removing the pillar around which Stewart policy in the region had been built and forcing the king to turn to the MacDonalds. In 1436, James recognised Alexander's claims to Ross and by January 1437 Alexander was styling himself 'earl of Ross' in his charters.[38]

Alexander was now the greatest power in the northern and western Highlands as well as in the Isles. With Ross, moreover, came important properties in Buchan and the Mearns, which gave him a landed interest far beyond his Highland domain.[39] Having obtained this position of dominance, however, Alexander was content to work with the crown in the government of the Highlands. In the aftermath of the assassination of James I in February 1437, this policy of co-operation paid dividends. In a kingdom bereft of clear political leadership – there were only four adult earls including Alexander at liberty in Scotland at the time, reduced to three in October 1437 and two in 1439 – it was essential that he be accommodated into government. By February 1439, Alexander had been appointed justiciar north of Forth.[40]

After the drama of the early part of his career, the last decade of Alexander's life appears something of an anti-climax. He was, at first, much preoccupied in restoring order to and asserting his control of Ross. His surviving charters from the period show him to be based firmly within his new earldom, establishing bonds with the chief vassal families and religious institutions there and in the satellite territories east of Inverness.[41] Dingwall and the nearby royal castle at Inverness became his principal bases of operation, and there is little evidence for his presence elsewhere in his sprawling domain. This must have resulted in a shift in the balance of power in the Isles, with greater authority passing – intentionally or otherwise – to cadet branches of the MacDonald kin, notably to the Mac-Donalds of Dunyvaig and Antrim, led by Donald Balloch, who became dominant within Islay and Kintyre, to the Clanranalds, and to the MacIans of Ardnamurchan. It is possible that this trend had commenced in the late 1420s, when the Dunyvaig and Lochaber lines of the family had assumed the leadership in the struggle against the crown during Alexander's captivity. The establishment of lordships for Alexander's bastard sons, notably Lochalsh for Celestine and Sleat for Hugh, contributed to a further erosion of the landed base of the main line of the family.[42] Alongside this, domination of Skye and Lewis passed increasingly to the Macleods, while Maclean power in Mull and Mackintosh power in Lochaber became deeply entrenched.

Alexander's personal orientation had clearly moved beyond his ancestral domain. After 1437, Ross dominated his actions, the evidence of his charters showing a strong skewing towards the earldom. His position as justiciar reinforced this trend and probably accounts for the number of charters issued by him at Inverness, where he held his courts. While Islesmen remained prominent amongst his councillors, a new circle of men drawn from the principal vassal families of the earldom came inevitably to predominate. The extent to which he had become immersed in this new, mainland world was revealed tellingly at the time of his death. It was at Dingwall, the centre of his earldom, that he died in May 1449. Instead of being conveyed for burial to Iona, the spiritual heart of the Isles and burial place of his ancestors, he was laid to rest in the cathedral at Fortrose, the chief church of Ross and mausoleum of the earls. The MacDonald had cut himself off from his roots.

John II, 1449–93

The new lord, John, succeeded his father when not quite fifteen. Despite his youth, he immediately stepped into a central role in the government of his domain and, while certain of his lands in the south and east were placed in ward, there is no evidence that any of his kinsmen controlled the Lordship during his minority. In the complex Scottish political arena, where the young James II was beginning to flex his muscles, John's power – and his youth – made him the focus of attention for the rival factions in the kingdom. Surprisingly, it was the rapidly weakening Livingstone family, which had controlled government for much of the king's minority, that pulled off the coup of securing John's marriage to Elizabeth, daughter of James Livingstone. This success did not stave off the Livingstones' fall from power, Elizabeth only just escaping from Dumbarton to the security of MacDonald territory.[43] John stood by his wife, however, despite the collapse of her family's position. It was to prove just the first of the many political miscalculations that dogged his career.

John compounded his error by sheltering his father-in-law, who escaped from royal custody in 1450, and then by entering into a bond with the earls of Crawford and Douglas.[44] The purpose of the agreement may have been to provide for mutual defence against James II, as evidenced by John's rapid association in 1452 with James, 9th earl of Douglas, in his rebellion against the king following the murder at the king's hands of his brother, the 8th earl. For John, however, the rebellion offered the opportunity to pursue his own agenda in the central Highlands, where MacDonald power had declined significantly since the death of his father. Inverness Castle, which Alexander had held by virtue of his office as justiciar, and Urquhart, which had perhaps been promised to him as part of the marriage settlement with the Livingstones, were seized, as was Ruthven, the key to Badenoch, which James II had granted to the crown's new strongman in the north, Alexander, 1st earl of Huntly.[45] While Douglas looked for more effective action in the south of the kingdom, and succeeded in winning the support of that perennial trouble-maker, Donald Balloch, John was clearly more concerned with regaining the initiative in the north from the rising Gordon family, than with the political survival of the Douglases, who were in any case rivals for regional influence in Easter Ross and Moray.[46] This outlook was made manifest by his total inaction during the king's final destruction of Black Douglas power in 1455.

Reconciliation with James saw John retain control of Urquhart and resume an active role in royal government. The king's death in 1460, however, changed the political landscape and by 1461 the relationship had broken down. John defied edicts from Edinburgh, seized royal lands and revenues in the north and wasted properties around Inverness. He also responded positively to approaches from the English king, Edward IV, who saw him and his extensive kin in Scotland and Ireland as useful tools to be used to neutralise Scottish support for his Lancastrian enemies. Negotiations at Ardtornish led to a treaty concluded at London on 13 February 1462, by which John entered the service of the English crown.[47] Edward, however, was also negotiating with James III's government and this secret indenture was never put into operation. It was, though, a time-bomb ticking away beneath the MacDonald empire.

The bomb exploded in 1476 when Edward casually informed James of the fourteen-year-old treaty. The royal response was swift and devastating: after a show of defiance, which was met with a sentence of forfeiture, John submitted and attempted to salvage something from the wreckage. His survival was bought at heavy cost: Ross, Knapdale, Kintyre and the sheriffships of Inverness and Nairn were surrendered to the crown. The remainder of his domain was confirmed to him, with the formal grant of the title Lord of the Isles, and entailed on his legitimate sons and, if failing, on his bastard son, Angus Óg.[48] It was still a vast lordship, but it was one in which the nominal Lord of the Isles had to contend with the ambitions of the kinsmen and families who had been built up to compensate for the drift of MacDonald power into Ross. The signs for the future looked distinctly unfavourable.

The 1476 settlement blew the cap off long-simmering tensions within John's family. Elizabeth Livingstone distanced herself from her husband, claiming in 1478 that John had attempted to poison her. Their estrangement was clearly not recent, for in February 1476 she had been provided by the king with lands and income for her support from the forfeited portion of John's domain.[49] More serious was the response of Angus Óg, who, although confirmed as his father's heir, had seen the most valuable portions of his patrimony lost. He could count on the support of his kin, especially those such as Donald Balloch who had been excluded from the succession by the terms of the entail that lay at the heart of John's settlement with the king. The result was civil war in the Isles, with John supported by those families who had benefited from his patronage in the past – Macleans, Macleods and MacNeills – while Angus Óg had the backing of the Mac-Donald kin. In *c.* 1481, the conflict came to a head in a naval battle in Bloody Bay in the Sound of Mull, where Angus Óg's fleet routed that of his father. John's authority never recovered from this defeat and, while he remained the nominal head of the kin, his son ruled as *de facto* Lord in his stead.

Through the 1480s, Angus Óg continued his rebellion and set his mind to the recovery of Ross. By 1490, he had taken Inverness and stamped his authority on much of Ross, but this renaissance of MacDonald power was brought to a violent end with his assassination.[50] News of his murder stirred the crown into a more effective response and the king's uncle, John, earl of Atholl, with the connivance of Angus Óg's father-in-law, Colin Campbell, 1st earl of Argyll, launched a raid on Islay. His objective was the capture of Angus's son, Donald Dubh, now the MacDonald heir. The child was delivered into his grandfather's custody and shut up in the Campbell stronghold of Innischonnel on Loch Awe, where he remained until his escape in 1501.[51]

Donald Dubh's confinement did not end the crisis. Continuing to ignore John, Alexander of Lochalsh assumed the leadership of the kin and attempted to regain the initiative in Ross. He enjoyed some success, but defeat in 1491 at the hands of the MacKenzies of Kintail destroyed his credibility as a military leader in the eyes of the Ross kindreds.[52] This did not end the disturbances in the north and John now dithered between seeking an alliance with his still-powerful nephew and maintaining his loyalty to the king. Recognising that John's failure to provide strong leadership in the Isles was a significant contributory factor in this instability, James IV, under pressure from the few loyalists in the region, decided on a radical solution. Parliament at Edinburgh in May 1493 pronounced sentence of forfeiture against John, who quietly surrendered his lands and titles to the crown and sank into obscurity as a pensioner on the fringes of the court.[53] His death at Dundee in 1503 passed without comment by the *seannachies* who had once sung his praises, their silence a fitting epitaph for the man whose inadequacies as a leader had seen the vast power which he had inherited slip through his fingers.[54]

John's forfeiture in 1493 is often presented as the end of the story but, although the Lordship itself vanished, there remained men by whom the restoration of MacDonald supremacy was considered an attainable goal. James IV's failure to pursue a consistent policy in the West and his distraction to the grander stage of international diplomacy ensured that there was still a significant reservoir of support that would rally around Donald Dubh when he escaped from custody in 1501. Recaptured in 1506 and consigned to wardship in Edinburgh Castle, the middle-aged claimant to the MacDonald titles could still draw on the power of his ancestry when he regained his liberty in 1543. Once again the focus for rebellion against the crown, Donald Dubh, following in his grandfather's footsteps, allied with England. He stood poised to regain his heritage when, in 1545, he died at Drogheda in Ireland. His death finally closed one long chapter in the history of the Isles and, although his kinsmen continued to scheme and dream of a restoration of past glories into the 1640s, the MacDonalds' role as leader of the Gaedhil had passed firmly into the hands of the Campbells. Like the MacDonalds before them, the Campbells stood astride the cultural divide in late medieval Scotland, basing their might on the military reserves of their Gaelic lordship but building their power as active and responsive participants in royal government, fully at home within Lowland Scottish culture and society.

Notes

1   *Acts of the Lords of the Isles*, no. 3.
2   *Registrum Magni Sigilli Regum Scotorum i*, app. ii, nos 56–8.
3   *Acts of the Lords of the Isles*, no. 1.
4   *Ibid.*, no. 2.
5   *Regesta Regum Scotorum*, vi, no. 113.
6   Walter Bower, *Scotichronicon*, vol. 7, 253.
7   *Vetera Monumenta Hibernorum et Scotorum Historiam Illustrantia*, no. dlxxxviii.
8   *Acts of the Lords of the Isles*, no. 7.
9   R. Nicholson (1974), 178.
10 R. D. Oram (1999), 195–213 at 200–201.
11 R. Nicholson (1974), 178.
12 *Acts of the Lords of the Isles*, no. 4; S. Boardman (1996), 84.
13 *Chronica Regum Manniae et Insularum*, 42.
14 MacQuarrie (1984–6), 362–8.
15 R. Fawcett (1994), 75, 76, 137.
16 *RMS*, i, nos 412, 551.
17 *Acts of the Lords of the Isles*, no. 7; Boardman (1996), 90.
18 *Acts of the Lords of the Isles*, nos A8, A9, A10.
19 *Ibid.*, xxxi.
20 *Ibid.*, 287.
21 *Ibid.*, 291.
22 *Ibid.*, 293.
23 Nicholson (1974), 209.
24 *Acts of the Lords of the Isles*, no. 15, and discussion on p. 293.
25 Boardman (1996), 184.
26 S. Boardman (1992), 1–27 at 8.
27 *Ibid.*, 8–9.
28 Boardman (1996), 258–9.
29 *Acts of the Lords of the Isles*, lxxvi; Nicholson (1974), 234.
30 *Scotichronicon*, vol. 8, 75–7.
31 *Acts of the Lords of the Isles*, nos 11, 12, 13, 17, 18.
32 *Acts of the Lords of the Isles*, 300–301.

33 M. Brown (1994), 96–99.
34 *Ibid.*, 100.
35 *Ibid.*, 100–103; *Acts of the Lords of the Isles*, 302.
36 Brown (1994), 138–9.
37 *Ibid.*, 146.
38 *Acts of the Lords of the Isles*, nos 23, 25.
39 *Ibid.*, xxxi–xxxvii.
40 Nicholson (1974), 326.
41 See *Acts of the Lords of the Isles*, 37–76.
42 *Ibid.*, 303–5, 307–8.
43 C. A. McGladdery (1990), 53.
44 *Ibid.*, 63–4.
45 Ibid., 62.
46 Nicholson (1974), 362.
47 *Ibid.*, 401–2
48 *Ibid.*, 480–1.
49 *RMS*, ii, no. 1272.
50 *Acts of the Lords of the Isles*, 312–3; Nicholson (1974), 541.
51 Nicholson, 482, 545; N. Macdougall (1997), 179–90.
52 Nicholson, 542.
53 Macdougall, (1997), 100–101; Nicholson, 542.
54 *Acts of the Lords of the Isles*, 311.

CHAPTER ELEVEN

The House of Argyll:
the Rise of Clan Campbell

ANCESTOR HUNTING can be an uncertain art, particularly when there is an element of competition involved. The Campbells, never ones to be beaten, even produced a pedigree which traced their chiefs back to Adam himself – via Old King Cole, the Empress Helena and Joseph of Arimathea. More recently, a family of American Campbells found a copy of this family tree and were able to trace themselves back to the chiefly line and thence all the way back to the Garden of Eden. Few people can boast such a magnificent pedigree and they had it made into a splendid chart, illuminated with coats of arms and pictures of castles. Also attached was a notice, which ended with disarming frankness: 'not all historians are united on the accuracy of this document but we believe it to be true since the information it contains cost us $300 ...'

If only reliable ancestor identification was that easy! At times the Campbells have claimed a Dalriadic descent, a Norman origin, a mythical Celtic founder and an Ancient British source. Most if not all of these claims were tactical responses to political need, made when the Campbell chief needed extra authentication for the role he was then playing.

By the seventeenth century the official version of the pedigree had been constructed. Fragments of earlier versions exist, including that produced by the MacEwans, a family of Irish bardic origin, who held the lands of Kilchoan in Lorne for their services as sennachies and genealogists to the Campbell chiefs. All these early versions are notably short; later versions either managed to introduce new personalities into the list or padded the generations – usually by the repetition of names already used – in order to fill the necessary span of time.

Most obvious of these manipulations is the introduction of Diarmid O'Duine into the pedigree. He was a mythical Fingalian hero who, having had an affair with the king's wife, was ordered by his jealous rival to measure the length of a slain boar in his bare feet. As the king had foreseen, the boar's bristles pierced Diarmid's feet and he subsequently died of blood poisoning.

The fact is that the earlier versions of the pedigree do show a Duine. In a bid for increased status, this person was identified as the Duine who was the father of Diarmid, who is himself then introduced into the line. Indeed this opportunity was taken by the family – they did not use the name Campbell at this stage – to rename themselves as the 'Clan Diarmid', the sobriquet by which they are popularly known. In all the versions, however, one thing seems to be constant: the tradition of a descent from King Arthur via his son Smerievore, who can be identified as Merlin the sorcerer. Whether King Arthur or his son existed is a moot point; this would seem to be sennachies' shorthand for saying: 'we do not know for certain who these people are, but they are Britons from Strathclyde and of some standing.'

Tradition often claims, probably correctly, that the Campbells came to Argyll as part of a royal army bent on bringing this fringe area into the ambit of the Scottish Crown. In Argyll, their leader married an heiress, thereby becoming lord of, firstly, two thirds of the lordship of Loch Awe, with a subsequent marriage bringing all three parts into Campbell hands.

The first Campbell in written record is one Gillespie, who is possessor of the lands of Menstrie in far off Clackmannanshire. A later royal charter to his descendant grants the lands concerned to be held 'as freely as did his ancestor Duncan O'Duin'. We can surmise that Gillespie's father flourished around 1200. Gillespie was father of Sir Cailean Mor, who was killed in a skirmish with the neighbouring MacDougalls on the String of Lorne. He was shot in the back when an acrimonious meeting degenerated into bloodshed. His descendants as chiefs of the clan have all taken the Gaelic patronymic 'Mac Cailein Mor', meaning either 'Son of Colin the Great', 'Great Son of Colin' or possibly just 'Son of Big Col'.

Colin was succeeded by his son Sir Neil, boon companion and cousin of Robert the Bruce, whose vicissitudes of fortune he shared. He died the year after the victory of Bannockburn but his son Cailean Og – 'Young Colin' – was rewarded with a charter which granted him the lordships of all Loch Awe and of Ardscotnish, the area round Kilmartin and Duntroon. They had previously managed these lands for the Crown, as well as various other territory forfeited by the MacDougalls, who had backed Balliol and the English faction in the struggle for independence. If the account of the various marriages in the traditional pedigree were true this grant would have been superfluous. But Colin's father Neil is on record as being appointed thane of the king's lands of Lochawe, implying that the family were not the possessors of the territory before the grant of 1316.

The traditional pedigree was in trouble anyway. The old Gaelic practice of tanistry passed the chiefdom of a kindred to the person deemed most suitable within a defined degree of consanguinity, not necessarily to the eldest male heir (as was the rule with feudalism, which eventually supplanted tanistry). It was therefore important for the later official pedigree to show the chiefs descending from a long line of eldest sons, when in fact this was very far from being the case. In addition, the pedigree extended far back before the emergence of the clan proper and therefore needed further massaging.

In fact the present line of chiefs is not the senior one by primogeniture and in the early stages of the emergence of Clan Campbell there appears to have been considerable doubt over who should be the chief. One of the competitors to the Lochawe line, from whom the present chief descends, was the family of Strachur, descended from Duncan Dubh, who seems to have been the elder brother of Cailean Mor's father Gillespie. Duncan Dubh's son Sir Arthur Campbell, who gave his name to this family whose head enjoyed the Gaelic patronymic 'MacArtairr', was little (if any) less important than Cailein Mor or his son Sir Neil of Lochawe. He was granted a third of Lorne by Bruce and was made constable of the chief MacDougall stronghold in the region, Dunstaffnage Castle. One of his sons was another Arthur, engaged to marry the heiress of the MacRuari lands of Garmoran; a large territory was made over to him in a charter which still exists. But disputes over the grant persisted until 1427, when James I summoned the Highland and Island chiefs to meet him for what they fondly imagined was to be a party, but which turned out to be general imprisonment and the execution of several troublemakers. Among them was the then leader of the MacRuaris and one John 'MacArthur', who, it is thought, was still causing trouble over the charter granted to his ancestor.

It would appear that this rivalry between Strachur and Loch Awe persisted for some time. It was the latter who emerged as the chiefly line, though there seems to have been contention within that branch of the family for the leadership and the 'official' pedigree shows signs of early manipulation to support the ancestry of the eventual winner.

It was Sir Cailean Mor's son, Sir Neil, who shared most of Robert's adventures. Shortly after his death (around 1316) his son, Colin Og, was given the charter which established him beyond doubt as lord of Lochawe and Ardscotnish. Sir Neil and the king were related: they were second cousins, once removed, through Gillespie's wife Efferic of Carrick, first cousin of the king's mother. But if the association with King Robert can be said to have provided the platform from which the Campbells were elevated from a being small, local kindred, the ascent was by no means an uninterrupted one. It was almost immediately disturbed, following the death of King Robert, by an English invasion in support of the Balliol faction. The dissension which ensued led in due course to the forfeiture of land by several Campbells who had backed the wrong side.

But by now the power of Clan Donald, under the newly styled 'Lord of the Isles', was causing growing unease to the Crown. The Lordship of the Isles increasingly saw itself as a virtually independent kingdom and in the struggle for eventual control of the west Highland seaboard Clan Campbell increasingly became the counterweight to Clan Donald ambition. It has been said, 'if the Campbells had not existed we should have had to invent them'.

Power depended on manpower, and manpower depended on the lands to support it. It is not clear where the Campbells' original base in Argyll was. The mighty fortress of Innschonnel on Loch Awe was certainly their headquarters after Bruce's time but it seems unlikely that they built it; this would have been beyond their means at the time. The smaller Caisteal an Nighinn Ruaidhe on Loch Avich might seem a more likely contender, although the traditional accounts (which are somewhat confused) suggest that this was in Campbell of Craignish hands at an early stage. In due course, the chiefs moved from the inland waters of Loch Awe to saltwater on Loch Fyne. The need to have access to the ocean is given as the reason, but Inveraray is far up a long fiord and its selection was probably due more to its strategic location, commanding the routes from southern and mid Argyll and the Isles.

The move to Inveraray also brought the Campbell chiefs closer to the district of Cowal, where they were making steady property gains. This was largely due to connections with the Stewarts and their off-shoots, the Menteiths, who had earlier been used by the Crown to make inroads into Argyll from the direction of the Clyde in order to bring the area under control. Their interests were now increasingly directed elsewhere – the Menteiths to richer lands further east and the Stewarts to the Crown itself – and it was to the Campbells that these lands and the task that went with them were steadily transferred. Strangely enough, in view of the later popular view of the Campbells, there is little evidence of this increase in territory being achieved by any form of force. Marriage did play a considerable part, although two potentially major moves failed in their early stages.

The first, that of Arthur Campbell's betrothal to the MacRuari heiress, we have already encountered. The second was as a result of the marriage of Sir Neil to King Robert's sister, Mary. This produced a son, John, who was granted the earldom of Atholl, together with the many lands that went with it, by his cousin King David II. John, however, was among the slain at the battle of Halidon Hill in 1333. Had he survived and produced heirs, it would certainly have been his line and not that of his elder half-brother Colin that would have become the chiefs of Clan Campbell, whose centre of gravity would then have been well to the east of Argyll.

It must have been around the same time that the heiresses of the lands of Loudoun came into Campbell hands. While the Council prevaricated, Sir Neil and his cousin Sir Donald took matters into their own hands; by the time the royal edict ordering Sir Neil to relinquish the heiresses, the deed was done: Sir Neil had married one of the girls and the lands of Loudoun went with the other to Duncan, son of Sir Donald. From this union descended the powerful Campbells of Loudoun, who amassed much land, together with the hereditary sheriffdom of Ayr in that fertile county. Separated from their cousins in Argyll both geographically and by their lowland way of life, the Loudoun Campbells nevertheless retained a strong sense of their identity. Indeed it was George Campbell of Loudoun who in 1430 resigned to Duncan Campbell of Lochawe all the lands he held in the parish of Lochgoil 'for friendship and as chief of his kin'. When the old line ended in an heiress, the Campbells immediately put forward a candidate who became her husband, thus keeping the valuable lands of Loudoun in Campbell hands; the lucky man was Sir John Campbell of Lawers, who in 1633 was raised to the rank of earl of Loudoun.

Other marriages were also successful. In 1358, the lands of Glenorchy came into Campbell hands with the marriage of the heiress of Glenorchy to John, son of Sir Dougall Campbell and nephew of Sir Neil. Her male kin were the MacGregors, whose subsequent shortage of lands with which to reward their people was one of the major causes of MacGregor unrest. The lands of Glenorchy came to the chiefly main line with an internal Campbell marriage – one of major importance – when Colin Iongantach married his cousin Mariota Campbell, their marriage also bringing the lands of Menstrie (which had been in Sir Dougall Campbell's possesssion) back into the chiefly line.

The important branch of the Campbells of Cawdor was also based on marriage to an heiress – this time to Muriel, heiress to the substantial Calder or Cawdor family near Nairn. When her father died young without a male heir, it fell to the king to arrange her marriage and he eventually settled on the Earl of Argyll. Muriel was still a child and if she had died before reaching marriageable age the rich lands of Cawdor would have been restored to her male relatives. Muriel was a valuable prize and the Earl of Argyll sent Campbell of Inverliver with a posse to bring her to safety in Argyll.

What happened next is well known: when one of Muriel's relatives taunted Inverliver that the prize might yet elude them if Muriel did not come of age, he replied staunchly: 'Muriel can never die while there is a red-haired lassie on the shores of Loch Awe.' Whereupon Muriel's nurse, to prevent the substitution Inverliver was hinting at, bit off the child's little finger joint – a stratagem which would not, one suspects, have fazed the Campbells for long, had the need for a replacement become necessary. The Campbells set off for home with the child, followed by a gang of Cawdors, who caught up with them before they had gone far. Inverliver left his sons and their companions in a circle around an upturned basket while he put Muriel across his saddle and slipped away into the hills. He and his precious burden came safe home but his sons saw Argyll no more. From this eventful beginning sprang one of the major branches of the clan, who kept a strong presence in Argyll as well as enjoying their rich lands farther north.

Another marital initiative which bore at least some fruit was the marriage in 1567 of Mary MacLeod, the heiress of Dunvegan, to one of Campbell of Auchinbreck's sons. In return for a handsome dowry and the transfer of the rights to Trotternish in Skye and to North Uist, Mary's rights to the chiefship and the lands of Dunvegan were relinquished to her male cousin. The Campbells who had been sent to Skye to guard the child remained there as a reminder of the incident.

The Campbells were always very careful to ensure that other people did not take advantage of them through marriage, and when a situation like the Loudoun one arose it was made certain that a Campbell husband was found.

If the Lords of the Isles looked from outside in towards central Scotland and the Scottish Crown, the Campbell chiefs looked on Clan Donald from inside the kingdom. Perhaps the unique factor in the Campbell rise to dominance in the Western Highlands and Isles was this capacity to act as great chiefs in the 'Gaeltacht' in combination with partaking of the affairs of Scotland along with their lowland counterparts. It was a need to further their credentials with the latter which led to the introduction of a Norman strand into the traditional pedigree – an unlikely tale of a marriage to William the Conqueror's niece following a sojourn in France by an earlier O'Duin.

From modest beginnings the advancement of the Campbell chiefs was steady and relentless. In 1334, Sir Colin Campbell of Lochawe was granted the hereditary keepership of the Castle of Dunoon; his son Gillespie together with his grandson Colin were made king's lieutenants over the stretch of land from Tyndrum to Lochgilphead and from Loch Melfort to Loch Long. This office in due course became vested in the Campbell of Lochawe family. This latter Colin was styled 'Cailean Iongantach' because of his astuteness, which features in many tales.

His son, Sir Duncan, was created Lord Campbell in 1445. He was succeeded in this title by his grandson Colin, whose father had died early. With Colin the family fortunes really burgeoned: in 1457 he was created Earl of Argyll and also became Justiciar of all Scotland south of the Forth. Having acted as an ambassador to treat for peace with England in 1463 he was appointed Master of the Royal Household in 1464, a post which has remained in the family's hands to this day. In 1473 he was made Justiciar, Chamberlain, Sheriff and Baillie over the king's lands in Cowal and the following year he had a joint commission over Argyll, Lorne, Menteith and various other lands. In 1481 he was made keeper of Castle Sween and in 1483 he was appointed to the post of Lord Chancellor of Scotland.

His son and successor Archibald continued to advance the family fortunes but was cut down in the great defeat at Flodden in 1513. A considerable number of the leaders of Clan Campbell fell alongside their chief in the right wing of the Scots army, of which their chief and his brother-in-law the earl of Lennox had joint command.

Colin, the 3rd earl, was Master of the Household and High Justiciar of Scotland, offices which in 1528, together with the Sheriffdom of Argyll, were confirmed to him and to his successors. In 1517 he was made one of the Vice-Regents and Lieutenants of the Kingdom. In 1528, too, just over a year before his death, the king appointed him Lieutenant of the Borders and Warden of the Marches.

This remarkable growth in the power and status of the Campbell chiefs was greatly helped by two things. In 1493 the Lordship of the Isles had finally been forfeited, following continued Clan Donald misbehaviour and the realisation of the full implications of the 1462 Treaty of Westminster-Ardtornish. In this, the Lord of the Isles and Douglas agreed to join with the English king in conquering Scotland. Their reward, as his vassals, was to have been all Scotland north of the Forth. The forfeiture led to the break-up of the hegemony of Clan Donald and although the situation on the west coast still continued to be troubled, it became more manageable.

The strength of Clan Campbell itself had grown steadily with the extending of its territory. Powerful branches were added to the main Campbell stem, which in turn now grew their own subsidiary cadets. The great families were by now well established: of Loudoun, Glenorchy, Cawdor, Strachur, Melfort, Inverawe, Auchinbreck, Ardkinglas and, lastly, of Lochnell.

The 5th earl, Archibald, married the half-sister of Mary, Queen of Scots. Although a staunch Protestant, he did his best to further his sister-in-law's interests and commanded her forces at the battle of Langside in 1568, where, unfortunately, he had a seizure just as the battle was starting. The defeat of the queen's army led to her eventual capture and her unhappy fate, which is all too well known. An aspirant for the Regency of Scotland, the earl did not achieve his ambition but was, however, appointed to the post of Lord Chancellor the year before his untimely death in 1573. He was succeeded by his brother Colin – a remarkable man, whose power was such that he held the balance between the kingdoms of Scotland and England with a large and sophisticated following under arms.

Colin died in 1584 leaving two small sons. The question of their care and upbringing nearly brought about the downfall of Clan Campbell when a struggle for control of the young earl broke out among his guardians. The chief target was Campbell of Cawdor, who, it was felt, had usurped an undue degree of influence. This brought in Huntly in the north; he was at loggerheads with the Earl of Moray, whose mother, Lady Margaret Campbell, was the young earl's aunt. The plot was first to get rid of Cawdor and then to move in on the two boys. The main beneficiary, as heir to the earldom, would appear to have been Lochnell. He was aided by Ardkinglas and by Glenorchy, the latter's reward being, significantly, the original chiefly lordship of Lochawe. Not for the first or the last time there is evidence of the deep-seated ambition of Glenorchy to take over the leadership of the Campbells.

The actual plot involved two related incidents across Scotland. On 4 February 1592 Cawdor was murdered at his house of Knipoch in Lorne. He was shot through the window of the lighted room in which he was sitting and died instantaneously. Three days later, the 'Bonnie Earl of Moray'

PLATE 1: The results of Tertiary volcanic activity: the characteristic stepped landscape of Ardmeanach lavas on Mull. (copyright © C. Gillen)

PLATE 2: The results of Tertiary volcanic activity: the hexagonal columns of basalt lava at Fingal's Cave on Staffa (copyright © Graham Ritchie)

PLATE 3: The Paps of Jura, with a raised beach visible (copyright © C. Gillen)

PLATE 4: The white sandy beach at Kiloran Bay, Colonsay (copyright © C. Gillen)

PLATE 5: The Kildalton Cross, Islay: the minerals in the greenstone from which it is carved are weathering at different rates (copyright © C. Gillen)

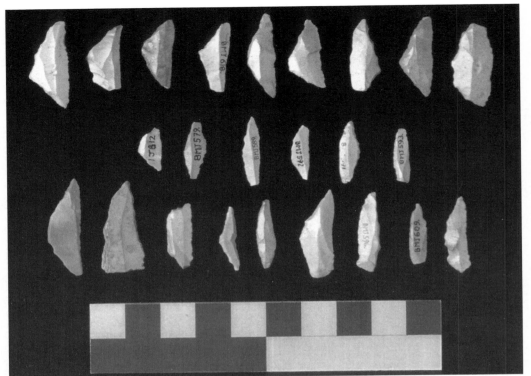

PLATE 6: Mesolithic flint microliths from Lussa Bay, Isle of Jura. Scale in cm.
(© The Trustees of the National Museums of Scotland)

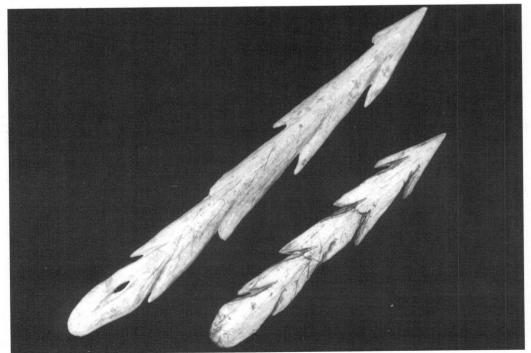

PLATE 7: Mesolithic barbed points made of red deer antler from MacArthur Cave, Oban. One has a basal
perforation to take a line. (© The Trustees of the National Museums of Scotland)

PLATE 8: The Neolithic chambered cairn of Nether Largie South, Kilmartin (Crown copyright: RCAHMS)

PLATE 9: One of the Neolithic to Bronze Age stone circles at Temple Wood, Kilmartin (copyright © Graham Ritchie)

PLATE 10: A cup- and ring-marked stone at Cairnbaan (copyright © Graham Ritchie)

PLATE 11: Stone circle and outlying standing stone at Lochbuie, Mull (copyright © Graham Ritchie)

PLATE 12: Neolithic axeheads of Irish flint from Auchenhoan, near Campbeltown, Kintyre. Scale in cm.
(© The Trustees of the National Museums of Scotland)

PLATE 13: Bronze Age jet necklace from Poltalloch (© The Trustees of the National Museums of Scotland)

PLATE 14: The Iron Age broch at Tirefour, Lismore (copyright © Graham Ritchie)

PLATE 15: Dunadd from the south-east (Crown copyright: RCAHMS)

PLATE 16: The 'Inomine' pebble from Dunadd and two other inscribed stones, on which designs for artwork have been sketched (Crown copyright: RCAHMS)

PLATE 17: Crucible and mould fragments from Dunadd (Crown copyright: RCAHMS)

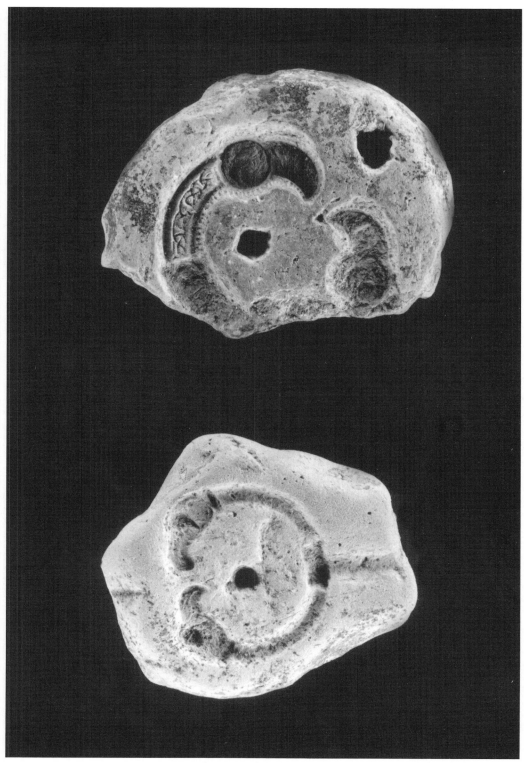

PLATE 18: Moulds for bird-headed brooches from Dunadd, one showing interlace decoration. The final brooches were about 2.5cm across. (Crown copyright: RCAHMS)

PLATE 19: Iona Abbey with the early Christian monastic vallum in the foreground
(Crown copyright: RCAHMS)

PLATE 20: Cladh a' Bhile burial ground, Ellary (Crown copyright: RCAHMS)

PLATE 21: Grave marker from Iona, inscribed in Latin: 'Lapis Echodi' (Crown copyright: RCAHMS)

PLATE 22: Iona, St Martin's Cross
(Crown copyright: RCAHMS)

PLATE 23: Iona Abbey. Originally founded by St Columba, the present
buildings derive largely from the period of the Benedictine monastery
and were restored in the nineteenth and twentieth centuries.
(Crown copyright: Historic Scotland)

PLATE 24: Iona Abbey: view of the interior from the west (Crown copyright: RCAHMS)

PLATE 25: Oronsay Priory, founded by John, first Lord of the Isles (copyright © Graham Ritchie)

PLATE 26: St Cormac's Chapel on Eilean Mór, with the tenth-century St Cormac's Cross marking the saint's grave in the foreground (Crown copyright: Historic Scotland)

PLATE 27: (opposite) A carved gravestone from Kilmory Knap Chapel, showing a ship, sword, and characteristic interlace shears (Crown copyright: RCAHMS)

PLATE 28: Aros Castle, Mull: the principal seat on Mull of the MacDonald Lords of the Isles. The original hall-house that dominates the site may originally have been built by their MacDougall kinsmen and rivals in the later thirteenth century. (copyright © Richard Oram)

PLATE 29: Lagg Pier, Jura, one of many piers constructed in the early nineteenth century as part of the drive to improve maritime infrastructure (Crown copyright: RCAHMS)

PLATE 30: Ardrishaig Lock on the Crinan Canal. The canal opened to traffic in 1801, and is still in use today. (copyright © Graham Ritchie)

PLATE 31: The planned village of Portnahaven on Islay was established in the 1820s to facilitate the exploitation of fishing in the area (Crown copyright: RCAHMS)

PLATE 32: Tobermory, Mull: one of many centres of the whisky industry in the nineteenth and twentieth centuries (copyright © Graham Ritchie)

PLATE 33: The planned settlement on the island of Ellanbeich, one of the slate islands which 'roofed the world' in the nineteenth century (Crown copyright: RCAHMS)

PLATE 34: The iron-smelting furnace at Bonawe (copyright © Graham Ritchie)

PLATE 35: Castle Sween, reputedly the oldest castle in Scotland, was built towards the end of the twelfth century (Crown copyright: RCAHMS)

PLATE 36: Duart Castle, Mull (Crown copyright: RCAHMS)

PLATE 37: Dunderave Castle (1598), an L-plan tower house, much restored and expanded in the early twentieth century (Crown copyright: RCAHMS)

PLATE 38: Colonsay House (1722), one of the first classical mansions in Argyll (Crown copyright: RCAHMS)

PLATE 39: Inveraray Castle (Crown copyright: RCAHMS)

PLATE 40: Craig Ailey, Cove, designed by Alexander 'Greek' Thomson (Crown copyright: RCAHMS)

PLATE 41: Hill House (Crown copyright: RCAHMS)

PLATE 42: John Francis Campbell of Islay (1822–85), an important collector of orally-transmitted Gaelic folktales, photographed here with, on the left, Lachlan McNeill (shoemaker) and, on the right, Hector Maclean (schoolmaster), Paisley, c. 1870.

was surprised in his home at Donibristle in Fife by a party of Gordons, who set fire to the house as they hunted the earl. He fled into the dark, but a spark caught in the covering of his helmet gave him away and his enemies cut him down. His mother had a picture painted of his nude body, disfigured by the many cuts and slashes inflicted upon him. This she had intended to use to arouse the king's wrath against her son's killers, but the anguish of grief was too much for her and she herself died almost immediately afterwards. The resulting rift in Clan Campbell was a serious one.

In spite of considerable efforts to bring the murderers to book, they seem to have survived and indeed managed to launch an attempt to poison the young earl and his brother. This too failed and both boys survived, but, whether or not this was due to the dangers he had gone through, the elder was not of an attractive disposition – indeed his sobriquet was 'Gillespie Gruamach' – 'Grim-faced Archie'.

He was not much loved by the king, who deemed him over-arrogant. When in 1594 he was defeated at Glenlivet by the earl of Huntly, against whom he had been given a commission, the king is said to have exclaimed with glee, 'Fair fa' ye, Geordie Gordon, for sending him back looking sae like a subject.' It was on this occasion that Lochnell was killed having, according to tradition, deliberately raised a yellow flag to mark the earl's position as a target for Huntly's artillery.

The 7th earl was a major prosecutor of the Clan Gregor and, as a reward for bringing them to heel was granted the former MacDonald lands of Kintyre in 1607. This was followed in 1611 by the purchase of Islay, also formerly in MacDonald hands, by Campbell of Cawdor – a move that severely overstretched that family's resources, particularly since they could not rely on receiving rents from their recalcitrant new tenants. In due course the imposition of a strong regime and the wholesale import of new Campbell tacksmen solved the problem. The same strategy was eventually followed in Argyll by the Marquess of Argyll, who brought in tenants from Ayr and Renfrew around 1650.

After his second marriage in 1617 the 7th earl converted to Roman Catholicism. His departure to the Low Countries led to a major power vacuum in the West Highlands, which seriously worried the government. The major figures of the Clan Campbell were summoned and a scheme was implemented for the governance of the area by their leaders, a move which necessitated the reforging of the bonds – still severely strained by the events of 1592 – that cemented the clan together.

The 7th earl died in 1638 and was succeeded by his son Archibald, the 8th earl, who was advanced to the rank of marquess in 1641. By now the Civil War had broken out. Argyll's position was somewhat anomalous since, a Royalist at heart, his loyalty to his religion was nevertheless superior, and he found himself the chief agent of the Covenanters when they turned against the king. Clan Campbell did not have a particularly 'good' war; Montrose's lieutenant Alexander MacColla invaded the country with his troops, forcing the marquess to flee on two occasions: once when Mac-Colla succeeded, by marching through the winter passes, in taking the town of Inveraray itself; and again when, by dint of a forced march through snowy mountains, he surprised and destroyed a pursuing force of Camp-bells at Inverlochy. The marquess took to his galley and sailed away to safety, leaving his captured commander, Sir Duncan Campbell of Auchin-breck, to choose to be either hanged or beheaded by the Royalist forces. '*Dha dhiu gun aon roghainn!*' – 'Two evils and a single choice!' he is said to have exclaimed.

The marquess has always had a bad press, but he was in fact a statesman of considerable stature, whose achievements are now beginning to receive due recognition by historians. Perhaps he was doomed to obloquy by a physical deformity that prevented him looking straight at anyone. Having crowned King Charles II as King of Scots, he hastened to greet him at the Restoration, but was rewarded with arrest and a trial that led to his execu-tion. His estates were forfeited and, when they were eventually given back to his son in 1663, the title of marquess was not restored.

The 1670s saw the last great expansion of Campbell land with the take-over of the estates of Maclean of Duart. Maclean had fallen into debt secured by pledges on his land; these debts had been bought by Argyll and, when he foreclosed, Maclean was unable to pay and ownership passed to the Campbell chief. However, it took more than one major expedition backed by government troops to impose the full effect of the law.

On the accession of the Roman Catholic King James VII, Archibald the 9th earl was soon in trouble; his refusal to sign the Test Act led to his being found guilty of treason and he was sentenced to death in 1681. With the help of his stepdaughter, Lady Sophia Lindsay, he escaped from Edinburgh Castle disguised as her page and fled to Holland. Here, with the duke of Monmouth, he planned the abortive rebellion of 1685, in which he led the Scottish invasion. The reaction of the clan was cautious and only a part joined their chief. His campaign was not a success and, while seeking fur-ther help from the Lowlands, he was captured near Glasgow and swiftly condemned to death in the same manner as his father.

The establishment of a Protestant monarchy at the Glorious Revolution of 1688 saw the Campbell fortunes restored once more. Among Archibald the 10th earl's many services to the Crown was the raising of a regular reg-iment of foot in 1689 – the Earl of Argyle's Regiment. The regiment achieved notoriety in 1692 when it carried out, under orders, the massacre of Glencoe; it subsequently went on to serve with great gallantry in the Low Countries before being reduced in 1697. Campbell of Glenorchy had also been much involved in attempts to keep the peace in the Highlands and had been given a large sum of money with which to gain the co-oper-ation of the Jacobite clans. His answer when called on to account for his expenditure might not be acceptable in today's business environment: 'The money is spent, the Highlands are at peace and there's no accounting between friends!' In 1701 the earl was created Duke of Argyll, Marquess of Kintyre and Lorne, Earl of Campbell and Cowal, Viscount of Lochow and Glenislay, and Lord Inveraray of Mull, Morvern and Tiree. He died two years later and was succeeded by his son John.

The 2nd duke was a remarkable soldier. For his services in promoting the Treaty of Union he was given the English peerages of the Earldom of Greenwich and Barony of Chatham and before he was thirty he had resigned from the Order of the Thistle on being appointed to the Order of the Garter. He served with distinction as a general officer under Marlborough and was at the battles of Ramillies and Oudenarde. He has been spoken of as a greater soldier even than Marlborough and, had the politics of the day gone otherwise, he and not Marlborough might have had the chief command. As it was, he went on to command the government forces that defeated the Jacobite attempt of 1715 and was one of the first two officers in the British Army to be given the rank of Field Marshal. Although he was attended by a sizeable body of Campbell gentlemen volunteers, not all his clan supported him: the followers of the Earl of Breadalbane, as Glenorchy had now become, came out on the Jacobite side. In 1719, the duke was created Duke of Greenwich but since he had no direct male heirs, this title lapsed when he died, laden with honours, in 1743.

He was succeeded by his younger brother, Archibald, who now became the 3rd duke. Another remarkable man, the new duke had already made his reputation as a brave and effective soldier before turning his ambitions to a civil rather than a military career. By the age of twenty-three he was Lord High Treasurer of Scotland and in 1706 he became one of the Commissioners for the Treaty of Union, of which he has been credited as the main architect. Later that year he was created Earl and Viscount of Islay and served as one of the representative Scottish peers at Westminster. His monument is Inveraray Castle, which he started building just as the 'Forty-five rebellion commenced.

The Campbells were now by far the most powerful force in the Highlands. Lord President Duncan Forbes of Culloden, in his report to government on the Highland clans, put their strength at five thousand – the aged Lord Breadalbane had learnt his lesson and had joined the fold – while the entire Clan Donald could muster less than half that number. In the event the Argyll or Campbell Militia – the two titles seem to be have been used interchangeably – took to the field at Culloden some two and a half thousand strong.

The battle of Culloden is often said to mark the end of the clan system and so it did. But the clan influence was still to play a strong part in the raising of the many Highland regiments that at one time figured in the army lists. The Campbells played a major role in this and no fewer than sixteen regiments of the line, militia, fencibles and volunteers were raised and largely officered by members of the clan.

The 3rd duke died in 1761; he was succeeded by his cousin, Lieutenant-General John Campbell of Mamore, later a full General and Knight of the Thistle. He died in 1770 and was succeeded by his elder son, 'Colonel Jack' of the 'Forty-five, who rose to the rank of field marshal, the second of the family to be so distinguished. Unfortunately the 6th duke, his elder son, was a rake, whose excesses very nearly brought down the family fortunes. His brother, who succeeded him, was however a man of great integrity, who worked hard to restore the house of Argyll. His son, the 8th duke, was a member of the Liberal cabinet, latterly as Secretary-of-State for India, and a member of both the Order of the Garter and the Order of the Thistle, an unusual distinction. In 1892 he was given another Dukedom of Argyll, this one in the peerage of the United Kingdom.

The social recognition of the family perhaps reached its apogee with the marriage of Princess Louise, Queen Victoria's daughter, to the Marquess of Lorne, later the 9th duke, in 1871. But something of the local standing of the Campbell chiefs can be gauged from the story of the old woman in Inveraray who exclaimed, on being told the news of the engagement: 'Och, the Queen'll be a prood wumman the day wi'her dochter gettin' mairrit on the son o' MacCailein Mor!'

Campbells are to be found all over the world today. Few of the old families still live on their ancestral properties, it is true, but if the award of a peerage may be taken as a indicator of success, it is notable that no less than four new Campbell peerages have been created in the last fifty years. And the Duke of Argyll, chief of Clan Campbell, still has his home at Inveraray, as his forebears have done for somewhat over five hundred years.

CHAPTER TWELVE

The Industries of Argyll: Tradition and Improvement

T HIS CHAPTER WILL CONSIDER some of the traditional industries of Argyll and the major developments that occurred during the era of improvement *c*. 1750 to *c*. 1850. This was a century of change in infrastructure, both social and physical, which witnessed the upheavals of both the agricultural and industrial revolutions – a period, in Argyll and the Highlands, that starts with the aftermath of conflict and ends with the scourge of the clearances. Both events were politically and socially damaging, with reverberations that can still be felt today; but these events were not the only things that disrupted and transformed the lifestyles of the inhabitants. There were other changes, which may seem rather mundane in isolation but when taken as a whole define the region during and after the age of improvements.

Transport

One of the defining changes of this era was in the types and modes of transport employed. From small wooden boats and sloops via sailing ships to steam-driven vessels, from rutted tracks and drove roads to metalled roads and the building of canals and, eventually, railways – Argyll had them all and shared in the technical aspects of the transport revolution that took place from the latter part of the eighteenth century.

Argyllshire was fairly undeveloped in terms of infrastructure in the mid-eighteenth century: all the centres of population were described as hamlets on Roy's maps of the period. Internal routeways were simple tracks over the moorland and mountainous terrain and there were few made-up roads. Indeed, the lack of good communications was what prompted the government of the day to build a network of roads in the region. These routes were constructed in fear of another uprising, but they also facilitated the movement of goods and people to and from markets. Early maps of the region show that the road system was rudimentary and the indented coastline meant that bridges and ferries were important components of the transport infrastructure. The most significant early improvements to

communications came during the first three decades of the nineteenth
century, a period which laid the foundations for a system that was still
apparent in the middle of the twentieth century.

Argyll was one of the six subdivisions of the Highlands created by the
Parliamentary Commissioners for roads, bridges and canals in the early
decades of the nineteenth century. They received many petitions from the
heritors of Argyll, mostly aimed at helping the fishermen of the area. New
roads would make it possible for the fish to reach the large southern markets, especially Glasgow, far quicker than had hitherto been possible. The
lack of a good communication network also hampered the industry by
making it difficult and expensive to bring the essential salt and casks north
to the centres of the fishing industry, mainly Loch Fyne. To meet the
needs of the industry, roads were built from Loch Fyne, through Glendaruel to Colintraive, by Loch Eck to Ardentinny and through Hell's Glen
to the head of Loch Goil. Various plans were also proposed for facilitating
the crossing of the high ground of the district, especially the old drove
routes around Loch Awe and Inveraray, to help the important cattle droving industry. The duke of Argyll also requested support to create more
efficient and direct routes for the movement of cattle from the island communities of Argyll to the mainland. A plan for a road on Mull from
Bunessan to the head of Loch Don never materialised but construction did
go ahead on Islay and Jura. The geography of the area meant that ferries
played a very important role in communications. Routes, tracks and roads
relied on the water crossings to cut down the time and expense of travel.

The social and economic history of the area is inextricably linked with
the sea. Most internal and all external communications were carried out via
water-borne transportation of one kind or another. Improvers, both local
landlords and government agencies, realised that new roads were not of
much use if they did not connect with the numerous crossings that were
in existence. The topography dictated that ferries operated in many parts
of the county, not only between the islands and mainland but also across
the many sea lochs and rivers. The communications infrastructure that was
improved upon or created during this period would have been familiar to
residents in the 1960s as well as the 1860s.

Ferry crossings abounded in Argyll, many of them centuries old. Most
were only for the movement of people, but as the eighteenth century progressed, the cattle drovers utilised some of these links on their way to the
trysts at Falkirk and Crieff. On the banks of Loch Fyne there were three
principal crossing-points, located at East Otter, Creggans and Inveraray.
Loch Leven's crossing-points were situated at Ballachulish and Glen Coe,
Loch Awe's near Kilchrenan and at Dalavich, Loch Etive's at Connel, and
Bonawe. Other crossing-points were the narrows between Appin and Lismore, Loch Creran from Appin at Rubha Garbh, and the Sounds of Seil
and Kerrera at several points. There were also numerous crossings between
the mainland and the islands of the administrative area. Ferries operated

between Port Appin and Port Ramsay on Lismore, from Port Askaig on Islay to Feolin on Jura, from Whitehouse on the Mull of Kintyre to Gigha and to Ports Askaig and Ellen on Islay. The growing commercial centre of Oban was connected to Colonsay, Kerrera, Lismore, Mull and Tiree, to name but a few.

It was recognised that the construction of new quays and piers would help improve these links and to that end a number of projects were instigated. The quays at Connel were rebuilt during the 1820s and the Commissioners for Roads and Bridges constructed piers at Tobermory and Corran around the same time. The improvements of ferry crossings was linked to other maritime changes; many piers, quays and harbours were constructed, most in conjunction with the planned village movement that flourished throughout the area or with the expansion of new industrial locations.

The early nineteenth century witnessed an explosion in maritime infrastructure building on the mainland and the islands of Argyll. The expanding slate industry was the reason for building quays with broad tops at Balvicar and Ellenbach; this allowed slates to be piled up prior to export. A similar type of construction was erected at Easdale, where a natural harbour was quayed on both sides. The new harbours at Cullipool and Tobornochy on Luing were built from slate spoil to a similar design. On Lismore, the limekilns at An Sailean required a pier from which the finished product could be exported. On Islay, rubble piers were built at Bruichladdich, Port Wemyss, Port Ellen, Bowmore and at Ardbeg, which also had a new sea wall. A harbour was constructed at Port Askaig, which re-developed a pier and quay from an earlier period. On Jura, Thomas Telford designed a straight massive-rubble pier with a rounded end, flanked by ferry ramps designed for the cattle traffic of the island. On Tiree the needs of the local community were catered for by the harbours built by the Northern Lighthouse Board at Hynish and the small pier at Scarinish, which allowed cattle to be exported from the island and peat to be imported from Coll and Mull. The larger planned settlements on the mainland were all at waterside locations and included substantial piers and harbours.

Another improvement that influenced development was the construction of canals. Scotland as a whole witnessed many proposals for canals during the improving period but only a small number of them were ever built. In the Highland area two ship canal projects, the Crinan and Caledonian, and one industrial canal were realised.

The first canal to be constructed outwith the developing central belt industrial area of Scotland was built between 1783 and 1791 to carry coal from Drumlemble to Campbeltown. The course of the canal is shown on Langland's 1793 maps of the area and again in 1801. Charles McDowall leased the coal deposits and it was he who instigated the project in order to get the coal to the market place. The overall length was 4.8 km and the level ground meant that no locks were required. By the late 1850s the canal was no longer in use. It was superseded by the next revolution in transportation – the railways.

Shipowners and merchants had long sought a method of avoiding the long, and at times dangerous, passage around the Mull of Kintyre before John Rennie's 1792 survey of the area identified a possible canal route. An Act of Parliament to license construction was passed in 1793; work began on the Crinan canal the following year and it opened to traffic in 1801. The construction costs at opening amounted to £140,760 for a link of 14.5 km, with fifteen locks, between Ardrishaig and Crinan. The depth of the canal had to be a minimum of 3.5m (12 ft) to accommodate sea-going vessels. This requirement and the difficult terrain meant that the original estimates were well below the actual costs of construction. Rather poor building methods meant that the repair bill was constantly rising, and in the 1840s major repairs were carried out along the route. As expected, the fishermen made very heavy use of this link in the early years, as did the slate trade. However, by the mid-nineteenth century coal and general goods supplied more than three quarters of its annual revenue. Although it was not until the latter part of the nineteenth century that this link became the important economic routeway of the area, its construction provided much-needed work and it certainly lowered the price of goods transported to and from the area.

Unlike Argyll's only other canal, the Crinan is still in operation today. Pleasure craft are the mainstay of its revenue, bringing visitors to an area that has been a tourist destination ever since the communications network was improved during the era under consideration.

Planned Settlements

The built landscape of Argyll is essentially late eighteenth and nineteenth century in origin. Estate houses abound and castles and mansions are numerous, as are the abandoned townships associated with the removal of the indigenous population. The area also contains a number of planned settlements, laid out to encourage new enterprises and to allow the new farming methods to be implemented.

The planned village movement in Argyll was mainly based on the exploitation of the herring shoals that abounded in the latter part of the eighteenth century, but the new villages were not exclusively associated with the fishing industry. The exploitation of other natural resources and the introduction of new industries were also catalysts for the laying out of new settlements. The best known of these settlements is Tobermory on the island of Mull. It was founded in 1787 by The British Fisheries Society as part of a grand design to establish settlements in the Highlands as bases for the herring industry. Although the unpredictable movement of the shoals frustrated the original intention, the town did develop as a commercial centre during the nineteenth century. The other major fishing settlement of the area was Campbeltown. A settlement founded in the early seventeenth century and given Royal Burgh status in 1700, it did not come to prominence until the development of the local fishing industry from 1750 onwards. The present Inveraray was a planned village of the mid-eighteenth century, when the 3rd duke of Argyll moved the site of the village a few hundred metres southwards to make room for his new castle. Along with new houses, a pier was also constructed in 1761 to facilitate trade and accommodate the fishing fleet. At Dunoon James Craig (of Edinburgh New Town fame) planned a small village in the early 1790s, before its expansion and improvement in 1795 for the 5th duke of Argyll. Lochgilphead was also laid out during the last decade of the eighteenth century. Its geographical location was exploited by merchants and seamen alike, once its connections had been improved by the completion of the Crinan canal and of road links to Inveraray and Campbeltown.

The only major settlement on the mainland that was not part of this movement was Oban. The town developed during the second half of the eighteenth century in a piecemeal fashion in response to increasing use of the natural harbour. The minister noted in the 1790s that a spirit of building arose here from about 1778. In 1800 Oban was described as a small straggling village, but the town developed considerably during the next decade. The construction of a new pier was the catalyst for change, but it would not become a flourishing settlement until the last quarter of the nineteenth century.

New settlements were also built to house workers at slate and quarry locations, for example the new village laid out at Easdale by the Marquis of Breadalbane. Similar settlements can be found at Cullipool and Toberanochy on Luing. The growing iron-smelting industry also provided accommodation for its workers at both Furnace and Bon Awe. The island communities did not miss out, and one of the earliest planned villages on the islands was at Bowmore on Islay in the 1760s. Nearly all the other settlements on Islay were laid out in the early 1820s, mainly to exploit the now legal whisky industry, but at least one – Portnahaven – was expected to exploit the fishing, as were the mainland villages of Bunessan and Port Ramsay. On Coll the tiny village of Aringour was established about 1800 in the hope that a linen industry would grow, and on Mull the twenty-six houses of the new village of Dervaig would herald a new spirit in husbandry among the inhabitants. On Iona efforts to expand the local economy through flax spinning, commercial fishing and marble quarrying had limited success; and in 1802, as part of the 5th duke's agricultural reforms, Iona was divided into individual crofts, thus ending the runrig or communal system of land use. Houses were built on these holdings and a new village street erected in its present location. This widespread spirit of change and improvement by lords, lairds and landowners led to an Argyll that is recognisable today.

People and Industry

An essay on the improving era cannot be about just the physical changes that occurred on and to the landscape. These changes had a cost in both economic and social terms. Culloden and its aftermath paved the way for re-organisation by removing from authority those who were in sympathy with the clan system. The reformers were able to plan and implement innovations with the backing of the ruling classes of the time. The new landowners, and many of the old who remained in power, approved and pursued the national enthusiasm for improvement in the hope of increasing their financial standing. The development of new forms of trade, especially those that catered for the growing industrialisation and population of southern areas, provided the incentives. Trade from Argyll began to expand prior to the 'Forty-five, but within twenty years the price of cattle had nearly doubled and by 1790 quadrupled. Similar price increases can be found in wool, kelp and wood. At the same time, the prospects for the fishing trade, especially herring, seemed to be enormous. Optimism abounded in the latter part of the eighteenth century, at least on the part of the landowners. It was expected that enclosure would succeed runrig and that the introduction of sheep would lead to some people being put off the land. The solution was planned settlements designed to provide those removed with a non- or semi-agricultural mode of living. Others would depart to the growing industrial areas of the south and find employment in the new industries. The land itself and what it could produce became more valuable to the owners than the retention of their people. Indeed, in much of Argyll the redistribution of a rising population within estates, from the interior glens to coastal areas in order to make way for sheep farming, was a major aspect of the improving movement. The duke of Argyll is quoted as saying, 'I am resolved to keep no tenants but such as will be peaceable and apply to industry.' This was a sentiment that many other landowners agreed with and one that echoes down the corridors of history to the present day.

From the late seventeenth century, the dukes of Argyll carried out social and economic reform, with the aim of increasing rents in order to finance their own ambitions rather than to enhance the lifestyles of their clan members. From the early eighteenth century, their lands were allocated less on the basis of kinship and more on the ability to pay higher rents. Some of the earliest removals were carried out by the Campbells, witness the 1669 mass evictions on Shuna, Luing, Torosay and Seil, long before 'clearance' became a byword for ruthless 'improvement'. This was the beginning of the end for the tacksmen of the area: those middlemen that had run the estates and organised the military might of the clans. Again, the Campbells of Argyll were at the forefront of this movement. They realised that more money would accrue to them if they reorganised the estates and leased the land directly through a system of competitive bidding. This policy more than doubled the rents from Tiree between 1703 and 1736. The aftermath of Culloden meant that many tacksmen were no longer required, as the landlords started to carry out improvements and adjusted to the new commercialism. Subsequently, many talented individuals left the area to seek their fortune elsewhere; most went overseas and took their extended families with them. At first, this was beneficial to the estate owners, but as economic conditions changed and the landlords again needed people to serve the new wealth-creating industries created by the Napoleonic Wars, worry about migration became apparent. The fear that there would not be enough people to work in the expanding industries led to measures ensuring that as few as possible could actually afford to leave. This policy of retention would be turned on its head in a few short decades, resulting in the eviction of the populations of whole townships and islands.

Kelp

A key factor in this need for people was the development of the kelp industry, which has been described as the greatest growth sector in the West Highland economy during the period 1750 to 1815. It provided employment in many communities that had witnessed a dramatic rise in population, whilst the introduction of the potato meant that the expanding numbers could be cheaply and easily fed. Eventually these two 'saviours' would exacerbate an already difficult situation.

The kelp industry involved the gathering and processing of the kelp to produce an alkali which was an important ingredient in the manufacture of glass and soap and in the bleaching of linen. It seemed to be an ideal industry for the area, which abounded in the raw material; the processing required no agricultural land and was labour intensive, without requiring any particular skills or specialised equipment. In addition, during the Napoleonic War period the price of the processed kelp was constantly rising and the finished product was easily transported from the region. The importance of the industry, and its subsequent revenue to the lairds, is reflected in the pronouncement of the then duke of Argyll that any adulterer of kelp would receive no shelter on his estate and that prosecution would follow. The number of individuals prosecuted for any such offences is unknown but a conservative estimate puts those dependent upon the industry in the whole of the Highlands at 50,000 in the early 1820s.

The *Statistical Accounts* provide an insight into the scale of the industry in the late eighteenth and early nineteenth century. Although the industry was an important source of income not every coastal community in Argyll participated to the same extent. In Kilfinan, only one kelper was employed in 1793 and in Kilmadon parish the writer notes that, although there are three miles of coastline available to parishioners, little kelp is made. The 10 to 12 tons of kelp made yearly in Kilmartin was reported as 'not so much considering the extent of shoreline'. Between them, the islands of Tiree, Rum, Canna and Muck manufactured 200 to 250 tons annually in the early

1790s. On Mull manufacture had been as high as 180 tons per annum in the 1780s. At Lochgoilhead about 20 tons were made, whereas in Morvern the manufacturing of the kelp was 70 tons in 1793, when kelp was worth £1 10*s.* per ton. In the parishes of Kilbrandon and Kilchatton, tenants gathered about 30 tons of seaweed per annum and the Laird, Lord Breadalbane, allowed them to decide whether to use it as manure or to turn it into an exportable item. The minister notes, 'in this they are directed by the price whether high or low'. Prices had been as high as eight pounds and as low as 50*s.* per ton in the preceding years.

The price fluctuations arose from a number of factors, the two main ones being imports from elsewhere and the use of substitutes in the soap and glass industries. In 1815, kelp prices fell when it became possible to import barilla as a substitute from Spain. It had been £20 a ton in 1808, but fell to £10 by the early 1820s. The manufacture of Leblanc alkali in Glasgow from 1825 meant that the price fell even further to £3 per ton, making it not worth the effort of gathering, manufacturing and transporting from the Islands and Highlands of Argyll. *The New Statistical Account of Argyll* records the demise of this once-important industry. In this report, only one parish still retains an interest in the industry. The inhabitants of Ulva were still manufacturing kelp 'because it is the best in the Highlands and commands the highest prices', but the 100 tons per annum is considerably less than the average amount of a few years previously. The common theme that emerges from these reports is one of change from enthusiastic endorsement to the distress, bankruptcy and poverty caused by the disappearance of an industry that once employed thousands.

During the Second World War seaweed again became a valuable commodity in the region and processing plants were set up in various locations in Argyll. Kilmelfort, Bellochantuy and Barcaldine saw the largest units but again, as in the past, it was a short-lived boom that ended soon after the war when trading with other nations was resumed.

Whisky

The production of whisky is probably the industry that most people associate with Argyll. However, the present-day trade, in both numbers of distilleries and volume of production, is but a shadow of its former self. The history of the industry in the Highlands and Islands was one, mostly, of illegal distilling and evasion of payment of taxes up until the 1823 Act, which reformed the law that had made it a profitable, although illegal, exercise for many an individual and indeed for whole communities. A reading of the *Old Statistical Account of Argyll* would lead one to believe that there was not a community that did not indulge in this activity. Indeed, industrial archaeology conducted in the area has found numerous remains of what have been identified as illicit stills. The most obvious of these are at Skipness in Kintyre, at Brackley in Lorne and at least two on the island of Lismore. The passing and subsequent enforcement of the 1823 Act led to the building of numerous distilleries and the production of malt whiskies that are now household names. However, a number of the buildings that became legal distilleries had been in operation for a considerable period prior to this. An example is the Oban distillery, which during the 1960s was advertised as the oldest in continuous production, having first distilled the malt in 1794. Due to the nature of the industry before this period, it is not always possible to be definite about the dating of the numerous distilleries that still operate in Argyll.

At present there are twelve operating distilleries in Argyll, very different from the hey-day of the late nineteenth century when Campbeltown alone was surrounded by thirty-four. The number in the town now stands at two, Glen Scotia and Springbank being the only ones left in production. The first of these was built by the Galbraith family in 1832, close to the Parliament Square in the centre of the town, and was initially named the Scotia. The second was established by the Mitchell family in the late 1820s and is notable as the only Scottish distillery still conducting all its own operations on site, from malting to bottling. Another continuity with the past is that the present chairman is the great-great-grandson of the founder. The demise of distilling in Campbeltown was due to indifferent distilling and the sale of immature whiskies, which gave the area a bad name. Other areas have had similar problems with production.

The distillery at Tobermory on Mull dates from around 1800 and was in continuous production until the premises were closed in 1928. From around that date onwards the buildings were used as a store and electricity generating station until 1972 when the structures were rebuilt and re-opened as the Ledaig Distillery (Tobermory) Ltd. A similar story surrounds another island distillery. It is said that there was distilling at Craighouse on Jura as early as the seventeenth century, but the present distillery only dates from around 1810. The buildings were owned by the Campbells, landlords of the Jura estate, but the stills and equipment belonged to James Ferguson, who operated the distillery for his own profit. In 1901, this arrangement ended and the equipment was removed. In 1958 two local landowners approached Scottish and Newcastle Breweries with a proposal to rebuild the distillery and 1963 saw the opening of the new enterprise under the name Isle of Jura Distillery Company, an enterprise that still provides employment to a number of islanders.

Today the stronghold of malt whisky production in Argyll is situated on the island of Islay, a location long associated with the distilling of the water of life. Whether one travels north, east, south or west on this island it is unlikely that the journey would not include an encounter with the whisky industry. The seven distilleries presently operating have a long and respectable history; two of them, Ardbeg and Laphroaig, are reputedly operating upon sites that were once the locations of illicit whisky-making. A Mr Simpson founded the Bowmore distillery, situated on the shore of Loch Indall, in 1779 and it is the oldest distillery on Islay. It was owned and expanded by James Mutter during the middle years of the nineteenth century, and in the 1890s it became the Bowmore Distillery Co. Ltd. There is an older claim, dating from 1742, concerning Lagavulin, but the modern distillery was probably built nearer to 1824. The whisky is best known for its use in the famous blend 'White Horse', the name it subsequently became known as in the 1920s. The remaining three distilleries in operation today started production in the nineteenth century. Bruichladdich is the most westerly distillery in Scotland, and was built in 1818 by the Harvey family at the beginning of the period of legal distilling. From 1886 onwards they ran their Islay distillery as the Bruichladdich Distillery Co. Ltd. The Coal Ila distillery was founded in 1846, at a time when demand was rising, and Bunnahabhain was first distilled in 1883 at the height of the whisky boom in Argyll.

Quarrying

Although Argyll is not blessed with an abundance of natural minerals, extraction industries have played an important part in the industrial heritage of the area. Quarrying activities can be traced back to the Middle Ages, the oldest being the extraction of sandstone, or free stone as it is often called in the Statistical Accounts. The quarries at Carsaig Bay on Mull provided building materials used on Iona as early as the twelfth century, a connection that was maintained during the later medieval period when a number of new buildings were constructed. In 1795 the parish minister noted that the free stone here was for gentlemen's houses. The last known industrial use for this site was in the late nineteenth century, when the quarry was re-opened to supply stone for restoration work on Iona Abbey. The outcroppings of sandstone were not only used for the construction of dwellings; they also provided the millstones which ground the cereals that provided the staple diet of many local communities. Another use to which the stone was put concerned the end of life. In at least one location, Innimore Bay, headstones dating from the thirteenth to the nineteenth centuries can be found. Free stone was used in abundance locally and there is also evidence of its being exported out of the immediate area. Blocks of sandstone from Ardentallan quarry were shipped north to be used in the construction of the Caledonian Canal. The white limestone of Lochaline has also provided employment and industry in the past. Mining of this large deposit was started in 1940 to provide raw material for the manufacture of glass; at this period it was the only source of this material for the war effort. By 1952 some 430,000 tons had been produced and the works employed around fifty people. Local rock was also used in two of the great nineteenth-century feats of engineering, the lighthouses at Skerryvore and Ardnamurchan. The stone for both came from a quarry opened in 1839 at Camas Tuath on Mull. Once extracted it was taken by ship to a yard at Hynish on Tiree, where it was shaped and worked before being sent to the construction sites.

Tiree was also the location for one of the most successful marble quarries in Argyll. The pink marble of Belephetrish is first recorded in 1764 when blocks were sent to Inverary and Edinburgh, mainly to be fashioned for ornamental use. In 1791 the 5th duke of Argyll leased the works to a commercial company, but this venture barely lasted three years due to problems of transport and finance. The mid-eighteenth century witnessed a number of attempts by the Marble and Slate Company of Nether Lorne to extract marble from sites at Armaddy and Caddleton, the latter site employing thirteen men in 1750. Both ventures were short-lived due to the difficulty the company had in attracting skilled labour to the region and also to the technical problems of extraction. One other site in Argyll has witnessed the intermittent quarrying of marble over a period of centuries. The marble of Iona was worked from the middle ages, but 1907–14 was the last period when it was profitable to do so.

The quarrying of limestone was also an important economic activity in the past. Although many minor outcrops were worked, Balephetrish on Tiree being the most notable, the industry was centred on the island of Lismore. The extraction of lime for agricultural and building purposes was carried out at three main locations on the island. At An Sailean commercial extraction and burning started shortly before the end of the eighteenth century. Before long a pier and store house had been constructed along with two pairs of lime kilns. The working of the fifty-metre-high limestone cliffs provided employment, albeit intermittently, into the early years of the twentieth century. The two other sites on the island did not have such a long history. The works at Port Kilcheran were begun in 1803 by Bishop John Chisholm upon the establishment of a seminary there, and they closed in 1828 when the Catholic priests left the area. The community at Port Ramsay combined the working of the limestone with fishing during the first half of the nineteenth century, after which the cost of quarrying and shipping made it uneconomical.

Slate

The cutting and shaping of slate was a feature of life in many areas of Argyll from the medieval period onwards. During the eighteenth and nineteenth century it came to dominate the industrial and economic life of two distinct areas: Easdale and Ballachulish. The area around Easdale had been worked from the medieval period and Ballachulish from the end of the seventeenth century. Great expansion was experienced at both centres during the nineteenth century, when industrial innovation expanded operations and that in turn created more markets at home and abroad. The quarry at Easdale ceased operations in 1914 and Ballachulish was declared unprofitable in 1955. The demise of the industry coincided with the trend for roof coverings that are easier to fashion, such as tiles and wooden shingles.

The quarrying at Ballachulish was principally carried out at West and

East Laroch, but many other smaller workings were also in production. The first quarry in this area was opened by a Mr Stewart of Ballachulish in 1693. By the end of the eighteenth century some seventy-four families were employed and slate was being exported to England, Ireland and America. A hundred years later 322 people were employed in the industry. Peak production was reached during the last quarter of the nineteenth century when 600 employees quarried 26 million slates per annum. The remains of the workings can still be seen and are testimony to the skills of the people employed in this industry. The quarries in this area were normal surface workings cut into the hillside unlike those at the other Argyll centres of slate production.

There have been many slate quarries opened and worked on the islands of Nether Lorne. The remains of workings can be found at Cullipool, Black Mill Bay, Toberanochy, Luing, Belvicar and Ardencaple. The most extensive were at Easdale and the smaller island of Ellanbreich, which in the first half of the nineteenth century became connected to Seil by a causeway of slag generated from the intense quarrying activities being carried out. On the islands of Luing and Seil, the best slate was located close to or below ground level. Quarrying here was greatly developed in the first half of the eighteenth century in response to demand from the Clyde region and eastern Scotland. During this period, slate was extracted from locations above the watermark. In 1745 8 crews, of 4 men each, quarried 500,000 slates annually. By 1771, 19 crews were working the slate and 20 years later 300 men were employed in the industry. The company books for 1795 show that 5 million slates were being produced annually.

The nineteenth century saw the use of industrial technology and innovation to allow the company to extract slate from below the tidemark. Water pumps, initially driven by windmills and later by steam engines, made it possible to remove the slate from ever-deepening works. By 1849 the principal quarry was at Ellanbreich, with workings, going down to a considerable depth, producing a peak production of 9 million slates in 1869. The last slate was quarried from this complex in 1914, thereby ending an activity that had been practiced in the locality for nearly four centuries.

Mining

Seams of coal are not plentiful in the region and of those that have been found only the deposits located close to Campbeltown have been worked to any extent. It is not recorded when the pits were first worked at Kilkivan but by the late eighteenth century the leasee of the mineral rights was so confident in the potential reserves that he built a canal from the pithead to the town, a distance of 4.8 km (3 miles). Construction began in 1783 and when the canal was opened in 1791 delivery to the town exceeded forty loads a day. When this pit was exhausted in 1881, another working was opened at Drumlemble and this continued production until severe flooding forced abandonment in 1928. By the end of the Second World War the Glasgow Iron and Steel Company had re-opened the mine but it was not until nationalisation of the industry took place that it began to flourish once more. By the late 1950s 250 men were employed, raising over 2,500 tons of coal weekly.

The mining industry in Argyll was not confined to coal alone; shafts were sunk from the early eighteenth century in the pursuit of metals. The most famous metal associated with Argyll is undoubtedly Strontium, a metal with special qualities when used in the production of alloys. It was discovered at the location from which the name is derived and the industry was centred on Strontian and on Lurga in Gleann Dubh, Morvern. But other metals have provided the bulk of extraction, the most important of which was undoubtedly lead.

The Morvern Company, formed to exploit the deposits of lead and copper recently discovered by Sir Alexander Murray of Stanhope, erected its terminal buildings at Liddesdale on the south shore of Loch Sunart, some 6 km north-east of the lead-mine at Lurga. In 1733 it was reported that there were several diggings and a road in the glen. This mining company was short-lived; within twenty years the workings had been abandoned. On the recommendation of a visiting Swiss geologist the Argyll family re-opened the workings in 1803, but the scale of operations was small and activity had ceased by mid-century.

The Strontian area boasted extensive mining operations during the eighteenth and nineteenth centuries. The main workings were at Whitesmith, Middleshope and Bellsgrove, with other ore veins worked at Corrantree and Fee Donald. The operations commenced in the third and fourth decades of the eighteenth century when, the owner, Sir Alexander Murray, leased the mining rights to a group of partners, who in turn persuaded the York Building Company to investigate the possible mineral wealth of the area. This company employed an estimated 500 workers in the mid-1930s, many of whom were skilled miners from the north of England. But the company found itself overstretched financially and a succession of subsequent lessees found the works too expensive for long-term working and the veins of ore were only exploited intermittently thereafter.

The middle of the nineteenth century witnessed the most profitable period for the extraction of metals from the mines in this area. Lead was not the only metal extracted; silver veins were also tapped. In 1867–68 the silver from Feedonald amounted to 746 tons and from all the workings in the Strontian area 3,970 tons were extracted between 1852 and 1865. The reasonable quantities of ore from this period led to the workings being re-opened in 1901 under the management of James Crookston and John Robertson. Fifteen people were employed in the operations by 1904, the year in which it was decided the operations were not profitable. A final abortive attempt to make the mining of ore a successful business was attempted in 1950 but, like many before, it was short lived.

TABLE I Strontian, Argyll, Mining Information: Lead and Silver

Year	Ore tons	Metal tons	Silver oz
1847	50	30	
1848	236	141	
1849	250.7	151	
1850	290.2	226.5	
1851	288	225	
1852	270	208	1,000
1853	310	239	1,070
1854	174	130	536
1855	100	74	
1856	31	23	45
1857	51	39.2	78
1858	44.2	34	
1859	44.3	34	162
1860	21.2	16	64
1861	39	29.5	59
1862	142	106	210
1864	168	119.5	296
1865	300	217	450

Geological survey notes three mines Bellsgrove, Feedonald and Corrantree.
Ownership:
   1860–61 Bradley & Company
   1862–66 Sir T M Riddle
   1878–85 Strontian Mining Company

Other locations in Argyll that have been associated with the extraction of lead ore and silver include Islay, possibly (according to tradition) from Viking times, but certainly intermittently since the end of the seventeenth century. Government papers from the late nineteenth century show that both lead and silver were found between 1862 and 1896 when the Islay Mining Company was working the reserves. Between those dates 18,406 tons of silver and 1,544 tons of lead were extracted. Silver deposits have also been exploited at Silvercraigs, near Lochgilphead, and in the vicinity of Inveraray, although the workings have been abandoned for many years.

Gold was also extracted in small quantities from workings at Ardrishaig in the 1850s and during early years of the nineteenth century. Varying amounts of zinc, nickel and cobalt have also occasionally been mined in the last two centuries. Copper extraction at Kilfinan, Shirvan, Loch Fyne and Islay can be traced in old records. These mines operated when labour was cheap, but the discovery of large deposits in America and Africa rendered the mines in Argyll uneconomical.

TABLE 2 Island of Islay, Argyll, Mining Information: Lead and Silver

Year	Ore tons	Metal tons	Silver tons	Value
1862	34	24	290	
1863	34	25.5	331	
1864	60	45		
1866	155	116	1,708	
1867	291	218.5	2,570	
1868	218	161	2,415	
1869	121.5	85	1,350	
1870	70	50	840	
1871	13	9.5	113	
1873	100	75		
1874	80	65	1,071	£1,200
1875	20	15		
1876	42	30.3	150	£576
1877	200	146.5	1,864	£2,700 (est)
1878	250	190	2,793	£3,000
1879	181	135	1,687	£1,991
1880	50	39	1,224	£475
1883	118	82.6		£1,062
1896	40	31		

Ownership:
    1864–72 Isle of Islay Mining Company
    1873–76 Islay Lead Mining Company
    1877–96 Islay Mining Company

Employment:	underground	surface	total
1896	8	8	16

Iron Smelting

A metal-related industry that did provide long-term employment in the area was iron-smelting but it relied upon the timber of the area to be profitable and not the raw material. Traces of old iron-workings occur in many areas of Argyll, with Kintyre displaying far more than most other areas. Who financed and operated these small-scale workings is not clear. What is evident is that these sites comprise the remnants of small bloomeries, usually identified as a mound of slag and cinders. It is thought that most are from the seventeenth and eighteenth centuries, but some may be much older. The first large-scale smelting in Argyll can be traced to Glen Kinglass *c.* 1725. The Irish operators located their furnace in this area because of the plentiful supply of trees which could be turned into the charcoal that fuelled the process. Within three decades, Argyll witnessed two more extensive iron works. The first, at Bonawe, was started in 1753 and the other, at Furnace, one year later. Both were operated by an English company. The choice of locations was determined by proximity to abundant forest reserves for fuel and an accessible sea route for imports of raw material and exports of finished products.

The operations at Glen Kinglass, which stood close to the shore of upper Loch Etive, are noted in old estate documents of the first quarter of the eighteenth century. In the early 1720s, timber rights were negotiated between local landowners and Mr Roger Murphy of Enniskillen and Captain Arthur Galbraith of Dublin. By February 1725 an iron forge 'had been erected and built' on the site. This venture did not last long, the last mention of its operations being in 1738, when the company lost its rights to timber extraction in the area.

In 1754–55 the Duddon Furnace Company of Furness in Cumbria negotiated with local landowners the right to establish a new iron-smelting works on the shores of Loch Fyne at a place called Craleckan. By 1799 a contemporary report notes that it was 'a considerable iron-work', now carried on by the Argyll Furnace Company. The ore was imported from the west of England, and the smelting performed by charcoal, made from the wood cut in the neighbourhood. The company was a partnership between the duke of Argyll and the Lake District company. By the time that the operations were closed in 1812, the average output had been around 700 tons per year. There were various reasons for the closure but the overriding fact was that new technology, in the form of coke smelting, made the operations redundant.

The third iron smelting location in Argyll was also the longest in production. The Bonawe Iron Furnace, located on the south shore of Loch Etive between Airds Bay and the mouth of the River Awe, was founded in 1752–53. A partnership, later to become known as the Newland Company, was headed by Richard Ford, an iron master from Ulverston in Furness. This partnership was a rival to the operators of the Argyll Furnace Company, both in Cumbria and in Argyll. Two long-term agreements, concerning wood rights, with Sir Duncan Campbell of Lochnell and the Earl of Breadalbane ensured a supply of charcoal for the fledgling works. This operation was intended to complement the companies' works in Furness by smelting raw materials into pig iron, which was then transported back to Cumbria. It has been estimated that the cost of processing in Argyll was, even with transport costs, slightly less it was at the iron works owned by the company in the Lake District. This was undoubtedly due to the abundance of locally made charcoal and possibly the use of local limestone sources in the fluxing process. In its heyday upwards of 600 people earned a living from the works. At the expiry of the original leases on wood rights, in 1863, a new lease was negotiated by a charcoal manufacturer who sub-let the furnace back to the company. The Lorne Furnace Company, as it was now called, carried on for another decade until it was finally closed down in 1874. Although it had survived as an iron-smelting complex for over a century the new technologies that were being utilised in the industry meant it could not compete any longer.

Other Industries

Numerous other industrial ventures have historical associations with the area; some, like those already noted, have left their mark on the landscape, whereas others can only be traced through contemporaneous writings. The gunpowder works at Melfort is in the first category and the Argyll shipyards in the latter.

The gunpowder works at Melfort were established in 1838 when the owners of the Lorne Furnace purchased the Melfort estate from Colonel John Campbell. The essential ingredients of gunpowder, saltpetre and sulphur, were imported from abroad. The only local ingredient was the packing agent – locally produced charcoal. The necessary manpower and waterpower were also found locally.

Shipbuilding is not readily associated with the area, but it flourished in the past. The extensive forests of the region were harvested to build waterborne craft throughout the ages, from hollowed-out logs to birlinns. However, the first evidence of modern shipbuilding techniques being used is in the work of John and Hugh Stevenson of Oban. They commenced operations in 1778 and at least ten vessels are attributable to them during the period 1790 to 1807, the largest of which was 145 tons. The full extent of their labours is unknown as is the exact time when the yard closed. The industry was revived in 1867 and provided work, although at times intermittently, till its final demise in 1951. Throughout this period shipbuilding, yacht and boat building, along with a period of seaplane servicing, sustained and maintained the workforce. Oban was not the only centre to harness the craft and engineering skills required. Both Campbeltown and Tobermory are mentioned in Parliamentary Papers as shipbuilding locations at the end of the eighteenth and the beginning of the nineteenth century. The number of vessels constructed at Tobermory is not given but Campbeltown is accredited with seven. Later in the century the Trench shipyard was opened here, employing 300 men at its height of production. During the next 45 years 116 vessels were built – 151,000 tons in total. The largest of these was the 4,363-ton *Roquette*, built in 1918. The same skills that were required in the larger centres have also provided employment in the many other small boatyards that have operated along the numerous sheltered bays and sea-lochs of the indented coastline of mainland and island Argyll.

Many other short-lived industries operated in Argyll during the age of improvements: intermittent rock extraction, marble quarries, linen and woollen mills – but none could provide long-term continuous employment to its workforce. Even the fishing industry, thought to be one of the area's greatest resources, did not deliver. It did employ at least 130 boats, each with a crew of three or four, during the hey-day of the herring shoals *c.* 1800, and continued to provide work for hundreds of people for decades after, but it did not and could not cater for the thousands who needed employment to pay rents. One reason for this was that fishermen from other areas of Scotland started to fish in Argyll waters. It was not unusual to find boats and crews from the Clyde, Ayrshire and Aberdeen chasing the shoals of herring. Longliners from these areas also looked for ling and cod, and east-coast merchants owned the leases for salmon. The commercialism of the fishing trade made it difficult for all but a few local fishermen to compete. The removal of a government subsidy for boats engaged in the herring fishing during the 1820s made it even more so.

Towards the middle of the nineteenth century the precarious economy of Argyll was struck a killing blow. A famine caused by the failure of the potato crop and the resulting unpaid rents led the landowners to look for more reliable ways of earning from their lands. The answer was an expansion of the sheep walks and removal of the people who could not pay arrears. The outcome was the 'clearances', from which almost no part of Argyll was exempt.

By 1827 the landlords, who had feared the consequences of outward migration and lobbied for controls, were now changing their minds. Tenants with money and ambition had been leaving while the poorer had stayed behind. The financial collapse of the kelp industry meant that many were struggling with rent payments and the landlords were losing revenue. By the late 1830s, and the first wide-scale potato failure, the need for change had become apparent. As already noted, a sheep economy had been making inroads to much of the area and it was this solution that many turned to. Eviction orders quadrupled in the next twenty years and the full weight of the law was brought to bear upon debtor tenants. *The New Statistical Account* abounds with accounts of removal and emigration.

The once-productive kelp islands of Ulva and Gometra were almost totally cleared between 1846 and 1851. The population of Iona fell sharply from 520 residents in 1831 to 236 less than 30 years later. On Tiree evictions left barely half the population still living there by 1880, 600 of whom were cleared to Canada in 1849. In the Ross of Mull, it was reported that the area was in total misery by 1849 due to removal, famine and poverty. Eviction started early on the small islands close to Mull, with Calgary Island cleared in 1822 and the Treshnish Isles finally emptied in 1834. On Jura, the population was 1,000 in the early nineteenth century, 1,300 by 1831 but, thanks to clearance policies, down to a few hundred by 1840. The 1840s witnessed a second period of potato crop failure, and this accelerated the process of eviction. It would be forty years before government addressed the plight of the remaining people. This intervention eventually led to the Crofting Acts of the 1880s.

The perception that the majority of clearances occurred towards the end of what is generally recognised as the improving period in Scottish history is based upon events in southern and central Scotland and not on events

TABLE 3 Population Argyllshire 1755–1951

Year	Total
1755 *	66,286
1795 *	76,101
1801	81,277
1811	86,541
1821	97,316
1831	100,973
1841	97,371
1851	89,298
1861	79,724
1871	75,679
1881	76,468
1891	75,003
1901	73,642
1911	70,902
1921	70,902
1931	63,050
1951	63,270

* The first figure is from Websters' survey and the second from OSA Sinclair.

in the western Highlands. To many observers the initial progress of improvement from an agrarian to an industrial society was complete by 1850. A new revolution was about to take place; science and engineering were being harnessed to make Britain, and especially central Scotland, the workshop of the world. In Argyll and many other parts of the west and north of Scotland the picture was somewhat different. The harsh and brutal facts of the new commercialism were about to make their mark. In 1850, there were no large-scale industrial towns or complexes in Argyll, no comprehensive transport system and no abundance of natural resources to be exploited in the manner they had been elsewhere in Britain.

CHAPTER THIRTEEN

Modern Argyll

THERE ARE FEW NATIONS that can point to a place, or a time of origin. The Scotland we are familiar with today originated at Dunadd in the ninth century, and Argyll has continued to play significant roles in this nation's recent history. Contributions from the lands of Argyll have come as cultural, religious, artistic, economic, military, social and industrial input to modern Scotland. The region has witnessed migration and resettlement for generations, yet Argyll is defined as much by tradition and identity today as in the time of Kenneth McAlpin.

To understand the county, one must be acquainted with its territory. The boundaries have undergone significant changes since title was conferred on the Campbells of Loch Awe in the middle of the fifteenth century. Argyll in the twenty-first century covers a wide area – a hundred miles from Appin to Campbeltown and eighty miles from Tiree to Helensburgh. Parts of the region are moderately populated, with a handful of main towns; only a few dozen of the countless islands are inhabited, with many dwellings spread over small settlements and isolated holdings.

Argyll County Council and Bute County Council administered this expanse of western Scotland from 1889 until the reorganisation of local government in 1975. Civic pride and local identities were diluted by the introduction of European regional authorities, and the public was confused by the obscure relationship between Strathclyde Regional Council and Argyll and Bute District Council. In 1975 Argyll lost the spectacularly desolate Ardnamurchan peninsula, busy Ballachulish, legendary Glencoe and the oddly industrial landscape of Kinlochleven to the Highland region. The re-introduction of single-tier authorities in 1996 restored Ardnamurchan and relieved Dunbartonshire of the relatively populous and picturesque districts of Helensburgh and Lomond.

The inclusion of Helensburgh and Lomond, including the Rosneath peninsula, within Argyll's boundaries has brought central Scotland closer, though there has been a naturally developing relationship between Lomond and Argyll as border districts for centuries. Today families travelling from Argyll think nothing of making a two- or three-hundred mile round trip for shopping in and around Glasgow, while opposite incursions into the countryside are made by city-dwellers on breaks, increasingly to their own holiday homes. The consequences of this alternating administrative landscape do not necessarily benefit the denizens of the upper Clyde, or the inhabitants of rural Argyll. Legitimate and convincing concerns have been raised by both sides: newcomers complain about high council tax subsidising unproductive rural areas, and Argyll veterans argue that larger population centres are favoured for deployment of development resources. Native couples struggle to compete for private housing while the influx of settling families has kept many village schools from closure.

But the historic links are incontrovertible. Helensburgh has long been a popular holiday and day-trip destination with visitors from Glasgow. Indeed Henry Bell, designer of the *Comet*, Europe's first commercially viable steamboat launched on the Clyde in 1812, was the town's first provost. The vessel was wrecked in Argyll waters, off Craignish point, fifty years later. From the first half of the nineteenth century to the 1960s, visitors borne on Clyde steamers descended in their thousands upon coastal towns on the Clyde and the Argyll coast. They spent their money in local shops, bars, hotels and guesthouses, and established a tradition of leisure breaks in the west Highlands that continues to this day. The advent of the railway in 1857 encouraged Helensburgh's expansion and its evolution into a wealthy Glasgow suburb. Notable villas by William Leiper and Alexander Paterson reflect the prosperity of the late Victorian and Edwardian eras, and Charles Rennie MacKintosh's Hill House is still a model of simplicity and elegance. Every Scottish schoolchild should know that the inventor of television, John Logie Baird, was born in Helensburgh in 1888. But it is doubtful if the curriculum teaches that nearby Faslane is the home of the United Kingdom's nuclear deterrent, the controversial Clyde Submarine Base. Garelochhead is home to the largest army training camp in Scotland, and between these sites the Ministry of Defence has established itself as Argyll's biggest employer.

The waters around the Firth of Clyde, Gare Loch and Loch Long have always been popular with yachtsmen and pleasure boaters. The neighbouring Holy Loch was, until 1992, the service depot for United States Navy submarines. Some tranquillity has been restored since the US withdrawal, but a few ugly installations remain in and around the loch. While American service personnel were stationed here, Dunoon enjoyed a revival of the fortune it had during the golden years of passenger steamer traffic. The town once boasted more taxis per capita than anywhere else in Europe, but those heady days, characterised by big spenders, dream weddings and unplanned pregnancies are long gone, and the fine seaside facades of Dunoon mask a community facing the considerable challenges of social and economic regeneration. Frequent ferries to Gourock and fast onward motorway and rail links to Glasgow should make the Cowal peninsula an attractive commuter base or an accessible and inexpensive holiday retreat. The Loch Lomond and Trossachs National Park, Scotland's first, extends into Cowal, affording extra tourism development potential for parts of Argyll, from which the entire county may benefit.

West of Loch Striven the narrows of the Kyles of Bute separate the Isle of Bute from the mainland. Until 1975 the County of Bute also encompassed the Isles of Arran, Inchmarnock and the Cumbraes, but these neighbours were lost during the creation of Argyll and Bute Council. The main settlement, Rothesay, is enjoying resurgent popularity as a touring destination, following decades of depression commensurate with the decline of the Clyde steamer trade. Mount Stuart supplanted twelfth-century Rothesay Castle as the seat of the earls of Bute in the 1680s. The present house was begun by the 3rd Marquis in 1877, and in 1995 was opened to the public. The attraction proved so popular with visitors that a striking new visitor centre was opened in 2001. John Stuart, 3rd earl of Bute, distinguished himself as the first Scot to hold office as Prime Minister of Great Britain in 1762. Ferries still operate between Rothesay and Wemyss Bay on the Clyde coast, offering similar commuting opportunities as Dunoon. The much shorter crossing between Colintraive and Rhubodach connects Bute more closely to the rest of Argyll, despite the long arm of Loch Fyne almost cleaving Cowal and Lomond from mid Argyll, Kintyre and Lorne.

Between Tarbet and Arrochar Major William Caulfield's military road and bridges are still visible from the mountain pass known as the Rest and be Thankful. Built between 1747 and 1749, the route was still in use as the arterial A83 until the 1930s, since when significant alterations and improvements have been made. The existence of military engineering so close to Glasgow demonstrates the unsettling impact the Jacobite uprisings of 1715 and 1745 had on government, and the considerable expense of imposing security, even in the comparatively accessible western Highlands.

The terminus of Caulfield's original route from Dumbarton was Inveraray, seat of the Campbells and the duchy of Argyll. Then the place was a fashionable new town, created to afford Archibald Campbell, 3rd duke of Argyll, more privacy in a new castle begun in 1745. Inveraray had become the first royal burgh in Argyll in 1648 and featured its own sheriff and court. The parish church in the main street dates from 1798, and was originally divided into two sections: one for services in English, one for Gaelic. The town prospered from the herring fishery in the eighteenth and nineteenth centuries, but dwindling stocks in Loch Fyne forced the burghers there and elsewhere to seek alternative revenue streams. Tourism has been at the heart of the local economy for over a century. Inveraray was on the pleasure steamer route from Glasgow and Ardrishaig, and remains a popular stop for road travellers. Military presence was felt here again during the Second World War when the court of offices at Cherry Park in the castle grounds were used as a Combined Operations Training Establishment.

While there is still limited employment in farming, creel fishing and forestry operations, Argyll Estates, fish farming and hospitality are the principal growth areas. Besides Inveraray Castle, the nineteenth-century courthouse and jail have been converted into a unique visitor attraction, and there is a maritime museum at the pier. The town sustains several large hotels, a caravan and camping site, and the famous Loch Fyne Oyster Bar is only a few miles away at Cairndow. A monument on nearby Cladich Hill honours Neil Munro, celebrated creator of *Para Handy* and one of the town's famous sons.

South of the town, on Loch Fyneside, the village of Inverleacann became Furnace in the late eighteenth century when abundant local supplies of oak were exploited for charcoal to fire the iron-smelting furnaces. Production ceased in 1843. Quarrying was established as the principal industry and is continued in the village today. After a long struggle against closure, nearby Crarae Gardens are now in the care of the National Trust for Scotland. Created in 1925 by George Campbell, this woodland setting is famous worldwide for its collection of rhododendrons, azaleas, eucalyptus and other Himalayan flora.

Lochgilphead replaced Inveraray and Dunoon as the administrative centre of Argyll in 1890 and in 1975 the then District Council moved to new headquarters in Kilmory. Kilmory House (affectionately or derogatorily known as Kilmory Castle) was acquired by Argyll County Council specifically for use by the new authority, and occupies an elevated site to the south of the town comprising formal gardens, mature woods and parkland. Lochgilphead, close to the heart of the ancient kingdom of Dalriada, prospered through the livestock trade, mills, herring fishing, a distillery, a ropeworks and the Crinan Canal. The connection with the rich prehistoric landscape of Kilmartin is strong. In 1997 an outstanding independent archaeological museum was opened in the village's former manse. The success of the project was predicated on the volume of traffic on the A816 between Lochgilphead and Oban, and in no small way relied upon firm community support. The museum and visitor centre has won international acclaim, and continues to welcome visitors from all over the world, all year round.

Ardrishaig, the eastern terminus of the Crinan Canal, grew from a fishing hamlet to a prosperous village, which continued to enjoy investment and development until the 1970s, when the seaward side of the main street was demolished to make way for car parking. Passengers from Glasgow would take the *Linnet* through the canal to Crinan, where they connected with the *Chevalier* bound for Oban and Fort William. The *Loch Fyne* was the last scheduled passenger vessel connecting Glasgow and Ardrishaig, and the service was withdrawn in 1972. Since the later part of the nineteenth century there has been a psychiatric hospital in Lochgilphead in one form or another, and today the Argyll and Bute Hospital is one of mid Argyll's largest employers.

The Crinan Canal was never finished to a satisfactory standard, nor did it convey the volume of commercial traffic necessary for profit. Commerce favoured the speed and associated lower costs of rail freight by the middle of the nineteenth century, and inland waterways fell into decline.

The 1960s witnessed a dramatic increase in the popularity of the automobile, and opened up the canal corridor to trippers not arriving or passing through by boat. This trend increased in the 1970s and 1980s, as improvements were made to the principal routes into mid Argyll from Glasgow, Oban and Kintyre via Ayrshire and Arran.

In addition to increased visitor numbers, settlement in mid Argyll rose as young professionals relocated from central Scotland and other parts of the UK, eschewing urban career progression in favour of self-employment in a flourishing rural economy. New wealth was created during this period by and in response to improvements to the hospitality and leisure industries. Refurbishment and extension of existing hotels and the construction of new ones, development of static caravan sites, self-catering units and marina facilities were at the forefront of the tourism economy. Local government reform precipitated the expansion of sub-regional headquarters, and new-build housing to accommodate the influx of personnel; and the new aquaculture industry – salmon, trout, mussel and oyster farms on varying scales – occupied most sea-lochs from around 1973 to 1990, intensively supported by subsidy in the early years from the Highlands and Islands Development Board.

The corollary of these changes, in canal navigation terms, was an increase in the number of pleasure vessels in local private ownership. With year-round sheltered moorings available to owners in nearby Lochs Craignish, Melfort and Sween, demand for passages between the Clyde and the western cruising grounds went into decline. Since the early 1990s British Waterways Scotland has sold six former lock keeper's cottages and the original canal manager's house to stem operational losses and meet ever-increasing maintenance costs. Nevertheless the Crinan Canal remains a lovingly preserved working transport monument, which has become a way of life for the communities that line its banks.

What is left of Loch Fyne's fishing fleet is headquartered in Tarbert, no longer the centre of the herring industry. Fewer boats are forced to farther waters in pursuit of ever-decreasing stocks of prawns, scallops, crabs and lobsters. Just one mile separates the East and West Lochs, and from this isthmus southward Kintyre proper begins. The ferry terminal at Kennacraig on the West Loch handles large volumes of vehicles and passengers bound for Port Askaig or Port Ellen on Islay, depending on weather conditions or the time of year, and Tarbert's hospitality and retail industries have benefited from the proximity of this service. In recent years the village has had difficulty sustaining a heritage-centre-cum-arts venue, indicative of a population focused more on labour than leisure. The village has always been popular as a tourist destination, particularly for yachts sailing the west coast. The Tarbert Series, one of the UK's premier sailing events, is held here every year, bringing competitors from all over the world and attendant economic benefits.

Kinlochkilkerran became Campbeltown in 1607 when the 7th earl of

Argyll founded a plantation settlement, importing families from Renfrew-shire and Ayrshire to help stabilise a troublesome locality. The town grew into a major fishing port and the fishing industry is still active. Between 1817 and 1880 no fewer than thirty-four distilleries were producing whisky, but the Prohibition years in the United States forced most to close by the 1920s. Springbank single malt is produced here to this day. More recent years brought textile production, a shipyard and a plastics factory. Large-scale dairy farming co-existed with the military installation at Machrihan-ish, until 1996 a joint British and American Air Force base with the longest runway in Europe. The civil air terminal still operates daily services to Glasgow, knocking two hours off the journey time by road. The former hangars and workshops are now used by a wind-turbine manufacturer, making ideal use of local assets. One of the most powerful wind-farms in the UK is being developed in Kintyre, and there are plans for more throughout Argyll. The projected reintroduction of the car ferry service to Ballycastle in Northern Ireland might help open the entire peninsula up to visitors and commercial traffic. Although Kintyre is a long way by road from Glasgow, Edinburgh, Inverness and the Highlands its ferry network (to the islands of Arran, Gigha and Islay and to Portavadie on the Cowal peninsula) renders the area one of Argyll's most important transport links.

Oban is really Argyll's principal town, its wealth and status founded on its links to the Hebrides. The powerful combination of steamship naviga-tion and the railway drove the town's population up from just 1,000 in 1819 to 5,000 in 1899. Transport and tourism remain the principal eco-nomic generators for the area: ferry services run to the islands of Barra, Coll, Colonsay, Kerrera, Lismore, Mull, South Uist and Tiree. The Vic-torians built splendid hotels to cater to this burgeoning trade, some of which survive more or less intact, and the town quickly established itself as the main town of the west Highlands for leisure and a connecting centre for persons or goods making onward journeys. Trains, though infrequent by nineteenth-century standards, still leave Oban for Glasgow, Mallaig and Fort William and the town is pivotally positioned for road routes to the north, south and east.

Banker John Stewart McCaig replicated Rome's Colosseum on the town's skyline in 1897. What began as a labour-creating act of civic phi-lanthropy was never completed, but the tower, or folly, has distinguished Oban for over a century. A squadron of Sunderland flying boats was sta-tioned here during the Second World War; adding a new dimension to a long and varied maritime tradition; today nearby Connel airfield is suc-cessfully run as a landing strip and refuelling stop for light aircraft. If the authorities could be persuaded to grant an operating licence for passenger planes, Oban's reputation as one of Scotland's transport hubs would be assured.

The proximity of sea and islands has had the most profound influence on the development or decline of most places in mainland Argyll. There are thousands of miles of engagingly ragged coastline, fjordic sea-lochs and a seascape of archipelagoes. *Earragael* – The Coastline of the Gaels – was won and settled centuries ago by seafaring folk whose descendants proudly defend their insular existence. For some, Argyll *is* the islands.

Mull is the largest of them and the easiest to get to. Forty-five minutes steaming with Caledonian MacBrayne is all that separates Oban from Craignure. The majority of residents and visitors are drawn to colourful Tobermory in the north-east, with its commanding views of Kilchoan on the Ardnamurchan peninsula. Mull's modern economy mirrors the rest of mainland Argyll, with one or two notable particularities. Island wildlife tours have flourished here for some years, including offshore whale-watching boat trips. A narrow gauge railway steams between Craignure and Torosay, a Scots baronial castle built in 1856. There was a dramatic population increase on Mull from the middle of the nineteenth century, peaking at 10,600 in 1861. The island of Ulva in Loch Tuath was notoriously cleared of its 500 inhabitants between 1846 and 1851 to make way for agricultural improvements – one of Argyll's few large-scale forced depopulations.

Pilgrims must negotiate the long single-track road to Fionnphort in the southwest, from where the ferry makes the short crossing to Iona. From the founding of a monastery by St Columba in the middle of the sixth century, this small island became the centre of the Celtic Church until political power was moved out of Argyll in the ninth century, the Church of Rome achieving pre-eminence around 1200. Today the Iona economy is supported almost entirely by visitors, even secular ones. Some crofting and farming still takes place and there is a modest fishing fleet, but visitors' needs are met by passenger boat trips to Staffa, two hotels, numerous guest houses and bed and breakfast establishments. Historic Scotland now manages the restored abbey, and the remainder of the island is in the care of the National Trust for Scotland.

Nowadays Tiree is more famous for international windsurfing competitions and its military communications 'golfball' structure than anything else. Seventy-five square kilometres of wind-blown machair and sand dunes, the island supported a population of 4,450 in 1831. Evictions and famines reduced numbers to 2,700 in 1881, a figure matched today only in the height of summer. There are miles of unspoilt sandy beaches that attract holidaymakers, and there is a thriving seasonal infrastructure to support them. Beyond tourism the principal industry is agriculture. Ferries connect the main township of Scarinish with Oban up to five times a week and there are daily flights to Glasgow and Barra. Neighbouring Coll is popular with visitors interested in its archaeological heritage, including an unusual island souterrain at Arnabost and the standing stones at Totronald. In common with Tiree, Coll has a windswept landscape, given over mostly to smallholdings.

Rich archaeological remains and Christian traditions closely associated with Iona are striking features of Lismore. The island is low-lying, fertile and productive. Limeworks augmented income from crofting and fishing, but could not support the population and many families emigrated to North Carolina from 1775. In 1831 the population was 1,497, and by 1885 was down to 600. There are fewer than 150 residents on the island today, but its splendid setting at the convergence of Loch Linnhe and the Lynn of Lorne, in the shadow of the great mountains of Morvern, has made it popular with visitors who have a choice of ferries from Oban or Port Appin.

Its position between Mull and Oban bay made Kerrera a natural droving station. Cattle landed from Mull were swum to the mainland. Nowadays its main industry is fish farming, but a home-workers' co-operative is well established and provides a base for a range of services on and off the island. A monument at the northern end of the island commemorates David Hutcheson, an early business partner of David MacBrayne, and the first man to establish scheduled ferry services between Oban and the Islands.

Clachan Bridge, designed by Thomas Telford and built in 1792, connects the Isle of Seil to the mainland twenty-four kilometres south of Oban. Seil and neighbouring Easdale, Belnahua and Luing produced much of Scottish slate in the eighteenth and nineteenth centuries. The settlements of Balvicar, Ellanabeich, Cullipool and Toberonochy were built on the industry, which came to end in 1965. Easdale island supports an award-winning museum, which tells the story of the slate islands, and is reached by a passenger-only ferry from Seil.

Islay is synonymous with whisky. There are seven operational distilleries on the island, producing very distinctive single malts and maintaining a profitable export business. The villages of Caol Ila, Bruichladdich and Bunnahabhainn, Laphroig, Lagavulin, Ardbeg and Bowmore were established by the whisky industry: Port Ellen and Port Askaig are ferry terminals, the latter connecting with Feolin on the Isle of Jura. Livestock farming is still Islay's main industry, despite the recent closure of the creamery, which was supported by local dairy herds.

The island is well served by hotels and other holiday accommodation, and is particularly popular with ornithologists. The wintering population of barnacle geese is in the region of 25,000, and is accompanied by about 4,000 white-fronts. A control system is in force, which allows farmers to cull or scare the birds in order to protect grazing and crops. As on most other islands, small fishing fleets prevail under increasingly difficult operating conditions, but traditional pursuits are gradually being replaced with tourism-related businesses. A splendid visitor centre, recently opened at Finlaggan, evokes the power of the Lordship of the Isles. Almost the entire western seaboard of Scotland was controlled from here and from Dunivaig at the south of the island. Clan Donald did not fully relinquish authority over these extensive territories until the Highlanders were defeated at Culloden in 1746.

Jura's only village, Craighouse, is home to the majority of the island's 200 inhabitants, the distillery, the hotel and the grass airstrip at Knockrome. The island is famous for a population of 5,000 red deer, which attract stalkers to sporting estates. Most islanders are engaged as estate workers, farm independently or work in forest operations. Literary enthusiasts trek 32 kilometres from Craighouse to Barnhill at the northern end of the island, in which isolation George Orwell wrote *Nineteen Eighty-four* in the summers between 1946 and 1949.

Fourteen kilometres west of Jura lie Colonsay and Oronsay. Warmed by the north Atlantic drift current, these islands feature breathtaking unspoilt beaches and abundant flora and fauna, which attract holidaymakers from home and abroad. The spectacular ruins of an Augustinian priory survive on Oronsay, just one of many sites alleged to have been visited by St Columba. A school of stonemasons produced grave-slabs and crosses here until the sixteenth century. The islands have *Iomairt aig an Oir* (Initiative at the Edge) designation – an initiative to assist the economic and social development of peripheral communities. Today Colonsay is the unlikely headquarters of a thriving independent publishing house, specialising in preserving Scotland's literary past and encouraging new talent.

In 2002 the Isle of Gigha, off Kintyre, became the property of its inhabitants. The island had had a succession of owners in the last thirty years, and was facing an uncertain future. When the island came up for sale yet again the islanders made a successful community purchase application to the Scottish Land Fund. A trust was established to raise money to settle a loan for a percentage of the purchase price, from various fund-raising activities, including the sale of Achamore House. This country mansion surrounded by exotic gardens is in the care of the National Trust for Scotland. The deal to secure heritable property for the islanders and their descendants echoed recent community buyouts in Knoydart, North Harris and the Isle of Eigg. The novelty of the situation has stimulated an increase in visitors, on which the island's economy largely relies. There is some fishing and a fish farming operation, and the creamery at Achamore produces a range of fine cheeses, which are exported worldwide. The ferry between Ardminish and Tayinloan on the mainland takes only twenty minutes and is particularly popular with day-trippers.

There are other islands, too numerous to mention, which together contribute enormously to the variety of Argyll. Large, small, flat, hilly, inhabited, empty, inaccessible, or connected to the mainland by strand or causeway: these places have special meaning for all of us who live on larger islands. The bond between land and people is complex and strong – stronger still on some islands where people have endured lifetimes of hardship.

Flourishing tourism economies on the islands and mainland of Argyll were stalled by two world wars, but technological advancement and increased wealth have assisted the industry's recovery. The number of ferry routes may have declined in the last thirty years, but the volume of vehicles secured to the decks of Caledonian MacBrayne and Western ferries has increased. Trains no longer pass through places that have stations, but these locations are no less popular in the era of the family car. The reality of modern Argyll is summertime motoring angst: drivers forced to glacial pace by any combination of HGV, coach, caravan or sightseer, each of whom is making direct contributions to a fragile economy. Forest Enterprise have addressed the road congestion and environmental impact issues of timber haulage by establishing a bulk sea freight service from Ardrishaig to the Ayrshire coast, thus minimising the use of heavy lorries on primary routes.

The appeal of Argyll is not, however, confined to its towns or island communities. There are so many scenic and interesting places to be found in the connecting landscapes of the hinterland. Appin, Benderloch, Etive, Orchy, Fyne, Awe, Craignish and Knapdale – each district supports villages and settlements, each with its own micro-economy and each with its own local pride and identity.

Civic identity is as transitory as the population. Gaelic has long been replaced by English as the dominant language of the region. Some settlements have a minority of inhabitants who can claim local ancestry over more than one generation, the greying skies of inevitability felt heaviest by those old-timers whose families moved away as soon as they could, and have never looked back. But there is a newfound passion for the rustic playground of childhood. Children born in the 1960s and 1970s have returned in extraordinary numbers to raise their own families in the places they themselves were brought up. The traditional pattern of being forced to go away to college or university, or even to find a job is facing challenges from flexible learning and modern employment opportunities. Vocational qualifications are made available through Argyll College, a partner in the laudably ambitious University of the Highlands and Islands project. Learning centres have sprung up in most population centres, offering a variety of training opportunities tailored to regional workplace demands. Breakthroughs in information and communications technology have moderated the remoteness of some locations, and long-standing obstacles no longer affect the ways in which certain types of business are conducted.

Entrepreneurial and creative individuals, from Argyll and elsewhere, have identified commercial opportunities or cultural vacuums and tried to make a difference, with varying degrees of success. Potteries, art galleries, arts venues and festivals, museums and heritage centres, recording studios and music labels, independent local radio stations, alternative therapy clinics, boarding kennels, equestrian centres, ballet schools, seaplane and helicopter services have all been introduced to Argyll in the last twenty-five years. Some ventures have endured and expanded; the time for others may not yet have come. All over the world businesses fail every

day, many facing lesser challenges than Argyll's geography, low population
density and endemic fondness for preserving traditions. The modern spirit
of enterprise may have evolved from a gritty native determination, or it
may have arrived with incoming families, but it characterises Argyll as a
microcosmic mercantile Scotland.

In February 2002 the population of Argyll and Bute was estimated at
91,000, less than 2 per cent of the population of Scotland. The official guess
is a decline to 80,500 by 2016, more through the effect of falling birth rates
than migration. As Argyll & Bute occupies nearly 9 per cent of the nation's
landmass, observers could be forgiven for assuming there is plenty of room
for more people. But housing in Argyll is in short supply. In some areas,
nowadays, demand exceeds supply to the extent that offering 50 per cent
over the asking price of a desirable house is routinely needed to clinch the
deal. Mid-range properties, a great many originally bought by local authority tenants, change hands infrequently, precipitating a need for new munic-
ipal housing. Housing associations have largely assumed responsibility for
building new houses, in partnerships between private developers and the
local authority, but waiting lists are long and lower-income families face
long periods in accommodation not particularly suited to their needs.
Planned housing 'zones' may have to be redrawn, and innovation applied
to development in scenic or environmentally sensitive areas if Argyll is to
maintain a healthy, socially improving and economically stimulating
settlement equilibrium.

Many of the features that attract visitors and settlers to Argyll were created or developed by owners of estates, great and small. From the late
eighteenth to the early twentieth century, wealth accumulated by colonial
trade and domestic industry was conspicuously applied to the creation of
spectacular country houses. Ardkinglass, Barbreck, Calgary, Glenbarr, Kilberry, Poltalloch, Minard, Scotnish – a cavalcade of outrageous
architectural curiosities, but each the seat of improved land management.
The improvement programs favoured large farms, the introduction of
sheep and efficient working practices. Much of the landscape at Kilmartin,
for example, was shaped during planned improvements in the nineteenth
century. Sporting forests of native deciduous trees were gradually replaced
with imported softwood plantations after the First World War, in a cycle
of intensive forestry which prevails to this day. These developments combined to drive rural populations down, and although Argyll does not have
much clearance history, some communities were undoubtedly forced to
move elsewhere. Some of the displaced found work and shelter in larger
regional towns or the Glasgow sprawl; others took ships to Canada and
America, establishing a pattern of settlement, migration and resettlement
still characteristic of Argyll today.

As wind farms take their place in the landscape, they typify the oddly
contradictory human dimension of Argyll. Residents opposed to them on
environmental grounds support the principle of harnessing renewable

energy. Critics of 'unsightly' installations could have much uglier things on their horizons. So far Argyll has resisted drive-throughs and multi-storey car parks, but consumer pressure is an ultimately irresistible force. Silage has replaced hay as the winter fodder of choice, bridges replace ferries, and village pubs and post offices close for want of custom, yet just along the road, new houses rub gables with the crumbling stonework left by earlier inhabitants. Gaelic is once again taught to schoolchildren, and small groups of adults absorb as much of it as they can at evening classes. The reintroduction of the language into mainstream society may be ambitious, but the culture of the Gael is everywhere evident. The origins of most place-names in western and highland Scotland are Gaelic: the Mod encourages and celebrates artistic expression in the native tongue, and the resoluteness of the Scottish people is a powerful inheritance of the ancient tradition.

Things change, and so they should. Argyll has an enduring and palpable faith in its regeneration, and in a cynical era excitement about the future is a refreshingly noble legacy. New technologies and a resurgent interest in Scottish ancestry herald the emergence of Argyll as a centre for cultural brokerage – richest and purest of history, and best equipped for people to access the experience.

CHAPTER FOURTEEN

The Early Families of Argyll

W HILE THOSE OF US who come of Argyllshire stock would no doubt find in our veins traces of the blood of the first hunter/gatherers who came to this part of the world on the track of the receding glaciers, and of the other peoples who followed them, it is not until the twelfth century that our first traceable ancestors appear. Most of what we regard today as the main clans do not emerge as identifiable political/military groupings until the late thirteenth and early fourteenth century, even though in many cases the pedigrees trace their chiefs to a much earlier date.

Most of the old Gaelic pedigrees lead back to Ireland via various routes and to such figures as Neil of the Nine Hostages, from whom the later O'Neils, High Kings of Ireland, descend. But pedigree-making or -faking is an old Celtic art; even the traditional account of the arrival of the Scots from Ireland in 500 AD in the persons of Fergus, Loarn and Angus, the sons of Erc, is now questioned.

Prior to the Scots, the inhabitants of the area were presumably Picts; the almost complete disappearance of the old Pictish nobility is one of the puzzles to which we will probably never know the answer. Legend – as so often, symbolic rather than historical – has it that Kenneth MacAlpine, king of Scots and Picts alike, decreed a great feast, at which each invited Pict sat with an attendant Scottish noble standing behind his seat. At a given signal the Scots stepped forward and slit the throats of the unfortunate Picts. But this would have been unnecessary if the Pictish succession was matrilinear. Marriage of an heiress to an incoming Scot and adoption of the Scottish form of patrilinear succession would have ensured a painless hand-over; the existence of the Dalriadic lion rampant in the heraldry of many of the great families of eastern lowland Scotland may support this latter theory.

The Vikings, who arrived c. 800, left some mark among the families of Argyll, although there was plenty of Norse blood in the Isles. Among the local clans with probable Norse origins are the MacCorquodales, whose name is thought to derive from 'son of Thorkettle' – an essentially Norse name. The MacCorquodales had their headquarters at Fantelans – a small castle built on an islet in shallow Loch Tromlee between Taynuilt and Loch Awe, which they held until the Civil Wars. Montrose's troops had been told to leave MacCorquodale alone when withdrawing from Argyll, but as misfortune would have it, as they skirted the loch, one of the

MacCorquodales is said to have found the temptation too great and fired his musket, killing one of them. The party turned aside and razed the castle to the ground. The chiefly family sank from sight in the eighteenth century, although they may be represented in the distinguished family who made a fortune on Merseyside, and who include Barbara Cartland and her daughter, Raine, Countess Spencer.

One of the first characters whose descendants are recognisable today was Anrothan, a prince of the *Ua Neill*, whose descendants inherited the districts of Knapdale, Glassary and Cowal. He is said to have married the daughter of 'the king of Scotland' in around 1000. From the lands his descendants inhabit it would seem that she was the heiress of Comghall, grandson of Fergus, since these lands were his portion. *The Book of the Clan Sween* says that Anrothan took them by the sword – perhaps he had to exercise force to establish his position as his wife's husband. From him descend the chief clans of Cowal and Glassary – the MacLachlans, the Lamonts, the MacGilchrists of Glassary, the MacSorleys, the MacEwans of Otter, possibly the MacNeills – there are conflicting theories as to their origins – and the MacSweens.

Of these, the greatest in their day were the MacSweens descended from Suibhne (or Sween) the Great, whose castle on Loch Sween was the earliest proper stone castle in all of Scotland, built around 1200. Ignored by most historians, the MacSween chiefs held unrivalled power in Argyll in their day. But by the middle of the 1200s they had 'lost the place' and Castle Sween had gone to the Stewart earls of Menteith. When Haakon of Norway brought his fleet south in 1263 to settle the ownership of the Western Isles with the king of Scots, he was joined by Murchadh, the MacSween chief.

During the Wars of Independence, Murchadh's successor was courted by King Edward of England with promises to restore his former possessions, but the fortunes of war went the other way. Although MacSweens still remain in Argyll (some of them at least are from the unrelated clan of Norse descent of the same name from the Outer Isles), the main part of the family moved back to Ireland, from whence they had come half a millennium before. Here they became professional mercenary soldiers or *galloglaich*. As they were extremely good at the job, much sought after and richly rewarded, the fortunes of the family fully revived. It was said that no king in Ireland could be considered as such without his own force of MacSween *galloglaich* at command.

The other descendants of Anrothan remained in Argyll, centred on Cowal and Glassary. The most important family was that of the Lamonts, who possessed the southern end of the Cowal peninsula, although the reputed self-description of the chief in the 1440s as 'Lamont of all Cowal' is most likely an exaggeration. The Lamonts maintained a generally friendly relationship with their expanding neighbours the Campbells, but the latter wreaked a terrible vengeance on the Lamonts, who had changed

sides in the Civil Wars. In response to the Lamont slaughter of a Campbell garrison, over a hundred Lamonts were rounded up and killed by the
Campbells at Dunoon. The Lamonts have now lost their lands in Argyll
and their chief is a Roman Catholic priest in Australia.

Their cousins the MacLachlans were in much the same situation; at the
beginning of the 'Forty-five their chief asked Argyll, with whom he was on
friendly terms, if he and his men might have free passage to join the Jacobite forces. This was readily granted but at the same time it was made plain
that the concession would apply only to the outward journey. In the end,
the return journey did not worry the chief, who was lying dead on the far
field of Culloden. His family, who had been bombarded out of their castle
by the navy, were given warning of his death by the arrival of his grey
charger, which swam the loch in advance of the remnants of his companions. But today MacLachlan of MacLachlan still resides in a new Castle
Lachlan by the shores of Loch Fyne.

The Maclachlans descend from Lachlan Mor, grandson of Gilchrist, the
brother of the great Sween. Gilchrist had three sons, all of whom shared
in the lands of Glassary. One line came to an end with the marriage of its
heiress to Master Ralf of Dundee, who was listed in Balliol's sheriffdom of
Argyll in 1292. His great grand-daughter Agnes *de Glasareth* – 'of Glassary'
– married Sir Alexander Scrymgeour, the Royal Banner-bearer of Scotland
and Constable of Dundee. Their descendent Alexander Scrymgeour, Earl
of Dundee, has the title of Lord of Glassary and is once more the owner
of his ancestral stronghold, Fincharn Castle on Loch Awe.

Other families who share descent from Anrothan include the
MacGilchrists of Glassary (nothing to do with those other MacGilchrists,
who are Macfarlanes), the MacSorleys, the MacEwans of Otter, the Mac-
Neills of Taynish and the Livingstones or Maclays. If the MacEwans of
Otter have vanished from the area it is all the more pleasant to record that
Alasdair Livingstone, Baron of Bachuil, hereditary guardian or *Dewar* of
the crosier or staff – the *bachuil* – of Saint Moluag, Columba's contempo-
rary, is still in possession of the lands of Bachuil on the Isle of Lismore.
The lands are held by the family for their service in keeping the holy relic,
which is still in their possession.

But if the descendants of Anrothan held much mainland territory, the
coastal and island part of Argyll was early to find itself in the hands of a
new emergent power in the person of Somerled. Of mixed Norse/Gaelic
descent, he led a rising against the Norse and carved out a kingdom for
himself in the Isles and along the coast, until, becoming too ambitious, he
moved against the king of Scots, meeting his death in battle at Renfrew in
1164.

From him descended three sons, who shared his kingdom. They were,
in order of seniority, Dougall, Ranald and Angus. Ranald had two sons,
Donald and Ruari, from whom two formidable kindreds descended.
Having absorbed the MacRuari inheritance through marriage with the

heiress, the Clan Donald chief eventually emerged as the most powerful of all Somerled's descendants, being, as Lord of the Isles, to all intents and purposes ruler of his own kingdom in the west. The earldom of Ross was also obtained after another marriage to an heiress, by which time the extent of the MacDonald chief's influence extended from the glens of Antrim to the Outer Isles and to beyond Inverness in the east. This strength was also a weakness: the Lordship of the Isles was eventually forfeited in 1493 when the extent of the Lord's ambition and his dealing with the English to conquer Scotland was finally recognised. Clan Donald broke up into warring factions, allowing the Clan Campbell to take over the headship of the Gael.

As well as the lesser branches of Clan Donald stock, such as the Macalisters in Kintyre and the Macintyres of Glennoe up Loch Etive, the Lordship attracted a number of clans, to whom were granted great territories as recompense for their service. Of the latter, probably the greatest in Argyll were the Macleans, whose origins may have lain in a professional priestly family from Galloway. The chiefs of the Macleans were eventually given most of the islands of Mull, Coll and Tiree. When the head of the MacInnes/MacMaster kindred reputedly infuriated the then Lord of the Isles by complaining that he smelt, Maclean was given the nod to move into mainland Morvern, with the resulting extinction of the MacInneses as any sort of power in the land.

Although the Clan Donald became without doubt the most powerful line of the descendants of Somerled, this had by no means been the case prior to the establishment of the Lordship. The eldest of Somerled's sons was Dougall and he inherited the largest share of his father's kingdom. Dougall's family used the designation *de Ergidia* – 'of Argyll'. Their mainland possessions had included Lorne, Benderloch and Appin as well as the islands of Mull, Coll and Tiree. When Haakon of Norway called on Ewen de Ergidia to accompany him, he was met with refusal, for Ewen declared that he could not serve two masters and chose to retain his mainland possessions and follow the king of Scots. But all went wrong during the Wars of Independence when the Lord of Lorne's brother-in-law, Comyn, was killed by Bruce in a scuffle and the MacDougalls espoused the cause of Balliol and his English supporters.

This of course was the losing side and, when Bruce finally won, the MacDougalls were much reduced. John of Argyll fled the country, but his career continued to be a notable one: as 'Jean Dargael' he is listed among the first Admirals of the Fleet in the Royal Navy when, in the reign of Edward II, he captured the Isle of Man for the English. The MacDougalls had lost their island possessions, with the exception of Kerrera, to Clan Donald. But this is not the end of the story. Bruce's death was the signal for an English-inspired Balliol invasion and the overturning of several of King Robert's decrees. So it was that the MacDougalls, now lords of Lorne, the northern portion of Argyll, were re-established with much of their old mainland territory returned to them.

They never recovered their former position, however. In due course, they lost the lordship of Lorne through the marriage of an heiress to the Stewarts, from whom it passed to the Campbells. But the male heir of the family established himself at Dunollie in a new, smaller castle, built on the site where Loarn, one of the sons of Erc, had established his fortress a millennium earlier. Although the lordship is long lost, the eldest daughter of the MacDougall chief is still informally styled 'the maid of Lorne'.

Several of the major Argyllshire clans were incomers, having arrived, so it is said, in the train of the king's army when he was bent on subjecting the west to the rule of the Scottish Crown. Precisely when this happened is unclear, but the Campbells probably arrived in this way around 1220. The most credible version of their origins has them come from the neighbouring Lennox, part of the ancient British kingdom of Strathclyde, with its seat of power at Dumbarton. From the same stock spring such families as the MacArthurs, the MacIver Campbells and the MacTavishes.

The definition of an incomer is actually rather indeterminate – several families claim to descend from Loarn through his descendant Feradach Finn, although few of them remained in Argyll throughout. The Mac-Millans' arrival at Knap from Lochaber would seem to be due to a marriage with MacNeill of Taynish's daughter, from whom they took on the keepership of Castle Sween. From this same descent through Feradach the MacKinnons, the MacQuarrys, the MacPhees, the MacNabs and the MacGregors are said to come.

The Stewarts of Appin descend from an unofficial union of the last Stewart lord of Lorne. The outcome of this union, Dougal, was given a portion of lands in north Argyll, where his family, friends and the existing inhabitants – MacColls, MacDunsleaves (otherwise Livingstones or Maclays) MacCombichs and Carmichaels among them – formed the new clan.

It is a mistake to think that incoming powers killed or displaced their predecessors; population was wealth and in most cases the previous occupants stayed on, working for a new lord. Their former master might also still be there, but now one place down at the high table and acting for the new lord. Here we may faintly discern some of the oldest families in Argyll. Fergusson of Glensellich in Strachur bears the coat of arms of the chief of the Fergussons, Fergusson of Kilkerran, with whom he has no blood connection, with, for difference, the white wand denoting his position as Officer of Strachur for the incoming Campbells. The last chief of the tiny Clannfhearguis made extravagant claims for the antiquity of his clan, who may well have been there before the arrival of the Clan Campbell.

So too Macilvernock of Oib (at the head of Loch Sween) rejoiced in the position of Hereditary Trumpet Bearer to Campbell of Auchinbreck, lord of the surrounding district. Oib itself had been split into two, one half going by the name of Oib Macilvernock, the other, Oib Campbell. The actual trumpet did apparently exist up to the nineteenth century, and the responsibility for summoning all the locals to attend Auchinbreck's twice yearly baron-courts at Kilmichael-of-Inverlussa was in all probability a vestige of Macilvernock's former lordship of the area, a position taken over by the Campbells for whom he now acted.

In the same way the MacEachrans of Killellan and the MacKays of Ugadale held hereditary positions as Mairs of Fee (administrators) of South and North Kintyre respectively, areas of which they had almost certainly been the former lords. But the oft-repeated fact that Ptolemy's map of Britain showing a tribe called the *Epidioi* inhabiting Kintyre, a name which means much the same as the Gaelic derivation of MacEachran – 'Son of the Horse Lord' – is probably no more than coincidence.

These Mackays have nothing to do with the famous clan of that name who hail from Sutherland, but are part of a seafaring kindred found on both sides of the North Channel, in the Rhinns of Islay and under the names of MacGee and MacGhie in Ulster and in Galloway.

On occasion claims are made for the egalitarian nature of Highland society. This is very much not the case. While kinship was readily acknowledged, the system was in fact extremely hierarchical. Reference to the early Irish law tracts of the seventh and eighth centuries reveals a system of honour price, by which people of certain callings are clearly graded both against each other and within their own category. This reveals the existence of a professional 'middle-class' of various professions ranging from the Church, whose leaders ranked with kings, to skilled craftsmen, who could rank with important landowners, down to the relatively modest callings of physician and even harper.

These professional families are to be recognised in Argyll at an early date, their knowledge being jealously guarded within the family and passed down for the most part orally through the generations. They defended their status even if it meant diversifying into another speciality. Some of these families are identifiable purely by their use of a workname; others form distinct kindreds with a name of their own, while others are distinguishable families within a larger clan. In the first category are such names as Macintyre ('son of the wright') MacSporran ('son of the purse-bearer') MacLaverty ('son of the spokesman'), Stewart ('steward'), Scrymgeour ('skirmisher'), MacNocaird ('son of the whitesmith'), MacinLeister or Fletcher ('arrowmaker'), and the church-related Clerks, MacPryors, MacPhersons, MacVicars and Macinespics, the last three being the sons, respectively, of the prior, the parson and the bishop.

The Argyllshire MacPhersons have nothing to do with the famous Badenoch clan of the same name, and are said to descend from an early Campbell priest. The Campbells not unnaturally kept a strong link with the Church, producing many senior churchmen, including one family – the Campbells of Auchinellan – known in Gaelic as 'the race of the bishops' due to the number of princes of the Church they produced. The MacVicars seem to have been early kindred around Inveraray, where a standing stone in the castle grounds is said to mark the border of their lands with those of the MacIvers. Although they continued on in the area, they were overcome by their powerful neighbours the Campbells, with whom they effectively merged.

Membership of the Church usually involved being literate and educated. Many people so trained found profitable lay employment in the train of great lords as men of business and administrators. The Lochaweside MacArthurs were clearly such a family, and appear again and again in early records as churchmen. Charles MacArthur, like his father before him, was employed by the earl of Argyll, who rewarded him in 1510 with the lands of Terivadich. He and his family were obviously able and within a few generations possessed a number of small lairdships along the shores of Loch Awe. Less well known were the MacUghtres, who performed the same function for the earl at the same time and received the lands of Kildalvan in Cowal for their services. There were other dynasties of churchmen, such as the MacCalmans from around Taynuilt, the MacCauises and the MacPhails from the same area, the MacPhilip family from Kintyre, the MacLachlans of Kilbride and, more recently, the MacLeods of Fiunary, whose ancestors had followed another profession as smiths and armourers to the MacLeod chief.

The profession of medicine was surprisingly lowly rated in early days. The most famous medical kindred was of course the Beatons, whose leading family was based on Islay in the service of the Lords of the Isles, and whose knowledge was such that no less than seventeen families by that name were established around the north of Scotland and Ireland on lands held for their skills – whether they were all of the same blood is another question. Other medical families included the O'Conchobars, established in Lorne, the MacPhails in Muckairn, physicians to Campbell of Barbreck and to the MacDougall chiefs, and the MacLachlans of Craigenterive at the southern end of Loch Awe, who were medical men for the earls of Argyll.

In the same way that MacArthurs were to be found as armourers and pipers on Islay, so the MacLachlans were found at Kilbride as a family of noted churchmen and antiquaries, holding a famous collection of manuscripts. Another branch of the same family relieved a family of MacArthurs as captains of the Campbell stronghold of Innischonnell on Loch Awe in 1617, when the latter were found guilty of theft.

The profession of poet, bard and sennachie – the earlier distinction between these became blurred – was carried on notably by the MacVurichs or Curries for the Lords of the Isles, and by the MacEwans for the chiefs of Clan Campbell. These MacEwans had nothing to do with the Lochfyneside family of the same name; it appears that they were of Irish stock descended from the bardic family of O'Hosey. The Morrisons or more strictly O Muirgheasains on Mull, probably descended from the hereditary abbots of Clonmany in Ireland, carried out the same function for the Maclean chiefs, to whom they were also standard-bearers.

There were many other professional kindreds; MacBraynes were hereditary judges on Islay, where their judgement mound is still to be seen by the roadside just south of Bowmore. The MacLucases and the MacGillechonnells or MacWhannells were wrights and boatbuilders, while in the musical field the Galbraiths or MacBhreatnichs in Mull and Gigha were famous harpers, as were the Mackellars in Glen Shira, and the MacShennogs or Shannons in Kintyre. These last held land from the Lord of the Isles for their music. Piping families abound: the Rankins were pipers to the Maclean chiefs and notable dynasties of pipers were produced by the MacGregors, the Macintyres and the Campbells.

Space does not allow a closer look at such interesting families as the Macnabs of Barachastelain near Dalmally, who were jewellers and armourers, nor the Brodies/O'Brolchains, stonemasons from Kintyre who were of Irish origin. The adoption of alternative names by members of larger clans accounts for many names which are not mentioned here. The 'gentrification' of names – making respectable by anglicising and disguising many old Highland names or adopting those which had approximately the same sound and which were better known – is a subject by itself, and affected many Argyllshire names.

People of Argyll descent are today found around the world. At home, few of the great chiefs and lairds still live on their ancestral acres. Professional dynasties do still exist – one need only mention the great dynasty of churchmen headed by the late Lord Macleod of Fiunary or the MacCallums, who continue to produce pipers and dancers of note in large number. Further afield, it is no coincidence that one of Canada's leading young pipers is a MacCrimmon or that one of the most successful traditional musical groups from Nova Scotia is 'The Rankin Family'.

Visitors to Argyll are astonished by the wealth and variety of historical monuments scattered through the countryside. Although people of Argyllshire descent are widely dispersed and the area itself is now largely populated by relative newcomers, these same visitors might well be astonished by the number of people still living here whose roots in Argyll stretch back over many centuries. Such people form a living historical tapestry no less fascinating than the more visible links with the past that the landscape contains.

CHAPTER FIFTEEN

The Castles and Mansions
of Argyll

W E MAY THINK of Argyll today as somewhat remote, but for many centuries the sea gave both empire-builders and invaders quick and relatively easy access to islands and littoral lands. The huge jagged coastline of Argyll was continually contested between the seaborne Scots and the Norsemen, who were not finally expelled until the Battle of Largs in 1263. There is much built evidence of these continuing security and counter security measures. Even in more settled times, and until relatively recently, the sea was the principal means of access for new estate owners from the Lowlands and England, for holidaymakers from Glasgow and for cargo in both directions.

It was only in 1266 that formal royal dominion over the Western Islands was accepted under the terms of the Treaty of Perth. Local power was thereafter distributed among the MacDougalls, the MacLeans and the MacSweens. And it was here that Clan Donald began its rise to prominence, acting for the crown in the creation of the Lordship of the Isles. From the late thirteenth century until its forfeiture (abolition) in 1493 by the king, the lordship was a kind of state within a state stretching from the Western Isles to the glens of Antrim in Ulster. The MacDonald power base was at Loch Finlaggan on Islay on two islands connected by a causeway, but there is little remaining above ground of this fortified settlement and council chamber. The Lordship had expanded from the thirteenth century, replacing the Stewart scion, Walter, earl of Menteith at Castle Sween and at Skipness on Kintyre. The eventual loss of the lordship was a cultural catastrophe, the effects of which are, arguably, felt to the present day. '*Ní h-éaibnheas gan Chlainn Domhnaill.*' 'It is no joy', as the poet wrote, 'without Clan Donald.'[1]

The rule of kinship and clan chieftainship was replaced by the rule of law under Clan Campbell, whose modus operandi was more attuned to the modern world of legal titles. Clan Campbell first rose under the patronage of the power brokers of Clan Donald, Dougall and MacLean, but it eclipsed them all from the sixteenth century in alliance with the centralising authority of the Stewarts. The two main branches of Clan Campbell were based at Breadalbane and Inveraray. The Breadalbane branch was a cadet which proved less powerful and enduring in the long term but was responsible for one of the most spectacular of Argyll's castles – Kilchurn on Loch Awe. On the islands and coastline of the west, power was enforced by sea. Inland this was achieved through the natural communication lines of the glens, hence the wedge-shaped land holding created by the Glenorchy or Breadalbane Campbells expanding out of Argyll into Perthshire. Land and island holdings were determined by communication routes and safe harbours; castles were placed at strategic points. Ultimately, the MacDonalds, who ruled the islands by means of the swift 'birlinn' galley, lost out politically to the Campbells, who were on the side of the crown in their final power struggle with the lordship in the later fifteenth century. The architectural relics of these struggles still exist in abundance.

Castles

The definition of a castle is simple enough in the earlier part of our survey. Castle Sween is one of the earliest in the country, designed like the Iron Age duns or forts principally as a defensive structure. However, as these fortifications evolve into comfortable dwellings, it is less clear when a castle becomes a mansion house, or even a villa. The elegant and sophisticated Carnasserie (1565–72), built as a residence for John Carswell, Bishop of the Isles, is a case in point. Much later, at Inveraray, Archibald Campbell, the cosmopolitan and highly anglicised 3rd duke of Argyll, destroyed an existing castle and its clustered settlement to build a great modern mansion with baronial pretensions expressed in the massive corner turrets. The new town of Inverarary was placed at a distance. Inside, the house was as up-to-date a duke's residence as could be achieved, using English designers and no less a 'job architect' than William Adam. Argyll's mansion pre-dated by many years the Robert Adam-inspired baronial tendency which gripped the county and peaked in the sublime Edwardian grandeur of Ardkinglas on Loch Fyne. Between these extremes there are countless houses trying to be mansions, mansions trying to be castles and villas trying to be both. The architectural dynamic created by these tensions remains occasionally unresolved, but when it works, the results can be awe-inspiring.

Argyll is a relatively modern political creation, whereas its castles attest to ancient power struggles. Mull and Lorne were traditionally under the control of the MacDougalls, who built Dunstaffnage and Dunollie before 1275. The entire western coast and archipelago of Argyll is the rugged setting for some of the most romantic, but essentially practical castles and fortified houses in Scotland. The earliest were mostly castles of enclosure or enceinte, that is settlements built of timber or stone protected by massive masonry walls. The most complete surviving example of this type is **Castle Sween.** Reputedly the oldest castle in Scotland, Castle Sween was built by Suibhne towards the end of the twelfth century. It was developed by the MacSweens (MacSween – 'son of Suibhne') throughout the following century and further strengthened by the new lords of Knapdale, the Stewart earls of Menteith, and later the Lords of the Isles, into whose hands the castle had inevitably fallen. One of the earliest Gaelic poems records an unsuccessful seaborne attempt in 1300 by the dispossessed MacSweens to regain their castle – '*marcaigh ag tráchtadh na dtonna*' (horsemen travelling the billows).[2] The earls of Argyll held the castle after the forfeiture of the Lordship of the Isles in 1493.

The main feature of Castle Sween is the great curtain wall, onto which were added habitable corner towers – a pattern that was to be followed throughout the region. Within the courtyard, ranges were constructed at various dates. In castles of this type the 'courtyard' was often entirely filled with timber or stone buildings. The final addition at Castle Sween was a squat rectangular tower added to the north-east of the courtyard with a kitchen and spacious hall above. It was not uncommon at first for castle kitchens to be detached from the main building, mostly because of the danger of fire. However, they were soon incorporated on a lower level. At Castle Sween we have a transitional phase of detached kitchen with hall above, but the pattern of development through the centuries is towards the self-contained residence. It was not until the eighteenth century that the idea of a 'kitchen wing' re-emerged, this time in order to keep cooking smells out of the main house.

Skipness Castle is another important example of the enclosure castle. In an unlikely position for a place of strength, standing on a gentle slope near the shore of Kilbrannan Sound, the complex consists of a great curtain wall protecting a tower. Here, a very early fortified 'hall house' survives. The other main building within the courtyard is a sixteenth-century tower house, one of a number built at the time for the Crown in pursuance of the 'pacification' of the Islands. Again, the castle was built by the MacSweens but was soon gifted by the king to Walter Stewart, earl of Menteith as Lord of Lorne. Skipness came under the control of the Lords of the Isles in 1325 and stayed in their possession until the lordship's final forfeiture in 1493. In 1502 the lordship of Lorne passed to Argyll through the marriage of Dugal Stewart's daughter and, like much of the lordship's holdings, the castle passed to the earls of Argyll. Its strategic importance rapidly diminished and it was abandoned in the late seventeenth century. Skipness was taken into state care as early as 1933.

Dunstaffnage Castle was built from the thirteenth century in the then typical form of a very high curtain wall of stone protecting stone or timber domestic buildings within. The ground plan and courtyard utilise the land available atop a natural rock. The huge wall follows the rock's edge, growing into great towers at the seaward corners. The castle belonged to the MacDougalls, who held the islands of Mull, Coll, Lismore and Tiree. Robert the Bruce crushed the MacDougall clan after Bannockburn, took

FIG. 22.—Castle Swin. View from North-West.

FIGURE 27 Castle Sween: view from north-west (MacGibbon and Ross, vol. III)

Dunstaffnage and placed it in the hands of the Campbells. In 1388 the lordship of Lorne, and therefore the castle, was passed to the Stewart earls of Menteith but by 1470 it was back in the possession of the earl of Argyll, who created the hereditary post of 'captain' of the castle for his first cousin.

Opposite Dunstaffnage on the island of Mull is another early Mac-Dougall stronghold, **Duart Castle**. Of the western 'sea' castles Duart is one of the most dramatic; its great curtain wall dominates the Sound of Mull from the south. The original castle was a simple fortified dwelling of the MacDougalls but the main part of the complex was built by the MacLeans, who erected a tower house incorporating the existing wall with the remaining walls utilised as a courtyard. The tower is on four levels with the usual first-floor hall. The MacLeans were dispossessed in the 1670s but Sir Fitzroy MacLean bought the castle in 1911 and joined a growing band of wealthy industrialists and émigrés in 'reclaiming' their heritage through castle recreation. The most famous of these castle 'restorations' was Major John MacRae-Gilstrap's grandiose scheme to convert Eilean Donan Castle (1913–32). At Duart, MacLean employed the Glasgow architect Sir J.J. Burnet to re-cast the complex as a modern baronial residence.

Duntrune Castle near Kilmartin is a much smaller version of the 'sea curtain', fifteenth-century enclosure castle. The house inside is later, of the seventeenth century and L-planned to fit into the restricted space available.

FIG. 10.—Duart Castle.   View from North-East.

FIGURE 28 Duart Castle: view from north-east (MacGibbon and Ross, vol. III)

Rothesay Castle is a different category of fortification, protecting not a sea passage but a safe harbour. It is probably the most grand in the region, because of its close royal connection. Rothesay has its origins in a castle of the Stewards of Scotland, predecessors of the royal family of Stewarts who acceded to the throne in 1371 when the castle immediately became a favourite royal retreat. The great curtain wall is the earliest part of the structure. A notable difference between Rothesay and other castles of enclosure is the refinement of the stonework. The walls are constructed of ashlar (worked stone) but they were later heightened in rubble, so the contrast is quite clear. New royal apartments and a defensive 'forework' in a reduced version of the Stirling model were built in 1512. The whole complex fell into decay but was repaired at the beginning of the nineteenth century, the Bute family beginning a long association with heritage conservation.

Tarbert Castle in Kintyre has had a turbulent history. The castle was built, extended and modified between the thirteenth and sixteenth centuries. The position of the castle is at the isthmus of Tarbert (*tairbeart* – to draw across). This is traditionally where the Norse chief Magnus Barelegs dragged his boat across the head of the peninsula in order to define it as an island and therefore gain control of Kintyre as part of the conceding of the islands to the Norsemen. Tarbert remained strategically vital and Robert the Bruce took the castle soon after Bannockburn, underlining its continued importance. The complex consisted of a tower and later enclosing wall, built probably at Bruce's bidding. The small town became a royal burgh in 1329. A second tower house was built onto the complex – probably by James IV – in 1494. Little of either tower now remains. Tarbert Castle was the scene of the main Scottish event of the Monmouth Rebellion when in 1685 the earl of Argyll raised 1,200 men against King James VII. The rebellion failed and Argyll was captured and executed for treason.

Tower Houses

The other main type of fortified dwelling is the tower house, built either as a separate residence (Dunollie, Dunderave, Barcaldine, Gylen) or as an addition to existing curtain wall enclosures (Skipness, Duart, Kilchurn). Scotland's devotion to its own brand of castle-like architecture throughout the seventeenth century was unique in Europe. But this adherence went beyond an unwillingness to shed traditional forms because of conservatism or through a fear of marauding neighbours. In a complex political situation, the use of castle-like forms represented both a survival and a conscious revival of 'traditional' architecture. Internally, much of the developing desire for prestige was expressed through a new segregation of living accommodation and the construction of grandiose staircases.

The exterior of tower houses was equally important. New ideas about the privacy of the person extended even to the environs of the house. At old Inveraray Castle, and on a smaller scale elsewhere, whole communities were banished from around the main house to live in a newly built, 'improved' town. The tower as a secure dwelling was of course common throughout Europe, but in Scotland the building type lasted much longer and was also greatly elaborated over time. The main features of the tower house are its height, its compactness, its stacked uses (cellar, kitchen, hall, bedroom), and of course its security – enough to withstand a minor attack by lightly armed men. The tower houses that have come down to us are of stone and were mostly built in the fifteenth and sixteenth centuries, often behind already existing curtain walls. Many castles were also built as single residences or places of strength.

Carrick Castle (late fourteenth century) is a simple promontory castle which guards Loch Goil and its land route to Loch Fyne and the Campbell heartland. Carrick is oblong except for a diagonal check in one corner. **Castle Stalker** (1540–2) performs a similar 'sentinel' function and was built for the Stewarts of Appin on the order of James V. The dramatically-sited, hard-edged and militaristic tower acted as an outpost of the Scottish Crown. In the early seventeenth century the Campbells took it over and rebuilt the upper levels. By 1686 the castle had gone back into Stewart hands but it was forfeited after that family's support of the Jacobite cause in

FIGURE 29 Carnasserie castle: view from south-west (MacGibbon and Ross, vol. IV)

the '45. The castle is accessed by boat over shallow water at the mouth of Loch Laich. The simple tower of **Dunollie Castle** near Oban was built in the later fifteenth century by the MacDougalls to command the channel between the mainland and the island of Kerrera, on which the same clan built the dramatically sited, L-plan **Gylen Castle** (1582) with its beautifully sculptured details.

Few tower houses in Argyll reach the self-contained complexity of the later tower houses of the Lowlands or the north-east of Scotland. One that does is **Dunderave Castle**, Loch Fyne (1598). This MacNaughton castle is one of a series of buildings, essentially Lowland in character, identified as the 'Haggs-Kenmure group'[3] of houses which exhibited forward-looking tendencies in Scots architecture of the later sixteenth century. Dunderave is built on an L-plan with a square tower in the sheltered angle of the L. Inside the tower is a circular staircase and the entrance is decorated with classicising mouldings. The building was much 'restored' and extended by Sir Robert Lorimer in 1911–12 as a counterpoint to his Ardkinglas just across the water (see below).

During the sixteenth century many castles and tower houses were expanded to meet new demands for comfort. The usual manner of such expansion was through the addition of wings, creating L-plan or Z-plan houses. However at **Carnasserie Castle**, an older plan type, which combined a hall and a tower, was invoked This was really an evocation in miniature of the earlier royal palace of Linlithgow. However, the hall and tower were not separate: the dining room is in the hall and the drawing room is on the same level but in the tower, thereby creating a horizontal suite of accommodation in contrast to the vertical stacking which tower houses necessitated. The hall and tower is therefore also a compositional architectural device. John Carswell, Bishop of the Isles, massively enlarged the earlier structure at Carnasserie in 1565–72, using masons engaged on Stirling Castle and the latest court-style classical decoration. Clearly at Carnasserie we have something quite close to a sophisticated modern 'mansion', displaying up to date classical detailing within the framework of a recognisable building type.

Kilchurn Castle on Loch Awe is a traditional tower house elaborated into an enclosure complex, making it one of the most celebrated castles in the country. Standing at the head of the loch and often shrouded in mist, it is one of the most romantic of Scotland's many ruined castles. This large and imposing building is largely the work of the first Lord of Glenorchy (d. 1475) but it was re-modelled by that family's celebrated 'Renaissance prince', the 7th laird of Glenorchy, Sir Duncan Campbell or 'Black Duncan of the Castles', who supervised the move to Balloch Castle (Taymouth) and consolidation there. The Glenorchy Campbells were members of a cadet branch of the clan who expanded into Perthshire, away from the main Campbell power base in mid-Argyll, and who became, relatively briefly, one of the wealthiest families in the country. Lord Breadalbane trumped Inveraray Castle with his own astonishingly lavish version of the Gothic mansion at Taymouth (A. and J. Elliot, 1802–6). The original builder of Kilchurn, the first earl of Breadalbane was the uncle and tutor of the earl of Argyll, for whom he built old Inveraray Castle. His great grandson Sir Duncan Campbell was one of the first to begin estate improvement in the Highlands around 1600: commercial forestry and landscaping. This 'improvement' also included the outlawing and 'clearing' of the MacGregors (the Glenorchy Campbells' erstwhile Praetorian Guard and keepers of Kilchurn) from the ever-expanding and now legally held lands. Kilchurn consists of a tower house with a laich (low) hall added to the complex at the end of the fifteenth century. The group of buildings was continually added to and re-ordered throughout the period of Glenorchy/Breadalbane expansion in the sixteenth and seventeenth centuries. A private barracks block was incorporated into the curtain wall in the 1690s, adding to the picturesque grouping. Black Duncan also built **Barcaldine Castle** (1601–09), this time as a 'stand-alone' tower house. Barcaldine is at the outer edge of the Glenorchy Campbells' sphere of influence but the house seems quite domestic in character. Like Dunderave, Barcaldine is an L-plan tower with its entrance as usual in the angle giving access to a staircase. The wing or 'jamb' was entered on each floor from the main block.

FIGURE 30 Barcaldine Castle: view from south-east (MacGibbon and Ross, vol. III)

Classical Houses

Scottish lairds hung on to their tower houses longer than their European counterparts. Consequently, the earliest, unambiguously 'classical' mansions were not built until well into the eighteenth century. None is in the outstanding category, but there are several medium-sized classical houses worthy of note. The first classical mansion was perhaps **Colonsay House** (1722) but this was an extremely plain 'box', with later Palladian wings. **Lochnell House** (1737–9) is more elaborate, with an arched first floor, decorative urns and central pediment. However, the development in this type of smaller laird's house is towards the sophistication of **Barbreck House** (1790). Major-General John Campbell built Barbreck when he regained the estate his family had forfeited after the 1745 uprising. It is a simple enough five-bay classical house which maintains its dignity – in a country of castles – through its height. The house is set back on a wide flat plain, which adds to its presence in the landscape, its low service wings reinforcing its height. Like the earlier **Airds House** (1738), the main front has a projecting three-bay central section but at Barbreck this part is constructed of ashlar (finely worked masonry). The rest is harled, but was probably originally rendered and 'lined' out to imitate stone. Barbreck has all the usual kit of parts, an Inveraray on a small scale with a battlemented Gothic folly, walled garden, and pretentious pyramidal mausoleum.

Strachur House (1785) is another version of the mini Georgian 'improved' estate. Here, the main house is all rendered with stone dressings, but to compensate there is a central, three-arched 'Palladian' window (answered on the garden front with a full-height bow window), an arched entrance from the main road and a beautifully detailed, Adam-style estate bridge mimicking the Inveraray exemplars. **Asknish House**, Lochgair was built in the 1780s in a curiously mannerist style, the effect of which is heightened by the use of coursed and 'pinned' rubble. The house also employs a first-floor Palladian window, with a diminutive version above. Asknish was probably the first stone classical house in Argyll. However, no estate could hope to compete with that of Argyll, famously 'the biggest fish that ever swam'. Inveraray had been built forty years earlier than Barbreck or Strachur but the influence of its layout, if not its aesthetic, was carried through well into the nineteenth century, where the challenge of Gothic was at last taken up through a re-assessment of Scottish national architecture.

Inveraray Castle

From the mid eighteenth century, a step was taken towards bringing the nascent romantic attitudes to landscape and scenery into the field of new building. This step was to build new houses in the style of castles, while continuing to incorporate into them up-to-date symmetrical plans and modern conveniences. The first, largest, and for many years the only example of this movement was the new house built at Inveraray from 1745 by Archibald, 3rd duke of Argyll, a staunch champion of Whig unionism who (with his brother the 2nd duke) had dominated Scottish politics for several decades. In common with many 'improving' lairds, in the 1740s he embarked on an extensive programme of estate improvement, including the demolition of the old castle and the building of a new, comfortable 'seat'. In building his new castle, he was probably anxious to display a combination of confident progressiveness and ancestral 'roots'. As early as 1720, Alexander McGill had made plans for adding wings to the old castle. Now, however, a completely new design was drawn up, probably in 1744, by the military engineer Dugal Campbell, who designed the crow-stepped, classical Governor's House at Edinburgh Castle in 1742, and who would later take part in the anti-Jacobite war of 1745–6. Campbell's plan envisaged a 'House ... designed in the Castle Stile', with a polygonal fort-like outer wall and symmetrical splay-planned corps de logis. Campbell's proposal was not built, and instead the duke engaged the English architect Roger Morris (whom he had previously employed on work in London).

Morris consulted William Adam in Edinburgh in 1744 and built the new house in 1746–9. His design retained Campbell's castellation and dry moat. It comprised a simple square box with pointed windows and central tower and round towers at the angles, later capped by high 'candle-snuffer' roofs. Inside, the house had classical interiors, later richly remodelled by Robert Mylne from 1780.

The two designs for Inveraray, by Campbell and Morris, between them anticipated many of the future permutations of new castle-building. This fashion would only catch on slowly – the next really large example was John (and probably James) Adam's Douglas Castle of 1757, a tall, U-plan design of which only one side was built – but it would eventually be taken to a new pitch of elaboration by Robert Adam. What distinguished this castle-building from the old seventeenth-century affection for dynastic homes was its combination of classical order with romantic reliance on the studiedly 'irrational' architectural past. In Argyll there was little development of the baronial tendency until the early years of the nineteenth century. William Burn's **Gallanach** (1814–17) is mildly baronial but still symmetrical and therefore, broadly, classical. James Gillespie Graham's **Torrisdale Castle** (1815) takes a tentative step towards the asymmetrical but it is still an 'Elizabethan' house in a Scottish setting. The beauty of the new movement towards asymmetry was that it would, ironically, permit a 'rational' plan within an 'irrational' form.

Twenty years later, W. H. Playfair took a major step towards the 'convenient' plan with **Stonefield Castle** (1836–40; formerly 'Barmore' House now Stonefield Castle Hotel), which also made an important contribution to the development of a more 'academic' or convincingly 'national' baronial revival in architecture. Stonefield was one of a series of houses by Playfair, who resented the later success of William Burn in the field of the informal 'baronial' country house. Playfair wrote that Burn 'carries all before him ... creating blots upon the landscape'. To counter Burn, Playfair built a series of baronial houses or enlargements. Key examples were Craigcrook Castle (1835) near Edinburgh and Barmore/Stonefield, with its crowstepped gables and tall twin corbelled turrets flanking the main entrance. All of this pre-dated the 'correcting' of the baronial with authentic features recorded by the artist and antiquarian R. W. Billings. Prior to the publication of Billings' series, *The Baronial and Ecclesiastical Antiquities of Scotland*, in 1845–52, much of the architecture, like much of the culture, was avowedly 'North British'. Stonefield is therefore an important milestone on the road to the creation of a truly 'Scotch' baronial, but this was of a type that had never widely existed in Argyll. The exemplars for the revived baronial were castles of the north-east and the Lowlands: Fyvie, Castle Fraser, Maybole. There was no attempt, generally, to design the revived castles for their local context.

Carradale House was built in 1844 by the baronial specialist and sometime partner of William Burn, David Bryce. There are clear similarities with Torosay Castle (below) but Carradale is at least one level of expense cheaper. There are two harled stories, crammed with pepperpot turrets and gables (asymmetrical of course) where Torosay is of a much larger order with a full service basement and two and a half storeys above. Nevertheless, Bryce clearly demonstrated at an early date the potential for the application of the baronial style to villas, which proliferated, particularly in the west. Of particular note is the introduction of the diminutive square bartizan turret which derives from the early seventeenth-century work of Sir James Murray of Kilbaberton (Pinkie House, Scottish Parliament, Edinburgh Castle Great Hall). **Torosay Castle**, Mull (1858) is also a relatively minor work of Bryce, who peppered the country with modern castles from Orkney to the Borders. It was originally called Achnacroish House, and it was as much a 'marine villa' as an attempt at a Highland estate for a Glaswegian estate owner, Colin Campbell of Possil. Like Carradale House, Torosay is a rather economical version of the full-blown Bryce of the Glen or Castlemilk House, but with its rubble stonework and astragalled windows the house sits well in its context. The later baronialist or 'Traditionalist', Sir Robert Lorimer added the wonderful terraced gardens, complete with a statue walk of nineteen sculptures. William Burn's own curiously English Jacobean masterpiece in Argyll is at **Poltalloch House** (1849–53). Here we have a true 'mansion house' with all its parts: themed 'Jacobean' east and west lodges to match the main house, gate piers, private chapel, bridge and experimental home farm at Barsloisnach. All of this was carried out by the Malcolm family, who had bought the land in 1796. The estate was developed with huge profits from trading and land holding in Jamaica. The family also had two large town houses combined for single use in Royal Circus, Edinburgh. Soon, however, the fortune was spent and the family retreated to the more modest Duntrune Castle (above).

The general form of the later nineteenth-century mansions in Argyll was baronial in the manner of Bryce or Burn. There were also personal versions of the style. Peddie and Kinnear's **Glengorm Castle** (1858–60) is a post-clearance power statement for James Forsyth of Quinish. It has all the baronial elements associated with the style as developed in that firm's urban public buildings and the entire designed street in Edinburgh linking Waverley Station to the Old Town, Cockburn Street. John Burnet's **Killean House** (1875) is something of an exception to the familiar Billings-inspired formula. Built for the shipping magnate James Macalister Hall, the house has a blocky composition more akin to later nineteenth century work, which was moving away from the by now exhausted, spiky Burn/Bryce baronial. The 1890s saw a brief interest in English Arts and Crafts, particularly in the marine suburbs and exemplified in Argyll at William Leiper's **Tighnabruaich House** (1895).

Sir Robert Rowand Anderson made an earlier, equally important contribution to the issue of historic architecture for an important client with clear ideas about the proper form for buildings of this type. John Patrick,

3rd Marquess of Bute, was the leading force behind the revival of conservation in the nineteenth century. Bute was one of the world's richest men and, in common with many of his class, spent large amounts of money on buildings, largely of a romantic, neo-medieval cast. When in 1878 Bute came to rebuild his own house, **Mount Stuart**, he commissioned Anderson, who drew on his own studies of secular medieval architecture in the south of France and northern Italy. The result was very different from the 'national' style which had been developed and also from the fantasy-castles built for Bute in Wales by W. Burges. At Mount Stuart Anderson designed a rectangular 'palazzo' block, with sheer unbroken walls, an eaves gallery and a bellcast roof. Bute's intense mysticism was reflected in the astrological decoration of the interior, including the focal space of 'a vast hall, gleaming with light ... lined with rarest marbles, pavonazzetto, emperor's red, and pink-flushed alabaster'. Yet at the same time, the house was fitted with the latest technology; it was the first in Scotland lit by electricity.

Architecturally, the influence of a house like Mount Stuart was felt more in compositional than in stylistic terms. In the early twentieth century, Sir Robert Lorimer, who had been Anderson's pupil, re-assessed the whole issue of baronialism and 'Gothic'. Lorimer had become dissatisfied with the polite simplicity of his early houses and restorations. At Rowallan in Ayrshire (1902), and to a greater extent at **Ardkinglas** (1905–1907) on the shores of Loch Fyne, he developed a much more monumental, rhetorical manner of bare rubble walls, ancient-looking detail and tight massing; he referred to this as his 'Scotch' style. The plans of these houses, with their first-floor principal apartments, were also based on Scots Renaissance precedents but there was little trace of the historic Billings exemplars; the idea of pasting in details from historic castles was gone. MacGibbon and Ross had systematically researched the whole subject of Scotland's 'castellated' architecture.[4] The point was now to be inspired by the past, not to imitate it. The tension between monumental assertion and Traditionalist restraint reached a peak at Lorimer's Formakin (1912–14), in Renfrewshire – 'the purest Scotch I've ever done.' In this final baronial domestic conversion Lorimer had learned a great deal from his earlier work on actual examples of Scottish Renaissance buildings, particularly **Dunderave** (1598), restored and extended in 1911–12. At Dunderave Lorimer's new wings were 'matched' to a rubble structure which had lost its traditional covering of harling. Lorimer's most celebrated Scots Renaissance monument is the Scottish National War Memorial (1924–7) at Edinburgh Castle.

There is one last true mansion worthy of mention. **Cour House** (1921–2) is one of the most remarkable, or perhaps even strangest houses in Scotland. It was designed by Oliver Hill, who in 1953 went on to write a beautifully illustrated account of Scottish castles and tower houses. But Cour is certainly not inspired by Scotland. Its massive, irregularly-shaped and heavy roofs are clad in Purbeck stone slates. The house itself is low and crouches on the rise of a hill. Nevertheless the effect is breathtaking. Hill was an English architect, landscape architect and garden designer. A friend of Lutyens, he was first apprenticed to a builder and then became an architect. The style of his country houses took Lutyens' experiments in Arts and Crafts design to a romantic conclusion. Thereafter Hill followed a less productive path as a Modernist architect but had more success designing gardens and became a Fellow of the Institute of Landscape Architects. Hill's most celebrated building is the Art Deco Midland Grand Hotel in Morecambe.

Marine Villas and Mansions

Argyll has a very fine collection of 'marine villas', fairly large coastal mansions designed for wealthy city dwellers, mostly from Glasgow. One of the earliest of these, **Castle House**, Dunoon (1822), was built for a Lord Provost of Glasgow, James Ewing. The house sits in a commanding position on Castle Hill and was designed by David Hamilton of Glasgow in a whimsical Gothic style. This element of whimsy filtered down into more modest villas and also inspired buildings like the remarkable '**Dunselma**' (1885–7), designed as a summer residence on the coast at Strone for a member of the millionaire Coats family. There is another cluster of dramatic clifftop dwellings nearby at the mouth of Loch Long at Cove. These grandiose mansions include at least one by Alexander 'Greek' Thomson at **Craig Ailey** (1852), and John Honeyman and William Leiper's superb **Knockderry Castle**, recast in 1896 for the carpet manufacturer Templeton, for whom the architect had built the celebrated factory on Glasgow Green. These were true 'marine' villas, reached by sea direct from Glasgow, but now the railway played its part in bringing fashionable mansions to Helensburgh, on the Firth of Clyde.

The altogether more suburban character of this planned town nevertheless contains very high-quality villas such as Leiper's **Cairndhu** (1871), built for another Glasgow Provost, John Ure, and A. N. Paterson's version of 'artistic' baronial **Long Croft** (1901), built for the architect himself. Here we also have one of the world's masterpieces of domestic architecture, Charles Rennie Mackintosh's **Hill House** (1902–4). Built for the Glaswegian publisher Walter Blackie, from the outside the white harled building was reticent to the point of being grim, particularly in contrast with the architectural fireworks going off nearby. Mackintosh managed to achieve a much desired whiteness through the novel use of Portland cement for the main walls, rather than stone. Externally however, there were only a few hints of the lightness of the interior, such as the jutting square bay window, which pointed to a Modernist breaking down of the external and internal divide. Generally, in Mackintosh's external architecture, the stress was close in spirit to Lorimer's 'national' architecture. The only true model, in Mackintosh's view, could be Scotland's historic architecture, and at Hill House he employed a tight L-plan group, complete with service stair in the re-entrant angle. The understated entrance to the house is on the west flank, where the composition conforms most closely to the contemporary Arts and Crafts work of Voysey and others. Inside, all the main rooms face south, including the small library and business room located, as was traditional, close to the entrance. Next was the drawing room which was at the very heart of the house in all its 'feminine' splendour. The billiard room and den had been dropped from the plans at the client's insistence, leaving the tiny library and smaller dining room as the only traditionally 'male' spaces. The service wing was on the east flank, with a day nursery, children's bedrooms and school room above. A traditional stair turret gave easy access to all floors for the servants and, externally, echoed five centuries of Scottish architecture.

Notes

1 *Bardachd Albannach, Verse from the Book of the Dean of Lismore*, Scottish Gaelic Texts Society, Scottish Academic Press, 1978, ed. J Watson, line 39
2 Ibid., line 873
3 see M. Glendinning, R. MacInnes and A Mackechnie *A History of Scottish Architecture from the Renaissance to the Present Day*, Edinburgh University Press, 1996, Chapter 3
4 The publication between 1887–92 of the five-volume set of David MacGibbon and Thomas Ross *The Castellated and Domestic Architecture of Scotland* was of immense importance to the study and appreciation of Scottish architecture. The move towards a more 'archaeological' rather than picturesque approach to the subject was gradually being made but their massive effort gathered up all the individual pieces of antiquarian knowledge and presented it critically. Their main target was Billings. Perhaps with some irony, they wrote: 'Our sketches are not intended to imitate or rival the beautiful and artistic etchings of some of our Scottish edifices which have, from time to time been published.' Instead they wished to record, to measure, and to classify according to plan type.

CHAPTER SIXTEEN

Agriculture

ARGYLL, stretching from Campbeltown in the south to Ardnamurchan in the north, is one of the most varied counties in Scotland. Every aspect of farming is affected by the Atlantic and the warm moist air from the Gulf Stream. No part of Argyll is far from the sea. It is said that Argyll, with all its inlets and sea lochs, has a longer coastline than France. Farmers and crofters farm sand, clay, loam, peat bogs, screes, heathland, rocks and mountains up to 915 m. Few areas of Britain can have a more varied soil and climate.

Some districts are dominated by large estates and tenanted farms while others are mainly owner-occupied. There is no such thing as a typical farm size. Some hill farms require several thousand hectares to keep enough sheep to make a living. Even in the more arable areas the size of a farm can vary from 2 ha (5 acres) to 200 ha (500 acres). Small farms are often part-time businesses with the farmer and/or his wife working in forestry, tourism, bed and breakfast, roads, ferries, the service industries, or whatever is available to ensure the family has a reasonable income.

Crofts and crofting townships are still to be found all over the county, although they are more common on the islands. Tiree and Iona, for example, are almost all crofts. In recent times many changes have come to the crofters. They can now buy their crofts if they wish, the purchase price being based on a formula equivalent to twenty years' rent. Not all crofters have taken up the offer and on some islands there has been positive resistance to buying. Crofters have benefited from special grant aid, but there is always the fear that it may be withdrawn at any time. It is an out-of-date system, which different laws and schemes have so far failed to redress.

Sheep farming

Sheep, as one would expect, are the main livestock enterprise. On the higher ground the Blackface predominates. It is the most suitable breed for difficult terrain: very little stops a determined Blackface ewe; her ability to find the greener grass on the other side of the fence is one of her greatest assets. Before the Second World War, Argyll Blackfaces had the reputation of being a bit too small, but with improved husbandry methods and feeding the animals have improved in size and can now compete with Blackface sheep from any other part of the country.

There are three types of Blackface: the Newton Stewart is a medium-sized sheep with relatively short wool and is prolific, with lambing on the hill in excess of 100 per cent; the Perthshire is a large sheep with long, quality wool, but is a shy breeder with lambing of less than 70 per cent; the Lanark is more or less between the Newton Stewart and the Perthshire in productivity and is the best suited to Argyll.

In the 1970s Swaledale tups were brought up from the north of England and crossed with Blackface ewes on the hill. The Swaledale produces more milk than the Blackface and is considered to be a better mother. Some farmers considered the cross to be better than the pure Blackface, but there were problems finding enough cross ewes to keep the system going. The Swaledale tups had an influence, but it was improved husbandry that started to make a real difference in sheep farming.

A few farms tried a rotation system. The hill land is divided into five or more large paddocks and the sheep are moved around. The ewes went first in the rotation, followed by the hoggs (young sheep), so that the ewes were always on fresh grazing. The number of lambs increased and in some cases the number of ewes. The annual output increased considerably, but the drawback was the large initial financial outlay. The system was criticised by the transitional hill shepherd, who feared that sheep no longer hefted to the hill would lose their hardiness.

A much more popular system was to provide lambing and tupping paddocks. These areas would be kept free of stock for most of the year, and had many advantages. Firstly, at tupping time it is much easier to supervise a small paddock to ensure that the tups are working properly and that the ewes have been served. By using coloured crayons fitted to the tups it is easy to see which ewes have been served, and to identify infertile tups and remove them. On the open hill barren rams are often not detected until the following spring. In addition, ultrasonic examination can determine the number of lambs in the womb. Ewes expecting twins can be separated out and given extra feed to ensure that good healthy lambs are born and that the mother has enough milk to feed two lambs. Then, at lambing time, the ewes can be observed several times a day, whereas on the hill it is difficult to find and help any ewe having difficulty lambing. Each ewe can be monitored to ensure that all the lambs are suckling. Any lamb not sucking can be taken away and put on another ewe, or, as a last resort, fed artificially, though this is usually avoidable. Lastly, the ewe and lamb(s) can go back to the hill as soon as they are fit. Any medicines required can be given and the male lambs castrated before the sheep go back to the open hill.

A further refinement of the paddock system is lambing inside a shed or plastic tunnel. All the advantages of the paddock are intensified, very few lambs die at birth, and birth problems are seen and resolved quickly. The advantages to shepherds are considerable. They have much more control of the husbandry than when working outside in the wind and rain, and can look at the sheep at night, sometimes even using closed-circuit television. The sheds should be as open as possible, to prevent condensation, and only slightly warmer than the outside. As soon as the sheep are fit they should again go outside, where they will have a better chance than those born outdoors.

The life cycle of the hill ewe in Argyll is usually seven years or five lamb crops. Each autumn the ewes are examined; all barren ewes and those over seven years old are culled from the flock. Those with good teeth and in fair condition are sold for further breeding to low-ground farms. The ewes with poor teeth and all castrated male lambs are sold to arable farmers from central and east Scotland to be fattened up for meat. The best female lambs are kept for replacement stock. Twenty-five to twenty-seven ewe-lambs are required per hundred ewes to maintain the flock; the more ewe-lambs per hundred ewes, the more choice there is. If the ewe-lamb numbers fall below twenty-five per hundred, the farmer may be forced to keep poor ewe-lambs, the flock will go into decline, and the farm is likely to fail.

The sheep of the low ground or arable land are of two types, resulting from the crossing of a cast hill ewe with a suitable tup to produce a cross low-ground, and from the mating of these cross low-ground ewes with purebred low-ground rams, usually Suffolk or Texel. The husbandry of these two types is similar. The cast hill ewes are likely to have a lambing percentage in the region of 120. The female lambs are used as replacements for low-ground flocks; the castrated males are sold to arable areas for fattening, but the demand for them is often poor. The lambing percentage of cross low-ground ewes mated with a pure low-ground tup is often 170 to 190. Islay and Lismore have a reputation for producing quality cross low-ground stock.

With field sheep the normal system is to rotate them round the grass fields along with or behind the cattle. Fresh ground helps to control parasites, which can be a major problem in field sheep. Lambing in sheds is popular but by no means universal. Some lambs are sold fat off the farms, especially from Kintyre, but the main sales are for lambs to be fattened in the central belt of Scotland. In the 1970s more lambs were fattened in Argyll, but changes in the system of subsidies in the 1990s meant that this ceased to be economical.

Cattle and Dairy Farming

Cattle have always been important to the economy of Argyll but have, like cattle everywhere, had their ups and downs. Environmentalists tend to believe that cattle are good and sheep are bad for our hills. But without both of these animals our hills would change beyond recognition.

Two pure breeds are found in Argyll: Highland and Luing. The Highland folds belonging to farms such as Achnacloich and Cladich are well known. Oban is the main sales centre for Highland cattle. Animals sold go all over the world, though in recent years Germany has been the principle foreign buyer. The recent problems with British beef have seriously affected the foreign market. Heifers are keenly sought after, either for pure breeding or for crossing to produce hardy hill cows. The unwanted male calves can be a problem. They can take three years to fatten and are not popular on arable farms. Some are sold to wildlife parks and some are bought as a tourist attraction. At Inveraray Castle, for example, Highland cattle are always kept in the fields adjacent to the castle. Highland cattle look fierce, but are generally gentle and placid, and very suitable for public parks, with one caveat. It is not wise to approach a Highland cow with a young calf; they are excellent and very protective mothers. The breed is very hardy and can withstand our wind and rain, but, like any animal, they must receive adequate food, although there are those who have suggested they could live on heather alone! They are not a prolific breed and calving is often no better than 90 per cent.

Luing cattle are one of the few new breeds to be established in the twentieth century. The Cadzow brothers on the island of Luing believed that it should be possible to create a pure breed of cattle suited to the Argyll hills, instead of continuing the existing system of crossing pure Highland with another breed to produce a suitable cow. In the 1950s they took pure Highland cows and tried various crosses, beginning with Devon and Shorthorn. Shorthorn crosses produced the best results, and attempts were then made to create a type of cross that would breed true. Success led to the formation of the Luing breed, which, although it has never expanded to the extent expected, has nevertheless become a significant breed.

As already mentioned, the main type of cattle used on the hills are Highland cross cows. A look around Argyll reveals that the cows have become very variable indeed, with almost every first of second cross imaginable. In many cases it would be more desirable to go back to the more traditional cow. Cast cows from the dairy herd can be very successful beef breeding cows on the more arable land, if given adequate hay and silage. In the past, a number of herds were based on Galloway cross cows, but they have disappeared. Continental sires were introduced almost thirty years ago. The Charolais was tried first, but proved unsuitable: the bulls were too large for the cows and calving problems were often serious. Numerous breeds were tried and Simmental and Limousin became the most popular. It is uncommon to find Aberdeen Angus or Hereford cattle in Argyll.

Between the wars, dairy farms were to be found all over the county, but there has been a steady decline in numbers since the 1950s. The dukes of Argyll brought farmers, mainly from Ayrshire and Renfrewshire, into several parts of Argyll during the eighteenth and nineteenth centuries; a large number were settled in Kintyre and a creamery was set up in Campbeltown.

Islay was another dairying centre, with a cheese factory at Port Charlotte. The year 2000 saw the end of dairy farms on Islay, apart from one to supply local milk. The problems on Islay began to arise after the demise of the Milk Marketing Board in 1994. The equipment in the cheese factory needed updating to comply with new EEC regulations, so the creamery was closed. Local dairy farmers, however, raised capital and formed a co-operative. Though it did well at first, outside sale prices soon made the cheese and butter uneconomical to produce. Islay cheese had a wide reputation for quality and was in demand, but in spite of this the factory could not continue and so the remaining dairy farms had to stop producing milk.

The island of Coll was a surprising place to find dairy farms, especially if you consider that the ferry to Oban takes five hours. Again there was a history of farmers coming in from the south-west. The Coll creamery survived until the 1950s; its manager moved down to the Islay creamery and, sadly, saw the closure of that too.

Gigha had only dairy farms, the reason being that the Horlicks family owned the island until the 1980s and a condition of tenancy of a farm was that the farmer had to dairy. The motive was to keep the creamery built by the Horlicks family viable. Unfortunately, the creamery could no longer comply with hygiene regulations and had to be closed. The milk then had to be ferried to the mainland and transported to Campbeltown. In March 2002 the island was taken over by the Gigha community in the form of the Isle of Gigha Heritage Trust. The farms have been reorganised and by early 2004 there were four larger dairy farms of the original nine supplying milk to the Campbeltown Creamery.

The Cowal peninsula was another centre of dairying. Any milk not sold locally was sent to the mainland or, more regularly, to Rothesay on the island of Bute. Lorne had many small dairy farms just after the Second World War; the milk was taken to Oban creamery, where it was treated and bottled for local use. The summer tourists fitted in with the seasonal production of milk. The Ayrshire breed once predominated, but slowly Friesians were introduced.

A number of factors have led to the decline in dairy farms. The compulsory introduction of pasteurisation saw the end for many small farms which retailed milk. The output was often too small to justify the capital outlay required. Dairying can only be carried out for local consumption of milk, or near a creamery. Farms producing milk in bulk were often too remote from a creamery. Coll, for example, only needs milk for a population of about a hundred and fifty. A dairy farmer on Coll or Islay has nowhere to sell his milk; the only creamery now in Argyll is at Campbeltown. The decline in dairy farming can also be attributed in part to the reluctance of younger farmers to work the long hours necessary or be tied to the strict routine of the dairy.

Arable Crops

Today arable crops do not figure highly in Argyll. It was traditional to grow oats and potatoes for consumption on the farm, and to sow grass seed under an oat crop in the spring. In the last few years there has been a move to sowing grass seed direct in either the spring or autumn. Spring and winter barley are grown in small areas of Cowal and Kintyre. Swedes and kale are still grown on some of the dairy farms. A number of sheep farmers grow rape for feeding lambs in the autumn and sow grass the following spring.

For generations hay had been made to feed the cows in the winter, but the post-war years saw a great change with the introduction of silage. At first it was made and stored in pits at some convenient place on the farm. Later some of the larger farms erected towers, which produced a better product. However, pollution regulations caught up with silage storage. The pits and towers had to be sealed and made waterproof, and became more expensive and difficult to maintain. This problem was solved by the introduction of baled silage with plastic wrapping.

Experimentation and Diversification

In the last half century there have been many experiments and changes in Argyll's agricultural economy.

Deer farming has been seriously considered over the last twenty-five years, but has not developed as was once expected. There is money to be made from deer stalking on the estates and from the sale of the carcasses of the animals culled. The Red Deer Commission count the deer regularly and recommend the numbers to be culled. This is important to the health and well-being of the herds. In a mild winter more animals survive, the hill becomes overgrazed and the quality of the animals declines. It is important to cull out sickly animals as well as the poorer quality stags. Some estates feed the stags to keep them in good condition.

Hotels and restaurants like farmed venison. Chefs say that the meat is easier to cook and that any culinary treatment is more predictable than with wild venison.

In the 1970s deer farming was seen as a possible diversification enterprise. The Highlands and Islands Development Board established a deer farm at Rahoy, Morven, to monitor deer farming. All aspects of the husbandry were examined and most problems likely to be encountered were ironed out. However, the economics of the enterprise posed serious problems. The capital required to set up a project is considerable: all fences must be two metres high and special handling facilities are essential; the government does not offer any per head subsidy to help, as it does for cattle and sheep farming. There are few financial returns in the first three to four years, when expenditure is at its greatest and the farm is still collecting deer calves to set up a breeding unit. In the 1990s the Rahoy experimental unit was closed; the HIDB felt they could not continue the farm any longer.

The rearing of goats is another enterprise that has had some attention in Argyll, the production of cashmere being the target. Problems over the supply of cashmere from Russia led the cashmere weavers to look for a new source. All goats have cashmere wool, the fine fibre next to the skin; the coarse outer hair is mohair. The cashmere goat produces the finest fibres but unfortunately is not always happy in our climate. The Hill Farming Unit at Lephinmore on Loch Fyne carried out some grazing experiments with goats and sheep, and it was shown that a mixture of goats and sheep is more efficient than either goats or sheep on their own, as each have different eating preferences. But goat farming posed some of the same problems as deer farming from a business point of view, in that it took a long time before any return was obtained and the cashmere quality was unpredictable. Wild goats were collected from the islands to try to increase the female stock and build up herds. One farm in Kintyre went into cashmere in quite a big way, but after some five years had to abandon the project before the goats bankrupted the farm.

Nothing has changed the farming face of Argyll as much as forestry. Mid-Argyll and Cowal were heavily afforested during the heyday of the Forestry Commission. The Commission was given a yearly planting target with few restrictions as to where and how. They were very successful in reaching their targets. In the period after the war, the Commission were offering prices per acre at least two to three times the agricultural value of land. In Cowal the number of farms decreased from 120 in 1965 to fewer than 50 in 1990. It is the side effects of forestry which are most important to those farmers left. Contractors carry timber as their main business and stock floats have to be hired from outside the district. Social effects can be serious as well: schools close, travelling shops stop coming, churches empty, buses are no longer viable and the community spirit is undermined.

Increasing awareness of environmental issues has also had a major effect. Argyll has many Sites of Special Scientific Interest – more than most other counties of Scotland. These sites are subject to a management agreement or conditions, which often restrict farming activity. In some cases monetary compensation is available, but money is not always what the farmer wants. The farmer usually has no say in the setting up of a conservation area, and farming for conservation can be a stressful and difficult business.

The SSSIs on Islay are mostly for the protection of birds. About sixty pairs of choughs breed on the island and many birds pass through on migration, including the osprey. But it is geese that have posed the greatest conservation problems on Islay, which is the major wintering area for Barnacle and, to a lesser extent, Greenland White-Fronted geese. In the 1950s approximately 10,000 geese wintered on the island; now about 40,000 come each year and the numbers are still rising, so much so that other islands and the Mull of Kintyre are being affected.

At one time the Barnacle goose was considered an endangered species, but numbers have now recovered. The geese on Islay breed in Greenland and come south to winter. Another group of Barnacles breeds at Spitsbergen in Norway and winters on the banks of the Solway in Dumfriesshire. The effect on farming can be considerable. Geese are grazing animals and it is estimated that five geese can eat as much as one sheep. It is easy, therefore, to calculate the number of extra sheep that could be farmed on Islay. In recent years farmers have been compensated by a grant to try to offset the loss of grazing, but the grant is not automatic and has to be fought for each year.

Again money does not offer a complete solution. The geese graze all the early grass and so cattle have to be kept indoors on conserved food for at least two weeks longer each year. In the autumn, turnip and kale crops are also eaten by the geese. Many attempts have been made to control the movements of the geese, with mixed success. In one scheme, the geese were scared off the fields by people employed to wave their arms about and shout. This worked for a while, but geese are intelligent animals and soon got the measure of the scarers! The Royal Society for the Protection of Birds had the idea of buying a farm and enticing the geese to stay there by providing good grass and scattering grain in the winter. This was partly successful, but the grass soon became scarce and the geese moved on to better pastures.

Fish farming has become a major industry in Argyll, and has had an important influence on the agricultural economy. The first fish farm was set up in the 1970s. Established on American principles, it was located on the shores of Loch Fyne and was entirely land-based. Now almost every sheltered sea-loch has fish cages. Salmon, rainbow trout, mussels and oysters are farmed and the Marine Research Station near Oban is currently investigating possibilities for farming many of the sea species. Fish farming is an important source of income and employs workers from farms and crofts.

Tourism has also had a major influence on the countryside, and brings in useful income to many farms. The summer B&B now helps to keep many households solvent and allows families to stay in the area. Two wildlife parks have been established in the last twenty years. A rare breeds park near Oban has replaced a sheep farm and has up to 80,000 visitors a year. Near Inveraray a wildfowl park has replaced a dairy farm and is an equally popular visitor attraction.

It is difficult to see what the future of farming and crofting will be. Will conservation and tourism take over completely? Probably not, because tourism does to some extent depend on agriculture to maintain the area and provide an infrastructure. Tourists need people to provide accommodation and food; most are unlikely to come to a wilderness with no facilities. Another pressing question is whether future governments will be prepared to give grants and subsidies to maintain farming, and, if so, on what terms?

CHAPTER SEVENTEEN

Oral Traditions/Folklore
of Argyll

S INCE MEDIEVAL TIMES Argyll, including the islands of Mull, Coll, Tiree, Jura and Islay, has provided evidence of an oral tradition rivalled only by that which has come to light in the Outer Hebrides from the nineteenth century, then beginning with the work of John Francis Campbell and Alexander Carmichael. This shared lore, largely orally transmitted and dating from the time of the first Gaelic settlements in Argyll from Ulster by the Dál Riada from sometime before 500 AD, embraces a wide variety of genres: custom and belief, songs of all kinds, international folktales, hero tales and romances, legends, word games and ritual formulae.

From these earliest times we have short religious legends associated with places in Argyll. Adamnán in his seventh-century life of St Columba (521–597 AD) provides accounts of prophesies and miracles on the island ecclesiastical centre of Iona, including one performed on the day of the saint's death whereby no poisonous reptiles would injure cattle or men on the island (as long as the Commandments were observed). On more than one occasion the saint and his companions, through fasting and the chanting of psalms, were able to obtain a steady, favourable breeze that speeded their return to Iona in their skiffs and curachs (Anderson 1991, 134–5, 174–75). A number of early saints' legends have persisted into modern folklore; one recorded in Tiree recounts how St Patrick, arriving on the same day each year to visit his temple on the island, was aided by a south-west wind on his journey to the island, and by a north-east wind on his return journey.[1] Another, possibly of more recent origin, concerns a religious debate on Iona between St Columba and Odhran, which Odhran determined to settle once and for all by having himself buried in a grave to test the church's views on the afterlife. Upon being disinterred three days later Odhran opened his eyes and declared neither heaven or hell to be as asserted in the scriptures, whereupon St Columba addressed his companions saying 'Ùir, ùir air sùil Odhrain mun dùisg e 'n còrr carmaisg' ('Earth, earth on the eye of Odhran before he wakes more controversy').[2]

Custom and Belief

A valuable account of oral traditions associated with custom and belief in the region some three centuries ago is to be found in Edward Lhuyd's record of his journey to the Highlands in 1699–1700. Prior to setting out from Glasgow, Lhuyd, a Welsh polymath, compiled a folklore question-naire and contacted sources in the Highlands in his search for games and customs and 'any other fashions that you know peculiar to the Highlands'. In the course of his journey he visited Kintyre, Knapdale, Lorne, Mull and Iona; the traditions noted down include proverbs, riddles, and beliefs con-cerning death and second sight. Much of the material was contributed by the Rev. John Beaton, Kilninian, Mull, the last in a long line of learned physicians.[3] The next methodical collections of custom and belief were made at the end of the 1800s by the Rev. John Gregorson Campbell of Tiree, and included extensive materials on witchcraft (J. G. Campbell 1900; 1902). During the following decade an extensive repertoire of games was assembled, many of them containing a strong verbal component. These included counting-out games, puzzles, funeral games, feats of long breath, incorrect speaking and many others known elsewhere throughout the Highlands (MacLagan 1901).

Song

Throughout the twentieth century many hundreds of songs were recorded from singers in Argyll, embracing the well-known Gaelic genres: love songs, panegyrics, songs of exile, waulking songs for shrinking the tweed, humorous and satirical songs, sea songs, and religious songs. Many are attributed to specific bards such as Duncan Ban MacIntyre and the earlier MacLean bards of Mull, but a good number, as is universally characteris-tic of Gaelic song, are anonymous. Modern fieldwork bears witness to the survival of a lively and vigorous community song tradition. The wealth of older songs recorded in Tiree since the 1950s is complemented by a dynamic tradition of song-making from local bards; locally-composed songs have played a central part in the social life of the community at all levels and have survived in great numbers. Of these, the oldest composi-tions go back to the middle of the eighteenth century (Cregeen and MacKenzie, 5). Often they are associated with the numerous families of song composers, some of whom have been active for two centuries (*op. cit.*, 12). Like other songs, these have been passed down primarily by oral trans-mission, often set to well-known airs, and dealing with favourite topics such as love, religion, politics, and satirical commentary. In the light-hearted but effective verse translated below, the bard laments the death of a horse in a mock-elegy (transl. *op. cit.*, 21):[4]

Yesterday my gelding died
That late was nimble, playful,
In leap and canter sure of hoof,
The clods of earth disdaining.
Great my sorrow that the hoar-frost
Now his eye is veiling.
Ah men! death is an ugly thing,
Over the beasts prevailing.

The Rev. Patrick MacDonald, minister of Kilmore, is an important source of information regarding Gaelic song in late-eighteenth-century Argyll. During his years there he heard and noted down 'the airs that are most common in that part of the country' (MacDonald 1784, 2). The items ('Argyllshire Airs' *op. cit.*, 31) include airs to ballads from the Finn Cycle, a lullaby, love songs, local panegyrics, a waulking song, and instrumental tunes. A sketch of what actual performance occasions may have been like comes down to us from the Swiss traveller Necker de Saussure's account in his Tour of the Hebrides (1822, 42–43). He visited Iona and described a dance held there, complete with fiddler (and toddy for the dancers), where choral songs were performed. These consisted of rowing songs (*jor-rams*), waulking songs, heroic ballads and humorous songs; these last were performed to great hilarity with the singers seated in a circle: 'We were astonished to see, under so foggy an atmosphere, in so dreary a climate, a people animated by that gaiety and cheerfulness.'

Less than a decade later Alexander Campbell, a Gaelic-speaking music teacher journeying through the Highlands in 1815, spent a number of days in Ulva, off Mull, as a guest of the owner, Ranald MacDonald of Staffa. The purpose of his journey, undertaken with the financial support of the Royal Highland Society of Scotland, was to amass songs for a 'great National Repository of Original Music and Vocal Poetry' (Alexander Campbell 1815, ix).[5] Staffa's hospitality extended to assembling local singers, from whom Campbell was able to take down a large number of songs. While visiting in Dervaig, Mull, Campbell examined manuscripts of Gaelic song and melody compiled there by ladies of the gentry; nearby in Ballochroy he describes a further manuscript book containing eight Gaelic airs noted down by the daughter of the Laird of Coll, as well as the singing of local Gaelic songs to accompaniment on the 'improved harp'. In the course of his visit to the island, he also describes a number of fiddlers, most notably Angus MacDonald of Clachy near Aros in Mull, a cabinet maker and jack-of-all-trades who, Campbell says, 'draws a bold, rough fiddle stick, and is no mean dab at a dancing measure of any sort' (*op. cit.*, 17–18, 21–22, 27–29).

Folk Tales

The importance and popularity of the recitation of extended folk tales in Argyll from early times is evidenced by Bishop Carswell's condemnation in 1567 of the 'darkness of sin and ignorance and design of those who teach and write and cultivate Gaelic, that they are more designed, and more accustomed, to compose vain, seductive, lying and worldly tales about the Tuatha De Danann and the sons of Mil and the heroes and Finn MacCoul and his warriors and to cultivate and piece together much else which I will not enumerate or tell here, for the purpose of winning for themselves the vain rewards of the world ...' (R. L. Thomson 1970, 11).

Over three centuries later, the effect of Carswell's admonitions against storytelling on the common people of Argyll can be measured from the description provided in 1891 by the Tiree minister John Gregorson Campbell (1891, xi–xii):

> and a person who was about seventy years of age, a few years ago, in giving an account of old Highland habits to the writer, said that when, *e.g.*, the people of a place assembled to build a boundary dike, some one would observe that they should wait until so-and-so came, and when he appeared, as the day was good and long, one or other would remark that the new comer might tell, before they began, some incident in the history of the Fian bard. The whole party then sat around the story-teller, and listened to his marvellous account. By the time that he was done the sun was drawing westward, and some would say that it was hardly worth while beginning that day, and that he might tell some other story suggested by the previous narrative. When the second story was finished the sun was well nigh setting, and the parties separated after agreeing to meet next day, as nothing had been done that day.

The storytellers of Argyll, like their Gaelic-speaking counterparts throughout the Highlands, commanded repertoires that covered a wide variety of tales: international tales known on the Continent (and often far beyond); the romantic and hero tales that had existed as part of the oral and manuscript tradition shared with Gaelic Ireland; historical legends including clan sagas; local legends; and a host of personal and family memorates, many of which are now beyond recovery. The surviving tales are derived from all strata of society. The elaborate, sometimes formal romances and hero tales represent an aristocratic, learned tradition, in the transmission of which manuscripts have played an important role. The isle of Mull was once the home of a large number of Gaelic manuscripts and Edward Lhuyd's account of 1700 of the contents of the Rev. John Beaton's manuscript library lists a number of specific tales found there. They include some of the better-known romances from late medieval Ireland, as well as older stories from the Ulster and Mythological Cycles. Often the written and the oral interacted, and tales of literary origin passed into the unlettered oral tradition. We cannot discount the possibility that here, too, tales were read aloud publicly from manuscripts as they evidently were in Skye around 1700 (Bruford 1969, 60, 66). There are also accounts from oral sources in Argyll of the *Cliar Sheanchain*, a colourful band of professional performers, who wandered throughout the region, possibly until as recently as the early eighteenth century, demanding hospitality from their not always enthusiastic hosts (Carmichael 1913, 324–27; MacLeod 1952, 446–47).

The impressive manuscript antecedents, however, should not obscure the importance of oral transmission, and it is clear from modern sources that many reciters have been capable of learning long and complex tales without recourse to written sources. From his boyhood John Francis Campbell of Islay (1822–85) kept company with unlettered storytellers on the island, among them James Wilson, a blind fiddler who provided a notable version of 'The Slim Swarthy Champion' (*An Ceathairneach Caol Riabhach*), an entertaining and linguistically-complex hero tale whose origins lie as far back as the sixteenth century (J. F. Campbell 1890–93, 1, 297–329). Campbell, though well aware of manuscripts, was a pioneer in his time in the collection of orally-transmitted folk tales. His collecting activities, carried out with his co-workers, covered much of Argyll, including Islay, Mull, and the mainland, and extended to vast areas of the Highlands and the Gaelic Diaspora communities in the Lowlands. In the course of his fieldwork, which began in 1847, one of the major contributions made by Campbell was in the area of international folktales. One such international tale, a version of the type known in English as Chicken Little[6] (J. F. Campbell 1940, 62–66), was noted down from a nursemaid in Islay; others were taken down from Gaelic-speaking travellers elsewhere in Argyll.

In addition to writing down the important store of romances and international tales from reciters among ordinary Gaels, the activities of J. F. Campbell and his co-workers uncovered a vast store of historical legend, much of it specific to the region. One of Campbell's main assistants, John Dewar, compiled a monumental collection of local legend, still largely unpublished, now known as the Dewar Manuscripts.[7] The materials are concerned largely with local and clan histories throughout Argyll and have been transmitted to a high standard. A notable example of Dewar's work and the traditions it embodies is the legend of Somerled (Somhairle mac GilleBhride) who established Clan Donald and the Lordship of the Isles. The account, which is supported by versions from other sources, describes at first hand, as it were, the rise of Somhairle, his alliance with and eventual leadership over Clan MacInnes in Morvern in their struggle against the incursions and threat of domination from the Norsemen, and his use when vastly outnumbered of a clever ruse by which the Norsemen were defeated and routed.[8]

Of no less significance in the nineteenth-century collections are materials from Gaeldom's main epic, the Finn Cycle. These interrelated

narratives, often interspersed with sung ballads, recount the exploits in
Ireland and Scotland of Fionn mac Cumhail, the Pan-Gaelic hero, and his
band of warriors. Many are associated with place-names in Argyll, particularly in the Glen Etive area. One of the earliest examples of a modern
folk-tale manuscript, taken down in 1803 in Mull at the instigation of Mac-
Donald of Staffa, contains materials from the Finn cycle including the
story of Oisean – the last survivor of Fionn's company of warriors.[9] Further tales from the Finn cycle appear in the important collection *Waifs and
Strays of Celtic Tradition* (Argyllshire Series, 5 vols.), printed at the end of
the nineteenth century with support from Lord Archibald Campbell. The
tales were collected, edited and translated by local scholar-clergymen, the
best known of whom was John Gregorson Campbell of Tiree (Duncan
MacInnes 1890; James MacDougall 1891; J. G. Campbell 1891). The
extensive and detailed Fenian materials are complemented by some international tales, but a significant part of the collection is concerned with local
materials, particularly legends. The accompanying notes and essays by
Alfred Nutt, a renowned scholar, placed the works firmly within the
domain of international scholarship.

Field recording over the past fifty years has yielded important and memorable performances in this central storytelling tradition. Fionn's pursuit
of Diarmaid and Gràinne is one of the most poignant of the stories from
the Finn Cycle, and persisted in the oral repertoire until a generation or
so ago. For his second wife Fionn chose Gràinne, a younger woman, who
soon persuaded Diarmaid, the son of Fionn's sister, to elope with her. The
pursuit continued through many dramatic episodes, including Diarmaid's
victory over the Irish warrior Ciuthach Mac-an-Doill and his joining his
endangered comrades-in-arms in a battle against the Lochlannaich (Norsemen). The capture of the eloping couple was often hindered by the
warriors in Fionn's own company, who held Diarmaid in high regard.
Finally Fionn challenged Diarmaid to hunt a wild boar that no warrior
before had escaped from alive. Diarmaid, armed only with a spear, succeeded, whereupon Fionn asked him to measure the boar by pacing
barefoot beside it, knowing full well that there was a spot on the sole of
Diarmaid's foot which, if pierced, would bring about his death. When
Diarmaid, at Fionn's request, measured the animal for a second time, this
time 'against the bristles', a bristle penetrated the vulnerable spot. As he
was dying, Diarmaid entreated Fionn to carry him water from the stream
in his palms, saying that a drink of it would save him. On his way back,
however, Fionn, remembering Gràinne, let the water drain between his
fingers, and Diarmaid died. Gràinne, after protesting Diarmaid's inno-
cence and asserting that he 'never lay down without placing a sword
between us', threw herself into the grave alongside him.[10]

Also persisting among storytellers active within living memory are legends whose function has been to entertain and at the same time explain the
nature or origin of things. The Mull version of *Cailleach Bheurr*, with its

place-name associations, provides a good example of the tales passed on at
the house céilidhs held in every community until the early decades of the
last century.

Now there was a giant – the last in Mull, I believe – known as the
Cailleach (Old Woman of) Bheurr, who lived in the island of Earraid.
That island is well-known these days from books in English, but in
former times no one lived there except for the Cailleach Bheurr and
her three milch cows that she used to send out to pasture every morning. Now the Cailleach Bheurr must have been a tremendous size,
and from what folk tradition tells us, she had a single eye set in the
middle of her forehead.

On one occasion as she was gazing out to the west she said, 'When
I was a young girl the sea was forest and trees.' Whenever she
spoke aloud – and she very seldom did – everyone in her territory (and
probably in places beyond as well) could hear her.

Now you might think the old woman foolish, or even misleading in
saying that what is sea now was forest and trees when she was a young
girl. But why should we not believe her? Is it not likely enough? Well,
if not all of you have seen the Torann Rocks, you have heard tell of
them. Looking out from the island of Earraid toward the Dubh Artach
there are dangerous skerries extending seventeen miles out to sea,
which in past times could have been the summits of hills or high
ground which subsided as the result of an earthquake or something
of the kind. So we cannot say for sure that the Cailleach Bheurr was
not right in saying , 'When I was a young girl the sea was forest and
trees.'

Now there was one thing concerning the Cailleach Bheurr: at the
end of every hundred years she had to bathe in Loch Bà, up at the
other end of Mull; all of you have heard of Loch Bà, a pretty loch,
and very long and deep. And as soon as she had bathed – which was
always in May – her youth was restored and she became a young girl
again. Now you may doubt this, but as you know many a strange thing
happens in this world and has done so since times long past, which we
never know except for what comes down to us through storytellers.

She used to set out every day from the island of Earraid with her
three cows, driving them through the Island of Mull and down to the
Mull of Kintyre. The cattle must have taken extremely long steps to
travel all the way down to Mull of Kintyre, where they would start
grazing until they began on their way back home. But it's not so
strange when you think of the kind of woman the Cailleach Bheurr
was, for she would complain when she reached Crùn Lochan – you're
familiar with the place – not far from Glen More in Mull:

Crùn Lochan deep and dark,
The deepest loch in the universe;

The Sound of Mull would only reach my knees,
But Crùn Lochan would come up to my thighs.

There was only one place where the Cailleach Bheurr's cattle would
go to be watered when she was away from Mull, and that was at a well
halfway down to Mull of Kintyre. Now the well had a great stone lid,
and as soon as she arrived there in the morning she would lift the lid
so that the cattle could drink when they were thirsty. But if she were
to leave the lid off until sunset, water would gush forth from the well
and flood the entire world ... One time as she sat by the well – by
then she was growing older, and growing weak, just like any old
woman – sleep began to overcome her. Suddenly she awoke: a force
of bitter water was issuing from the well just as the sun was setting,
with only a little of the upper part of it remaining in view, so she leapt
up and pushed the lid down on the well and thus saved the world from
being submerged in the flood; but a part of the overflow remains to
this day and people call it Loch Awe.

So there you have the story of the Cailleach Bheurr. But the poor
thing, she came on one time and took the cattle to the island of Earraid. Soon it would be summer, and the month of May about to begin,
and it was coming time for her to go and bathe. Now she could only
bathe if she did not hear a dog's bark, and before she could hear the
little bird's chirping in the bushes, for if she should hear either of
those she was done for. On this day she set out in a leisurely fashion,
carrying a stick and descending the slope to the side of the loch on
her way to bathe. And just as she was at the shore's edge there was a
shepherd living not far away whose dog gave a bark. No sooner had
she heard the bark than she collapsed in a heap. Now the shepherd
knew very well that it was time for the old woman to visit and he had
always tried to keep the dog inside until she had had a chance to bathe,
but this night the dog happened to be out and for that reason it barked
when it saw her on her way down. She collapsed in a heap and the
shepherd ran to her as fast as he could to see if there was anything he
could do. She was not yet entirely gone, and she was singing a sad,
melancholy song. I can't sing, but it went something like this:

Early today the dog barked
The dog barked, the dog barked,
Early today the dog barked
On a calm morning above Loch Bà.

That's how the song went, and it had many verses, but that's the air.

Now, anyone who does not believe this story need only go up to
Barrachandroman and row up through Abhainn nan Slat and on the
left-hand side you'll see the Cailleach Bheurr's stairway ascending
to where she used to live. And to this day the place is known as the

Cailleach Bheurr's dwelling-site.
Now I don't know whether you believe the story or not, but that's the
way I heard it. And if it's a lie from me it was a lie to me.[11]

Tales in Gaelic have continued to be recited through the second half of
the twentieth century and down to the present period. Many of these were
recorded from such accomplished reciters as Donald Sinclair (Dòmhnall
Chaluim Bàin) in Tiree, and some have appeared in print recently (MacK-
innon 1997). The massive language shift away from Gaelic over the past
century has had its effects on the storytelling repertoire. Extended narratives such as complex international folktales and hero tales have gone
out of usage, while local legends, historical legends, ghosts and fairy
stories are among the genres that have survived. A significant number of
the lengthier narratives in Gaelic from Argyll have been maintained among
Sutherland travellers whose origins are largely in Argyll; these have been
extensively documented since the 1950s. Further Gaelic-based Argyll tales
have been maintained among another branch of the travellers, this time in
Scots, from Duncan Williamson, a traveller-storyteller, born beside Loch
Fyne, who learned them as a young man while working on dry-stone dyk-
ing in Auchindrain (Duncan and Linda Williamson 1987, 18–19).
Williamson, arguably the finest living storyteller from Argyll, describes
storytelling scenes from his childhood. On winter nights in a tent with a
paraffin lamp and a fire in the middle of the floor, he would listen to tales
told by his grandmother and his father (Williamson 1994, 6). Contemporary repertoires and performances on the mainland are predominantly in
English, often featuring personal narratives, but can contain much derived
from local tradition. Such items occur in great variety, ranging from the
evacuation of children in the Second World War to accounts of the lives
of fishing communities, history, semi-mythological materials, and work
and activities in a rural setting. Characteristically, stories told in the contemporary setting tend to reinforce community, social status, and the
region (Armstrong 1990, *passim*).

Notes

1 SA1960/197/A4
2 Carmichael 1928–71 2: 338–40. Carmichael observes that the legend was widespread; versions in the SSS archive were recorded in the Outer Hebrides,
  Lochaber, and in fragmentary form from Donald Sinclair of Tiree in 1968 by
  John MacInnes (SA 1968/26/B2).
3 Rev. Beaton gave Lhuyd information on folklore from Mull and the contents
  of his library during a meeting in northern Ireland, probably in Coleraine in
  February 1700 (J. L. Campbell and D. Thomson: xix, 12). See also Folk Tales
  below.
4 Original Gaelic in Cameron 1932, 173.

5 Campbell returned to the Society with 191 items, a selection of which appear in *Albyn's Anthology*.

6 AT 2033 in the Aarne-Thompson classicification system for international tales.

7 A selection appears in John Mackechnie, ed. *The Dewar Manuscripts*. Glasgow: W. MacLellan, 1964.

8 Somhairle mac GilleBhrìde of the Cave (Dewar MSS vol. 5 A, 123–28, 154–59).

9 A widespread tale known as *Oisean an Déidh na Féinne* 'Oisean after the Fenian Band'. The Staffa MS is now listed as National Library of Scotland Adv. MS. 73.2.1.

10 SA 1960/70. Recorded from Donald Sinclair, Tiree by John MacInnes.

11 SA 1953/49/B5,6. Recorded by Calum I. Maclean 13 April 1953 from Cap. D. MacCormick, Mull.

CHAPTER EIGHTEEN

Literary Argyll

THE NON-GAELIC LITERATURE of Argyll can be considered in two categories: the literature written in English (and in Latin in the earliest period) by natives or long-term residents in Argyll; and the works produced by visitors, in the form of descriptive accounts, fiction and poetry inspired by Argyll's landscape and history.

The native tradition

The earliest recorded Argyllshire centre of learning and literature is the monastic settlement on Iona. There is a considerable body of poems and hymns attributed to St Columba (521–97) and his followers, a selection of which was published under the title of *Iona, the Earliest Poetry of a Celtic Monastery* (Clancy and Markus eds. 1995). The *Life of St Columba*, written by a later abbot, Adamnán (*c.* 625–704), although not based on first-hand knowledge of the saint, is a key text for the early history of Celtic Christianity and its spread among the Dalriadic Scots of Argyll and beyond into the Pictish kingdoms.

It is a remarkable commentary on the strength of Gaelic and the oral tradition in Argyll that we have to wait until the nineteenth century to find significant Argyllshire writers using the English language.

The Rev. Norman MacLeod (1783–1862), '*Caraid nan Gaidheal*' (the Friend of the Gaels), was a significant Gaelic literary figure, and his son Norman (1812–1872), born at the manse of Campbeltown and largely raised at his grandfather's manse of Morvern, was one of the most popular religious writers of the Victorian period. His editorship of the mass-circulation magazine *Good Words* from 1862 to 1872 gave him a large British readership. He combined literature, and parochial duties in Loudoun, Dalkeith and Glasgow, with a chaplaincy to Queen Victoria, whose favourite preacher he became. His delightful volume of memoirs of his family and his Highland childhood, *Reminiscences of a Highland Parish* (1867), also acts as a useful counterblast to the stereotypical picture of a joyless Highland Presbyterianism: 'A striking characteristic of the manse life was its constant cheerfulness. One cottager could play the bagpipes, another the fiddle. The minister was an excellent performer on the latter, and to have his children dancing in the evening was his delight.'

Another Argyllshire clergyman writer was George Matheson (1842–1906), who for eighteen years was minister of Innellan in Cowal. Matheson lost his sight at the age of eighteen but completed his studies for the ministry of the Church of Scotland and, aided by a secretary, successfully carried out all his duties at Innellan and later in Edinburgh. Matheson is today best remembered for the popular hymn 'O Love that wilt not let me go'.

Susan Edmonstone Ferrier (1782–1854), born in Edinburgh, was a frequent visitor to Inveraray Castle, accompanying her lawyer father, who was the Duke of Argyll's 'man of business'. She set her novels *Marriage* (1818) and *Destiny* (1831) partly in Argyll.

Kenneth Grahame (1859–1932), the author of *Wind in the Willows* (1908), spent the first five years of his life in Inveraray, where his father was Sheriff Substitute.

The first significant novelist to come from Argyllshire was Neil Munro (1863–1930). Munro was born in Inveraray; his mother was a kitchen-maid, his father reputedly a member of the ducal house of Argyll. After an uncongenial early career in an Inveraray lawyer's office he left Argyll, aged eighteen, to go to Glasgow to follow a career in journalism, rising to become editor of the *Glasgow Evening News*. Munro combined an active journalistic career with a commercially successful and critically esteemed career as a novelist and short-story writer. The success of his first collection of Highland short stories, *The Lost Pibroch* (1896), was followed by the novels *John Splendid* (1898), *Doom Castle* (1901) and *The New Road* (1914), which led to his being seen as the natural successor to Scott and Stevenson in the creation of Highland historical novels. Honorary degrees in 1908 and 1930 from Glasgow and Edinburgh Universities are evidence of his contemporary standing.

Munro spent his working life in and around Glasgow and eventually settled in Helensburgh, but in his emotional commitment and writing he remained firmly focused on Inveraray and Argyll. Munro acknowledged, on the occasion of his being awarded the Freedom of Inveraray in 1909, that he had never been able to keep Inveraray and Argyll out of any story of his.

A major theme in Munro's novels is the process of change in the Highlands – this is perhaps most graphically illustrated in *The New Road*, where the lines of General Wade's military roads stretching over the Highlands, bringing order and trade, spell the end of the old feudal, unruly but romantic Highlands – a blessing but a mixed one. The novel's hero Æeneas remarks: 'It means the end of many things, I doubt, not all to be despised – the last stand of Scotland, and she destroyed. And yet – and yet, this New Road will one day be the Old Road, too, with ghosts on it and memories.'

A by-product of Munro's journalistic career was his enormously success-
ful series of humorous short stories which originally appeared in his weekly
'The Looker-On' column in the *News*. In these columns first appeared the
shrewd Glasgow waiter and kirk beadle Erchie MacPherson; the pawky
travelling salesman, Jimmy Swan; and above all, the perennially popular
Peter MacFarlane – Para Handy – and the rest of the crew of the puffer
Vital Spark. The adventures of Para Handy and his crew in and around the
Clyde and Loch Fyne have charmed readers for over ninety years, even surviving television and film adaptations. Munro had an ambivalent attitude to
these comic creations and used the pseudonym of 'Hugh Foulis' to distance
them from his more serious literary output. Despite such authorial reser-
vations, the Para Handy stories were for a time in the late twentieth century all that remained in print of Munro's work; however in recent years
there has been an increasing academic and public interest in Munro, a
growing number of his titles have been reprinted and with this has come an
appreciation of his significant place in Scottish literature.

If Neil Munro is the pre-eminent novelist of Mid-Argyll, Kintyre may
claim John MacDougall Hay (1879–1919) as its great native novelist. Hay
was the son of a Tarbert herring-buyer and educated at Tarbert Academy
and Glasgow University. On leaving university he worked as a freelance
journalist and as a schoolteacher before entering the ministry of the
Church of Scotland. In his brief life Hay wrote two novels, one of which,
Barnacles (1916), is almost unknown. His other novel, *Gillespie*, however,
still keeps Hay's name before modern readers.

The 'kailyard' has been used as a pejorative description of a dominant
strand in the Scottish literature of the late nineteenth and early twentieth
centuries – the couthy portrayal of small-town life, often depicted by cler-
gyman-writers such as S. R. Crockett and 'Ian Maclaren'. *Gillespie* is indeed
a picture of small-town life, set in Tarbert, renamed Brieston for the occasion, and it was written by a Church of Scotland minister – but there the
resemblance ends. It is a dark and bitter portrayal of the rise and fall of
Gillespie Strang, a man for whom the making of money becomes an all-
consuming passion. The novel was a conscious reaction against the
kail-yard school and an impassioned attack on what Hay saw as the growing materialism of Scottish society. The quotation on the novel's title-page,
drawn from the Book of Proverbs, 'He that is greedy of gain, troubleth his
own house', aptly sums up the character of Gillespie and the plot of the
novel. Published in 1914, and dedicated to Neil Munro, *Gillespie* has held
its place as a key text in twentieth-century Scottish literature. In its Calvin-
istic emphasis on divine justice as the only answer to man's sin it looks back
to an earlier Scottish tradition, while its concern with religious doubt and
the failure of religion to ease the physical and spiritual suffering of Brieston
and its people looks forward to a more secular literary outlook.

Naomi Mitchison (1897–1999) lived at Carradale in Kintyre for over
seventy highly productive years. Her range of fiction was wide and

included historical novels set in the ancient world and Scotland. In this latter category particular mention may be made of *The Bull Calves* (1947), based on her own (Haldane) family's history in the post-Jacobite period. She also wrote contemporary works arising out of her own active political and social concerns. Her 1952 novel *Lobsters on the Agenda* – in which she herself has a walk-on part – was particularly inspired by her own experiences of Kintyre life, economic and social development and politics.

'George Orwell' (Eric Blair, 1903–50) was something more than a passing visitor to Argyll, if hardly a native or indeed a long-term resident. He lived at Barnhill in the north of Jura between May 1946 and January 1949 and while there finished *Nineteen Eighty-four* (1949), his bleak masterpiece of life under the all-seeing eye of Big Brother.

Helensburgh, then part of Dunbartonshire, now administratively within Argyll and Bute, had a remarkable literary connection from 1928 to 1932. Larchfield, a local preparatory school, enjoyed the services of the poets C. Day Lewis (1904–72) and W. H. Auden (1907–73) as English teachers – Day Lewis from 1928 to 1930 and Auden from 1930 to 1932. Helensburgh was also the home of the playwright 'James Bridie' (O. H. Mavor, 1888–1951) and is the setting for his play *The Baikie Charivari* (1953). The prominent Scottish publisher, Walter W. Blackie (1860–1953), commissioned a family home in Helensburgh from Charles Rennie Mackintosh – The Hill House, built in 1904 – and in so doing created perhaps the finest Scottish building of the century.

Angus MacVicar (1908–2001), the popular author of thrillers, children's stories and a successful series of memoirs such as *Salt in my Porridge* (1971), lived in Southend, Kintyre.

Robin Jenkins (1912–) was born in Lanarkshire and taught overseas for many years before settling in Dunoon. While much of his fiction reflects his foreign experiences, many of his finest works, such as *The Cone Gatherers* (1955), have a Highland setting.

George Campbell Hay (1915–84), the son of James MacDougall Hay, was a distinguished poet in English, Scots and Gaelic. Born in his father's manse at Elderslie, Renfrewshire, he returned to Tarbert on Macdougall Hay's death and was educated there before going to Oxford University to read modern languages. Among his Scots and English poetry is the collection *Wind on Loch Fyne* (1948), which includes his celebration of the Loch Fyne ring-net fishermen and their boats, 'Seeker-Reaper':

> She's a seeker, thon boat. She's a solan's hert.
> She's a solan's look. She'll strike doon oot o nowhere
> 'Cast off!' she says 'Cast off!' red mad tie stert
> 'The loch is wide wi wanderin' watter.
> Lowse me! Drive me! Go there!'

Strachur on Loch Fyne was the home of the travel writer Fitzroy MacLean (1918–96), whose *Eastern Approaches* (1949) gave a vivid account of his pre-war adventures as a diplomat in the Soviet Union and of his war-time career with the Yugoslav partisans.

Maurice Lindsay (1918–) the poet and broadcaster, though born in Glasgow, spent much of his childhood at Innellan and celebrated the area in *Clyde Waters* (1958).

Marion Campbell of Kilberry (1919–2000) was the author of historical fiction for adults and children and the author of a fascinating historical account of the area, *Argyll, the Enduring Heartland* (1977).

Equally at home in Gaelic and English was Iain Crichton Smith (1928–98); he wrote in Gaelic as Iain Mac a'Ghobhainn. Born in Glasgow and raised in Lewis, he taught English at Oban High School from 1955 to 1977 before retiring to concentrate on writing, settling in Taynuilt. His novel of the Highland Clearances *Consider the Lilies* (1968) has become recognised as a modern Scottish classic and his considerable output of novels, short stories, plays and poetry in the two languages established his secure reputation as one of Scotland's leading literary figures. Smith also translated from the Gaelic, notably such works as Duncan Ban Macintyre's *Praise of Ben Doran* and Alasdair MacMhaighstir Alasdair's *Birlinn of Clanranald*.

Moira Burgess (1936–) the novelist, short story writer and literary historian was born in Campbeltown. Her *Imagined City* (1998) provides a comprehensive overview of Glasgow fiction.

Lorn Macintyre (1942–) was born in Taynuilt and has written many short stories as well as an on-going novel series, *The Chronicles of Invernevis*, set in Argyll.

Angus Martin (1952–), born in Campbeltown, is a poet and short-story writer as well as a social historian whose works such as *Kintyre Country Life* (1987) record a largely vanished way of life.

The prolific children's author and illustrator Scoular Anderson is a native of Argyll and lives in Dunoon.

Of the late twentieth century's wave of young Scottish novelists Argyll has produced Alan Warner (1964–), whose *Morvern Callar* (1995) was set in the author's birth place, Oban.

The Literary Visitors

Among early Scottish visitors to Argyll who left valuable descriptions of the area was Sir Donald Monro, High Dean of the Isles, (*fl.* 1550–70) whose *Description of the Western Islands of Scotland* (1594) is a brief but significant work. Martin Martin (*c.* 1660–1719), a native of Skye, wrote a *Description of the Western Islands of Scotland* (1703) which proved an inspiration for many later travellers.

The Rev. Richard Pockocke (1704–65), an early literary traveller, included Argyll in his explorations of Scotland between 1747 and 1760.

Thomas Pennant (1726–98), the Welsh-born naturalist, made two important tours in Scotland, one in 1769 which included much of mainland Argyll and one in 1772 which also included some of the islands, such as Jura, Islay, Staffa and Iona. Pennant was a perceptive and inquiring traveller, of whom no less an authority than Samuel Johnson remarked: '. . . he's the best traveller I ever read, he observes more things than anyone else does.'

A regular traveller to Argyll and the Highlands was John Knox (1720–90), whose *Tour of the Highlands of Scotland and the Hebride Isles* was published in 1786. Knox travelled to report on potential developments in the fishing industry but despite these practical concerns his *Tour* is an important source for the period.

Tobias Smollett (1721–1771) was born in the neighbouring county of Dunbartonshire and set part of his masterpiece, the epistolatory novel *Humphry Clinker* (1771), in Argyll. One character observes that the Highlanders: 'regale themselves with whisky, a malt spirit, as strong as geneva, which they swallow in great quantities, without any signs of inebriation. They are used to it from the cradle, and find it an excellent preservative against the winter cold, which must be extreme on these mountains.'

Another traveller who enquired into whisky, or 'what it is that makes a Scotchman happy', was Samuel Johnson (1709–84) who, with his friend and biographer James Boswell (1740–95), made one of the most famous of all literary tours in the late summer and autumn of 1773. They spent memorable days in Argyll, visiting the islands of Coll, Mull, Ulva and Iona, and returned south via Inveraray. Their passage to Coll was marked by a gale which greatly alarmed Boswell and drove Johnson below in the grip of sea-sickness. These distressing experiences were redeemed by the visit to Iona, described by Johnson as: 'that illustrious Island, which was once the luminary of the *Caledonian* regions, whence savage clans and roving barbarians derived the benefits of knowledge, and the blessings of religion.' He concluded: 'That man is little to be envied, whose patriotism would not gain force upon the plain of *Marathon*, or whose piety would not grow warmer among the ruins of *Iona!*'

Many late-eighteenth-century travellers came to Argyll to see the sites associated with Ossian – the hero of the legends collected and given written form or, as some insisted, invented by James MacPherson (1736–96). The international furore created by the publication of *Fingal* (1761) and *Temora* (1763) brought visitors eager to see the lonely glens and sea-lochs where the Fingalian warriors had fought and loved.

In the post-Jacobite era, as travelling conditions became easier and the Highlands became safer, the trickle of daring visitors to Argyll became a flood. Certain key locations attracted the literary and scientific tourist: Iona was a major cultural draw; the spectacular rock formations of Staffa and Fingal's Cave, first described to the outside world by Joseph Banks in 1772, were immensely attractive; and the new Inveraray Castle and its accompanying planned town formed another focus of touristic activity. The castle, planned by the 3rd duke of Argyll in the mid-eighteenth century, prompted Dr Johnson to comment, 'What I admire here, is the total defiance of expence'; it would win the praise of many other visitors.

One foreign visitor to Inveraray and Staffa in 1784 was Barthélemy Faujas de St Fond (1741–1819), a geologist and naturalist, who provides an insight into local life from the perspective of a cosmopolitan French visitor. He even commends the ducal table at Inveraray, where, he noted: 'the dishes are prepared after the manner of an excellent French cook, everything is served here as in Paris, except some courses in the English style, for which a certain predilection is preserved.'

Not every literary visitor to Argyll was quite so complimentary. Robert Burns (1759–96) called at Inveraray Inn in June 1787 and found the management and staff preoccupied with travellers planning to call on the duke of Argyll at the castle. Burns, however, had the last word:

Who'er he be that sojourns here,
I pity much his case,
Unless he comes to wait upon
The Lord their God, his Grace.

There's naething here but Highland pride,
And Highland scab and hunger;
If Providence has sent me here,
'Twas surely in an anger.

Argyll has another Burns connection, as the home of Mary Campbell, 'Highland Mary', with whom the poet planned to emigrate to Jamaica. Her sudden death resulted in the abandonment of these plans and ten more years of active poetic creation in Scotland. A statue commemorating Mary Campbell stands the foot of Dunoon's Castle Hill.

Thomas Campbell (1777–1844) a Glasgow-born poet of Highland descent spent the summer of 1795 as a tutor at Sunipol on Mull. Here he learned of the legend which he later used in his ballad 'Lord Ullin's Daughter' and found the subject for his poem 'The Pleasures of Hope':

'Tis distance lends enchantment to the view,
And robes the mountain in its azure hue,
Thus, with delight we linger to survey
The promised joys of life's unmeasured way.

In 1796 the intrepid Mrs Sarah Murray (1744–1811) travelled extensively through Scotland and published a lively account of her travels in *A Companion and Useful Guide to the Beauties of Scotland* (1799). She revisited Scotland and enlarged her *Guide* in 1803. Mrs Murray starts off on a severely practical note: 'Provide yourself with a strong roomy carriage,

and have the springs well corded ...' and recommends carrying one's own
bed-linen, towels, 'a blanket, thin quilt, and two pillows.'

She describes the visitors arriving in Oban on their way to Staffa: 'Some
are in such a hurry to get away that they run to and fro like maniacs, hear-
ing everyone's tale of the voyage ...' But she too paid the obligatory visit
to Staffa and Fingal's Cave and was suitably impressed: 'When I faced the
mouth of the cave, what I could see of the inside, and what I gazed at on
the outside, made my blood thrill through every vein; but when I got
within it I forgot the world and everything it contains.'

In 1803 William Wordsworth (1770–1850), his sister Dorothy
(1771–1855) and Samuel Taylor Coleridge toured extensively in Scotland.
Coleridge fell ill and left the Wordsworths on the boundary of Argyll but
William and Dorothy pressed on to Loch Fyne and Loch Awe and north
through Appin to Glencoe. Returning south they called at the Inveroran
Inn, near Bridge of Orchy, where Dorothy reported in her *Recollections of
a Tour made in Scotland* (1894) a sad disappointment over breakfast: 'the
butter not eatable, the barley-cakes fusty, the oat-bread so hard I could not
chew it, and there were only four eggs in the house, which they had boiled
as hard as stones'. William composed several poems on this visit including
the 'Address to Kilchurn Castle'.

The Lake poets were followed to Scotland by John Keats (1795–1821),
who had an unfortunate experience in 1818 on the classic route into Argyll
– the pass from Loch Long to Loch Fyne through Glen Croe by the 'Rest
and Be Thankful'. Keats and his friend Charles Brown misinterpreted their
map and assumed that 'Rest and Be Thankful' indicated an inn, rather than
a seat and viewpoint. He wrote: 'We were up at 4 this morning and have
walked to breakfast 15 miles through two tremendous Glens – at the end
of the first there is a place called rest and be thankful which we took for
an Inn – it is nothing but a Stone and so we were cheated into 5 more miles
to Breakfast.'

John MacCulloch (1773–1835) carried out a series of annual tours in the
Highlands between 1811 and 1821. He published his account of these tours
as *Travels in the Highlands and Western Islands of Scotland* (1824).

In 1814, the year of publication of his first novel, *Waverley*, Walter Scott
(1771–1832) sailed around the coasts of Scotland with the Commissioners
of the Northern Lights in the lighthouse yacht *Pharos*. His diary of this
journey appeared in John Gibson Lockhart's *Life of Sir Walter Scott* and has
recently been reprinted as *The Voyage of the Pharos* (1998, Scottish Library
Association). Part of Scott's reason for the trip was to absorb local colour
for his long poem 'The Lord of the Isles' (1815) and the Argyllshire part
of the voyage, and his earlier visits to Inveraray, doubtless also helped in
such works as *A Legend of Montrose* (1819). Scott's diary descriptions of the
places visited on his cruise are vivid and entertaining. Of Tobermory he
noted that 'the new part is reasonably clean, and the old not unreasonably
dirty,' displaying a nice balance between romanticism and practicality. The

party landed on Skerryvore where the engineer Robert Stevenson and the Commissioners planned to build a lighthouse. Scott noted this would be 'a most desolate position for a lighthouse – the Bell Rock and Eddystone a joke to it.'

Robert Louis Stevenson (1850–94), the grandson of Robert Stevenson, visited Argyll in 1870 with his father, Thomas, to inspect the construction of the Dubh Heartach lighthouse. Their visit to the shore station for the project, on Erraid off Mull, (which was also the service base for Skerryvore) was later used by Stevenson in *Kidnapped* (1886); the hero, David Balfour, is stranded on this tidal island after the wreck of the *Covenant*. David eventually finds his way to Mull and then to the mainland, where he is caught up in the Appin Murder. In the sequel, *Catriona* (1893), he returns to Inveraray to give evidence at the trial of James Stewart of the Glen for the Appin Murder.

Stevenson, reluctant as he was to follow in the family tradition of lighthouse building, did not entirely reject his heritage. He named his villa in Bournemouth 'Skerryvore' and wrote for it a poem, inspired by the lonely Argyllshire lighthouse:

> For love of lovely words, and for the sake
> Of those, my kinsmen and my countrymen,
> Who, early and late in the windy ocean toiled
> To plant a star for seamen, where was then
> The surfy haunt of seals and cormorants:
> I, on the lintel of this cot, inscribe
> The name of a strong tower.

The French novelist Jules Verne (1828–1905) was one of many nineteenth-century foreign literary tourists who were attracted to Argyll; his 1859 visit to Staffa resulted in his novel *The Green Ray* (1882) being set there.

In the twentieth century Argyll continued to attract many travel writers including J.J. Bell, George Blake, Seton Gordon, H.V. Morton and W.H. Murray.

CHAPTER NINETEEN

Gaelic Language and Literature in Argyll

G AELIC IS INSEPARABLY LINKED with Argyll. Not only has the area been Gaelic-speaking throughout many centuries, but it has also made an important contribution to the development of Gaelic literature in Scotland. In the present day, when indigenous Gaelic is relatively rare on the Argyll mainland and strongly maintained only in the more westerly islands such as Tiree, it is very easy to overlook the deep, pervasive and longstanding connection that Gaelic has with the whole region. The Gaelic legacy is, however, still very evident even in those parts which have lost the living language. It can still be read and heard in place-names. The enduring record, outlasting active Gaelic speech, has been supplemented by folklore collectors and dialectologists who have recorded vanishing dialects, songs and stories on tape. It is preserved pre-eminently in the work of many Argyllshire composers, whose contribution passed into manuscript and print. Indeed, there are few parts of the old county which cannot claim at least one significant writer or composer who originated there and who made a mark on modern Gaelic literature.

The Gaelic language

Gaelic is likely to have reached Argyll, *Oirir Goidel* ('Coastland of Gaels'), by at least the third and fourth centuries AD, when substantial numbers of settlers from Dál Riata in Antrim crossed the narrow stretch of water separating the Mull of Kintyre from the north coast of Ireland. From the new Dál Riata, the *Scoti* spread northwards and eastwards, taking Gaelic with them. By the twelfth century Gaelic had reached as far as the eastern seaboard of Scotland, and was spoken in most of the country, except Caithness, Orkney and Shetland.

As vernacular Gaelic took root in Scotland, it developed a significant number of regional, sub-regional and local dialects. It is convenient to speak of 'Argyllshire Gaelic' or 'Perthshire Gaelic', but any such labelling disguises considerable dialectical diversity. Argyll was something of a buffer zone between the dialect areas of the mainland central Highlands, the

Outer Hebrides, and the southern Hebrides; thus the Gaelic of eastern Argyllshire shaded into that of western Perthshire, while that of Tiree, the furthest west of the Inner Hebrides, has features in common with Barra Gaelic, to the extent that, at first encounter, it may be difficult to distinguish a Barra Gaelic speaker from a Tiree one. Yet Argyll had, and continues to have, numerous distinctive Gaelic dialects. Mull has at least two sub-regional dialects, that of the 'north end' and that of the Ross. Some features of the latter are found in the Gaelic of the west end of Tiree, with which the Ross had close connections. Ardnamurchan Gaelic, which has western and eastern dialect zones, is distinguished by its preponderance of low back vowels and its broad consonants; Tiree Gaelic has a high incidence of palatalisation; and the Gaelic of Ballachulish is noted for its pronunciation of broad *l* as *w*, though this feature is found more rarely elsewhere. Thus, while sharing features with neighbouring islands and districts, each island and mainland community had, and in some cases continues to have, its own dialect of Gaelic. This is well exemplified in the case of Islay. Dr Seumas Grannd's recent study shows with great clarity how the Gaelic of Islay relates most closely to that of neighbouring islands and districts: it shares 81.8 per cent of 'tested' features with Jura, 79.8 per cent with Kintyre, 69.2 per cent with Arran and 32.8 per cent with Tiree. This means that there are some 20 per cent of features which are distinctive of Islay Gaelic alone. Regional variation did not create insuperable difficulties in communication for Gaelic speakers in Argyll, any more than elsewhere.

The distinctive features of Argyllshire dialects were preserved to some extent by the isolation of the speakers in their own districts. The shared features of the dialects were doubtless part of a wider common core, but some would have been introduced by the penetration of other dialects through travel, trade, marriage and (most recently) media intrusion. The arrival of non-Gaelic-speaking people has had much more serious consequences for Gaelic. From the mid-eighteenth century the Gaelic dialects on the southern edges of Argyll, and indeed the very language itself, were being threatened by the arrival of Lowlanders who knew no Gaelic. The industrial belt of Lowland Scotland on the Argyll doorstep has exterted a potent influence across the years, while clearance, education, and many more subtle processes of assimilation to 'external' cultural values have accelerated the de-Gaelicisation of the region, particularly since the Second World War.

The medieval literary tradition

Gaelic has been a medium of great literary creativity in Argyll from the early Middle Ages. Scribes and composers, operating within the bounds of the old kingdom of Dál Riata, made major contributions to the growth of Gaelic literature. We can trace the region's earliest recorded literary tradition to the island of Iona and the work of Columban and post-Columban monks in their island 'university' in the sixth and seventh centuries. The Iona monastery was a highly literate community, engaged in the making and copying of manuscripts, recording in Latin events of local and national significance, and maintaining close links with other Columban houses in Ireland. Literary activity, ranging from the copying of manuscripts to the writing of books, was also very evident in Argyll in the time of the Lordship of the Isles. The Lords of the Isles acted as patrons to the poets until the end of the Lordship in 1493. Their patronage, and that of the Campbells, is reflected in some of the poems in the early sixteenth-century manuscript, the Book of the Dean of Lismore (1512–42). James MacGregor, one of its scribes, was titular Dean of the cathedral church of Lismore, near Oban. The Book of the Dean of Lismore is a priceless anthology of medieval Gaelic verse from both Ireland and Scotland. It contains a number of poems with a close connection with Argyll, including a fine salutation to John MacSween, a member of the displaced family of the MacSweens of Knapdale, who had taken up residence in Ireland by c. 1260. Around 1310 John apparently tried to retake his family's fortress, Castle Sween, which stands in ruined magnificence on the eastern shore of Loch Sween. Unlike the MacSweens, some kindreds grew in significance and in patronage after the demise of the Lordship. The MacLeans, including the MacLeans of Duart and the MacLeans of Coll, mantained poets of considerable stature. Island lairds too were often skilled in song. The cultivation of Gaelic literature in Argyll after 1492 owed much to the Campbells, who were also patrons of the Gaelic arts, as the background of the first Gaelic printed book amply demonstrates.

Prose

The very first Gaelic printed book to appear in Ireland or Scotland was published in Edinburgh in 1567, but it was produced in Carnasserie Castle, which stands in a beautiful spot just above the main road through mid Argyll, and looks across Kilmartin Glen. The occupant of the castle in the 1560s was a powerful and influential clergyman called John Carswell (c. 1520–72), who enjoyed the patronage of the 5th Earl of Argyll, and was known and long remembered in Gaelic as Carsallach Mòr Charnàsaraidh ('Big Carswell of Carnasserie') because of his great height (seven feet). The lintel of the main door bears the words Dia le ua nDuibhne ('God [be] with Ua Duibhne', Ua Duibhne being the Campbell Earl of Argyll). With the warm support of the 5th earl, John Carswell became a Protestant at the time of the Reformation, and translated into Gaelic a fundamentally important book of the Scottish Reformation, namely John Knox's Book of Common Order. The Book of Common Order was a directory for the conduct of worship in the Reformed churches. Carswell's translation, Foirm na *nUrrnuidheadh*, was of great importance for the implantation of Reformed doctrine in this part of the Highlands. It would have been used by Gaelic-speaking ministers, like Carswell himself, who were formerly priests in the pre-Reformation church. But the book was of even more importance for the future of Gaelic; it established the tradition of printed Gaelic, and it used the Classical Gaelic of the Middle Ages as the vehicle for the transmission of Protestant doctrine. It also laid down a standard – the Classical standard – for the spelling of Gaelic.

This is important because other scribes who have at least a nominal link with Argyll, notably the compilers of the Book of the Dean of Lismore, were operating mainly in Fortingall on the eastern edge of the Highlands, and employing a spelling system for Gaelic which was based on the systems of Middle and Early Modern Scots. If the scribes of the Book of the Dean had beaten Carswell to the printing press, the spelling of Gaelic might have been very different; it might have resembled that of modern Manx. Carswell's foundational book ensured that there would be continuity between the Gaelic literary conventions of the Middle Ages and those of the modern era. The vision which inspired Carswell's work was not only that of a Protestant west, embracing Scotland and Ireland; it was also a vision of a region whose literary culture had made a successful transition from script to print. He had an important message for the traditional scribes, labouring with their quills:

> *Is mor-tsaothair sin re sgriobhadh do laimh, ag fechain an neithe buailtear sa chló ar aibrisge agus ar aithghiorra bhios gach én-ni dhá mhéd da chriochnughadh leis.*
>
> (It is a great labour to write that by hand, considering how swiftly and speedily whatever is put through the printing press is completed, however great.)

Since Carswell's time, clergymen of the Reformed Church in Argyll have played a major part in the creation of Gaelic literature, particularly Gaelic prose literature. Clergymen were not so keen to compose original Gaelic poetry, though Carswell did fashion a poem to send his book on its way. They did, however, contribute massively to the development of Gaelic prose, especially religious prose. Ministers of the seventeenth-century Synod of Argyll, following Carswell's example, translated catechisms into Gaelic, and even set to work on a translation of the Bible into Gaelic. The Old Testament reached completion by 1673, and was apparently available in manuscript. Sadly, it did not reach print because of the political and ecclesiastical turmoil of the times. When the Bible was eventually translated into Gaelic, between 1755 and 1801, Argyllshire men again played their part in the task, the most notable Argyllshire contributor being the Rev. Dr John Smith (1747–1807), a native of Glenorchy and minister of Campbeltown, who translated the Prophetic Books in a revolutionary manner resembling the 'dynamic equivalence' versions of today, in which contemporary idiom takes precedence over literal translation. His work annoyed some of his colleagues, and it was later brought into line with the 'word equivalence' of the other translators.

The manse of Morvern is another clerical mansion which contributed extensively to the diversification of Gaelic prose literature, notably in the nineteenth century. It was the home of a family of MacLeods with roots in Skye. The Morvern MacLeods produced a distinguished succession of ministers, whose best known modern representative was Lord MacLeod of Fiunary. The manse of Morvern was the boyhood home of the Rev. Dr Norman MacLeod, otherwise known as 'Caraid nan Gàidheal' ('The Highlanders' Friend'), whose father was the parish minister of Morvern. MacLeod was the editor of the first Gaelic periodicals to be devoted to the regular publication of prose and verse. These periodicals were *An Teachdaire Gaelach* (1829–31) and *Cuairtear nan Gleann* (1840–43). MacLeod was successively minister of Campbeltown (1808–25), Campsie (1825–35) and St Columba's, Glasgow (1835–62). He established the two periodicals in an attempt to provide a wide-ranging diet of good, informative reading in natural idiomatic Gaelic for the large numbers of Highlanders who were becoming literate in Gaelic through the work of the Gaelic schools and General Assembly schools from the opening years of the nineteenth century.

Norman MacLeod's work may seem unexciting nowadays, but in its own time it was very important in extending the range of Gaelic prose. Much of the available Gaelic prose material written before his time consisted of translations of English puritan prose works, and it was heavily weighted towards doctrinal knowledge. MacLeod provided a variety of new prose styles, including dialogues, essays and short stories. The aim of the periodicals was didactic, but it was a broad-minded type of didacticism. In his venture he was ably assisted by two other Argyllshire men. One of these was his own son-in-law, the Rev. Archibald Clerk (1813–87), a native of Glen Lonan, who was latterly minister of Kilmallie. Clerk edited MacLeod's collected works. The other Argyllshire man who helped Norman MacLeod was Lachlan MacLean (1798–1848), a native of Coll, who was a merchant in Glasgow.

Archibald Clerk has a further claim to distinction. He was the first editor of the Gaelic Supplement of *Life and Work*, first published in 1880. Donald Lamont (1874–1958), a native of Tiree, edited the Gaelic Supplement for over forty years (1907–51). During most of this period, he was parish minister at Blair Atholl, Perthshire. Under Lamont's ceaselessly provocative pen, the Gaelic Supplement became the main vehicle for thematic and stylistic experimentation in Gaelic; it carried sermons, essays and short stories. Lamont had a particularly lively imagination, and was not afraid to create 'factional' characters and scenarios, and to use these to carry the message he wanted to communicate. Often he poked fun at the Established Church. He was obviously aware, to a remarkable degree, of the opportunity he had, as a clerical writer, to contribute constructively to the well-being of the Gaelic language. His concept of a Gaelic Supplement was not one that ran in the rails of ecclesiastical convention, restricted by doctrinal rigidity and enslavement to purely homiletic styles.

The tradition of printed Gaelic prose was established primarily by writers from the mainland of Argyll, but, as the contributions of MacLean and Lamont indicate, writers from the islands were of great significance to the growth of modern written prose. One very fine writer of Gaelic prose came from the island of Jura. He was Donald MacKechnie (1836–1908). MacKechnie, who was resident in Edinburgh for most of his life, wrote essays in which he empathised with the animal world – cats, dogs, and deer – and discovered a close affinity between them and himself. He was the first Gaelic writer to internalise the influence of Darwin's theory of evolution, and to acknowledge its implications for the relationship between humans and animals. He had a wonderful sense of humour too, writing a splendid essay on the theme of 'going to the ant'. He describes vividly how he sat down on an ant-hill on the Salisbury Crags, and, having got 'ants in his pants', had to pull off his trousers in dire emergency. His dog, seeing his master in this 'state of nature', went slightly crazy ... and the whole chaotic scenario was witnessed by a rather proper, well-to-do lady, who fainted at the scene. The moral of the story is that one must not take proverbs too seriously, lest primordial chaos and embarrassment should be the result. In his satirical and (philosophically) existential approach to life, MacKechnie differed markedly from his contemporaries, and not least from his close friend, Professor Donald MacKinnon (1839–1914), a native of Colonsay, who became the first Professor of Celtic at the University of Edinburgh in 1882. MacKinnon contributed extensively to the Gaelic periodical, *An Gàidheal*, from the 1870s onwards, and was the first major literary critic to write in Gaelic. He expounded, rather ponderously, the meaning and philosophy of Gaelic proverbs, and provided assessments of the works of Gaelic poets.

The era which stimulated the writings of the first Professor of Celtic in Scotland also produced John Francis Campbell of Islay (1822–85). The son of the last Campbell laird of Islay, he was perhaps the first Gaelic scholar to acknowledge the special importance of the prose tales which circulated in oral transmission. He organised a band of collectors, who wrote down the tales from the mouths of reciters, and later, between 1860 and 1862, a selection of these tales was published in four volumes entitled *Popular Tales of the West Highlands*. Campbell's *Popular Tales* were no more than a small sample of the immense richness of the Gaelic story-telling tradition. More such material was edited by another scion of the Campbell house, the rather eccentric Lord Archie Campbell (1846–1913), who produced a series of useful books called *Waifs and Strays of Celtic Tradition*. Among the contributors was John Gregorson Campbell, a native of Kingairloch, who was parish minister in Tiree from 1861.

Story-telling was very much part of Gaelic culture in Argyll, as elsewhere, and the county produced a number of minor writers, who had some considerable significance in their own time. Henry Whyte (1852–1913) from Easdale was a stalwart of the late nineteenth-century Highland cèilidh circuit in Glasgow, and produced volumes of humorous tales. His brother, John Whyte (1842–1913), was a significant Gaelic journalist who wrote for various late nineteenth-century papers, including John Murdoch's radical, anti-landlord organ, *The Highlander*. The Whytes were the sons of John Whyte, who was manager of the earl of Breadalbane's quarries in Easdale. A small group of influential Mull writers is also evident. It included John MacCormick (d. 1947), who produced a novel *Dùn-Aluinn* (1912), and John MacFadyen (1850–1935), with his series of books of humorous tales and poems, of which *Sgeulaiche nan Caol* (1902) is an example.

Poetry

Gaelic poetry, like Gaelic prose, has a long history in the county, and it is pre-eminently with poetry that the literary activity of Argyll is connected in the popular mind. A tour of the places associated with Argyll poets would take us to the native areas of some of the greatest poets of Gaelic Scotland. Dalilea and Islandfinnan (Inverness-shire) were the early stamping-grounds of the formidable poet, Alexander MacDonald (*c*. 1698-*c*. 1770), otherwise known as Alasdair mac Mhaighstir Alasdair, who served his reluctant time as a schoolmaster in Ardnamurchan, before becoming Prince Charles' Gaelic poet-laureate, and lampooning the Campbells with his barbed wit. Later, after the 'Forty-five, MacDonald became baillie of Canna. MacDonald is widely regarded as the greatest of the eighteenth-century Gaelic poets, certainly in terms of intellectual fire. His volume of poems, *Ais-eiridh na Seana Chànoin Albannaich*, was the first volume of verse by a Gaelic vernacular poet to be put in print. It appeared in 1751, but, because of its Jacobite sentiments, it is said to have been burnt by the public hangman in Edinburgh. Only a few copies of the original printing of the book have survived.

MacDonald's poetry had a profound influence on his contemporaries in Argyll, notably (it would seem) Argyll's best known poet, Duncan MacIntyre, better known as Donnchadh Bàn Mac an t-Saoir (1724–1812). MacIntyre is the Gaelic nature bard par excellence, describing the wonderful productivity which can be achieved when humanity and nature are in a co-operative harmony. His poem, 'Moladh Beinn Dòbhrain' ('In Praise of Ben Dobhran'), is perhaps the finest poetic description ever made of the wildlife of any region in the British Isles:

> *An t-urram thar gach beinn*
> *Aig Beinn Dòbhrain;*
> *De na chunnaic mi fon ghrèin*

'S i bu bhòidhche leam;
Monadh fada rèidh,
Cuile 'm faighte feidh,
Soilleireachd an t-slèibh
Tha mi sònrachadh.

(Honour above all hills
upon Beinn Dobhrain;
of all I've seen beneath the sun,
I think her loveliest;
a long, smooth upland,
a storehouse of the deer,
the silhouette of the hill
I am contemplating.)

Duncan MacIntyre was unable to read or write, but many of his poems were written down by a native of Glenorchy, the Rev. Donald MacNicol, parish minister of Lismore. His verse was first published in 1768.

Gaelic poets and songsters of lesser stature than Donnchadh Bàn were active throughout Argyll. There was an almost inexhaustible number of poets, particularly of the local 'township bard' type, who commemorated events and personalites within their own districts. Representatives of the nineteenth-century poetic tradition on the mainland include Dr John MacLachlan (1804–74), Rahoy; Calum Campbell MacPhail (1847–1913), Dalmally; Iain Campbell, Ledaig; Evan MacColl (1808–98), Lochfyneside; and Dugald Gordon MacDougall, a native of Dunach in Kilbride parish. MacLachlan and MacPhail, in particular, observed, and commented on, the patterns of social change as their areas were transformed by 'improvement' and clearing. MacLachlan's poignant elegies on cleared townships are deeply moving, as the physician expresses his sorrow at the immense loss of human companionship. The ability to compose light lyrics survived in mainland Argyll into the twentieth century; Edward Pursell (1891–1964), a native of Campbeltown who learned Gaelic, was the composer of several popular Gaelic songs and tunes, including the words and melody of 'Fàgail Liosmòr' ('Leaving Lismore').

The 'township bard' is well attested in most island communities, especially in the context of crofting, after 1800. Tiree was particularly rich in poets of this kind. Pride of place belongs to John MacLean (1827–95) of Balemartin, who composed the well-known humorous song, 'Calum Beag' ('Little Callum'), about the imaginary sea-going adventures of one of his neighbours. Callum travelled through stormy seas to Glasgow by way of the Crinan Canal, which held out many temptations, particularly since it offered ready access to a range of hostelries such as Cairnbaan Inn:

Nuair ràinig tu Aird Driseig bha na h-ighneagan an tòir ort;
Chùm iad ann ad chabhaig thu toirt caithreim dhaibh air òrain;

Do ghillean 's iad air bhuidealaich an cuideachd Mhic an Tòisich,
Is chaidh thu thar na còrach ag òl sa Chàrn Bhàn.

(When you reached Ardrishaig, the girls there pursued you;
they kept you in a hurry singing songs for their amusement:
your lads were fired up mightily in MacIntosh's company,
and you went beyond your limit as you boozed in Cairnbaan.)

MacLean also composed political songs, which helped the cause of the
crofters in the local Land League in the 1880s. Some island poets achieved
major recognition within the wider Gaelic area. Islay, for example, was the
home of one of the best of the nineteenth-century Gaelic bards – William
Livingston (1808–70), who composed memorable verse on the effect of the
clearances in Islay. Two editions of his poems were published.

The Gaelic poets of Argyll, like those of other parts of the Highlands
and Islands, had a tremendous appreciation of the value of their own local
communities. A sense of place has always been important to Gaelic writers, but it has probably been more evident in verse than in prose. Argyll
itself has been not only the home of poets; it has also been the creator and
inspirer of poets, right down to our own time. One of the greatest Gaelic
poets of the twentieth century was George Campbell Hay (1915–84),
whose roots were in Tarbert, Loch Fyne, and who celebrated the beauty
of the Kintyre landscape and the achievements of its people, particularly
the fishermen who were among the last custodians of the Gaelic language
and culture of the area:

Sìth o Dhia air màthair m' altraim,
le spreigeadh gràidh chan fhaigh mi clos;
sòlas duit, Chinn-tìr, is sonas;
cuim nach molainn crìoch gun lochd?

(God's peace upon my fostering mother,
with love's incitement, I cannot keep quiet;
joy to you, Kintyre, and happiness;
why should I not praise a flawless place?)

Concluding Overview

Across the centuries, Argyll has been highly productive of Gaelic literature,
both prose and verse. Literary activity has extended from the Middle Ages
down to the present century, and the region contributed greatly to the
development of Gaelic literature. Perhaps the most important contribution
that Argyll has made to that development lies in facilitating the transition
from oral tradition to manuscript, and from manuscript to the modern
printing press, thus ensuring that there was, and is, a modern Gaelic

printed literature. Writers born in Argyll led the field in producing Gaelic printed books; the first Gaelic printed book comes from the county, and almost all the main composers and collectors mentioned above published printed volumes of their works. A native of Mulindry in Islay, Archibald Sinclair (1813–70), established the highly influential Celtic Press in Glasgow in the second half of the nineteenth century, to ensure that Gaelic material was printed. In this he and his son and grandson gave a singular service, not only to natives of Argyll, but to all Highlanders until the 1920s, when the business was taken over by Alexander McLaren. Argyllshire men likewise made key contributions to the modern media, and helped to extend the range of outlets available to Gaelic writers. In Gaelic broadcasting, for instance, Hugh MacPhee (1899–1980), a native of Ballachulish, laid the foundations of the Gaelic service of the BBC, operating from Broadcasting House, Glasgow.

What made this county so productive of Gaelic composers and literary leaders? The fundamental reason is surely that throughout the centuries Argyll had a Gaelic literate class who were used to plying their literary crafts and expressing their thoughts on vellum, parchment and paper. Literary creativity was given a high place from the time of the Lordship of the Isles, and patronage continued through the Campbells and other local families. The value of literacy was maintained by the schools. When formal schooling began to come to the Highlands, Argyll was provided with parochial schools and grammar schools from an early stage in the seventeenth century. Not all of these schools were sympathetic to Gaelic, but in 1706 the parochial school in Lochgoilhead (for example) had a teacher who was capable of writing Gaelic, and he may have taught his scholars to do the same.

If schoolmasters were not always sympathetic to Gaelic, the clergy of Argyll certainly used the language, and greatly aided its development as a literary medium. The Protestant clergy in Argyll were less tied to doctrinal straitjackets than their colleagues in other parts of the Highlands. The evangelicals of the northern Highlands tended to regard Argyll as a rather 'moderate' region. It is certainly true that the more profoundly world-denying evangelical movements which altered the religious shape of the northern Highlands and Outer Hebrides were less influential in Argyll, though they were by no means absent. These post-1800 movements came to Argyll very late in the day, and did not displace the foundation of broad-minded humanism (in the Renaissance sense) which had already been laid by Carswell and his successors. This allowed sacred and secular to breathe together more freely, and even the ministers of small, intensely evangelical groups such as the Baptists had a high degree of cultural awareness and published volumes of hymns. Duncan MacDougall, a native of Brolas in Mull who had close connections with the Ross of Mull, became the founding father of Tiree Baptist Church (1838), and put his hymns into print in 1841. His sister, Mary MacDonald (1789–1872), who continued to live in the Ross of Mull, was the composer of a Gaelic hymn, 'Leanabh an Aigh', famous today as the carol 'Child in the Manger'. Mary also composed secular verse. The proportion of ministers who were natives of the region and contributed constructively to the development of Gaelic literature *per se* is thus probably higher in Argyll than in any other district of the Highlands. The county had a liberal and liberating atmosphere in which writers could pursue their callings. This continuing feeling of liberation may partly explain why Gaelic writers from other parts of the Highlands still find it a congenial place.

The openness of Argyll was created not only by its religious complexion but also by its geographical position as a threshold area of the Highlands. This was its weakness as well as its strength. People from Argyll travelled backwards and forwards to the Lowlands with relative ease. As a consequence, the fashions of the Lowland south entered Argyll more quickly than they did other parts of the Highlands; witness, for example, the ready reception of Protestantism in the region shortly after the Scottish Reformation. Printing accompanied Protestantism, allowing Gaelic tradition to take printed form faster in Argyll than in any other part of the Highlands and Islands. Argyll was a multicultural, cosmopolitan region, but this had dangers for Gaelic. The overall result is very evident. Today the use of the language is restricted to the Inner Hebrides, and there are very few active Gaelic writers who are natives of Argyll. The primary roles in developing and maintaining Gaelic literature in Scotland have passed mainly to writers who are natives of the northern Highlands and the Outer Hebrides.

Note: An earlier version of this chapter was published in the journal, *Laverock*, 3 (1997).

CHAPTER TWENTY

The Place-names of Argyll

T HE ARGYLL THAT WE KNOW TODAY was once of much greater extent,
extending perhaps as far north as Loch Broom in Ross. But the extension of Norse power in the ninth century, and its dominance of the western
coastlands had a profound influence on the political situation, and on the
names used for the whole coastal zone.

In Middle Irish, the fledgling Gaelic kingdom was known as *Airer Gáidel*,
later *Oirer Ghaidheal*. The first part of the name is composed of two Gaelic
words, *oir* 'edge' and *tir* 'land', giving the modern Gaelic *oirthir* 'coastland',
'littoral', so the whole means 'coastland of the Gaels'. The modern form is
Earra-Ghàidheal, in which *oirthir* is contracted and the original meaning
is blurred.

Like many of the old district names of Scotland, we find the origins of
some district names in Argyll to be personal names. The four major tribes
of sixth century Dál Riata were those of Congall son of Domongart, Loarn
Mór son of Erc, Gabrán son of Domongart and Oengus son of Erc. Two
of these names survive in Argyll – *Lorne*, from Loarn, which basically
meant 'fox', and *Cowal*, from Comgall. The other district names are geographically descriptive. In North Argyll, *Ardnamurchan* is thought to derive
from Gaelic *aird na muir-chon* 'promontory of the sea-dogs', alluding to
otters, while *Morvern*, usually referred to as *a' Mhorbhairn* with the definite article, can be broken down into two words, *muir* 'sea', and *bearna*
'gap', giving 'the sea-gap'. This is very likely a reference to the great sea-
loch of *Loch Sunart* which lies between Morvern and Ardnamurchan. This
is a Norse name *Sveina-fjordr* 'Sveinn's fjord', but it is almost certain that
its pre-Norse name was *a' Mhuir-bhearna*, and the district to the south
retains this form.

On the east shore of the Firth of Lorne lies *Appin*, between Loch Creran
and Loch Leven. This comes from Middle Irish *apdaine* 'abbacy', 'abbey
land'. The Argyll Appin, which may have been the property of the monastic community of Lismore, is of old referred to as *Apuinn nan Stiubhartach*
'the Stewarts' Appin', to distinguish it from other abbey lands in the Highlands, in particular *Apuinn nam Mèinnearach* 'the Menzies' Appin', which
lies to the east, in the form of the Appin of Dull in Perthshire.

In the south lies *Kintyre*, *Ceann-tír* 'head of the land', the long peninsula
which runs south from *Knapdale*. This is a Norse formation, probably

ON *knoppr* 'lumpy hill', 'knob', and *dalr* 'valley'. It is certainly a landscape which consists of lumpy hills breached by many small sea-lochs and inlets, so it is aptly named.

The island names of Argyll are among the most difficult as regards derivation. The three major islands of Argyll – Mull, Jura and Islay – all pose different problems as far as their origins are concerned. *Jura* is most likely from ON *dýr-øy* 'deer island' (the deer population remains high) and we have no clear-cut pre-Norse name for it, although a native of Jura at the beginning of this century informed Prof. W. J. Watson that it was traditionally known as *An t-Eilean Bàn* 'the blessed isle', where *ban* 'white' has the secondary meaning of 'holy'. *Mull* is generally equated with a name *Malaois*, an Old British name recorded by writers during the Roman period. But we do not know what the name means. In modern Gaelic the island is called *Muile*, and a man living there would be called a *Muileach*.

Islay is referred to by Adamnán as *Ilea insula*, and is in Gaelic *Ìle*, or *Eilean Ileach*. Watson and others suggested a derivation from Early Celtic meaning 'to swell', giving a term which describes the island's shape. But there has been much speculation on this name, and we will probably never be certain about its derivation.

Even more complex is the name *Iona*. Adamnán refers to it as *Ioua insula* and the misreading of *u* as *n* gives us the present form. In fact *Iona* is an adjective formed from the name of the island, although Gaelic speakers today refer to the island as *Ì*, gen. *Idhe*, and a man of Iona is *Idheach*. Mediaeval forms of the name often combine it with that of Columba, as *Icolmkill* '*Idhe Coluim Cille*', or in its fullest translation 'Iona of Colm of the Church'. The full account of serious scholarly discussion is too long for the scope of this article, so it is recommended that W. J. Watson's analysis in his *History of the Celtic Place-Names of Scotland* (1926, 87–90) should be studied.

Of the other Argyll islands, many are referred to in Adamnán's writings, since they frequently had contacts with Iona, and with Ireland. *Colonsay* is ON *Kolbeins-øy* 'Kolbein's island', in Gaelic *Colbhasa*. *Coll*, however, is equated with the island called *Colosus* in Adamnán's text. In modern Gaelic it is called simply *Colla*, but we are left in the dark as to its derivation. Adamnán refers to *Tiree* as *Ethica Terra* or *Ethica insula*, while the Irish Book of Ballymote mentions it as *tír iath seach íle* 'Tir-aith beyond Islay'. Although we have many references to Tiree in early writings, such as *Tiri-eth* (twelfth century), *Tiryad* (1343), *Tereyd* (1354) and *Tyriage* (1390), we are still uncertain as to its true meaning. The Norse referred to it as *Tyrvist*, and a man of Tiree is therefore known as *Tirisdeach*. Most people in Argyll refer to it as *Tireadh*, with the stress falling slightly on the first syllable.

Two other significant islands are *Lismore* and *Gigha*. The first of these was the site of an important monastery, founded by St Moluag (d. 595) shortly after Columba's establishing of Iona. The name *Lismore* is simple

– Gaelic *lios mór* 'big garden' or 'big walled enclosure', presumably either because of the fertility of the island, or the specialised use of *lios* as a monastic site (cf *Lesmahagow*). *Gigha* first appears in the Norse *Hakon's Saga* as *Guðey*; thereafter it is *Gudey* (1263), *Grythe* (1335), *Geday* (c. 1400) and *Giga* (1510). Speculation on the derivation has raged for years. ON *goð*, *guð*, suggests 'God's Island', but *gja* 'chasm', 'rift' is just as likely, and we are again left with a doubtful meaning for the name.

Most of the smaller Argyll islands have conventional names, some of Norse origin. *Kerrera* is written *Kjarbarey* in a Norse saga, and may be from ON *kjarr* 'brushwood'; *Luing* is ON *Longa-ey* 'long island'; and *Scarba* may be form *skarf-ay* 'cormorant island'. *Oronsay* to the south of Colonsay, and connected to it at low tide, is an example of the many islands which can be reached at the ebb. This is ON *oirfiris-ey* 'tidal island'. *Eriska* off the mouth of Loch Creran may be 'Erik's island'.

As we have seen, Argyll is an area with a highly indented coastline. Glacially produced sea-lochs give the county a fjord-like littoral, with many sea-lochs of lengths varying from a few miles to over thirty in the case of Loch Fyne. This enabled penetration deep into the interior of Argyll, as well as affording good communications for what essentially a coastal population.

In general, the names of sea-lochs, at least those of Celtic origin, have as their basis the name of the rivers which run into the head of the lochs. This is certainly true of *Loch Fyne*, into which the River Fyne, *Abhainn Fíne* in Gaelic, runs through Glen Fyne, *Gleann Fíne*. Watson (CPNS, 437) discusses the term *fíne* 'vine' in connection with this river, suggesting that it was a 'stream of virtue' and equating it with Latin *vinea* 'vine'. A number of such pure, clear streams acquire this term in early Gaelic Scotland, as well as several wells called *Tobar an Fhìona* which were often associated with religious sites. We thus have the progression river – glen – sea loch, which Loch Fyne illustrates well. *Loch Long* seems to be from *long* 'ship', but *Loch Striven*, in Gaelic *Loch Stoigheann* is obscure in origin. *Loch Melfort* and *Loch Killisport*, however, contain the ON *fjord* as their final element; *Loch Craiginish* similarly is Norse, from *kraka-nes* 'crow-point'. *Loch Sween* most probably comes from ON *Svein*, the personal name, and *Loch Stornoway* in Knapdale is probably derived from ON *steorna-vágr* 'steerage inlet', in the same way as Stornoway in Lewis.

One of the most unusual names is that of *Loch Etive*, in Gaelic *Loch Eíte*. Again, the river-name is similar. The origin is in a feminine proper name *Éitig* 'foul or horrid one', and Gaelic speakers earlier in the twentieth century referred to this hag as *Eiteag* 'the little horrid one', who lived in *Gleann Salach* 'the foul glen', which runs into Loch Creran above Barcardine. She frequently called up furious storms on Loch Etive, which make it a dangerous stretch of water.

Across in North Argyll, the two significant sea lochs are *Loch Aline* 'beautiful loch' on the Sound of Mull, and *Loch Sunart*, already described.

In Mull, we have several important sea-lochs, including *Loch Scridain* 'loch with the scree side' (although up to *c.* 1790 it was known as Loch Leffan), *Loch Spelve* 'stony loch', and *Loch Buie* 'yellow loch'. *Loch na Keal*, originally *Loch Scaffort* is a puzzle, as the present name dates only from 1801. Some authorities derive the name as 'loch of the churches' but there is no real evidence for this (see Charles Maclean, *The Isle of Mull*, 1997, 149).

The term *tairbeart*, from *tairm-bert* 'over-bringing' and 'isthmus', occurs in situations where two major bodies of water are connected by a short neck of land. Several of these occur in Argyll, usually in the form *Tarbert*, the best known of which connects Loch Fyne with the Sound of Jura. On Jura itself, there is another Loch Tarbert, and *Glen Tarbert* lies between Loch Sunart and Loch Linnhe in North Argyll, while we find another Tarbert in Gigha.

Loch Linnhe itself is curious in that it is a 'manufactured' name, from Gaelic *linne* 'pool'. The part inside the Corran narrows as far as the mouth of the River Lochy, is referred to as *An Linne Dhubh* 'the black pool', and originally was *Loch Abar*. Outside the Corran, the wider, more salty sea-loch is *An Linne Sheileach* 'the salty pool'. Both of these were used by Gaelic speakers in the area.

Few of the rivers of Argyll are substantial, falling as they do from a watershed which lies relatively close to the coast. No extensive streams such as the Tay, Forth or Spey, exist in Argyll. The valleys of important streams certainly existed in pre-glacial times, but are now largely occupied by the great sea-lochs which have already been discussed.

Settlement Names

The settlement of Gaelic speakers in Argyll from the sixth century under Fergus mac Erc resulted in a group of settlement names which set the pattern for place-names in all parts of Scotland where Gaelic was spoken, so we look on Argyll, the ancient Dál Riata, as the heartland of Gaelic speech and nomenclature. This settlement was preceded by p-Celtic; but the overlay of Gaelic proved to be so powerful and all-embracing that few p-Celtic names are immediately recognisable in Argyll, apart from those island names which are largely obscure in derivation, and which pre-date the Gaelic settlement. The other factor which plays an important role in the story is the Columban church. This provides us with a number of generics that are directly the result of Christian activity from the sixth to the eleventh centuries, when the establishing of churches became a central part of the life of the Dalriadic population.

The introduction of Norse naming, from the mid-ninth century on, becomes an important element in place-names in certain parts of Argyll, especially the islands of Tiree, Coll, Mull, Jura and Islay. The adjacent mainland contains fewer Norse names, especially those which indicate habitation (habitative names), but there area substantial numbers of Norse topographic names throughout Kintyre, and along the shores of Loch Linnhe.

The early church in Argyll leaves its mark in a large number of place-names. Not only were churches established to become a focus of local activity, but Columban monastics set up cells and hermitages in secluded places and, indeed, in sites near populated areas as well. The original parish names of Argyll demonstrate clearly the extent and influence of the early church since 22 of them contain the element *cill*. This was thought to come from the Latin *cella* 'church', and is by far the most common of the ecclesiastical terms from the early Gaelic period. Many of these names, generally anglicised to *kil-*, commemorate early saints of the Celtic church, such as *Kilarrow*, Islay (St Maelrubha), *Kilberry* (St Berach), *Kilchoman*, Islay (St Comman), *Kilmaronag*, Loch Etive (St Conóc), *Kilfinnichen*, Mull (St Findchan, a contemporary of St Columba), *Killundine*, Morvern (St Fintan), *Kilviceun*, Mull (the church of the sons of Eoghan) and *Kilchammaig*, Knapdale (Camoc's church). Another group commemorates biblical figures, such as *Kilmichael* in Glassary, where the archangel is featured, or *Kilmartin*, which was dedicated to St Martin of Tours (*c.* 316–*c.* 400), apparently a favourite saint in the Celtic church, and the patron saint of France. The name *Brigid* (which, according to the chroniclers, was borne by no fewer than fifteen female saints) was extremely popular, so it is no surprise that we have places called *Kilbride* 'Brigid's church' in Seil, Lorn, Islay, Tiree and Coll, as well as at least sixteen in other parts of Scotland. *Kilmorich*, Cowal, is named after *Muireadhach*, Abbot of Iona (d. 1011), and *Kiloran* in Colonsay is named after *Odrán*, Columba's kinsman and disciple, who died during Columba's lifetime.

In the early period of Christian settlement, stone-built churches were referred to as *clachan*, and the communities which grew up around them were often called by the same word. So the name *clachan* 'hamlet' frequently gives us a clue to a place's origin. Dalmally in Glenorchy, for example, was of old called *Clachan an Diseart*, from Latin *desertum*, and Irish *díseart*. This term, which also occurs in the name *Dysart*, Fife, meant 'deserted place' – in other words, a site where monks sought solitude for contemplation. One of the few examples of *clachan* that survives in Argyll is *Clachan Seil*, although one has to be careful with this term as *clachan* can also mean 'stepping-stones' or 'causeway'.

The term *annaid*, from O.Ir. *andoit*, is found throughout Scotland from Galloway to Sutherland, and meant a 'parent' church, or one which contained a relic of the founder. Normally, the name is found in a simple form, such as *Annat* in Appin, and *Annat* in Kilchrenan, Loch Awe. Some are compound forms, like *Achnahannet* 'field of the Annat' in Morvern, and in Glen Lonan, east of Oban, we have *Cladh na h-Annaide* 'the cemetery of the Annat'. Most of the names containing *annaid* are in remote places; few are connected with a known saint, but they are all close to an ancient chapel or cemetery, such as the Appin Annat, which lies close to the site of the parish church.

Other names connected with the church include *Bachall* in Lismore, which is recorded in 1544 as *Peynabachalla*. This term is from Latin *baculum* 'staff', and in Gaelic *bachall* 'crozier'. The hereditary custodian of the crozier of St Moluag is the family of Livingstone, and the head of the family is known as *Baran na Bachaill* 'the Baron of the Crozier'. Originally, the land granted to the custodian was *Peighinn na Bachaill*, 'the pennyland of the crozier', but the generic has fallen out of use for a long time. Another relic was the *arbhachall* or 'great crozier' of St Maol-Rubha of Applecross, which was in the possession of its keeper, the Dewar. This name comes from the name of the relic itself, *deòradh* 'pilgrim', and survives in the name *Ballindeoir* in Muckairn – 'the dewar's town'.

Contemplative monks were often associated with a seat, in Gaelic *suidhe*, so we find *Suidhe Bhaodain* 'Baodan's seat', a large block of stone near Ardchattan, while Glen Lussa in Knapdale contains *Suidhe Bhacoch* 'Bacoch's Seat'.

The major farms in Gaelic Argyll were named according to a system that flourished in Ireland, and used a system of generics which can still be found there. The standard term for 'farm' is *baile* anglicised to *Bal-* or *Bally-*, the latter being more common in Ireland. Originally it meant 'farm' or 'farmstead', very similar to the Scots 'ferm-toun'. In Argyll Gaelic, the term *baile-fearainn* was common, to distinguish it from *baile* 'settlement' and *baile mór* 'town' or 'city'. All these *baile*-names were applied to important farms, and there are over a hundred in Argyll, mostly in areas where agricultural land was most fertile and extensive, such as South Kintyre, Lorne, Islay and Tiree, but there are about a dozen in Mull and several on fertile Lismore. The term is scarce in North Argyll and Appin, and absent on Jura. A number of these farm-names contain personal names, indicating ownership, or occupational names, *Balephetrish*, Tiree (Peter's farm), *Ballygrant*, Islay (Grant's farm), *Ballinaby*, Islay (the abbot's farm), and *Ballygown*, Mull (the smith's farm) are examples of these. Others are descriptive of size, location or status, such as *Baile Mór* 'big farm' on Kerrera, *Ballibeg* 'little farm' near Lochgilphead, *Balnagleck* 'ravine farm' in Kintyre, and *Ballimenach* 'middle farm' near Campbeltown.

Of several habitative elements, one of the most common in Argyll is the Gaelic *gart* 'enclosure'. This comes from O.Ir. *gort*. Originally it meant 'field' or 'cornfield', and eventually 'corn' or 'standing corn', as applied to farm holdings which were in land fertile enough to grow a good grain crop. The diminutive, *goirtean* is very common as a field-name in Argyll, Bute and north as far as Skye. In Islay, where the generic is popular, we have *Gartacharra* 'the standing-stone enclosure', *Gartachossan* 'the enclosure of the little nook' and *Gortanilivorrie* 'MacGillivray's enclosure'. *Gortanronach* 'the bracken enclosure' is near Lochgair, while *Gartavaich* 'byre-field' is in Kintyre, *Gortenanrue* 'the little field of the headland' is in Mull, and *Gartnacopaig* 'the field of dock-leaves' is in Southend parish, Kintyre.

The Gaelic *tír* means 'land'. It is fairly rare in farm-names, but *Tirfergus* 'Fergus' land' in Kintyre and *Tirarragan* in Mull 'St Fergan's land' are examples. *Tigh* 'house' occurs in several places in Argyll: *Tayvallich* 'the house of the pass' and *Tighavullin* 'mill-house', both in Knapdale; *Tayintruain* 'house of the streamlet', and *Taylinloan* 'meadow-house' in Kintyre; and *Taynuilt, tigh an uillt*, 'the house of the burn'.

The mediaeval period saw the development of land measures in the south-west of Scotland, including Galloway and Carrick, as well as Argyll. This was based on the silver penny, so we find *Pennyland* and *Pennysearach* 'the pennyland of the foal' in Southend, *Pennycross* 'pennyland of the cross' in Mull and *Peninver* 'pennyland of the confluence' in Saddell. The Gaelic form, *peighinn* is divided into *leth-pheighinn* 'half pennyland' which contracts to *Leffin* or *leffen*, as we note in *Lephincorrach* 'the rough half-pennyland' near Carradale, *Lephinmore* 'the big half-pennyland' in Stralachlan, and *Lephenstrath* 'the half-pennyland of the strath' in Southend. There is a further division made in the quarter land or *ceathramh*, as in *Keramenach* 'middle quarter' in Southend. Even smaller was the *ochdamh* 'eighth', which we find in such Islay names as *Octomore* 'big eighth', *Octofad* 'long eighth' and *Octovullin* 'the eighth of the mill'.

By far the most common habitative term in Argyll place-names is the Gaelic *achadh* 'field'. This is almost exclusively found on the mainland, although there are substantial numbers on Mull as well as a few in Lismore. It is absent as a settlement name on Tiree, and only a couple of instances occur on Islay. This is the standard field term in Gaelic, coined later than *baile* and probably related to the infilling process that took place once the main farms were established. Most of these *achadh* names (usually anglicised to *ach-* or *auch-*), are descriptive names, and a small sample will suffice out of over two hundred recorded. *Achafors* 'waterfall field' and *Achnatra* 'shore field' are in Morvern; *Achluachrach* 'rushy field' is in Seil; *Achindarroch* 'oak field' is in Appin; *Achnamoine* 'field of the peat' is in Benderloch, and *Achavaich* 'barn field' near Dunstaffnage. *Achadun* 'field of the dùn' is in Lismore, and *Achnacraig* 'field of the rock' near the mouth of Loch Don in Mull. *Auchalick* 'flagstone field' is in Kilfinan, Cowal, and *Achamore* 'big field' is almost the sole example on Jura.

A more specialised field-name describes the alluvial flats which are found beside major rivers, and which in south-eastern Scotland take the Scots term *haugh*. These 'water-meadows' were important grazing areas, and were frequently suitable for arable land where the river could be depended upon to be relatively flood-free. In early times these situations were much sought-after for settlement, especially in hilly terrain where arable land was scarce. The Gaelic term *dail* 'meadow', originally from a p-Celtic source, *dol*, found in Brittany and Cornwall, as well as in Wales, provides us with a set of place-names which are invariably found in these riverside situations.

Argyll examples are *Dalmally*, 'St Maillidh's haugh', *Daltot* 'foundation haugh' in South Knapdale, and *Dalnahasaig* 'ferry haugh' on the Moine Mhór though which the River Add flows; *Dalmore* 'big haugh' in north of Tayinloan in Kintyre, and *Dalilea* 'grey haugh' is in Ardnamurchan.

Other terms which suggest the presence of good arable land, and hence habitation, are scarce in Argyll, apart from the Norse names which are discussed later. A few deserve mention, including the old term for a kneading-trough, *losaid*. Two examples in Argyll are *Lossit* in the Rinns of Islay, and *Lossit* near Machrihanish, both in particularly good arable situations. *Croit* 'croft' occurs in *Cretshengan*, just north of Kilberry. It is unusual in that *seangan* is the word for 'ant', suggesting that ants were a plague in the place, but it could equally mean *seang* 'narrow'. Older habitations, often abandoned, were given the term *larach* 'footing', 'foundation', so we have *Larach na Gaibhre* 'the goats' foundation' near the mouth of Loch Caolisport, and *Corrlarach* in Cona Glen, Ardgour, where *corr* means 'together' or 'joining'.

Topographical Names

Many settlements were named after a nearby topographic feature, and do not contain a habitative element at all. These simply adopt the name of a nearby hill, river-bend, stand of trees or loch, or they may simply describe the nature of the landscape in which the settlement is located. In this brief survey, it is impossible to cover the whole range, but we may examine the most common of these.

Aird 'height', 'promontory' is usually coastal, or found on the shores of the major lochs. *Arduaine* 'green height' on Loch Melfort, *Ardanaiseig* 'ferry headland' on Loch Awe, *Ardgour* 'goat height' and *Ardfin* 'white headland' on Jura, *Ardentallan* 'height of the salt inlet' on Loch Feochan, and *Ardnacross* 'height of the cross' in Saddell, Kintyre are typical. The term can occur as a final element, such as *Coeclard* 'narrow promontory' in Appin and *Toward* 'hole promontory' in Cowal.

Airigh 'shieling' is not strictly a topographical term, but denotes areas where summer grazing was important. Many of these old shieling sites achieved the status of permanent settlements. *Arinanuan* 'lambs' shieling' in Glen Barr, Kintyre, *Ariundle* 'shieling of the fair meadow' in Ardnamurchan, *Arinagour* 'goats' shieling' in Coll, and *Arienas* 'Angus' shieling' in Morvern are good examples, while *Fiunary* 'white shieling' in Morvern and *Salachary* 'willow shieling' in Kilmartin display the element in a final position. This term was borrowed into Old Norse as *aergi*, and we find a number of names in a Norse word-order, especially in Mull and Ardnamurchan.

Ath, 'ford' denotes places of settlement at sites where a crossing-place provided a focal point of routes. *Acharcle* in Ardnamurchan is 'Thorkild's ford'; *Aruadh* 'red ford' is in the Rinns of Islay; and *Ath na Croise* in Mull is 'ford of the cross'.

Barr 'point, 'height' is very common in mainland Argyll, especially in Lorne, Knapdale and Kintyre. Many of the specifics (the compounded descriptive elements) are words relating to woodland and vegetation, such as *Barcaldine* 'hazel height', *Barrandroman* 'ridge height' and *Barbreck* 'speckled height' in Lorne, and *Barachleit* 'height of the rocky eminence' in Mull. The innumerable small rocky hills in Central Argyll are largely given the term *barr* which also means 'tip' or 'point' in Gaelic.

Camas is the term used for a small, horseshoe-shaped bay, either on the sea-coast or on major inland lochs. *Camasinas* 'Angus' bay' in Sunart, *Camasnangall* 'bay of the foreigners' in Ardgour, *Camaslaich* 'muddy bay' in Seil, *Kames* in Cowal, on Loch Melfort, and on Loch Awe, are examples of this. It is similar to the O.N. *vík*, which we shall discuss later.

Cùl 'nook', 'back' is applied to secluded or sheltered places, often in wooded areas. It is widespread throughout the Gaelic area, and common in Argyll. *Cuilimuich* 'pig-nook' on Loch Goil, *Cuilnashemraig* 'trefoil-nook' on West Loch Tarbert, and *Cuil* in Appin, a simplex form, are three of the many instances.

Leth 'half' occurs in several Gaelic generics in Argyll, combined with terms like *tír* 'land', to give *leth-tír* or *leitir* literally 'half-land', but applied to situations where the steep sides in the glaciated valleys give a regular slope on one side of a glen. *Letterwalton* in Appin, *Lettermore* and *Letterbeg* in Mull, *Coileitir* 'wooded slope' in Glen Etive, *Lettermay* 'slope of the plain' near Lochgilphead, and *Gairletter* 'short slope' near Ardentinny are typical, while the term occurs in a simpler form in the case of *Leitir* on the north shore of Loch Awe.

Sailean is a salt-water inlet, a smaller version of *camas*. It is most common in north and mid Argyll, Mull and Jura. Two important settlements, both in a simplex form, are *Salen* in Mull and Ardnamurchan, and there is *Sailean* in Lismore. *Ruantallen* 'point of the inlet' in Jura is heavily anglicised, as is *Kentallen* 'head of the inlet' in Appin. There are, incidentally, numerous small inlets which contain this generic, including *Sailean nan Cuileag* 'the inlet of the flies' in Ardnamurchan, which was reputed to have the most ferocious midges in Argyll.

Sròn is one of the many promontory features, both coastal and inland, which occur in settlement names. The best known are *Strontian* 'point of the fairy hill' in Ardnamurchan, *Stronesker* 'point of the fisherman' on Loch Awe, and *Strone* on the Holy Loch.

Finally, we may consider a number of place-names which contain the suffix *-ach* or *-och*. This means 'abounding in' or 'place of' and is widespread in the north and west. *Polanach* 'pool place' in Appin, *Fernoch* 'alder-place' in Kilmory and Lochgilphead, *Keppoch* 'tillage-place' in South Knapdale, *Dunach* 'fort-place' in Kilbride, *Carnach* 'cairn-place' in Glencoe and *Carnoch*, with a similar derivation, at the head of Loch Sunart give us

an idea of the range of these names. An unusual example is *Succoth* in Glen
Loin, which is an anglicised form of *socach* 'place of snouts or promontories'. All of these names take the definitive article in Gaelic, so Gaelic
speakers would refer to a man living in Keppoch, for example, as *anns a'*
Cheapaich 'in the place of tillage'.

Mountain and Hill Names

A survey of mountain names in Argyll must of necessity be brief. The standard term *beinn* 'mountain', anglicised to *ben*, is a relative term, and implies
prominence in a topographic situation rather than actual height. *Beinn*
Hough, in Tiree (388 ft ASL), could scarcely be termed a mountain, while
Beinn a' Bheithir in Appin, at 3361 ft certainly qualifies. The latter, 'the
peak of the thunderbolt', is made up of a number of peaks, including *Sgurr*
Dhonuill (3284 ft), *Sgurr Dhearg* (3361 ft) and *Creag Ghorm* (2470 ft). A
number of words are used to describe a variety of peak types – in terms of
height, aspect, shape, texture and outline. Among these are *sgurr* 'peak', *stob*
'pointed peak', *meall* 'lump' (the standard word for 'hill'), *cruach* 'stack' and
cnoc 'hill', with its diminutive, *cnocan*. Also found in Argyll are *carn*, 'cairn',
creag 'rock', *cnap* 'lump' or 'lump-shaped hill', *bidean* 'sharp-pointed peak'
and *aonach* 'desert place', which is applied to very high mountain ridges or
plateaux.

Occasionally, mountains receive fanciful names, such as *Am Buachaille*
'the herdsman' in Glen Etive, *Am Bodach* 'the old man' at the east end
of *Aonach Eagach* 'the toothed ridge', in Glencoe, and *Mainnir nam Fiadh*
'deer-enclosure' in Mull. But most mountain names are descriptive of height,
colour, shape or general appearance, and are usually fairly conservative in
nature.

Coastal Names

Argyll's highly indented coastline has resulted in a plethora of names,
which involve a large number of terms. Like the mountain landscape, the
coastline with its sea-lochs, promontories and hundreds of small inlets, has
been the site of much human activity in the past.

Promontory terms, such as *rubha* 'headland', *aird* 'promontory', and *gob*
'point' are widespread, as well as *sròn* 'nose'. Most of the headland place-
names use these four terms. There are occasional exceptions such as *corran*
'gravel spit' and *oitir* 'sandbank'. *Oitir* give us the relatively rare example of
Otter Ferry.

Bays and inlets are usually named *bàgh* 'bay' if they are reasonable size,
òb 'inlet' if they are sheltered, or *sailean* 'shallow inlet'. Fiord-like inlets
usually contain the element *loch*. The Latin *portum* gives us the Gaelic *port*,

widespread throughout the Gaelic area, with hundreds of Argyll examples, ranging from *Port nam Marbh* 'port of the dead' in Ardnamurchan, where coffins were brought ashore, to *Port nan Ileach* 'the Islayman's port' on Scarba. These inlets range from substantial harbours to small inlets just large enough to allow a small boat to be beached.

The rocky chasms which are more common in the Western Isles are usually given the term *sloc* 'pit' in Argyll, so we find *Sloc an Eithir* 'boat-pit' on Lismore and *Slock a' Bhiorain* 'stick-pit' on Seil (where floating logs were washed up). *Geodha* from ON *gjá* is the standard term in the Outer Isles, but is rare in Argyll, even in the islands. The other common inlet term is *poll* 'pool' which is found in *Poll a' Bhrochain* 'porridge pool' on Seil.

Rocks and skerries usually take the term *sgeir*, from ON *sker* 'sea-rock', and a submerged rock is normally *bogha*, from ON *boði*. Many of these are small, and sometimes not on the map. *Leac* 'flagstone', *stac* 'sea-stack' and *carraig* 'crag', 'outcrop' are also common coastal terms. Some are dangerous, and individual names were coined for them. *A' Bhratag* in Kilmore and *An Sgorag* in Lismore are both feminine terms for unpredictable rocks. Noisy rocks include *Plocach* 'the plopper' in Glaceriska Bay, and the delightful *Tudan* 'farter' off Seil. Many take animal names such as *Na Gamhainn* 'the stirks' in Morven, *Lair Bhàn* 'the grey mare' off Shuna, and *Madadh a' Bhealaich* 'the dog of the sea-pass' between Lunga and Scarba. The names of the smaller islands are partly Norse and partly Gaelic. *Pladda* 'flat-isle', *Sanda* 'sandy isle', *Lunga* 'long isle' are Norse, while *eilean* is the Gaelic word for island and usually applied to islands large enough to supply grazing for a few head of sheep or goats. *Innis*, the archaic form, is scarce, although *Inchkenneth* off Mull is one that has survived.

Norse Names

Most of the habitative names of Norse origin occur in Islay, Tiree and, to a lesser extent, Mull. The most common generic is ON *ból*, which itself is from *bólstaðr* 'farmstead'. This has developed in the form *-bols*, *-bolls*, or *-bus* in Islay and even to *-boll* or *-poll* in some cases. In all we are left with some thirty names containing variants of this generic. The Islay names are clustered in the Oa, where we find *Cragabus*, perhaps 'crow-farm', *Risabus*, *Cornabus* 'corn-farm', *Coillabus* and *Kinnabus*. In the north-east of the island we have *Scarrabus* 'Skari's farm', *Robolls*, *Persabus*, *Eorrabus* and *Coullabus*. In Mull we have *Scobull* in Ardmeanach, and *Assopol* in the Ross, while Tiree contains names like *Crossapoll* 'cross-stead', *Kirkapoll* 'church farm', *Barrapoll* 'barley-stead' and *Hellipoll*, perhaps 'holy-stead'. The only mainland *-bol* is *Resipole* 'horse-stead' on Loch Sunart in Ardnamurchan. In Coll, we find *Arnabost* 'Arni's stead', with an ending similar to that found in Lewis and Skye.

Few of the other Norse settlement generics have survived in Argyll, although ON *staðir* 'farm' is found in *Olistadh* 'Olaf's farm' in the Rinns of Islay, and *Consiby*, a substantial farm also in the Rinns, beside Loch Indaal, is probably *konungs-býr* 'king's farm'. *Soroby* 'sour or muddy farm' was in Tiree.

The majority of Norse names in Argyll, however, relate to topographic features, although many have achieved settlement status. Foremost is the ON *dalr* 'valley', which gives endings in *-dal* and *-dale*. There are close to a hundred of these in the county, the majority being in Kintyre, Islay, Jura, Mull and North Argyll, with few if any found north of Loch Awe, and east of Loch Linnhe. Names like these do not necessarily indicate Norse settlement, but rather a sphere of Norse influence, and were very likely coined in a period when both Gaelic and Norse were spoken, probably *c.* 1000–1250.

Examples of *-dalr* names include *Laudale* 'low-dale', and *Liddesdale* 'sloped dale', on Loch Sunart, *Scamadale* in Lorn, *Carradale* 'brushwood-dale' and *Borgadale* 'fort dale' in Kintyre, while Islay has *Margadale* 'mark-dale', and Jura *Brosdale*. When the Norse language died out, Gaelic speakers in some parts of Argyll added the Gaelic *gleann* 'glen' to some of the *-dalr* names, giving such names as *Glenegedale* in Islay, *Glenborrowdale* 'fort-dale' in Ardnamurchan and *Glenlibidil* in Mull.

Coastal names of Norse origin are frequent in Argyll. The most significant are those names in *vík* 'bay', 'inlet', which usually give the ending *-aig* in Gaelic. Although these are mostly found in the Argyll islands, e.g. *Cornaig* 'corn-bay' in Coll, *Sandaig* 'sandy bay' in Tiree and *Dervaig*, *Carsaig* and *Cragaig* in Mull, we get a few instances on the mainland, such as *Plocaig* in Ardnamurchan. *Carsaig*, *kjarr-vík*, 'brushwood bay' in Knapdale and *Eignaig* in Morvern.

The word for 'promontory' or 'point' in O.N. is *nes* 'nose', and it is found in many place-names which end in *-nish* or *-nis*. So we get *Craignish* in Lorne, *Ardmenish* 'narrow point' in Jura (prefixed by Gaelic *aird*), and many in Mull, where they apply to extensive promontories such as *Mishnish*, *Quinish*, *Mornish* and *Tresnish*.

A landscape as complex and indented as Argyll has required an extensive nomenclature over the centuries. A detailed investigation of the place-name record reveals a great deal of the history, language and culture of the area, not to mention aspects such as land-use, husbandry, fishing, natural history and archaeology. Place-names also reveal the impact that man has made on the landscape, and the various resources which have been exploited over the years. Many of these minor names have now passed out of use, with the decline of Gaelic, and with the reduction in the rural population. The Ordnance Survey of the nineteenth century recorded many names, but thousands have been lost. They were never recorded, but they formed part of the oral tradition of the community. Nevertheless we are left with a remarkable legacy of nomenclature, which reveals a great deal of Argyll's complex past.

CHAPTER TWENTY-ONE

Communications

The Earliest Travellers

As the ice retreated at the end of the last great Ice Age small nomadic bands of men and women started to colonise what is now Scotland. The earliest trace of these Mesolithic people can be dated back to about 7000 BC. Their economy was based on seasonal gathering, hunting and fishing, mainly on coastal sites and near river courses or lochs. Argyll, with its relatively mild climate and deeply indented coast, was particularly attractive.

Movement over land, much of it then thickly forested, was difficult and of necessity on foot. What is remarkable is that even at that early time the sea was not the obstacle to travel that might be supposed. Archaeological evidence confirms the presence of these Mesolithic incomers on our islands. Clearly they were capable of constructing and navigating seaworthy craft. Unfortunately, we have as yet little idea of the shape or structure of these vessels.

As millennium succeeded millennium, the way of life evolved with the domestication of animals, the growing of crops, the introduction of metal and thence out of pre-history into the period of recorded history. From then on, written records exist to back up archaeological evidence, giving a progressively clearer picture of technical advance. For a long period, until two or three centuries ago, the means of transport and communications changed little in its essentials. Before the eighteenth century, overland movement in Argyll was still on foot or hoof through wild, lawless country and it necessitated fording or swimming fast-flowing rivers. Only the rich and powerful could afford the cost of a messenger to convey important information. News was carried informally on the lips of travellers. It was the sea that offered direct, if intermittent, connections for coastal and island traffic.

The Western Seaways

The earliest historical evidence we have for significant maritime traffic relates to the fifth century and probably earlier when scholarship has suggested that Kintyre was settled from northern Ireland, just twelve miles (19 km) or so across *Struth na Moaile* (the North Channel) from the Scottish coast. This settlement by the Gaelic *Scotti* expanded into the whole of what was to become Argyll. It is clear that this could not have been achieved unless these settlers were skilled in seamanship. The process was consolidated decisively around 500 when Fergus Mòr Mac Ercc moved his seat of power from Dunseverick in Ireland to Argyll, establishing the Scottish kingdom of Dalriada.

The most graphic early description of an Argyll sea voyage is given by Adamnán in his life of Columba. Trained as a monk, Columba (in Gaelic Calum Cille) was of warring Irish royal lineage from both parents. A dispute over his copying of a codex of the Gospels and his subsequent part in leading a bloody rebellion led to his banishment from Ireland. In disgrace, he set out with twelve companions in a currach (hide-covered boat) to make amends by winning souls in Argyll and beyond. In May 563 he landed on Iona, where he established his monastic community.

From this island base Columba's evangelising influence spread firstly along the 'coastland of the Gaels' – Earra Gàidheal or Argyll – and then, it is said, among the Picts. Columba was only one of many Gaelic saints who navigated the seaways of the West Highlands and beyond. The records also confirm that the Dalriad kings were highly mobile and able to range by sea from Orkney to Ireland and the Isle of Man.

The light, strong, seaworthy currach of the Dark Ages, equally suited to war and trade, was the means by which this mobility was made possible. It was arguably a key factor in the rise of the Argyll dynasty and their ultimate siring of the Scottish and later British royal lines. According to Irish tradition it was in such a craft that Brendan the Navigator made his epic voyage to Iceland and America. The currach is still in use today on the west of Ireland and we may presume that the design was in use long before it is revealed to us by historical record – surely a civilising artefact of world significance. Unfortunately, because of the perishable nature of the materials with which these vessels were built, no example of a medieval currach survives in Argyll or anywhere else.

The dominance of the currach ended in 795 with the sudden and violent appearance in Argyll of the Vikings. These Norse raiders and traders used the sea as their highway to power and, for a while, to superiority over a dominion that was to stretch from Dublin to Greenland and, briefly, America. This territory included the Argyll Isles and parts of mainland Argyll. What gave the Vikings their edge, apart from their pragmatic ruthless vigour and seamanship, was their manoeuvrable wooden ships, capable of sailing closer to the wind than any previous design. Several examples of Viking ships of that time have been preserved in Scandinavia.

Around 1150, Somerled, the half Norse-half Gael ruler of Argyll, began a Gaelic resurgence in the west. The end of Norse dominance came with the defeat of Haakon's fleet at Largs in 1263, but the Viking maritime legacy was to live on. Somerled's progeny became Lords of the Isles, who held their island domains together by means of an improved version of the Viking galley – the birlinn. Like the Viking longship, the birlinn had a prow at each end, with one mast and a square sail, but the introduction of the rudder in place of the old steering oar improved manoeuvrability. The birlinns of the chieftains of the Lordship criss-crossed the seaways of Argyll and the Isles. The Council of the Isles at the Lord's headquarters at Finlaggan on Islay attracted men and birlinns from all directions in a concentration of Gaelic power so great that it was effectively beyond the rule of the Scottish kings. It is telling that the coat of arms of the Lordship featured a black *lymphad* or birlinn on a gold field. The power of the Lordship was finally broken by James IV in 1493 under the terms of the Statutes of Iona, which ordained that all the birlinns of the Lordship be destroyed – and they were. None survive.

Land Communications

In succeeding centuries, until the beginning of the modern period, maritime trade was carried on by sailing vessels identical to those found generally in Scottish waters. But the sea was losing its dominance. After the fall of the Lordship of the Isles, the dominant power in Argyll was the Earldom (later Dukedom) of Argyll, based at Inverary. The maintenance of the earls' power depended on their influence at the main centres of power such as Stirling, Edinburgh and Glasgow. To facilitate such travel, be it for the earl and his full retinue, or for his agents and messengers, a barge was maintained at Inverary. A quick crossing to St Catherine's linked with a short overland journey to Lochgoilhead and a further sheltered boat trip or trips to a landfall convenient for the overland journey to the selected lowland destination. Other magnates in Bute, Arran and elsewhere in the region maintained similar facilities.

The routes of movement and trade started to shift as land travel improved. The droving trade became a major economic force. For millennia cattle have been a mobile and convertible store of wealth in Scotland, hence the prevalence of cattle raiding in the Gaelic tradition. By the sixteenth century, as times became more settled, Argyll cattle were being driven to the Lowlands for sale. This trade was to grow greatly over the next two centuries. Cattle of course moved themselves comfortably over land but a water crossing presented a challenge.

It was possible to swim beasts over narrow sounds, hence the place-name Colintraive (Caol an t-Snaimh – the swimming narrows). Where swimming was impracticable it was necessary to ship island cattle to the mainland. To minimise the cost and hazard of shipment over water, the shortest feasible crossings were used. Thus from Islay cattle were ferried from Port Askaig to Feolinn, driven to Lagg, then ferried to Keills, from where they embarked on their leisurely journey to the trysts of Crieff or Falkirk. Beasts from Colonsay were ferried to Loch Tarbert, Jura, thence driven either to Keills or Kinuachdarach for a further ferry passage to the Argyll mainland. From Coll and Tiree the route was by sea to Kintra or Carsaig in Mull, overland to Grasspoint, by ferry to Kerrera, and across Kerrera for a final swim to Oban. From Cowal the ferry was from Dunoon to Cloch Point.

The New Roads

The 1707 Act of Union and the 1715–19 Jacobite Rising generated tensions in the Highlands. In 1724 General George Wade was commissioned to subdue the rebellious clans. Between 1725 and 1736, using military labour, Wade built some 250 miles (400 km) of roads. The Highlands' first strategic network was further extended after 1746. Long-distance wheeled transport, though still uncommon and slow, became possible. Pioneering though they were, the military roads were poorly made. By the end of the eighteenth century they were falling into decay. The Highland people meanwhile suffered demoralisation and destitution in the post Forty-five economic and political climate. Of course people and goods were also shipped long distances by sea – including in due course thousands of dispossessed Highlanders to North America!

Around the turn of the century schemes were mounted to address these problems. One of the inconveniences of navigation between the Clyde and the West Highlands was the need to round the hazardous Mull of Kintyre. To obviate this sea passage of 85 miles (137 km), construction of the nine-mile (14 km) Crinan Canal was commenced in 1793. Equally significant was the creation, under the auspices of the British Fisheries Society, of fishing stations to exploit the rich west-coast herring shoals. The society's surveyor and engineer was Thomas Telford.

In 1801 the Treasury instructed Telford to plan communications. As a result of Telford's recommendations, two commissions were established in 1803 to construct roads and bridges in the Highlands and to cut the Caledonian Canal between Inverness and Corpach – highly ambitious undertakings, given the lack of skills and facilities in the area. Telford was appointed engineer to the Commissioners.

The Commissioners set to work immediately. The difficulties were substantial, including bankruptcy of contractors, labour unrest and innumerable engineering problems.

Telford was also involved in a number of other schemes in the Highlands, including the provision of ferry jetties to facilitate better movement across sounds and sea lochs too broad to bridge. This massive project was funded by what today would be described as a 'public private partnership', funds being put up by the Government, banks and landowners.

Within nineteen years, Highland transport infrastructure was trans-
formed. By 1825 stagecoaches ran daily from Loch Lomond-side over the
Rest and be Thankful to Inveraray, to Dalmally and the west and through
Glencoe to Ballachulish and Fort William. New roads also opened up
Cowal, connecting Dunoon, Kilmun and Lochgoil with Lochfyneside.
Wheeled vehicles became commonplace and the tourist trade started to
develop. It is a testimony to Telford that much of the system he created is
still in use today.

The Advance of Steam

During this remarkable period, in 1812, another innovation in transport
occurred that was to have far reaching effects. Henry Bell, a Helensburgh
hotelier, started operating Europe's first commercial steamboat, *Comet*, on
the Clyde. Competitors appeared rapidly on the scene and within a few
years a well-established network of steamer services catered for the carriage
of passengers, goods and livestock on the Firth of Clyde. Regular services
were opened up to Argyll ports such as Lochgoilhead, Dunoon, Campbeltown, Tarbert Loch Fyne, Ardrishaig and Inveraray. Access was
revolutionised to such an extent that settlements like the tiny clachan of
Dunoon attracted prosperous Glasgow merchants to establish villas there.
Soon a string of resorts emerged along the picturesque Clyde coast, served
by ever-improving steamer services.

The West Highlands and Islands too were opened up to steam navigation. The innovation must have been startling to some. Captain James
Williamson in his seminal work, the *Clyde Passenger Steamers*, relates the
tale of the first arrival in Islay of a steamer, whose steward had a pet monkey on board. An islander who had not hitherto seen either steamboat or
monkey fled to the hills crying 'Mac an Diabhoil, Mac an Diabhoil!',
believing the devil to be the agent of propulsion. But acceptance came
quickly. By 1824 a through-service was available from Glasgow to Inverness and other West Highland ports via the Crinan and Caledonian
Canals. The trade was driven forward by commercial interests, but contracts to carry mail by steamship introduced a measure of state funding.

In the next decade both the composer Mendelssohn and the artist
Turner visited Fingal's cave by steamer. Music, painting, literature, news-
papers and posts facilitated the transmission of ideas as never before. The
romance and prestige of the West Highlands as a tourist destination was
promoted and confirmed by Queen Victoria's voyage from the Clyde,
through the Crinan Canal to Oban, Staffa, Iona and Fort William in
1847. The route from Glasgow to Oban, Fort William and Inverness was
advertised thereafter as the Royal Route. In 1851 the West Highland
steamers were taken over by David Hutcheson and his brother Alexander.
The Hutchesons greatly expanded the network, in particular by the

development of 'swift steamer' routes. From 1879, following the retiral of the Hutchesons, the business was carried on by their nephew David MacBrayne – a name that has become almost synonymous with West Highland travel.

Scotland's steam navigation was soon paralleled by the introduction of steam locomotion on the developing railways. By 1848 the lowland lines were linked with each other and with the English system, so creating a national network, but it took some time before the railway penetrated to Argyll. That was achieved by the construction of the Callander and Oban line, finally opened, after a series of difficulties, through to Oban in 1880, under the auspices of the Caledonian Railway.

From then on, Oban, which was already an important steamer interchange port, became a railhead for a wide range of onward steamer connections – earning it the epithet 'Charing Cross of the Highlands'. In 1897 the Caledonian Railway obtained permission to construct a branch from Connel on the main line to Ballachulish. The Oban line was in fact predated by an independent narrow-gauge line, opened in 1877, linking Campbeltown with a colliery at Machrihanish. The Campbeltown & Macrihanish Light Railway was upgraded to passenger operation in 1906 and became a popular excursion in connection with the new turbine-steamer summer services to Campbeltown.

By the end of the nineteenth century steam power had integrated the Argyll economy with that of the rest of Britain and its Empire. Manufactured goods and tourists came northwards and westwards by sea and rail. Local products such as livestock, fish and whisky were sent south by the same means. Roads served as local distributors, carrying horse-drawn traffic to railway stations or seaports.

The Modern Age

In the twentieth century Argyll transport reflected world trends. The internal combustion engine revolutionised road transport. Motor vehicles became the dominant transport mode for people and goods. Asphalt surfacing enabled existing roads to handle motor traffic. As the century progressed, growth in the numbers and size of vehicles necessitated new road and bridge schemes. These ranged from widening and improving the routing of single-track roads to major strategic projects. In the same period the telephone, radio, television and, most recently, the internet have brought instantaneous communication.

However, the rural railway network, nationalised in 1948, became a casualty of road transport competition. Branch-line closures, including that to Ballachulish, were followed by proposals in the 1960s to close virtually the entire Highland railway system. Well-orchestrated campaigning secured the retention of the main lines, including that to Oban, albeit in modified form. Replacement of steam by diesel trains and other technical advances reduced operating costs on these lightly-used lines, although state subsidy remains high.

Shipping operators also adopted motor propulsion, giving cost savings over steam. The dominance of road transport, however, led to a more fundamental reorientation of shipping services. In the 1970s and 80s new 'roll on-roll off' vehicle ferries were introduced to act as floating bridges linking islands with the mainland road system, partially superseding the pattern of routes which had evolved over the previous century and a half. In 1973 state-owned shipping interests were drawn together to form Caledonian MacBrayne, which operates about half the Scottish internal ferry services and is now subsidised by the Scottish Executive. Scotland's busiest ferry route, however, between Hunter's Quay (Cowal) and McInroy's Point (Gourock), is operated by private company – Western Ferries – and is profitable and run on purely commercial lines, as are a number of other seasonal operations. Other local ferry routes are funded by Argyll and Bute Council.

In the 1930s scheduled air services to Campbeltown and the more populous islands of the Inner and Outer Hebrides were developed from Renfrew (Glasgow) by John Sword. An early innovation was the air ambulance, whose commercial flights were supported by mail contracts. From 1947 the newly nationalised British European Airways (BEA) supplanted the independent operators on Highlands and Islands services. Subsequently privatised, the basic route-pattern has remained broadly similar for half a century. The main airports in the Highlands and Islands, upgraded during the war by the military, were transferred to the Civil Aviation Authority (CAA) and, more recently, to Highlands & Islands Airports Ltd., which, as an arm of government, was able to absorb operating losses.

In the mid 1970s the government sought to rationalise air services. A working-group, made up of representatives of BEA, CAA, the Scottish Office and the new independent airline Loganair, started a process of recasting the support for non-viable 'lifeline' services in the Highlands and Islands. In 1975, with the aid of government subsidy, Loganair took over the loss-making Glasgow – Tiree – Barra service, and later also the Glasgow – Campbeltown and Islay routes.

The Future

In comparison with some similar rural communities, for example in Norway, there is much still to be achieved. Arrears in road maintenance are storing up problems for the future; the Argyll islands are particularly inaccessible and this inhibits their development; there is no holistic, researched, long-term transport plan for rural Scotland to address the problems in an informed and objective way. But it is heartening that these issues are now subjects of concern and debate. With the application of innovative and dedicated minds to these problems, Argyll's transport and communications network could in the future be a model of excellence.

Bibliography

GAJ   *Glasgow Archaeological Journal*
PPS   *Proceedings of the Prehistoric Society*
PSAS   *Proceedings of the Society of Antiquaries of Scotland*
RCAHMS Royal Commission on the Ancient & Historical Monuments of
            Scotland
SGM   *Scottish Geographical Magazine*
SSt   *Scottish Studies*
TBNHS   *Transactions of the Bute Natural History Society*
TGSI   *Transactions of the Gaelic Society of Inverness*

SA   School of Scottish Studies Sound Archive

Acts of the Lords of the Isles (1986), Scottish History Society.

Aitken, W. G. (1955) 'Excavation of a chapel at St Ninian's Point, Isle of Bute', *TBNHS*, 14, 62–76.

Alcock, L. (1981) 'Early historic fortifications in Scotland' in G. Guilbert (ed.), *Hill-Fort Studies: Essays for A. H. A. Hogg*, Leicester, 150–180.

Alcock, L. (1987) *Economy, society and warfare among the Britons and Saxons*, Cardiff, University of Wales Press.

Alcock, L. (2003) *Kings and Warriors, Craftsmen and priests in Northern Britain AD 550–850*, Edinburgh.

Alcock, L. and Alcock, E. A. (1987) 'Reconaissance excavations ... 2, Excavations at Dunollie Castle', *PSAS*, 117, 119–47.

Allison, I., May, F., and Strachan, R. A. (eds) (1988) *An Excursion Guide to the Moine Geology of the Scottish Highlands*, Edinburgh.

Anderson, A. O. and Anderson, M. O. (1961) *Adomnán's Life of Columba*, Thomas Nelson, Edinburgh and London. Revised edition (1991), Oxford, Clarendon Press.

Anderson, J. (1895) 'Notice of a cave recently discovered at Oban, containing human remains and a refuse heap of shells and bones of animals, and stone and bone implements', *PSAS*, 29, 211–230.

Anderson, J. (1898) 'Notes on the contents of a small cave or rock shelter at Druim-vargie, Oban; and of three shell mounds on Oronsay', *PSAS*, 32, 298–313.

Armit, I. (ed.) (2000) *Beyond the Brochs*, Edinburgh, Edinburgh University Press.

Armit, I. (1990) 'Epilogue' in Armit, I. (ed.) *Beyond the Brochs*, Edinburgh, Edinburgh University Press, 194–210.

Armit, I. (1991) 'The Atlantic Scottish Iron Age: five levels of chronology', *PSAS*, 121, 181–214.

Armit, I. (1997) 'Cultural landscapes and identities: a case study in the Scottish Iron Age' in Haselgrove, C. and Gwilt, A. (eds) *Reconstructing Iron Age Societies*, Oxford, Oxbow Books, 248–253.

Armit, I. (forthcoming) 'Atlantic Roundhouses: a beginner's guide' in Turner, V. (ed.) *Tall Stories: the archaeology of brochs*, Oxford, Oxbow Books.

Armit, I., Dunwell, A. J. D. and Hunter, F. J. (forthcoming) *The Traprain Law Summit Project*.

Armstrong, K. (1990) 'Women's Stories: Creating an Identity in the Scottish Highlands', *Suomen Antropologi*, 3, 25–32.

Anderson, J. (1898) 'Notes on the contents of a small cave or rock shelter at Druimvargie, Oban; and of three shell mounds on Oronsay', *PSAS* 32, 298–313.

Ashmore, P. J. (1996) *Neolithic and Bronze Age Scotland*, London, Batsford/Historic Scotland.

Baird, W. J. (1993) *The Scenery of Scotland – the Structure Beneath*, Edinburgh.

Bannerman, J. M. W. (1974) *Studies in the History of Dalriada*, Edinburgh.

Barber, J. W. (1981) 'Excavations on Iona, 1979', *PSAS*, 111, 282–380.

Barber, J. W. and Brown, M. M. (1984) 'An Sithean, Islay', *PSAS*, 114, 161–189.

Barber, J. W. and Crone, B. A. (1993) 'Crannogs: a diminishing resource? A survey of the crannogs of southwest Scotland and excavations at Buiston', *Antiquity*, 67, 520–534.

Barclay, G. (1998) *Farmers, Temples and Tombs: Scotland in the Neolithic and Early Bronze Age*, Edinburgh, Canongate/Historic Scotland.

Barrell, A. D. M. (2000) *Medieval Scotland*, Cambridge, Cambridge University Press.

Barrow, G. *et al.* (1986) *The Seventeenth Century in the Highlands*, Inverness Field Club.

Boardman, S. (1992) 'The Man who would be King: the Lieutenancy and Death of David, Duke of Rothesay, 1378–1402' in Mason, R. and Macdougall, N. (eds) *People and Power in Scotland*, Edinburgh, 1–27.

Boardman, S. (1996) *The Early Stewart Kings. Robert II and Robert III, 1371–1406*, Tuckwell Press, East Linton.

Bold, A. (1989) *Scotland, a literary companion*, London, Routledge.

Bonsall, C., Sutherland, D. G., Russell, N. J., Coles, G., Paul, C. R. C., Huntley, J. P. and Lawson, T. J. (1994) 'Excavations in Ulva Cave, western Scotland 1990–91: a preliminary report', *Mesolithic Miscellany*, 15, 8–21.

Bower, W. (1987–98) *Scotichronicon*, eds Watt, D. E. R. *et al.*, 9 vols, Aberdeen & Edinburgh.

Boyd, A. M. (1978) 'The vernacular architecture of Tiree and Coll', *Notes & Queries* (Society of West Highland and Island Historical Research), No. 7, 10–14.

Bradley, R. and Edmonds, M. (1993) *Interpreting the Axe Trade: Production and Exchange in Neolithic Britain*, Cambridge, Cambridge University Press.

Bray, E. (1986) *The Discovery of the Hebrides*, London, Collins.

Broderick, G. (ed.) (1996) *Chronicles of the Kings of Man and the Isles*, Manx National Heritage.

Broun, D. (1994) 'The Origin of Scottish Identity in its European Context' in Crawford, B. E. (ed.) *Scotland in Dark Age Europe*, St Andrews, 21–31.

Broun, D. (1998) 'Pictish Kings 761–839: Integration with Dál Riata or separate development?' in Foster, S. M. (ed.) *The St Andrews Sarcophagus*, Dublin.

Brown, M. (1994) *James I*, Tuckwell Press, East Linton.

Bruford, A. (1969) *Gaelic Folktales and Medieval Romances*, Dublin, The Folklore of Ireland Society.

Burl, A. (2000) *The Stone Circles of Britain, Ireland and Brittany*, London, Yale University Press.

Burt, E. (1754) *Letters from a Gentleman in the North of Scotland to his Friend in London*. 2 vols, London.

Butt, J. (1965–66) 'The Scottish iron and steel industry before the hot blast', *Journal of the West of Scotland Iron and Steel Institute*, 73.

Butter, R. (1999) *Kilmartin: Scotland's richest prehistoric landscape. An Introduction and Guide*, Kilmartin, Kilmartin House Trust.

Cameron, D. (1990) *Glasgow's Airport*, Holmes McDougal, Edinburgh.

Cameron, Rev. H. (ed.) (1932) *Na Bàird Thirisdeach*, Stirling, The Tiree Association. (Anthology of Gaelic verse from Tiree)

Cameron, N. M. de S. (ed.) (1993) *The Dictionary of Scottish Church History and Theology*, Edinburgh.

Campbell, A. 'A Slight Sketch of a Journey made through parts of the Highlands and Hebrides; undertaken to collect materials for Albyn's Anthology by the Editor in Autumn 1815', *University of Edinburgh Special Collections, Laing MS Collection (La III. 577)*.

Campbell, A. (1816–1818) *Albyn's Anthology or A Select Collection of the Melodies and Vocal Poetry Peculiar to Scotland and the Isles*, 2 vols, Oliver and Boyd, Edinburgh.

Campbell, Lord A. (1889–1891) *Waifs and Strays of Celtic Tradition*, with various contributors, 4 vols, London.

Campbell, E. (1987) 'A cross-marked quern from Dunadd and other evidence for relations between Dunadd and Iona', *PSAS*, 117, 59–71.

Campbell, E. (1999) *Saints and Sea-Kings: The First Kingdom of the Scots*, Edinburgh, Birlinn/Historic Scotland.

Campbell, E. (2001) 'Were the Scots Irish?' *Antiquity*, 75, 285–292.

Campbell, I. (1884) *Poems*, Edinburgh.

Campbell, J. G. (1891) *The Fians … Waifs and Strays of Celtic Tradition, vol. 4* (Reprint, New York, AMS Press).

Campbell, J. G. (1900) *Superstitions of the Highlands and Islands of Scotland*, Glasgow, James MacLehose & Sons.

Campbell, J. G. (1902) *Witchcraft and Second Sight in the Highlands and Islands of Scotland*, Glasgow, James MacLehose & Sons.

Campbell, J. L. and Thomson, D. (1963) *Edward Lhuyd in the Scottish Highlands 1699–1700*, Oxford, Clarendon Press.

Campbell, J. F. (1860–1862) *Popular Tales of the West Highlands*, 4 vols, Edmonston & Douglas, Edinburgh. (Repr. (1994), 2 vols, Birlinn, Edinburgh)

Campbell, J. F. (1940, 1960) *More West Highland Tales*, ed. MacKay, J. G., 2 vols, Oliver & Boyd, Edinburgh. (Repr. (1994), 2 vols, Birlinn, Edinburgh)

Campbell, M. and Sandeman M. (1962) 'Mid Argyll: an archaeological survey', *PSAS*, 95 (1961–62), 1–125.

Carmichael, A. (1913) 'Traditions of the Land of Lorne', *The Celtic Review*, 8, 314–333.

Carmichael, A. (1928–1971) *Carmina Gadelica*, 6 vols, Edinburgh, Scottish Academic Press.

Carswell, J. (1970) *Foirm na n-Urrnuidheadh*, ed. Thomson, R. L., Edinburgh.

Checkland, S. and Checkland, O. (1982) *Industry and Ethos: Scotland, 1832–1914*, London (New History of Scotland Series, vii).

Childe, V. G. and Thorneycroft, W. (1938) 'The vitrified fort at Rahoy, Morvern, Argyll', *PSAS*, 72, 22–43.

Christison, D. (1905) 'Report on the Society's excavations of forts on the Poltalloch Estate, Argyll, in 1904–5', *PSAS*, 39, 259–322.

Chronica Regum Manniae et Insularum. A Facsimile of the Manuscript Codex Julius A. Vii in the British Museum (1924), Douglas.

Clancy, T. O. (1995) 'Annat in Scotland and the origins of the parish', *Innes Review*, vol. 6, part 2, 91–115.

Clancy, T. O. and Markús, G. (eds) (1995) *Iona: the Earliest Poetry of a Celtic Monastery*, Edinburgh, Edinburgh University Press.

Clarke, D. V. (1968) 'Two jadeite axes, and two arrowheads of Antrim porcellanite and Rhum bloodstone from Scotland', *PSAS*, 100, 185–188.

Clerk, A. (ed.) (1867) *Caraid nan Gaidheal: The Gaelic Writings of Norman MacLeod D. D.*, Glasgow.

Coles, B. (1990) 'Anthropomorphic wooden figures from Britain and Ireland', *PPS*, 56, 315–333.

Coles, J. M. (1983) 'Excavations at Kilmelfort Cave, Argyll', *PSAS*, 113, 11–21.

Collins, G. (1776) *Great Britain's Coasting Pilot*, London. (First published, 1689)

Connock, K. D., Finlayson, B. and Mills, C. M. (1992) 'Excavation of a shell-midden site at Carding Mill Bay near Oban, Scotland', *GAJ*, 17, 25–38.

Cowan, E. J. and McDonald, R. (eds) (2000) *Alba: Celtic Scotland in the Medieval Era*, East Linton, Tuckwell Press.

Cowan, I. B. (1995) *The Medieval Church in Scotland*, ed. Kirk, J., Edinburgh, Scottish Academic Press.

Cowie, T. (1986) 'A stone head from Port Appin, Argyll', *PSAS*, 116, 89–91.

Craw, J. H. (1930) 'Excavations at Dunadd and at other sites on the Poltalloch Estates, Argyll', *PSAS*, 64, 111–146.

Crawford, B. (1987) *Scandinavian Scotland*, Leicester University Press.

Cregeen, E. R. (ed.) (1964) *Argyll Estate Instructions 1771–1805*, Edinburgh, Scottish Historical Society.

Cregeen, E. and MacKenzie, D. (1978) *Tiree Bards and their Bardachd*, Coll, Society for West Highland and Island Historical Research.

Crone, A. and Campbell, E. (forthcoming) 'A crannog of the 1st millennium AD; excavations by Jack Scott at Loch Glashan, Argyll, 1960', *Society of Antiquaries of Scotland Monograph Series*.

Denison, S. (2001) 'Earliest evidence found of settlers in Scotland', *British Archaeology*, 60, 4.

Dewar MSS, ed. J. MacKechnie (1960)

Ditchburn, D. (2000) *Scotland and Europe – The Medieval Kingdom and its Contacts with Christendom, 1214–1560, Vol 1, Religion, Culture and Commerce*, Tuckwell Press, East Linton.

Duckworth, C. L. D. and Langmuir, G. E. (1967) *West Highland Steamers*, Prescot.

Duke, J. A. (1937) *History of the Church of Scotland to the Reformation*, Oliver and Boyd, Edinburgh & London.

Dunwell, A. J. and Strachan, R. (1995) 'Brown Caterthun', *Discovery and Excavation in Scotland, 1995*, 13.

Dunwell, A. J. and Strachan, R. (forthcoming) *Excavations at Brown and White Caterthun, Angus, 1995–7*.

Fairhurst, H. (1960) 'Scottish clachans', *SGM*, 76, 67–76.

Fairhurst, H. (1967) 'The archaeology of rural settlement in Scotland', *Transactions of the Glasgow Archaeological Society*, 15, 139–158.

Fawcett, R. (1994) *Scottish Abbeys and Priories*, London.

Feachem, R. W. (1966) 'The hillforts of northern Britain' in Rivet, A. L. F. (ed.), 59–87.

Fenton, A. (1968) 'Alternating Stone and Turf – An Obsolete Building Practice', *Folk Life Journal*, VI, 94–103.

Fergusson, J. (1951) *Argyll in the Forty-five*, London, Faber.

Finlayson, B. (1998) *Wild Harvesters: the First People in Scotland*, Edinburgh, Canongate/Historic Scotland.

Fisher, I. (1994) 'The monastery of Iona in the eighth century' in F. O'Mahony (ed.), *The Book of Kells: Proceedings of a conference held at Trinity College, Dublin, 1992*, 1–16, Dublin.

Fisher, I. (1997) 'Early Christian Archaeology in Argyll' in Ritchie, G. (ed.), 181–204.

Fisher, I. (2001) *Early Medieval Sculpture in the West Highlands and Islands*, Edinburgh, RCAHMS/Soc. Ant. Scot.

Fraser, I. A. (1976–78) 'Gaelic and Norse Elements in Coastal Place-names in the Western Isles', *TGSI*, vol 1, 237–255.

Fraser, I. A. (1988) 'The Place-names of Argyll: an Historical Perspective', *TGSI*, vol. liv, 174–207.

Gailey, R. A. (1960) 'Settlement and population in Kintyre, 1750–1800', *SGM*, 76, 99–107.

Gailey, R. A. (1962a) 'The peasant houses of the southwest Highlands of Scotland: Distribution, parallels and evolution', *Gwerin*, 3, 1–16.

Gailey, R. A. (1962b) 'The evolution of Highland rural settlement', *SSt*, 6, 155–177.

Gillen, C. (2003) *Geology and Landscapes of Scotland*, Harpenden.

Gilmour, S. (1994) 'Iron Age Drystone Structures in Argyll', Unpublished MA Dissertation, University of Edinburgh.

Gilmour, S. (2000) 'First Millennia settlement development in the Atlantic West' in Henderson, J. (ed.), 155–170.

Glenn, V. (2003) *Romanesque and Gothic Decorative Metalwork and Ivory Carvings in the Museum of Scotland*, National Museums of Scotland.

Goring, R. (ed.) (1992) *Chambers Scottish Biographical Dictionary*, Edinburgh, Chambers.

Graham, A. and Gordon, J. (1987) 'Old Harbours in Northern and Western Scotland', *PSAS*, 117, 353–358.

Graham-Campbell, J. and Batey, C. E. (1998) *Vikings in Scotland*, Edinburgh, Edinburgh University Press.

Grannd, S. (2000) *The Gaelic of Islay: a Comparative Study*, Aberdeen.

Grant, S., McDonald, J., Swanson, C. and Wood, J. S. (1983) 'A survey of deserted settlements at Braleckan and Brenchoillie, Argyll', *GAJ*, 10, 143–156.

Gray, M. (1978) *The Fishing Industries of Scotland 1790–1914*, Oxford.

Groome, F. H. (1901) *Ordnance Gazetteer of Scotland*, Edinburgh.

Haldane, A. R. B. (1952) *The Drove Roads of Scotland*, Edinburgh. (New edn 1997, Edinburgh, Birlinn).

Haldane, A. R. B. (1962) *New Ways Through the Glens*, London.

Hambrey, M. J., Fairchild, I. J., Glover, B. W., Stewart, A. D., Treagus, J. E. and Winchester, J. A. (1991) *The Late Precambrian Geology of the Scottish Highlands and Islands*, London.

Harding, D. W. (1984) 'The function and classification of brochs and duns' in Miket, R. and Burgess, C. (eds) *Between and Beyond the Walls*, Edinburgh, John Donald, 206–220.

Harding, D. W. (1997) 'Forts, duns, brochs and crannogs: Iron Age settlements in Argyll' in Ritchie, J. N. G. (ed.) *The Archaeology of Argyll*, Edinburgh, Edinburgh University Press, 118–140.

Harding, D. W. and Gilmour, S. (2000) *The Iron Age settlement at Beirgh, Riof, Isle of Lewis, Excavations 1985–95*, vol. 1 (Calanais Research Series No. 1), Edinburgh, University of Edinburgh, Department of Archaeology.

Harman, M. (1977) 'An incised cross on Hirt, Harris', *PSAS*, 108 (1976–77), 254–258.

Harvie, C. (1981) *No Gods and Precious Few Heroes: Scotland 1914–1980*, London (New History of Scotland Series).

Haselgrove, C., Armit, I., Champion, T., Creighton, J., Gwilt, A., Hill, J. D., Hunter, F. and Woodward, A. (2001) *Understanding the British Iron Age: an agenda for action*, Salisbury, Trust for Wessex Archaeology.

Hay, G. C. (2000) *Collected Poems and Songs of George Campbell Hay*, ed. Byrne, M., Edinburgh.

Heald, A. (2001) 'Knobbed spearbutts of the British and Irish Age: new examples and new thoughts', *Antiquity*, 75, 689–696.

Henderson, J. (ed.) (2000) *The prehistory and early history of Atlantic Europe* (BAR International Series, 861), Oxford, Archaeopress.

Henderson, J. (2000) 'Shared traditions? The drystone settlement traditions of Atlantic Scotland and Ireland 700 BC – AD 200' in Henderson, J. (ed.), 117–54.

Henshall, A. S. (1972) *The Chambered Tombs of Scotland, Vol. 2*, Edinburgh, Edinburgh University Press.

Highland Roads and Bridges Commission 1821, *9th Report 1816–21*, 10 (1821)

Hill, J. and Buist, D. A. (1994) *Geological Field Guide to the island of Bute, Scotland*, London.

Holley, M. (2000) *The artificial islets/crannogs of the central Inner Hebrides* (BAR British series, 303), Oxford, Archaeopress.

Holley, M. and Ralston, I. B. M. (1995) 'Radiocarbon dates for two crannogs on the Isle of Mull, Strathclyde Region, Scotland', *Antiquity*, 69, 595–596.

Holmer, N. (1938) *Studies on Argyllshire Gaelic*, Uppsala.

Holmer, N. (1962) *The Gaelic of Kintyre*, Dublin.

Horne, D. J. (1980) *The Geology of Jura*, Jura.

Hunter, J. (1976) *The Making of the Crofting Community*, Edinburgh, John Donald (new edn 2000)

Keay, J. and Keay, J. (1994) *Collins Encyclopaedia of Scotland*, London, Harper Collins.

Lamont, D. (1960) *Prose Writings of Donald Lamont*, ed. Murchison, T. M., Edinburgh.

Lane, A. (1990) 'Hebridean pottery: problems of definition, chronology, presence and absence' in Armit, I. (ed.), 108–130.

Lane, A. and Campbell, E. (2000) *Dunadd: an Early Dalriadic Capital*, Oxford, Oxbow Books.

Larsson, L. (1989) 'Late Mesolithic settlements and cemeteries at Skateholm, southern Sweden' in Bonsall, C. (ed.) *The Mesolithic in Europe*, Edinburgh, John Donald, 367–378.

Lawson, J. D. and Weedon, D. S. (eds) (1992) *Geological Excursions around Glasgow and Girvan*, Glasgow.

Lenman, B. (1981) *Integration, Enlightenment and Industrialisation: Scotland 1746–1832*, London (New History of Scotland Series).

Lethbridge, T. C. (1952) 'Excavations at Kilpheder, South Uist, and the problem of brochs and wheelhouses', *PPS*, 18, 176–193.

Lindsay, I. and Cosh, M. (1973) *Inveraray and the Dukes of Argyll*, Edinburgh.

Lindsay, J. (1968) *The Canals of Scotland*, Newton Abbot.

Lindsay, M. (1979) *The Discovery of Scotland*, London, Hale.

Livingston, W. (1882) *Duain agus Orain*, Glasgow.

Livingstone, Duncan. There is no printed collection of the poet's work, but see article by MacThòmais, R. (1982), *Gairm*, 119, 257–268.

MacBain, A. (1922) *Place Names, Highlands and Islands of Scotland*, Stirling.

MacColl, E. (1836) *Clàrsach nam Beann*, Glasgow.

MacCormick, J. (n. d.) *Dun-Aluinn no an t-oighre 'na dhiobarach*, Glasgow.

MacDonald, A. (1973) 'Annat in Scotland: a provisional review', *SSt*, 17, 135–46

MacDonald, A. (1996) *Alasdair mac Mhaighstir Alasdair: Selected Poems*, ed. Thomson, D. S., Edinburgh.

MacDonald, C. (1997) *Moidart, Among the Clanranald*, ed. Watt, J., Birlinn, Edinburgh.

MacDonald, J. (1964) *Orain Iain Luim*, ed. MacKenzie, A. M., Edinburgh.

MacDonald, P. (1784) *A Collection of Highland Vocal Airs*, Edinburgh.

McDonald, R. A. (1997) *The Kingdom of the Isles: Scotland's Western Seaboard c. 1100–1300*, Tuckwell Press, East Linton.

MacDougall, D. G. (1959) *Bràiste Lathurna*, ed. MacMillan, S., Glasgow.

MacDougall, D. (1841) *Laoidhean Spioradail a chum cuideachadh le cràbhadh nan Gael*, Glasgow.

MacDougall, James (ed.) (1891) *Folk and Hero Tales. Waifs and Strays of Celtic Tradition, vol. 3* (Reprint, New York, AMS Press).

Macdougall, N. (1997) *James IV*, Tuckwell Press, East Linton.

Macdougall, N. (2000) 'Achilles Heel? The Earldom of Ross, the Lordship of the Isles and the Stewart Kings, 1449–1507' in Cowan, E. J. and McDonald, R. A. (eds) *Alba: Celtic Scotland in the Medieval Era*, Tuckwell Press, East Linton.

MacEacharna, D. (1976) *The Lands of the Lordship: the Romance of Islay's Names*, Port Charlotte.

MacFadyen, J. (1890) *An t-Eileanach*, Glasgow.

MacFadyen, J. (1902) *Sgeulaiche nan Caol*, Glasgow.

McGladdery, C. A. (1990) *James II*, Edinburgh.

MacInnes, Duncan (ed.) (1890) *Folk and Hero Tales. Waifs and Strays of Celtic Tradition, vol. 2* (Reprint, New York, AMS Press).

MacIntyre, D. (1952) *The Songs of Duncan Ban MacIntyre*, ed. MacLeod, A., Edinburgh, Oliver & Boyd/Scottish Gaelic Texts Society.

MacKechnie, D. (1910) *Am Fear-Ciùil*, Edinburgh.

MacKenzie, M. (1776) *The South Part of Argyle Shire* [map/chart], London.

MacKie, E. W. (1963) *Dun Mor Vaul: an Iron Age broch on Tiree*, Glasgow, University of Glasgow Press.

MacKie, E. W. (1975) 'The vitrified forts of Scotland' in Harding, D. W. (ed.) *Hillforts*, London, Academic Press.

MacKie, E. W. (1997) 'Dun Mor Vaul revisited: fact and theory in the reappraisal of the Scottish Atlantic Iron Age' in Ritchie, J. N. G. (ed.), 141–180.

MacKinnon, D. 'The Place and Personal Names of Argyll', series of seventeen articles in The Scotsman, *9 November 1887 to 18 January 1888*.

MacKinnon, D. (1956) *Prose Writings of Donald MacKinnon*, ed. MacKinnon, L., Edinburgh.

MacKinnon, F. (1997) *Tiree Tales/Sgeulachdan a Tiriodh*, 2nd edn, Tiree, published by the author.

MacLachlan, Dr J. (1880) *The Gaelic Songs of the Late Dr MacLachlan, Rahoy*, ed. Gillies, H. C., Glasgow.

MacLagan, R. C. (1901) *Games and Diversions of Argyllshire*, London, David Nutt/the Folk-lore Society.

Maclean, A. (1981) *The Place-names of Cowal*, Dunoon.

Maclean, C. (1997) *The Isle of Mull – Placenames, Meanings and Stories*, Dumfries.

Maclean, D. (1983) 'Knapdale dedications to a Leinster saint', *SSt*, 27, 49–65

MacLean, L. (ed.) (1835–1836) *An Teachdaire Ur Gaidhealach* (periodical), Glasgow.

MacLean, L. (1837) *Adhamh agus Eubh*, Edinburgh.

MacLeod, Angus (ed.) (1952) *The Songs of Duncan Ban MacIntye*, Edinburgh, Oliver and Boyd.

McNeill, P. G. B. and MacQueen, H. L. (1996) *Atlas of Scottish History to 1707*, The Society of Medievalists and the Department of Geography, University of Edinburgh, Edinburgh.

MacNeill, N. (n. d.) *Guide to Islay*.

MacPhail, C. C. (1947) *Am Filidh Latharnach*, Stirling.

MacQuarrie, A. (1984–6) 'Kings, Lords and Abbots: Power and Patronage at the Medieval Monastery of Iona', *TGSI*, vol. liv.

Maltman, A., Elliott, R., Muir, R. and Fitches, W. (1990) *A Guide to the Geology of Islay*, Aberystwyth.

Mann, L. M. (1915) 'Notes on the relics discovered during excavations in 1913 at the cave at Dunagoil, Bute and in 1914 at the fort of Dunagoil, Bute', *TBNHS*, 8, 61–86.

Mann, L. M. (1925) 'Notes on the results of the exploration of the Fort at Dunagoil, Bute', *TBNHS*, 9, 56–60.

Marsden, J. (2000) *Somerled and the Emergence of Gaelic Scotland*, Tuckwell Press, East Linton.

Marshall, D. N. (1977) 'Carved stone balls', *PSAS*, 108, 40–72.

Marshall, D. N. (1978) 'Excavations at Auchategan, Glendaruel, Argyll', *PSAS*, 109, 36–74.

Marshall, D. N. (1983) 'Excavations at MacEwen's Castle, Argyll, in 1968–69', *GAJ*, 10, 131–142.

Marshall, D. N. and Taylor, I. D. (1977) 'The excavation of the chambered cairn at Glenvoidean, Isle of Bute', *PSAS*, 108, 1–39.

Marshall, J. N. (1915) 'Preliminary note on some excavations at Dunagoil fort and cave', *TBNHS*, 8, 42–49.

Marshall, W. (1794) *A General View of the Agriculture of the Central Highlands of Scotland*, London.

Meek, D. E. (ed.) (1995) *Tuath is Tighearna*, Edinburgh.

Meek, D. E. (1997) '"Norsemen and Noble Stewards": The MacSween Poem in the *Book of the Dean of Lismore*', *Cambrian Medieval Celtic Studies*, 34, 1–49.

Meek, D. E. (ed.) (2003) *Caran an t-Saoghail: The Wiles of the World*, Edinburgh.

Mellars, P. (1987) *Excavations on Oronsay: Prehistoric Human Ecology on a Small Island*, Edinburgh, Edinburgh University Press.

Mithen, S. (ed.) (2000) *Hunter-gatherer landscape archaeology: the Southern Hebrides Mesolithic Project 1988–98*, Vols 1 & 2, Cambridge, McDonald Institute.

Morrison, A. (1984) 'Recent work at Auchindrain, 1981–83', *Vernacular Building* (Scottish Vernacular Buildings Working Group), 8, 25–27.

Munro, J. (1986) 'The Earldom of Ross and the Lordship of the Isles' in Baldwin, J. R. (ed.) *Firthlands of Ross and Sutherland*, Edinburgh.

NMS (1995) 'Newfield, Lismore' in *Discovery and Excavation in Scotland 1995*, 66.

Necker de Saussure, L. A. (1822) *A Voyage to the Hebrides*, London.

Newton, N. (1988) *Islay – a Geological Guide*, Glasgow.

Nicholson, R. (1974) *Scotland: the Later Middle Ages*, Edinburgh.

Nicolaisen, W. F. H. (January,1969) 'Point of the Otters', *The Scots Magazine*, 375.

Nicolaisen, W. F. H. (1976) *Scottish Place Names*, London.

Nieke, M. R. (1984) 'Settlement patterns in the Atlantic province of Scotland in the First Millennium AD: A Study of Argyll', unpublished PhD, University of Glasgow.

Nieke, M. R. (1988) 'Literacy and power: the introduction and use of writing in Early Historic Scotland' in Gledhill, J., Bender, B. and Larsen, M. T. (eds), *State and Society: The emergence and development of social hierarchy and political centralization*, London, 237–252.

Nieke, M. R. (1990) 'Fortifications in Argyll: Retrospect and Future prospect' in Armit, I. (ed.), 131–142.

Nieke, M. R. (1993) 'Penannular and Related Brooches: Secular Ornament or Symbol in Action?' in Spearman, R. M. and Higgitt, J. (eds) *The Age of Migrating Ideas: Early Medieval Art in Northern Britain and Ireland*, Edinburgh, 128–134.

Nieke, M. R. and Boyd, W. E. (1987) 'Eilean an Duin, Craignish, Mid-Argyll', *GAJ*, 14, 48–53.

Nieke, M. R. and Duncan, H. B. (1988) 'Dalriada: the establishment and maintenance of an Early Historic kingdom in northern Britain' in Driscoll, S. T. and Nieke, M. R. (eds), *Power and Politics in Early Medieval Britain and Ireland*, Edinburgh, Edinburgh University Press, 6–21.

New Statistical Account of Scotland (1845), *Vol. 7 Renfrew and Argyll*, Edinburgh, Blackwood.

Ó Baoill, C. (ed.) (1979) *Bàrdachd Chloinn-Ghilleathain: Eachann Bacach and other MacLean Poets*, Edinburgh.

O'Sullivan, J. (1994) 'Excavations of an early church and a women's cemetery at St Ronan's medieval parish church, Iona', *PSAS*, 124, 327–65

Oram, R. D. (1999) 'Alexander Bur, Bishop of Moray, 1362–1397' in Crawford, B. E. (ed.) *Church, Chronicle and Learning in Medieval and Early Renaissance Scotland*, Edinburgh, 195–213.

Origines Parochiales Scotiae (1850), ed. Innes, C., Vol. II, Part i.

Peltenberg, E. J. (1982) 'Excavations at Balloch Hill, Argyll', *PSAS*, 112, 142–214.

Pennant, T. (1790) *A Tour in Scotland and a Voyage to the Hebrides, 1772*, 4th edn, 2 vols (new edn. 2000, Edinburgh, Birlinn).

Phillipson, N. T. and Mitchison, R. (1970) *Scotland in the Age of Improvement*, Edinburgh.

Pollard, T., Atkinson, J. and Banks, I. (1996) '"It is the technical side of the work which is my stumbling block": a shell midden site on Risga reconsidered' in Pollard, T. and Morrison, A. (eds) *The Early Prehistory of Scotland*, Edinburgh, Edinburgh University Press, 165–182.

Powell, T. G. E., Corcoran, J. X. W. P., Lynch, F. and Scott, J. G. (1969) *Megalithic Enquiries in the West of Britain*, Liverpool, Liverpool University Press.

RCAHMS (1971) *Argyll. An Inventory of the Ancient Monuments: 1. Kintyre*, Edinburgh, HMSO.

RCAHMS (1975) *Argyll. An Inventory of the Ancient Monuments: 2. Lorn*, Edinburgh, HMSO.

RCAHMS (1980) *Argyll. An Inventory of the Monuments: 3. Mull, Tiree, Coll and Northern Argyll*, Edinburgh, HMSO.

RCAHMS (1984) *Argyll. An Inventory of the Monuments: 5. Islay, Jura, Colonsay and Oronsay*, Edinburgh, HMSO

RCAHMS (1988) *Argyll. An Inventory of the Monuments: 6. Mid-Argyll and Cowal (Prehistoric and Early Historic monuments)*, Edinburgh, HMSO.

RCAHMS (1992) *Argyll. An Inventory of the Monuments: 7. Mid-Argyll and Cowal (Medieval and later monuments)*, Edinburgh, HMSO.

RCAHMS (1999) *Canna: The Archaeology of a Hebridean Landscape*, Broadsheet 5, RCAHMS/National Trust for Scotland, Edinburgh

RCAHMS (1999) *Colonsay and Oronsay. An Inventory of the Monuments extracted from Argyll Volume 5*, Edinburgh, RCAHMS.

RCAHMS (1999) *Kilmartin: Prehistoric and Early Historic Monuments. An Inventory of the Monuments extracted from Argyll Volume 6*, Edinburgh, RCAHMS

Raferty, B. (1998) 'Knobbed spearbutts revisited' in Ryan, M. (ed.) *Irish antiquities: essays in memory of Joseph Raferty*, Wicklow, Wordwell, 97–109.

Ralston, I. B. M. (1979) 'The Iron Age (c. 600 BC – AD 200): B. Northern Britain' in Megaw, J. V. S. and Simpson, D. D. A. (eds) *Introduction to British Prehistory*, Leicester, Leicester University Press, 446–496.

Regesta Regum Scotorum (1961-) eds Barrow, G. W. S. *et al.*, Edinburgh.

Registrum Magni Sigilli Regum Scotorum (1984, repr.) eds Thomson, J. M. *et al.*, Edinburgh.

Reid, A. and Osborne, B. D. (eds) (1997) *Discovering Scottish Writers*, Motherwell, Scottish Library Association.

Rennie, E. B. (1984) 'Excavations at Ardnadam, Cowal, Argyll, 1964–1982', *GAJ*, 11, 13–39.

Report on the State of Farms on the Barony of Ardnamurchan and Sunart. Thom. Anderson, Strontian, 1st January, 1829 (National Archives of Scotland, AF 49/3).

Richards, M. P. and Sheridan, J. A. (2000) 'New AMS dates on human bone from Mesolithic Oronsay', *Antiquity*, 74, 313–315.

Ritchie, G. (ed.) (1997) *The Archaeology of Argyll*, Edinburgh, Edinburgh University Press.

Ritchie, J. N. G. (1967) 'Keil Cave, Southend, Argyll: a late Iron Age cave occupation in Kintyre', *PSAS*, 99, 104–110.

Ritchie, J. N. G. (1971) 'Iron Age finds from Dun an Fheurain, Gallanach, Argyll', *PSAS*, 103, 100–112.

Ritchie, J. N. G. and Crawford, J. (1978) 'Excavations at Sorisdale and Killunaig, Coll', *PSAS*, 109, 75–84.

Ritchie, J. N. G. and Lane, A. M. (1980) 'Dun Cul Bhuirg, Iona, Argyll', *PSAS*, 110, 209–229.

Rivet, A. L. F. (ed.) (1966) *The Iron Age in northern Britain*, Edinburgh, Edinburgh University Press.

Roberts, J. L. (1998) *The Highland Geology Trail*, Edinburgh.

Roberts, J. L. and Treagus, J. E. (1977) 'Dalradian rocks of the Southwest Highlands', *Scottish Journal of Geology*, 13, 87–184.

Robertson, J. (1788) Paper read to the Society of Antiquaries of Scotland. MS in Antiquaries Library, Vol. 2, Folio 23, Unpublished Communications.

Robertson, I. M. L. (1967) 'Changing form and function of settlement in southwest Argyll, 1841–1961', *SGM*, 83, 29–45.

Robson, J. (1794) *General View of the Agriculture in the County of Argyll*, London.

Ross, A. (1967) *Pagan Celtic Britain: studies in iconography and tradition*, London, Routledge.

Royle, T. (1984) *Macmillan Companion to Scottish Literature*, London, Macmillan.

Saville, A. (1997) 'Palaeolithic handaxes in Scotland', *PSAS*, 127, 1–16.

Saville, A. (1999) 'A cache of flint axeheads and other flint artefacts from Auchenhoan, near Campbeltown, Kintyre, Scotland', *PPS*, 65, 83–123.

Saville, A. and Hallen, Y (1994) 'The "Obanian Iron Age": human remains from the Oban cave sites, Argyll, Scotland', *Antiquity*, 68, 715–723.

Scott, J. G. (1960) 'Loch Glashan Crannog, Argyll', *Discovery and Excavation Scotland*

Scott, J. G. (1960) 'Loch Glashan Crannog, Argyll', *Medieval Archaeology*, 310–311.

Scott, J. G. (1961) 'Loch Glashan Crannog, Argyll', *Archaeological Newsletter*, Vol. 7, No. 2, 20–21.

Scott, J. G. (1964) 'The chambered cairn at Beacharra, Kintyre, Argyll', *PPS*, 30, 134–158.

Scott, J. G. (1969a) 'The Clyde cairns of Scotland' in Powell, T. G. E. *et al.*, 175–222.

Scott, J. G. (1969b) 'The Neolithic period in Kintyre, Argyll' in Powell, T. G. E. *et al.*, 223–246.

Scott, J. G. (1989) 'The stone circles at Temple Wood, Kilmartin, Argyll', *GAJ*, 15, 53–124.

Scott, Sir Walter (1998) *The voyage of the Pharos: Walter Scott's cruise around Scotland in 1814*, Hamilton, Scottish Library Association.

Seright, S. (1984) 'The Mesolithic on Jura', *Current Archaeology*, 90, 209–214.

Sharpe, R. (1995) *Adomnán of Iona: Life of Columba*, Penguin Books, London

Sharpe, R. (2000) 'The thriving of Dalriada' in Taylor, S. (ed.), *Kings, clerics and chronicles in Scotland 500–1297*, Dublin, 47–61.

Simper, R. (1974) *Scottish Sail, a Forgotten Era*, David & Charles, Newton Abbott.

Sinclair, C. (1953) *The Thatched Houses of the Old Highlands*, Edinburgh.

Sinclair, J. (1983) *The Statistical Account of Scotland, 1791–1799*, Vol. 8 [Mainland], Wakefield, E. P. Publishing.

Sinclair, J. (1983) *The Statistical Account of Scotland, 1791–1799*, Vol. 20 [Western Isles], Wakefield, E. P. Publishing.

Skelhorn, R. R. (1969) *The Tertiary Igneous Geology of the Isle of Mull*, Colchester.

Smith, J. (tr.) (1786) *The Gaelic Old Testament*, Vol. IV, Edinburgh.

Smith, J. (1813) *General View of the Agriculture of the County of Argyle*, Edinburgh.

Smith, R. (2001) *The Making of Scotland*, Edinburgh.

Smout, T. C. (1969) *A History of the Scottish People 1560–1830*, London.

Sound Archive of the School of Scottish Studies, University of Edinburgh.

Steer, K. A. and Bannerman, J. W. M. (1977) *Late Medieval Monumental Sculpture in the West Highlands*, RCAHMS, Edinburgh.

Stephenson, D. and Gould, D. (1995) *British Regional Geology – the Grampian Highlands*, London.

Stevenson, J. B. (1984) 'The excavation of a hut circle at Cul a' Bhaile, Jura', *PSAS*, 114, 127–160.

Stevenson, R. K. B. (1949) 'The nuclear fort of Dalmahoy, Midlothian, and other Dark Age capitals', *PSAS*, 83, 186–98.

Stevenson, R. B. K. (1966) 'Metalwork and some other objects in Scotland and their cultural affinities' in Rivet, A. L. F. (ed.), 17–44.

Storrie, M. C. (1961) 'A note on William Bald's plan of Ardnamurchan and Sunart, 1807', *SSt*, 5, 112–117.

Storrie, M. C. (1965) 'Landholdings and settlement evolution in West Highland Scotland', *Geografiska Annaler*, 47, 138–161.

Stott, L. (1992) *Robert Louis Stevenson and the Highlands and Islands of Scotland*, Aberfoyle, Creag Darach Publications.

Stott, L. (1995a) *The Ring of Words: Argyll*, Aberfoyle, Creag Darach Publications.

Stott, L. (1995b) *The Ring of Words: Literary Loch Lomond*, Aberfoyle, Creag Darach Publications.

Survey of the lands of Ardnamurchan and Sunart by William Bald, 1806–7 (National Archives of Scotland, RHP 72/5 & 72/6). The westernmost extremity of Bourblaige is on RHP 72/5. The greater part of Bourblaige, plus Tornamony and Camusangaal, is on RHP 72/6.

Taylor and Skinner (1776) *Survey and Maps of the Roads of North Britain or Scotland*, London, Wakefield, E. P. Publishing.

Thomas, F. W. L. (1881–82) 'On Islay Place-names', *PSAS*, 16, 241–276.

Thomas, J. (1990) *The Callander and Oban Railway*, David St John Thomas, Nairn.

Thomson, D. S. (ed.) (1993) *The Companion to Gaelic Scotland*, Oxford.

Thomson, R. L. (ed.) (1970) *Foirm na n-Urrnuidheadh*, Edinburgh, Oliver and Boyd.

Tocher (1971-present) School of Scottish Studies, Edinburgh University.

Tolan-Smith, C. (2001) *The Caves of Mid-Argyll; an Archaeology of Human Use*, Edinburgh, Society of Antiquaries of Scotland.

Trewin, N. (2003) *The Geology of Scotland*, London.

Valuation of the Estate of Ardnamurchan and Sunart, the property of Sir James Riddell, Bart., September, 1807 (National Archives of Scotland, AF49/2a).

Vetera Monumenta Hibernorum et Scotorum Historiam Illustrantia (1864) ed. Theiner, A., Rome.

Walker, B. (1989) 'Traditional dwellings of the Uists,' In *Highland Vernacular Building* (Scottish Vernacular Buildings Working Group, Regional & Thematic Studies No. 1), 50–70.

Warner, R. B. (1983) 'Ireland, Ulster and Scotland in the Earlier Iron Age' in O'Connor, A. and Clarke, D. V. (eds) *From the Stone Age to the '45*, Edinburgh, John Donald.

Watson, W. J. (1926) *The History of the Celtic Place-names of Scotland*, Edinburgh.

Whittow, J. (1992) *Geology and Scenery in Britain*, London.

Whyte, H. (1881) *The Celtic Garland*, Glasgow.

Whyte, H. (1898) *Leabhar na Céilidh*, Glasgow.

Wickham-Jones, C. R. (1994) *Scotland's First Settlers*, London, Batsford/Historic Scotland.

Williamson, D. (1994) *The Horsieman: Memories of a Traveller, 1928–1958*, Edinburgh, Canongate. (repr. 2002, Edinburgh, Birlinn).

Williamson, D. and Williamson, L. (1987) *A Thorn in the King's Foot*, Harmondsworth, Penguin.

Williamson, Capt. J. (1904) *The Clyde Passenger Steamers 1812–1901*, Glasgow.

Withers, C. W. (1984) *Gaelic in Scotland 1698–1981: The Geographical History of a Language*, Edinburgh.

Woodcock, N. and Strachan, R. (2000) *Geological History of Britain and Ireland*, Oxford.

Writers in Scotland Scheme Handbook (2001), Edinburgh, Scottish Book Trust.

Youngson, A. J. (1973) *After the '45: The Economic Impact on the Scottish Highlands*, Edinburgh.

Index

Note on the index:
Page numbers may have a suffix of *tbl.*, *map*, *cht.*, *fig.* These indicate a reference to a table, map, chart, figure respectively and have been omitted when the reference is clearly to a map or figure. A letter *n* after a page refers to a note on that page. Entries for names beginning 'Mc' are sorted as if spelt 'Mac'. 'St' with place names is sorted as spelt. Christian saints are filed under their first name.